BUCK, BUCK, MOOSE

# BUCK, BUCK, MOOSE

## RECIPES AND TECHNIQUES FOR COOKING VENISON

Deer, Elk, Moose, and Other Antlered Things

**HANK SHAW**

with photographs by HOLLY A. HEYSER

H|H

Published in the United States by
H&H BOOKS
www.honest-food.net
H&H books may be purchased for business or promotional use or for special sales. For information, please email hank@huntgathercook.com, attention Special Markets.

Distributed by SCB Distributors, Gardena, CA

Cover and page design by Laura Shaw
Food and prop styling by Hank Shaw and Holly A. Heyser
Photographs: Hank Shaw © 6, 10, 14, 28, 38, 43, 44, 45, 48, 49, 50, 51, 52, 54, 64, 66, 86-7, 111, 124, 151, 222, 247, 251, 252–3, 260, 290, 298; Shutterstock © page 68; Josh Valentine © pages 30, 32; Carlo DeFalco © pages 33, 37, 41, 47; Matt Greene © page 34

ISBN : 978-0-99694-484-7

1 2 3 4 6 7 8 9 10

Printed in the United States

Library of Congress Cataloging-in-Publication Data
Shaw, Hank, 1970—
Buck, Buck, Moose : Recipes and Techniques for Cooking Deer, Elk, Antelope, and Other Antlered Things / Hank Shaw
Pages cm    Includes index
Cooking (Venison) 2. Cooking (Elk) 3. Cooking (Game) I. Title.
2016908699

"Hank Shaw understands that great venison starts long before the pan gets hot. *Buck, Buck, Moose* is an essential field-to-table guide for anyone who wants to honor the animal, understand the meat, and cook every cut with confidence."

**—JESS PRYLES, meat expert, live-fire cook, and author of *Hardcore Carnivore* and *Prime Cuts***

"Hank Shaw has built a definitive reference for anyone who hunts, cooks and respects wild game. *Buck Buck Moose* belongs on the shelf of every serious outdoorsman and cook. This new edition raises the bar once again."

**—MICHAEL HUNTER, chef and co-owner of Antler Restaurant in Toronto and author of *The Hunter Chef Cookbook* and *Hunter Chef in the Wild***

"I've lived on a cattle ranch for twenty years, so venison in all its forms has always been a bit of a mystery to me. For that reason, I devoured every page of *Buck, Buck, Moose*. Hank Shaw lives, sleeps, eats, and breathes venison—and his passion is palpable. From laying out the ancient connection between man and deer to presenting clear, hands-on instructions for handling and cooking venison, no stone is left unturned. Hank has absolutely outdone himself, and I know this book will be enjoyed by venison enthusiasts and novices alike."

**—REE DRUMMOND, *New York Times* bestselling author of *The Pioneer Woman Cooks***

"If Hank's goal was to completely empower deer hunters and open up new perspectives on the possibilities of venison, then he has completely surpassed that with this book. It is a treasure, and—pardon the pun—a complete game-changer."

**—JESSE GRIFFITHS, chef and author of the James Beard–nominated wild game cookbook *Afield***

"Hank Shaw has done it! He has written the definitive guide to everything venison. Whether you are the hunter who wants to learn what to do with the buck you just shot, or the cook who has been given venison from a friend, Hank will tell you everything you need to know. With recipes drawn from traditions around the world, Hank has elevated cooking venison to an art form. Steak, tacos, stew, short ribs, meatballs, pot roast, curry, kebabs, and more. It's all here."

**—ELISE BAUER, founder of SimplyRecipes.com**

"This book is not for everyone. If you are among those game cooks who insist on submerging your game in a slow cooker loaded with salty, canned goo, then save yourself some money on an incredible resource you'll never use. Hank Shaw demystifies antlered game preparation with simple techniques that can be applied to anything from a whitetail tenderloin to the bony neck roast of a bull moose."

**—SCOTT LEYSATH, TV host, wild game cookbook author, food columnist**

"There is no reference that celebrates the outdoor lifestyle and dedication to responsibly harvesting everything antlered like *Buck, Buck, Moose*. As a chef and outdoors enthusiast I have been searching for a complete guide from hunt to table. It has now arrived."

**—BRYAN VOLTAGGIO, "Top Chef" finalist, deer hunter, and James Beard Award nominee**

Dedicated to the many readers of Hunter Angler Gardener Cook.
Without you, this book would never have happened.

# CONTENTS

Sunset on the Oklahoma plain after an evening sitting in the blind, waiting for deer.

# FOREWORD

Evolution and revolution. Evolution is the gradual development or changes to knowledge or processes over a long period. Revolution is an idea that causes sudden, rapid, and radical change in knowledge or processes.

I always understood food and cooking to be evolutionary, changing slowly, methodically, since we started using fire to make food more digestible, which increased our brain size. My evolutionary view of the pace of change in our gastro intelligence remained constant until I shared a camp with Hank Shaw. We were along Arizona's Mexican border, chasing quail, rabbits, Coues deer, and javelina.

As a lifelong hunter starting my fifth decade of chasing wild food, I had assumed everything was cooked how my grandparents did it. They'd emerged from the depression, pre-freezers. Meats were cured or cooked beyond recognition. Not because such torching was flavorful but because they'd known someone who had likely died from pathogens ingested with undercooked meat.

This was the cooking tradition I evolved from in Minnesota's Northwoods. Traditions die hard. Meat came in from the field or water with low expectations. Meals were mostly calories, eaten as a life necessity without much concern for variety or flavor. We thought tacos were ground beef dusted with spices from an instant recipe mix. Mild, of course.

Years ago, I read *Buck, Buck, Moose* and *Duck, Duck, Goose* in preparation for a podcast with Hank. I was impressed with the detail brought to those pages, starting from the moment an animal dies. The amazing photos provided high professional credibility, yet as I would come to learn, they mostly reflected Hank's ethos that wild food gave its life for this meal, so you are expected to give it the best effort you can.

Reading Hank's books (more than once) did not prepare me for Hank's exacting attention to every detail he demonstrated on our hunt. Within six days, my understanding of food combinations, history, and the secrets to improving every portion had expanded by volumes. As a lifelong hunter, I did not expect this.

Watching Hank made it clear that his books should be twice as thick. He has so much to offer. The owner of that much knowledge must feel abbreviated when books get condensed down to a few hundred pages of words and photos. *Buck, Buck, Moose* started a wild food revolution for many of us.

What I call "Hank's revolution" begins with his emphasis that meat quality starts the moment that buck, bird, or bass expires. I have a library of books, some cooking, some field dressing. None of those authors directly connect wild food quality to the knowledge and exertions the hunter applies to wild meat *before* it hits the kitchen. Hank does.

When hunting with Hank, not much time is spared for pictures or congratulations. It becomes abundantly clear that important work is at hand. The business of maximizing the potential of this meat starts now. And that is how Hank approaches his writing and his books.

Many may want to skip those chapters about getting meat from field to freezer, wanting to get right to one of his many amazing recipes. Don't! *Read them.* Read them again. And before season starts, read them as a reminder.

Hank will tell you he is a journalist, a writer, who loves to cook things. What goes understated in that brief biography is that Hank is a researcher and historian. Research requires studying people, cultures, and their food, for with no food culture, there is no society. Hank could teach graduate-level courses around those topics. Hank works his ass off to be an expert.

I've benefitted from Hank's talent applied to Arizona javelina, cuts taken from a Montana bison, and birds and fish in between. Every meal he prepared came with a deep history that is reflected in his cooking methods, combinations, and stories explaining why this meal, prepared in this manner, does justice to the wild thing we are eating. Hank does this in this book.

Hank's passion for improving our collective wild food skills drives him to refine and expand, as he has done with this new edition. Hank is sincere in his belief—a belief I share and that connects me to Hank—that wild food is far deeper than what modern media can provide in the insta-world of half-minute feel-good soundbites. Hank takes this stuff seriously. And he expects readers like me to put the same work into wild food that he invests in teaching us.

Hank's attachment to the land, the water, and the air that provides this wild food extends to the hard-working caretakers of those resources. Hank's countless stories about poor cultures rich in food history is experiential. He has lived with those people, toiled in their lands, and learned direct lessons about food security. Hank brings those stories to every dish he writes about, including many in this book.

Revolutionary ideas inspire others. Wild food cooking trends have exploded in the decade since this book was first released. Hank's work is a catalyst for this wild food revolution, based on not just his immense knowledge and his tireless energy but also his uncommon talent to connect the important values wild food expresses among people from diverse backgrounds. I know many participants in wild food, veterans and novices alike, who point to Hank as their influence.

Hank Shaw does not believe in shortcuts. He believes in honest food, acquired through our own labor, appreciated as a gift of life. Hank's revolutionary ideas are here in this book, improved and expanded in a way only possible from a hunter, a writer, a compassionate human who wants us all to be better, in the kitchen, in camp, in our communities. Appreciate this new edition. Use it as inspiration to experiment, to accept some failures as tuition paid for improvement, and to give an honest effort that does justice to the wild food you share.

**—RANDY NEWBERG,**
**BOZEMAN, MONTANA**

# INTRODUCTION

A mural in El Paso, Texas, of a whitetail doe running

## DEER MAKE US HUMAN

Deer and humans have evolved together. We have hunted deer, and deer have escaped us, for so long that neither of us are what we once were when this relationship began. Our dance with deer is primal, ancient, and ongoing.

There is growing evidence among anthropologists that the pursuit of hoofed animals—deer and their kin—helped us evolve. The hunt demands patience, memory, cooperation, and foresight. It asked us to read landscapes, to anticipate movement, to imagine outcomes. In doing so, it changed not only our bodies. It changed our minds. However you frame it—science, story, or something older—our relationship with deer runs deep.

Deer hunting is embedded in cultures across the world, and so is eating venison. Tell someone you're going deer hunting, and they'll probably shrug. Tell them you're hunting cranes, or bears, and you'll get a different reaction entirely. Humans hunt and eat venison; it's just what we do. It is, in many ways, the original red meat.

The word *venison* comes from the Latin *venari*, "to hunt." Over time, it came to mean the meat of any hunted animal, and in some places, it still does. But in this book, as in most modern usage, we're talking about the meat of deer and their relatives:

whitetails and mule deer, elk and moose, caribou, as well as pronghorn and wild bovids like nilgai, oryx, and even bison.

Given this long history, it's surprising that venison has so often been mishandled in the kitchen, although less so than it once was. When I first wrote this book, the clichés were everywhere: overcooked backstrap, buried under bacon or cream-of-mushroom soup, cooked gray and sad. Shoulders undercooked. Trim wasted. Good meat treated as something to be disguised rather than celebrated.

That has begun to change.

In the decade since this book first appeared, more people have come to wild food with curiosity instead of fear. We understand more now, about how animals live, what they eat, how that affects flavor. We've learned to age meat more thoughtfully, to break down animals with care, to match cut to method. New tools have entered the kitchen, too—sous vide, pressure cookers, even air fryers—all of which, used well, can make venison easier to prepare and better to eat than ever before.

And yet, the fundamentals remain the same.

Venison rewards attention. It asks you to notice things: how lean it is, how it carries heat, how each cut wants to be cooked. These are not obstacles. They are invitations. Because more often than not, the simplest preparation—the right cut, cooked properly, with a few well-chosen companion ingredients—is the dish that gets cooked again and again.

*Buck, Buck, Moose* has changed my life in the ten years since it was published. It has sold more than a hundred thousand copies, and it has introduced me to countless fellow deer and elk hunters, from backwoodsmen to Michelin-starred chefs, in every state and nearly every province in the US and Canada. I have learned much in that decade, not only from my own hunts and my own experiments in the kitchen, but also from skilled butchers, skinners, hunters, and cooks I've met along the way. This book is the distillation of that journey.

Cooking venison well isn't complicated. It just requires understanding. A handful of techniques. A dash of confidence. A guide. And maybe, now, another decade's worth of hard-earned knowledge gathered in one place. That's what this book is for.

Ready to begin?

## HOW TO USE THIS BOOK

In these pages you will find pretty much everything you need to know to fully enjoy the deer, elk, moose, antelope, or similar animal you bring home (most of the recipes will also work for bison, bear, beef, sheep, or goat)—everything from how the different species act in the kitchen to techniques on butchering at home to tricks and tips on working with the fundamentally lean nature of venison. You'll also find recipes for all parts of the deer, wonderful dishes made with unloved parts like shanks, flanks, necks, and offal, the wobbly bits. And those recipes will come from all over the globe. No matter where you live on this planet, at least one thing binds us all: a tradition of hunting and eating venison.

The book you are holding takes you from the moment after you've recovered your animal all the way to the dinner table. While much of the book is dedicated to specific recipes, within those recipes you'll learn the underlying techniques that govern them, allowing you to modify my recipe to suit your own tastes. I'll walk you through the science of marinating, storing, curing, cooking, and otherwise working a deer.

I hope these pages give you the tools you need to get the most out of your hard work in the field. Good luck out there, and enjoy!

## USING MODERN COUNTERTOP COOKERS

In the last decade, tools like pressure cookers, air fryers, and sous vide have changed how we cook venison at home, especially the tougher cuts. Used well, they make some dishes more accessible and more reliable than with traditional methods. Used poorly, however, they can damage texture and flavor. Here's how I use them now.

### SLOW COOKER (CROCK-POT)

- Best for shanks, neck, shoulder, stews.
- You'll need to brown venison first in a separate pan, deglaze the pan with stock or water, and add that to the slow cooker.
- Generally speaking, cook on low for seven to nine hours, or high for four to five hours.

### PRESSURE COOKER (INSTANT POT)

- Best for shanks, shoulder, ribs, stew meat. Ideal for Mexican Barbacoa (page 97).
- Reduces braising time dramatically.
- Typical time: thirty-five to sixty minutes at high pressure, then use the natural release.

### AIR FRYER

- Best for burgers, meatballs, cutlets like Country-Fried Venison Steak (page 134).
- Use at 375°F to 400°F

## A WORD ON SOUS VIDE

Thanks to cheap immersion circulators, sous vide cooking has swept through the wild game world. I get asked a lot about sous vide and wild game, and, frankly, I am not a fan. In most cases, cooking wild game in traditional ways produces a better result than a hot water bath. There are, however, a few areas where sous vide shines.

For those who don't know, sous vide is highly controlled "boil in a bag," which you may remember if you are, like me, of a certain age. You seal food inside a bag with a vacuum sealer, then drop it into water at a certain temperature and leave it until it's done.

I cooked sous vide when I started as a professional cook, back in the late 1980s. It was OK for cooking massive volume, but I never loved this method, and neither do most professional cooks I know.

Texture is a serious issue. Sous vide-cooked meat gets a weird, pasty-gummy texture if left too long. So if you do use it, watch your timing. You can always cook something more. You can't uncook it.

You will almost always need to sear or grill your wild game after it's out of the water bath. If you don't, your protein will be soggy and waterlogged. Because the meat is already cooked, you need very high heat and a quick sear.

Another huge issue is wild game's variability. One of the great things about sous vide with store-bought meats is that you can dial in a temperature and time and get consistent results every time. That won't work with wild meats.

How old was that goose? Young-of-the-year or thirty years old? Trophy buck or button buck? Bull elk or raghorn? How large is your cut? Store-bought meats are consistent in size. Wild animals are not.

This variability is easily handled in a pot or a pan. Is it done? Lift the lid and check. When you cook sous vide, you need to open up your sealed bag to check, and if it's not ready, you need to reseal the bag. By then you've defeated the convenience of the cook-in-a-bag method.

Sous vide does have a few good uses, though:

**CONFIT.** It's not as good as old-school French confit. But even I don't like that old-school confit requires a quart of fat or more. Sure, you can reuse it, but *still*. Packing confit in a vac bag and cooking it in a big stockpot of steaming water—note that there is no immersion circulator needed here—works well and allows you to confit in nifty fats like, say, rendered bison fat, since you don't need that much.

**SAUERBRATEN.** I've done this dish many ways, but the five-day marinade, all vac-sealed, and then that marinated venison cooked slowly but at 140°F, still pink but hot enough to break down connective tissue over many hours, and then served with the traditional sauce—so it's pink venison with that amazing sauce—is worth the loss in texture. See page 92.

**POTENTIALLY TOUGH CUTS LIKE CORNED VENISON.** Set your water bath to 140°F, add spices or fill with broth instead of water, and just drop the meat in to cook. No vacuum bag needed.

**PÂTÉ OR TERRINES, OR EVEN MEATLOAF.** Fill the water bath up to the neck of the vessel—either a terrine or loaf pan—set it at your target temperature, cover, and let it ride for a few hours. Incidentally, a regular two-quart terrine pan will need about three hours to get to the ideal internal temperature of about 148°F to 150°F. Again, no vacuum bag needed.

**POACHING SAUSAGES.** Again, no vacuum bag needed, but being able to submerge meat in water or a flavorful liquid at a precise temperature makes it easier to get a good result.

**ROULADES.** One of the things about vacuum-sealing is compression. And when that is combined with coagulating proteins from cooking, you can get a roulade of venison that is cooked medium and that holds it shape.

**PARTIES.** When you are serving a ton of people, use sous vide for the same reason we did in the restaurants: you can hold meats in the water, then open the bag and sear to order. Using your immersion circulator as one more cooking vessel can help a lot when you are cooking for a crowd.

Bottom line for me? Sous vide is an adjunct to traditional cooking, not a replacement.

> "If you are hunting deer, ignore the hares."
>
> —CHINESE PROVERB

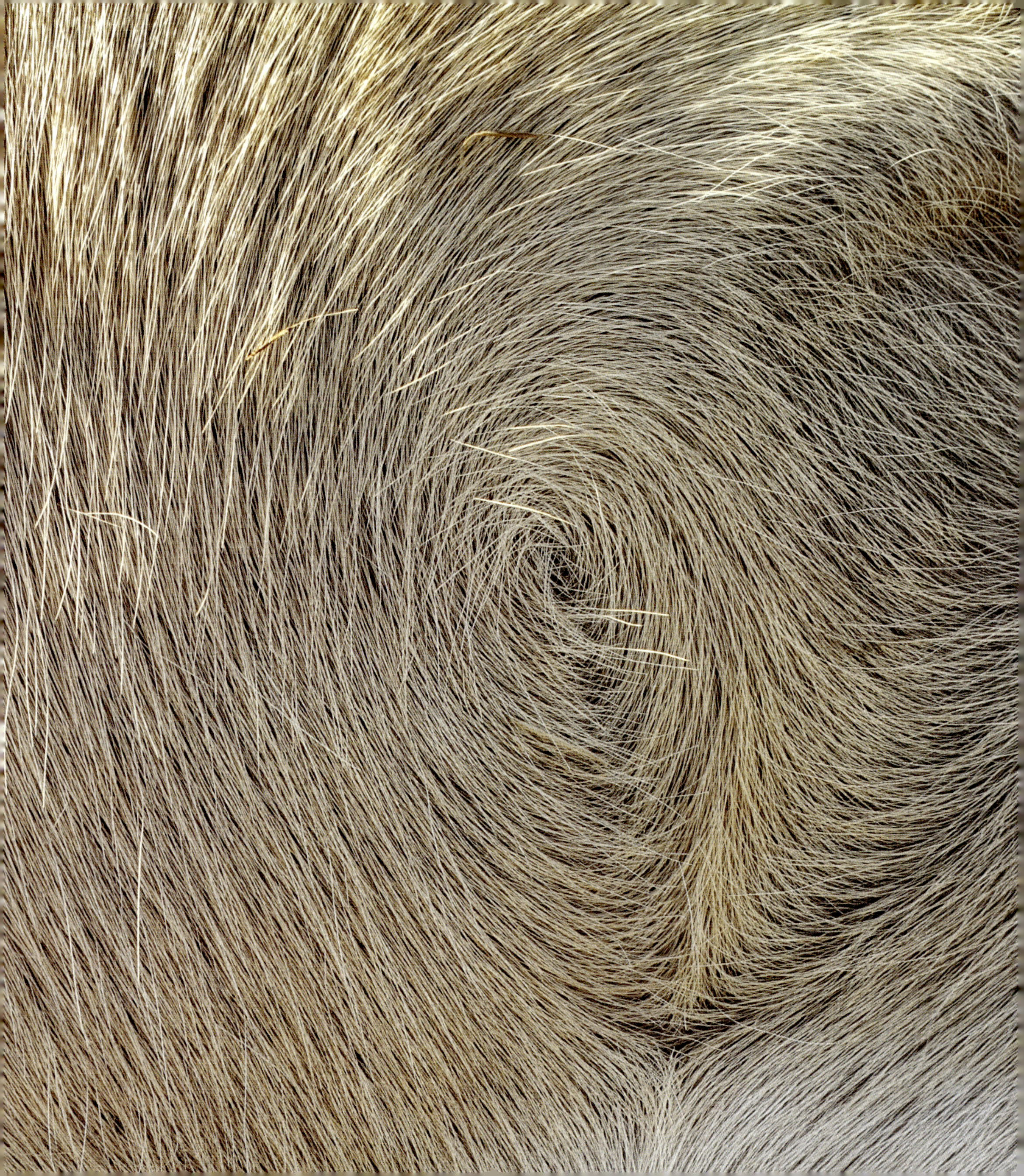

– Part One –

# DEER BASICS

This is, in many ways, the most important part of this book. Sure, I love the recipes, but the information you'll find in this section will ground you in all the best practices of field care, butchery, storage, and food safety. You'll learn about the different kinds of venison (an elk in the kitchen can be far different from an antelope in the kitchen), how to handle all parts of the carcass (including the odd bits), and even which beer or wine goes best with venison.

# VENISON IN ALL ITS FORMS

## A DEER IS NOT A MOOSE: VARIOUS TYPES OF VENISON

Any species of venison (deer, elk, moose, or antelope) can be used as the basis for any of the recipes in this book. However, there are some differences that you'll want to be aware of when working with each individual species in the kitchen.

### Size Matters

Venison comes in an astonishing range of sizes, from giant moose in the Yukon to tiny Coues deer in the Sonoran Desert. That's why I typically call for meat in weight rather than a specific cut, for example, a three-pound roast rather than a "sirloin" roast. In this way, you'll be able to use whatever sort of red meat you have available. I've become more rigid about this over time. Weight and thickness—or if it's a whole cut or a smaller portion of a larger, whole-muscle roast—matter far more than the name of the cut. Trying to force a "cut" onto animals of wildly different sizes leads to bad cooking decisions.

Here are a few size-related things you'll want to keep in mind as you explore the specific dishes later (don't worry, we'll review these again in Part Two).

For shank recipes with large animals, use a cross-cut shank (the kind you'd buy for osso buco in the supermarket) rather than the whole shank.

You can get more intricate with larger animals too, fabricating beef-like cuts such as skirt steak, short ribs, cheeks, or even hanger steak with bison, elk, moose, or large exotics like nilgai or oryx.

To avoid overcooking, the backstraps of most deer should be cooked in sections a foot long or so and cut into medallions only after the meat has been cooked. The backstraps of elk or moose, on the other hand, can be cut into steaks one or two inches thick before cooking. Don't cut them thinner because this makes them very difficult to cook rare-to-medium.

### They Are What They Ate

Diet affects meat flavor. Deer can eat more than a thousand different plants, and they've been seen eating fish and eggs, and even baby birds. Elk tend to prefer grasses, while moose love to eat marshy plants and the new shoots of trees. Caribou are big fans of lichen. A mule deer that has gorged on a farmer's grain will taste different from a mule deer that grazed on sagebrush.

To be sure, flavor differences aren't as dramatic in venison as they are in omnivores such as ducks, pigs, or bears, but perceptible differences do occur. I've had sage-y deer and even pond-y moose. Though not overpowering, it's definitely there.

What I've learned over time is that most "bad-tasting" venison isn't about diet, it's about handling. A well-handled deer that's been eating sage will still taste good. A poorly handled one won't, no matter what it ate.

### The Culinary Variety of Venison

Most deer hunters will tell you that they prefer elk to whitetail or mule deer. Many say mule deer meat can be slightly drier than meat of a whitetail. Whitetails in farm country tend to be better tasting than those in the deep woods of, say, the Adirondacks or the Appalachians.

Most people swear by moose meat as some of the finest venison in the world. Opinions on antelope vary wildly, though I suspect that most negative experiences stem from poor handling. The pronghorn antelope (the so-called speed goat), is, in my

## A Word About Bison

**A bovid, bison meat is very similar to beef, and its flavor and texture are virtually identical to grass-fed beef. I love bison, don't get me wrong, but it's more of a beef substitute than a venison substitute. Having said that, absolutely don't hesitate to substitute bison for venison in any of the recipes in Part Two. Just remember bison are big. A bison steak, being three times as large, will cook differently than a venison steak (though the tough cuts will cook the same). For stews, braises, and other slow-cooked recipes, bison makes a great venison substitute.**

opinion, the finest of all venison. However, it's worth noting that antelope must be gutted, skinned, and cooled quickly in the field. Let the meat heat up and it will be awful.

Among the exotic species, red deer is quite similar to elk in flavor, while axis deer will be almost sweet. These little Asiatic deer are, to many, the best tasting venison available in North America (though I rank them second behind a properly prepared antelope). Fallow deer are similar to whitetails and blacktails. Like bison, nilgai antelope and oryx, which can be found roaming around New Mexico and Texas, are large bovids, which means their fat is tasty, not waxy. Save it!

## Age and Toughness

Older animals are tougher. I used to think this mattered more than it does. With proper aging and cooking technique, even an old animal can eat very well. But you do need to treat it differently.

Of all the deerlike animals we chase in North America, the caribou is the earliest to mature. A good bull caribou may be only four years old; life's harsh in the Arctic. Whitetails and blacktail deer usually reach maturity between four and nine years, with blacktails tending to live longer. Mule deer can get even older, with average life spans between nine and eleven years in the wild.

A good bull elk is likely to be at least eight years old and could be as old as fifteen. A nice buck antelope will probably be at least seven years old and can live to fifteen years in the wild. The longest-lived of all is the moose, which routinely lives longer than ten years; a twenty-five-year-old bull is not uncommon. And if you think the meat on a twenty-five-year-old moose will be tough, then you'd be right.

## Boys Smell

Let's face it. Testosterone stinks. If you've ever been in a men's locker room after a game, you know what I mean. And while the body odor in male cervids isn't nearly as rank as it is in animals such as pigs or javelina, a buck in full rut will not make for the best eating. And there are other reasons besides odor that can adversely affect the meat of an animal in rut. A 1992 study in the *Journal of Animal Science* showed dramatic differences in tenderness and texture between those red deer of the same age and health that were slaughtered before the rut and those that were slaughtered after. The pre-rut bucks were fatter, larger, and more tender than the post-rut bucks. The reason is obvious. During the rut, bucks spend all day running around chasing does. Whatever time is left they spend fighting with each other. I'm not telling you *not* to shoot that giant, swollen-necked king of the forest who's been chasing all the ladies. Just know that unless you can age the meat, it's the ladies who'll taste better at the table.

## VENISON: NUTRITIOUS, LEAN, SUSTAINABLE

Venison is a lean alternative to beef. A typical venison roast or steak has about one-third the fat of a comparable piece of beef, and since deer and elk work for a living, they lack the intramuscular marbling we so prize in a ribeye. The composition of deer fat is significantly different from beef or bison fat, too (see page 21).

But fat is only one part of the story. According to USDA data, a six-ounce venison steak has about 260 calories and only six grams of fat. It could be even less if you are scrupulous about trimming your venison. Compare that to a similar cut of beef, such as a trimmed top loin filet. This same portion of top loin will have roughly 410 calories and, depending on the grade (choice, prime, etc.), about twenty grams of fat. Real data on this sort of thing can be unreliable, however, as fat content can vary widely among individuals. Venison also tends to be far higher in niacin and iron than beef and is a good source of vitamins B12, B6, and B2 (riboflavin) and minerals such as phosphorus, zinc, and selenium.

Not only is venison low in fat and nutritionally more dense, it's also about as organic as you can get without official certification. And speaking of official organic certification, it's worth noting that to meet USDA organic requirements, all feed must be certified organic, and it must come with the paperwork to prove it. Virtually no wild game can be officially certified as organic. For those of you who are concerned about organics, do be aware of deer herds that camp out in agricultural fields in which conventional or GMO crops make up most of the landscape. As I said, we are what we eat.

### Lamb and Goat as Venison Stand-Ins

Where bison is close in flavor but not in size to venison, lamb and goat are close in size but not in flavor. Lamb and goat cuts are very similar to those in a typical whitetail or blacktail deer, but the flavor of lamb and goat is much more pronounced. Believe it or not, lamb and mature goats are gamier than venison. But if you like lamb, it's a perfect substitute for venison, and, of course, it's readily available in stores. Kid goat is shockingly mild, with almost no off flavors or odors.

One cooking note, though. Lamb, being a young animal, will cook far faster than most wild animals. A venison shank normally takes two to four hours to fall off the bone. A lamb shank can get there in ninety minutes. So if you're substituting lamb for the real deal, keep an eye on things. Mutton and adult goat meat should be cooked like venison.

### Free Range and Humane

Where venison excels, though, is in the realms of humane animal husbandry and sustainability. You simply can't get more free-range, humanely harvested, or sustainable meat than wild game. Even farmed venison must be raised in a free-range way, because deer simply won't survive if confined like cows.

In terms of quality of life, every deer, antelope, elk, or moose we bring home to feed our families has led as free a life as nature allows: no confinement, no antibiotics, able to live as it was meant to live and to breed as it was meant to breed. As long as we hunters do our part to ensure a clean kill, the death of a deer is nearly as quick as in any slaughterhouse. When compared to death in the wild, a hunter's bullet or broadhead is a far cleaner way to go than by starvation or the claws and teeth of a predator.

Because venison is a wild, renewable resource, it is among the most sustainable sources of meat available. Venison requires nothing more than healthy, natural habitat for their own health and survival, whether that habitat be in the Rocky Mountains or on your farm or in your backyard. And since venison forage for their supper, the resource load and environmental impact of commercial feed is avoided. The North American hunting system itself is entirely based on sustainable management practices, and hunters are allowed to take only as many deer as wildlife biologists say we can. Population census and hunting tallies are carefully tracked, and the numbers are then used to determine how many deer can be harvested in any given year. If deer numbers are high, more licenses are issued and seasons are expanded. In this way, deer populations are kept in optimal balance with their associated ecosystems.

## Top Factors Affecting Meat Quality

I've talked with many, many butchers, deer hunters, meat experts, and cooks over the years about what they consider to be the most important factors affecting the flavor of your venison. Here's the consensus:

1. **FIELD CARE** By far the top cause of nasty-tasting venison is poor meat care. If you think strapping a buck to your truck and driving around with it is a good idea, I'm talking to you. Take your photos, then get to work. And I don't mean back in camp after a cup of coffee. I mean right out there in the field (unless it's beastly cold out). Cooling down the carcass quickly is the single most important factor in assuring good meat quality, especially in warmer climates.
2. **SHOT PLACEMENT** A good hunter is something of an assassin, killing silently, swiftly, and cleanly. Your animal should have no idea it's being hunted, and when shot, it should die quickly. A clean heart-lung shot on an unsuspecting deer will go a long way toward tasty venison. A liver shot (or worse) or a shot on a fleeing deer will flood the animal with adrenaline, which can taint the meat.
3. **HANGING TEMPERATURE** If you're hanging your deer, you need the temperature to be no higher than about 40°F; just above freezing is better. One of the reasons people get nasty venison back from meat processors is that in deer season, the door of their meat locker is opened and shut all day, letting warm air sneak in and allowing temperatures to creep up past 40°F. Processors don't like to talk about this, but it happens.
4. **THE RUT** Note that this is the first time the animal itself comes into play as a factor in meat quality. Rutting and post-rut bucks and bulls are in ragged shape. They've been running around and fighting for weeks, and they have a lot of hormones racing through them. They'll be leaner and tougher than before the rut.
5. **AGE AND SEX** All things being equal, a young doe or cow will be more tender than an old male. But keep in mind that a young male might be more tender than an old doe. You can get good venison from an old, rutting buck, provided that the first three factors are all done right.

6. **DIET** Grain-fed whitetails and mule deer will be fatter and nicer tasting than those deer subsisting on sagebrush or pine needles. That doesn't mean a muley that's shot in the sage won't be good, it's just that you might find yourself preferring the whitetail doe that you shot in the alfalfa field. That said, venison from all sorts of animals, with all sorts of diets, can be wonderful; these observations are the fine distinctions that can elevate your culinary awareness and enjoyment.

7. **BUTCHERY** Bad butchery, whether in the form of sloppy knife and saw cuts, meat ground with loads of sinew and no added fat, or failure to remove enough silverskin from roasts and stew meat, can seriously damage meat. This is why many of us choose to butcher our own deer and elk. Good butchers are like good mechanics. Hold onto them and treat them well.

## Demystifying Deer Fat

I've long been a proponent of using deer fat in cooking. In fact, the widely accepted injunction against using deer fat is one of the hunting myths I most like to puncture when I talk to other hunters about game cookery. After all, it makes sense that the fat on venison would taste good, especially if you're hunting either in the Corn Belt or wherever there are a lot of acorns. Most of us like the taste of grain-fed beef, and acorn-fed pork is some of the finest in the world. The same holds true for venison.

Still, the majority of sources on the subject will tell you to remove all fat from your deer, calling it gamy, "strong," or otherwise unpleasant. Even the normally sporty *The L.L. Bean Game and Fish Cookbook*, which I have great respect for, says venison fat is nasty (but, oddly, that moose and caribou fat isn't). Some critics skip the flavor aspect altogether and stress how quickly venison fat goes rancid, even in the freezer. There has to be something to this, right?

Turns out, there is—to both sides of the deer fat debate. Let me start with the obvious: Deer, elk, antelope, caribou, and moose are all separate critters, with different diets among the different species, compounded by regional differences within the same species and individual differences within the herd. The menu for an Arizona Coues deer is nothing like that of an Iowa whitetail deer, for example. And one buck may love acorns, while the one eating next to him prefers your azaleas. Given this enormous range of factors, any hard-and-fast universal ideas about the flavor or composition of deer fat should be taken with a grain of salt. Being wild, variability is the name of the game.

Nevertheless, all our "deer" are ruminant cousins of sheep, goats, and cattle. And ruminants tend to have a narrower range of flavor differences than do animals with a less intense digestive system and/or a wider diet. Ruminants all eat grasses, plants, and nuts; only rarely do they eat animal protein. Contrast that with ducks, bears, and wild pigs, which can all run the flavor gamut from abominable to sublime depending on what they last ate. A salmon-eating bear is foul-tasting; a berry-eating one fantastic. Deer taste like deer, with real, but far subtler, differences in flavor.

Not all fat is created equal. Muscle fat is different from body cavity fat. You will often see a lot of fat around the kidneys, as well as some stuck here and there within the gut cavity. This latter is suet. I tend to toss it or use it as waterproofing material (see page 23). Why? Body cavity fat (suet) is always harder than fat on working muscles. If you're a soap or candle maker, this stuff is golden. But the very qualities that make suet so good for the candle maker—particularly

its high melting point (around 150°F)—make eating it less than ideal. It tends to be very waxy. (By comparison, rendered wild duck fat melts at around 68°F.) Some people like beef and lamb suet. I don't. Birds love it, though, especially in winter. So if you live in a place with cold winters, save your deer suet for them.

Good data are hard to find on this subject, but they do exist, mostly from New Zealand, Scandinavia, and Great Britain, although there are a few studies from the United States, too. They all come to the same conclusion about deer fat:

- It is high in omega-3 fatty acids, due mostly to a diet of forbs and grasses. Deer eat more forbs, elk more grasses.
- Stearic acid is a main component of cervid fat because it's stable, with a high melting point; an animal with more stearic acid in its fat can withstand a colder winter. So yes, that means the fat on an Alberta whitetail will be far waxier than the fat on a Coues deer. I can confirm this through personal experience.
- Different cervids carry different percentages of stearic acid in their fat. Hot-weather deer will have the lowest, Arctic caribou the highest. Generally speaking, whitetails have the lowest, then mule deer, then elk, then moose, then caribou.
- Pronghorn, bison, nilgai, and oryx are not cervids, so their fat is tasty. Have at it!
- As winter progresses, the percentage of stearic acid increases. So the same animal in September will have softer fat than one in January.
- Diet is huge. Grass and grains result in lower levels of stearic acid. Forbs, bark, twigs, sagebrush, shrubs, and the like all increase it.

## Suet Boots

I like venison fat. A lot. But on a fat deer, there's often more than even I want to use for sausages or ground meat. Don't waste the excess! An old-timer's trick is to render down the fat into suet and use it to waterproof things, notably your hunting boots.

To render venison fat, cut it into little pieces about one inch across or smaller—the coarse die on your grinder is great for this—then put the pieces into a large, heavy pot. Cover with water and bring to a boil. Lower the heat to a simmer and cook the fat down until all the water has boiled away, which should take an hour or two, depending on how much fat you have.

When all the water has boiled away, most of the fat should have liquefied. Turn the heat down to low and keep cooking until the fat turns clear. Strain the fat through a paper towel into a wide-mouthed jar or can; I like to use a wide-mouthed pint or half-pint Mason jar. Let the fat solidify, and you'll have a jar of some of the best waterproofing material there is.

What's more, legend has it that with this stuff on your boots, you won't scare deer with your scent. Whether or not this is true, I have no idea, but I'd like to think it works.

Most saturated animal fats are composed of palmitic and myristic acid, which are present in all ruminants, including deer. As it happens, stearic acid, a third saturated fatty acid, is an anomaly. Diets high in stearic acid decrease the levels of "bad" cholesterol in people and may even increase the "good" cholesterol. At the very least, it is cholesterol neutral. Beef has some stearic acid, lamb more. But you know what has even higher levels of it? Chocolate. And it's this fact that will soon help explain something critical about eating venison fat.

So back to the question of hanging your deer. If you hang your deer with the fat exposed, will the fat begin to go rancid? Not really, and this busts the myth. All that stearic acid slows oxidation markedly. We trim deer fat not for rancidity but for texture.

A word on taste. Flavor in deer fat is all about meat care (which we just discussed) and diet. A deer that had been pillaging an alfalfa field or a cornfield will have fat that tastes a lot like beef or lamb fat. A deer eking out a living in the Great Basin or in the desert might not have any fat at all, and what fat there is may taste unpleasant. How can you tell? Render some in a pan with a little water, and if it smells good, it is good. Your nose won't lie.

That said, the primary carrier of individual flavor in animals is the fat, not the lean meat. If you like the flavor of lamb or beef fat, you'll like venison fat. Others might find it too strong. And that's fair, but I'm betting it isn't the flavor of the fat that's got them—it's the mouthfeel.

And this brings us to the final issue with deer fat: it can coat your mouth. Blame the stearic acid. You know why you love chocolate so much? One big reason is because that lovely flavor coats your palate. But when that coating is deer fat rather than chocolate, the experience is something else entirely—and not altogether pleasant. A little is fine, largely because it carries that nice venison flavor. But when I eat sausages I've made from venison alone, without other meats, they do taste fantastic, but I find that I need to drink something acidic, like red wine, to cut that very perceptible coating. Is it a deal-breaker? No. But it's something to be aware of.

So. Bottom line. If you want to eat your deer fat, I'd follow these guidelines:

- Save the fat when it's from deer that had been eating nice grasses, grains, or acorns. Remove the fat from deer inhabiting sagebrush or sketchy areas.
- Toss the suet (unless you want to make waterproofing material, candles, or soap or want to use it to feed the birds).
- Intramuscular fat will be softer than the fat on the outside of the muscles.
- Never use deer fat in dry-cured salami. Uncooked deer fat is nasty and chalky.
- Use deer fat sparingly in sausages and burger. A little adds a lot of flavor. A lot can give you that "coated mouth" thing.
- The fat on early-season or hot-weather deer can be downright fantastic. I discovered this by accident with a Coues deer in Arizona.
- Venison fat crisped on a roast or steak is awesome when eaten piping hot. You're welcome.

## VENISON AND FOOD SAFETY

Deer meat is among the safest meats around, and the incidences of food-borne illnesses linked to venison are few and far between. But it's not impossible to get sick from eating venison, and there are some basic food safety issues that you should be aware of when butchering, processing, and eating venison.

### Salmonella

Although salmonella is the most common food- borne illness in North America, infection from venison consumption is extremely rare. The lone recorded case of a person getting salmonella from eating venison was in Hawai'i in 2012, when a sixty-five-year-old man and his wife ate raw venison "sashimi" from a locally hunted deer. Deer feces can carry salmonella bacteria, but it too is pretty rare. A 2006 study of Nebraska deer found salmonella in only 1 percent of deer feces tested. A 2005 study in Scandinavia found no salmonella in 611 tested deer.

## E. coli

The nasty strain of *Escherichia coli* bacteria, *E. coli* O157:H7, is even rarer than salmonella in deer. Another Nebraska study, this one in 2001, found *E. coli* in only 4 of 1,608 total samples of whitetail deer feces. That's one-quarter of 1 percent. Likewise, that Scandinavian study cited earlier found no *E. coli* O157:H7 in its samples. One Georgia study, however, did find that of seventy-seven deer tested, 3 percent carried this nasty strain of *E. coli*.

In a wide study of the medical literature, I could find only five cases of people getting sick from venison-borne *E. coli*—two from blacktail deer, two from a whitetail deer, and one case with commercially raised red deer in Scotland. In one case, the disease was caused by deer feces contaminating the tenderloin; the whitetail case involved a gut-shot deer that hung for a while and whose gut cavity was not rinsed. Researchers suspected that the deer picked up *E. coli* O157:H7 from eating alongside cows, which are a far more common source of the bug. In another odd case in Minnesota in 2010, twenty-nine high school kids were poisoned by another strain of *E. coli* from whitetail deer. Most just got diarrhea, but two were hospitalized.

So can it happen? Sure. But it looks like you'd be more likely to get struck by lightning, live through it, and then be bitten by a shark. The takeaway: Exercise some common sense when dealing with any part of any animal's digestive tract. Work clean, and you should be fine.

## Trichinosis

According to the Centers for Disease Control and Prevention, only three cases of trichinosis could be traced to deer meat from 2002 to 2025. Given these statistics, I am highly confident in the safety of venison, both rare and well-cooked.

I am happy to say that since the first edition of this book was published, the USDA now recognizes that whole cuts of venison served at an internal temperature of 145°F are safe, although it still recommends cooking ground venison to 160°F. But as always, you should make up your own mind about it and do only what you feel comfortable doing. Remember, the immune systems of the very young, the very old, and the chronically ill are not as strong as those of young, healthy adults. Keep that in mind when serving raw or very rare venison.

## Chronic Wasting Disease: What You Need to Know

Chronic wasting disease (CWD) affects mule deer, whitetail deer, elk, moose, and other cervids (note that antelope are not affected by this disease, because they're not cervids). The disease makes them listless, emaciated, and generally sick. Ultimately, deer suffering from CWD die of general wasting, with pneumonia as the most likely proximate cause of death. Affected deer tend to be clumsy, too.

No one knows for sure what causes CWD, but many researchers point to a "rogue protein" called a prion that can wreak havoc on an affected organism, producing scrapie in sheep, bovine spongiform encephalopathy ("mad cow disease") in cattle, and Creutzfeldt-Jakob disease in humans.

This is one area where the conversation has changed since the first edition of this book. We know more now, but not everything. So the advice here reflects both updated science and a practical approach I've settled on.

The epicenter of CWD is an area of northeast Colorado, Wyoming, and the adjacent parts of Montana, Nebraska, Utah, and Kansas. The disease has also been detected in thirty-five states and five provinces in Canada, but many cases are restricted to deer farms. Areas where CWD has appeared in wild deer include New Mexico and far west Texas; North and South Dakota; Minnesota, Wisconsin, Iowa, and northern Illinois; West Virginia; Arkansas; Pennsylvania; Maryland; Michigan; Missouri; western Tennessee; Oneida County, New York; and in the Canadian provinces of Alberta and Saskatchewan.

For the most part, CWD is not a common affliction, although I saw one report of a herd in Colorado in which biologists estimated the rate of incidence at an alarming 40 percent. Elk populations in affected areas average around 2 percent infection, and incidences with moose or caribou are extremely rare, according to the Centers for Disease Control and Prevention.

There is no significant evidence that CWD is transmittable to humans; there appears to be a "species barrier" between us and the cervids. And since the first edition of this book was published, that barrier appears far stronger than previously thought. That said, chronic wasting disease does resemble mad cow disease, which has been shown to be able to jump the species barrier, and the possibility still exists of a new strain that could affect us in the future.

Bottom line: Every authority with whom I've consulted advises being safe rather than sorry. That means two things right off the bat: Deer brains are off the menu, and if you live in a CWD state, don't cut your venison into bone-in chops—fillet the whole backstrap off the bone instead.

Some advise against ever using bones from any deer shot in CWD country. I think this is a bit much, but I'll meet the authorities halfway and recommend that if you do live in areas where this disease exists, toss the spinal bones from the neck to the tail; if CWD is present, it will be primarily in the brain and spinal tissue, as well as the spleen and lymph nodes. So yeah, no Sicilian spleen sandwiches. (The spleen, by the way, is the pale, liver-like organ in the gut pile.) My advice: Use only the leg bones for stock.

If you're worried about CWD, here are some extra precautions that you can take when you are hunting in a state where the disease has been detected:

- First and foremost—and this is an ironclad rule for all hunting—don't eat any animal that looks weird or sick, or even if you just get a sense that something is wrong with it. Your instincts are generally good on this one.
- Wear latex, nitrile, or rubber gloves when gutting your deer or elk. I sometimes do this, and for a variety of food safety reasons, it's generally not a bad idea.
- Remove the bone from the meat. Don't saw through bone, and avoid cutting through the brain or spinal cord. I think this is wise in CWD areas, and it's not very different from how most people butcher their deer. The reason you don't want to saw through this stuff is that in theory, the saw could become contaminated and affect the meat itself.

- Be extra clean. Wash your hands, knives, and saws thoroughly after field dressing. Use hot, soapy water or a weak bleach solution.
- Don't eat the brain, spinal cord, eyes, spleen, tonsils, or lymph nodes of deer in CWD states.
- If you send your deer or elk to a butcher, tell him or her to process your animal individually, without adding any meat from other animals to the meat from your animal. Yeah, this happens a lot, especially with burger.

Note that many states forbid you from bringing home certain parts of deer and elk. California forbids all entry of heads and backbones, regardless of state of origin, but most states forbid entry of such from those states known to have CWD.

If you're interested in finding out if your animal might have had chronic wasting disease, consider taking advantage of the free testing offered by many state wildlife agencies, often available at check-in stations. The test itself takes only a few minutes, so if you do come across a testing station, it's well worth it. The results can take a week or two, however. And if your deer comes back CWD positive? That's your call. Some public health officials say you should toss the meat. If it were me, I would still eat the boneless meat, but I'd toss everything else. But remember, that is my personal choice.

## Lead and Venison

This is becoming less controversial these days. Lead bans are a political cause célèbre with anti-hunting groups all over the country, and in California, they've succeeded in banning lead ammunition altogether. But since the first edition of this book was published, the science has shifted from "Can you get lead toxicity from game?" to "Yes, it happens. How do we mitigate it?"

A 2022 study found that those who ate wild game had more lead in their blood than those who did not eat wild game. Lead levels were highest in those who ate not only venison but also other game. The study found that people who ate wild game had average lead levels of 1.4 micrograms per deciliter, compared with 0.84 in people who didn't eat game.

OK, that sounds bad. And it is, for children. The CDC's health guideline is 3.5 micrograms of lead per deciliter of blood, so we're talking about a significant level for young people. Chronic exposure to venison shot with lead bullets has also been linked to toxic levels of lead in the body.

Ultimately, it's your call. It's proven that if you shoot lead ammo, you will ingest micro-fragments of lead in your venison. Whether this is significantly harmful for most adults is unclear. What is more certain is that even tiny amounts of lead can damage development in a fetus or a young child, and most health agencies warn against pregnant women and young children eating lead-shot game. This is a warning I would heed.

Personally? I shoot copper.

## Other Heavy Metals

In some cases, deer and other cervids can bioaccumulate heavy metals in their meat and organs. Cadmium and other metals, as well as selenium (a mineral salt), can occasionally accumulate to levels that are potentially dangerous. Such cases are usually traced to specific local and regional environmental issues, such as the site downstream of a chemical spill in Michigan in the early 2000s that caused the local deer to pick up so much cadmium that the state health department advised hunters to avoid eating the deer's liver. Your body will rid itself of heavy metals over time, so a celebratory snack of your buck's kidneys or a meal or two of its liver isn't likely to give you problems. But if you live in areas that are troubled by heavy-metal contamination in likely deer habitat and you shoot a lot of deer, you might want to limit your intake.

## BUYING VENISON IN THE STORE

It has been illegal to sell truly wild venison in the United States for more than a century, thanks to various state and federal laws banning the practice. So how is it that you can buy venison in supermarkets?

The simple answer is that deer and elk can be farmed, and those farmed animals are legally considered livestock, not game. Although the number of deer and elk farms is growing in the US, most farmed venison sold in this country are red deer from New Zealand. Still, the US deer-farming industry is a $4 billion-a-year enterprise, with close to ten thousand farms, with high concentrations in Texas and Pennsylvania. Every state but Nevada and South Carolina has at least one farm. Unfortunately, most of the deer from these farms are shot by "hunters" seeking trophy bucks with minimal effort. Only about 20 percent are butchered and sold to the consumer market.

The quality of farmed deer varies wildly. While most cervids won't tolerate the tight, squalid conditions of a factory farm, even those farms that do offer acceptable accommodations for deer management and breeding are a far cry from natural, wild habitat. Meat from farmed deer tends to be lighter in color, softer, and less flavorful than that of a true wild deer. Deer from New Zealand is a step above most domestically farmed deer, since New Zealand deer tend to range wider than the deer on most American farms. And since most of the deer imported from New Zealand are red deer, a relative of our elk, the cuts are also larger and more beef-like.

Among the notable exceptions to this is the venison from Broken Arrow Ranch in Ingram, Texas. Broken Arrow Ranch is one of the few operations large enough to raise deer in a near-wild state, and it is one of the only outfits able to harvest their deer via sharpshooters, who can haul the carcasses immediately to a mobile USDA truck for butchering. This "one shot, one kill" method of harvest results in higher meat quality than that from deer sent to the slaughterhouse, which are often heavily stressed. Consequently, of all the farmed deer I've eaten over the years, Broken Arrow's is the closest thing to actual wild venison on the market today.

If you've eaten venison in a restaurant, Broken Arrow is likely the source, although several other purveyors, such as D'Artagnan Foods, also sell nationally. Nicky USA is an excellent purveyor in the Pacific Northwest.

If you want to buy venison, high-end supermarkets such as Whole Foods do sell it in the freezer section, but I've never seen it sold fresh. Broken Arrow and D'Artagnan sell online, as do several other outfits. But it'll cost you: steaks can run up to $50 a pound, and even burger can be more than $16 a pound.

Better to find a hunter.

# FROM FIELD TO FREEZER

We've come to the bloody section of the book. Here we'll cover skinning and gutting, field care, tips on getting the animal home, aging your meat, butchering your deer yourself, and storing it properly so you can enjoy it all year long.

## SKINNING AND GUTTING

OK, you have a deer, elk, moose, or whatever on the ground. Now what?

First, get the animal out of the sun if you can. If there's one thing I've become more adamant about over time, it's this: cooling the animal quickly matters more than almost anything else you do. Obviously, moving a moose or an elk in the field is not something one does casually. But keeping your animal out of the sun is especially important if you hunt in hot weather. If it's way below freezing, you can disregard this.

I like a scalpel-blade knife with a gut hook to get things going; a gut hook unzips a paunch quickly. You'll also want some sort of compact saw for the pelvis, which you'll need to crack open to remove the gnarly bits near the rectum. Heavy bolt cutters or loppers work here, too.

A good skinning knife is also a must. One good option is a trapper's pelting knife; these have been used for this purpose for several centuries. A better option, however, is a scalpel knife with disposable blades. I've never used anything sharper. In fact, the only caveat to using one is its sharpness. I've cut myself twice with one and barely knew it, once all the way to my knuckle. I had allowed myself to get distracted. Keep your eye on the ball and your wits about you, and you'll be amazed how easily things go with a scalpel blade.

I use gambrels to hoist a deer when I'm at a ranch or in a forest or if there are big trees around that I can use as attachment points. When I don't have gambrels, I typically skin one side of an animal then flip it using the skin as a mat for the other side. This works fine and is great in grasslands, where trees are scarce. It's also a perfect method for skinning on a truck's tailgate.

If you're backcountry hunting, you'll want to carry a game bag made from real cheesecloth, not the cheap stuff that lets flies in. Regular sealable plastic bags are handy for the heart, liver, and kidneys, as long as you have a cooler in the truck. If you don't have a cooler, washable mesh bags are good, or you can make a pouch from some cheesecloth. Zip ties are a good idea for attaching your tag, although leftover twist ties from a loaf of bread work, too. Some people like to wear nitrile or rubber gloves when they butcher animals, but I rarely do this when I'm working with deer, elk, or antelope.

### Skinning

Skinning a deer is fairly easy. I will normally start at the animal's hind leg at the first joint above the hoof. Pay attention to what you're doing and you'll only need the knife in those places where the skin sticks—you can literally peel the skin off most of the animal. Work both hind legs first, then the paunch, working all the way around to the backstrap.

If the animal has not yet been gutted, be careful around the paunch, as you don't want it open yet. Face the blade away from the gut and you'll be fine. Run the blade toward the genitals and then through the middle of the inside of the leg all the way to the last joint of the leg, if it hasn't already been skinned.

You'll need your knife to free the skin from the front legs, which you skin like the back ones, all

HughesNet

the way to the last joint before the hoof. I will typically wait to cut off the feet until I'm done skinning. You remove the feet with a good strong, stiff-bladed knife, working it between the joints, slicing tendons, and cracking the foot back against the way it ought to move. It's easy once you get the hang of it. Tree loppers or bolt cutters work too.

The hardest part is the neck, where the skin is tight to the meat. Just use short strokes with the blade to skin all the way up to the head. After skinning, slice deep, all the way to the bone at the base of the head. Here's the gruesome part: Yank the head in a circle, as though you were unscrewing the head from the neck, until it pops free. Slice the remaining bits with a knife and set the head aside. You'll want to skin this later for either a skull mount or to eat.

## Gutting

Time to gut the animal. Again, starting at the sternum with the blade facing away from the guts, run the knife to the genitals. Be aware that many states require that you preserve evidence of the sex of the deer, so don't toss them.

So you've opened the paunch and are staring at a bunch of stuff. What to do?

First, you'll notice a white, weblike membrane covering all the entrails. That is caul fat, and it's worth saving. It's clean-tasting fat latticing a thin but sturdy membrane. What do you do with it? Wrap things (typically meatballs—see British Meatballs, page 262). But caul fat also works wonders with lean cuts like backstrap or roasts. As they cook, the fat melts and bastes your meat, keeping it moist and lovely. Put it into a plastic bag and into the cooler it goes.

Now you'll need to let the offal fall. First, look toward the pelvis of the deer for a bag of liquid.

Hank removing the feet off a buck. This can also be done with a knife slipped between the bones of the shank and foot.

This will be the bladder, which may be full of urine. You need to remove this *carefully* or you'll get piss all over everything. I reach into where it attaches to the urethra and twist it once to close it off. Then I pinch the twist tight with one hand and cut off the bladder with the other. Toss it. *What happens if the bladder breaks and you get pee all over everything?* In most cases, you can wipe it off and move on, making sure to wash anything that the urine touched. If you're near a hose, this would be a good time to spray everything down.

On to the pelvis. Chances are that your deer will have some (ahem) bullets in the chamber. Mercifully,

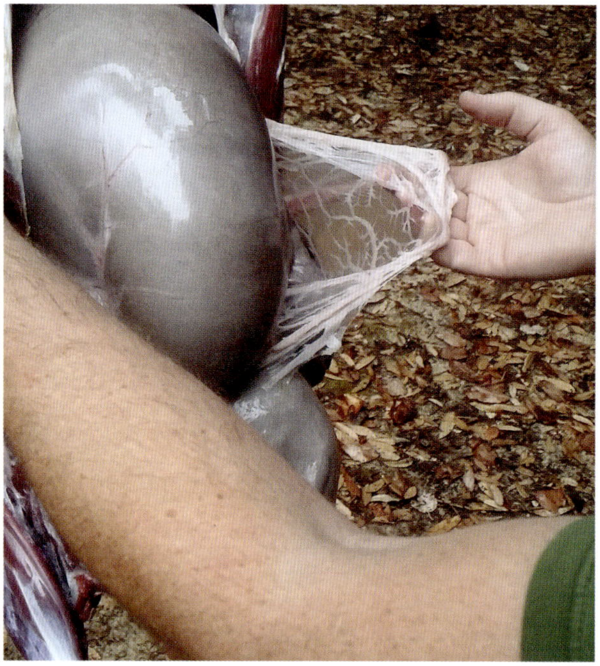

The stomach of a blacktail deer, full from his morning's meal. I'm pulling away the caul fat from it.

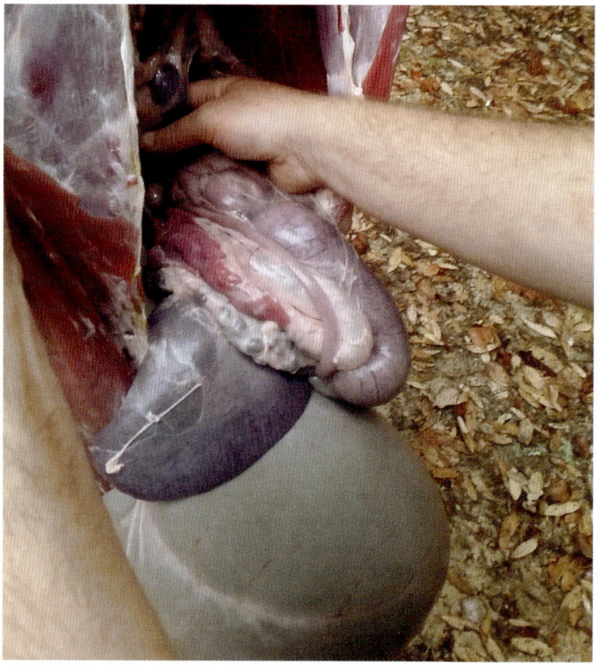

This is why they call it "offal." It's what "falls off" the carcass.

deer pellets aren't as toxic and stinky as pig shit, but you still don't want to be cavalier about it. You want to remove the rectum as cleanly as possible. An easy way to do this is with heavy-duty shears or loppers or a hand saw to cut through the pelvis so you can crack it open and lift the whole rectum out. This won't work on larger deer, though. For those, you'll need that hand saw. Saw through enough of the pelvis without rupturing the rectum underneath to crack the pelvis and lift the plumbing out. Tie it off with a twist tie if you have one.

Now you can basically pull everything out. I go to the front of the gut cavity and grab the windpipe, yank or slice it off (depending on the size of the animal), and pull everything free of the carcass. It will be steamy and bloody, especially where the lungs were.

But this won't work if the animal is on gambrels. In such cases, grab the stuff in the paunch and turn it out of the cavity, then slice any piping that's holding it to the front of the cavity, where the lungs and heart are. Then deal with the heart and lungs.

Be careful when you're removing the heart. It's encased in a slippery membrane called the pericardium, within which it is firmly attached. You will need both hands: one on the knife, one to grab the stuff holding the heart in. Carefully slice that off to free the heart. This is where most people cut themselves, so be careful during this procedure.

In this gut pile will be a large, burgundy organ. That's the liver. Take it and put it aside to cool. Once cooled, put the liver into a bag and into a cooler. Look at the inside of the carcass: You'll probably see the two little kidneys, which in deer look as

## Pee Needles

**One tip I've learned is to have a syringe at the ready for use in those cases where you have to deal with a really full bladder. Stick the needle into the bladder, being careful not to pierce the other side, and retract the plunger. This will create a vacuum that will suck urine into the syringe. Remove the syringe from the bladder, press the plunger to empty the urine, and reinsert into the bladder. Repeat the process until the bladder is not so taut with pee, then twist it off and cut as described. Make sure you put the cap back on the syringe and dispose of it properly later.**

you might imagine kidneys to look, only encased in heavy white fat. Save them, too.

If you are adventurous, you can save the stomach to make tripe. The stomach will probably be filled with green ick that must be cleaned out thoroughly. Cleaning deer tripe (see page 43) is something of a process, but if tripe's your thing, deer tripe is perfectly usable. I like it.

You want to save the tongue too. This can be tricky to remove, as it's a strong muscle, firmly attached to the base of the skull. The best way to remove the tongue is to come up underneath by slicing away the skin and tissue between the two mandibles of the lower jaw. Grab the tongue, pull it down through, and sever it as close to the base as possible, where there is a little forked bone. It's a bit grisly, but it's an effective method.

If you're dealing with an elk, moose, bison, nilgai, or other large animal, skin the head as best you can and carve out the animal's cheeks. They can be quite large on a moose or bison and are worth it, even in large deer. You remove them with a boning knife, slicing as close to the lower jaw as possible, up to behind the eye. It's exactly like removing a fish cheek, if you've ever done that.

Can you save other things? Yes, but I admit I have not. That pale, liver-like organ in there is the spleen. Italians eat spleen sandwiches, which I hear are edible. And of course, there are the intestines, which, if cleaned religiously, can be used for sausages or chitterlings. And finally, the lungs can be saved, rinsed free of blood, and ground into haggis.

If you're super dedicated, even the blood can be saved. There can be quite a lot in the cavity near the lungs. You'd need to pour it into a vessel somehow and then stir in about a tablespoon of red wine vinegar for every pint or so to prevent the blood from coagulating. You could then make blood sausages if you wanted to. I have not done this with deer, but it is possible.

Once you have all the wobbly bits you want to keep, use paper towels to thoroughly wipe out and dry the cavity. Water is your enemy until you can get the carcass chilled because bacteria like wet places above 40°F. If you're near a walk-in cooler, however, hose down the cavity and *then* dry it well.

### Dealing with Gut-Shot Deer

It's every deer hunter's nightmare: a poor shot, a wounded animal, and a long search that either ends in anguish or a rapidly decaying carcass. It's on your honor to tag that animal anyway and deal with the meat as best you can. Hunt deer long enough, and it is a near certainty that this will happen to you.

Deer are ruminants, and as such, they host beneficial bacteria in their digestive tracts that break down twigs, leaves, grains, and anything else the deer decided to eat. Those bacteria aren't harmful in and of themselves (*Escherichia coli* bacteria may sometimes be present, though it's rarely the *E. coli* O157 strain that can make us seriously ill.) But the digestive process is a stinky affair, no matter what animal you're dealing with; if the gut cavity is pierced and those bacteria are allowed to run free and extend their activity outside the gut, the meat can become tainted.

Time and temperature are the critical factors that will determine what you can salvage from a gut-shot deer. One year, I killed a mule deer buck with the infamous "Texas heart shot." I'd been aiming for the animal's neck, but he moved at the last second, and I put a bullet through the top of the buck's left hindquarter. It ripped through everything en route to a lung shot. Miraculously, the deer died of blood loss almost instantly, taking only a couple of steps before it dropped. My friend Randy and I were on this deer in an instant, and we gutted it as usual, using our bottled water to rinse any digestive ick off the meat. I ended up losing a little bit of that hindquarter and one tenderloin, but that was it. This was a best-case scenario.

I've seen deer shot in the paunch and then felled with a follow-up shot. There was little or no meat loss in these cases. Other times, however, I've seen deer shot in the guts and not recovered for hours—sometimes as long as a day. This is where things get tricky. What you can salvage depends on temperature and on how long the carcass has been exposed to its own gut contents. You're more likely to salvage more meat in freezing weather than in the August heat of California's A-Zone (the state's largest deer-hunting area). But remember that deer hides are tremendous insulators, so even in subzero temperatures, the meat can spoil if it has lain too long.

Whatever happens, open up the deer as usual and clean out the cavity. It will stink. Some hunters put Vick's VapoRub under their noses to disguise the smell, which can get into your nostrils and not go away. For some people, this can be traumatic enough to put them off eating that deer even months later, even if by that time, the meat has no smell at all. We create strong associations with smell, so beware of this effect.

I prefer to face the nasty business head-on. If I'm close to civilization, I'll use water bottles to clean out the carcass and then dry it with paper towels that I keep in my backpack. Then, when I get to the house or lodge, I'll forcefully hose out the cavity, dry it, and trim off any meat that appears to be contaminated.

But isn't water bad for a carcass? Not really. What's bad for a carcass is long-term contact with water above 40°F, which invites bacterial growth. In that case, water can be truly harmful. Clean water—not stream or pond water—is your friend, provided you can dry out the cavity afterward.

Once I've cleaned the carcass and dried it, I will very carefully smell the inside. In paunch-shooting situations where delay has been minimal, as in the two cases I described above, the smell will normally be acceptable. If the carcass stinks, it will need further treatment. And if the deer has been on the ground for hours, those digestive juices can ruin the meat, especially the tenderloin, which is exposed to them directly. First, try wiping down the inside of the carcass with vinegar, then dry it again. Let the animal hang a bit to dissipate any vinegar smell, then take another sniff. If it still stinks, you'll need to sacrifice those parts of the hind legs that are touching the paunch. Ribs are likely done for, too. But most of the animal should be OK. It won't be prime, mind you, but it should be safe to eat.

The reason that I urge you to face the situation of a gut-shot deer head-on and proactively should be clear—a quick response and a careful, thorough assessment are key to salvaging the most from your kill.

## The Dreaded Bone Sour

Should you fail to cool off a carcass fast enough (and remember, the larger the carcass, the harder this is to do), another creeping disaster awaits you. No matter how well you shot an animal, if it lies un-gutted and warm, it can get what's called "bone sour."

You'll know it when it happens. The meat will stink horribly of rotten flesh, and there will be a green tinge near the bone, much like gangrene. Basically, what has happened is that the carcass did not cool fast enough, and with no more immune response from the animal, existing internal bacteria explode within, rotting the meat from the bones outward. This is most common in larger animals like elk and moose, but it can happen in deer, too.

All cervids have body temperatures of at least 100°F, and mule deer can run as high as 104°F. You'll need to bring that temperature down below 80°F within the first hour, if at all possible. With a deer, this normally just means gutting it, unless it's hot out, in which case you'll need to quickly skin the animal, too. But with elk, moose, and even caribou, you must not only gut and skin the animal but also quarter it—unless it's really cold out.

Why? Airflow. A big elk hindquarter can be two feet thick, and without enough airflow around it to cool the ham, it can start to spoil right where the femur attaches to the pelvis, the most common origin for bone sour. An exception is cold-weather hunting. If you're in bitterly cold weather, quartering an elk, moose, or caribou is still a good idea, but leave the hide on as protection against freezing.

On the other hand, if you're elk hunting and it's very hot out, say 80°F or warmer, you might want to go one step further and use a knife to separate some of the large hind leg muscles from each other, cutting down to the bone, but not removing the meat from the femur. Prop the two muscles apart with a stick or something similar to cool down the meat even faster.

If you can't hang the quarters, prop them up off the ground or the truck bed with logs or PVC pipe—anything that will allow air to flow underneath those giant hindquarters. Do this for the front legs too once you have your hind legs squared away.

A few years ago, I saw one brilliant setup where the hunters laid sticks and branches and pine needles in a sort of bridge over a stream and set the meat on that. The airflow from the running water plus the natural cooling worked like magic to cool the meat. So keep this trick in mind if the situation ever presents itself.

## HANGING AND AGING DEER

Hanging and aging deer and other big game animals is one of the more controversial topics of deer hunting. Some swear by it, while others never age their deer and swear by that. I've eaten deer aged a month and deer aged a couple of days. Both were fine. So what's the real deal? What happens when you age meat, and what should you do once you have your deer up on the gambrels?

The short answer is that by aging meat, you are removing moisture and allowing enzymes present in the meat to break down connective tissue. The longer this goes, the more flavorful the amino acids that are created by this process—up to a point. Really old meat, even when perfectly aged, will begin to smell and taste like blue cheese. It's not bad for you, but it can be a little off-putting. Note that with game animals, which are lean, this blue-cheesy aroma is minimal compared to beef because it comes from aged fat, not muscle.

Before we get into aging and hanging deer, you need to know this: *Remove the tenderloins!* They don't need aging, and if you leave them on the carcass while aging, the rind that forms on them will need to be trimmed and there will be nothing left.

The perfect deer-aging scenario would look something like this: You'd shoot your deer in weather somewhere below freezing, say around 20°F. You'd gut it close to the truck (and save the offal) and get it to your locker. Yes, to properly age a whole carcass, you need a walk-in cooler or locker. If you had access to such an enviable appliance, you'd hang your deer, still in its skin, for up to three weeks between 33°F and 38°F, with the humidity in the cooler somewhere between 60 and 70 percent Then you'd skin the deer and butcher as normal.

Why is this perfect?

- The deer cooled down very quickly after the shot.
- The deer was hung in a perfect environment: humid enough to prevent the carcass from desiccating and cold enough to inhibit bacterial growth. Aging, remember, is enzymatic, not bacterial.
- You kept the skin on, which prevented that rind from forming on the outside of the meat. That rind needs to be cut away in dry-aging, which results in significant meat loss.

- The deer aged for three weeks, a duration that has been shown in a number of studies to yield the best combination of tenderness and "dry age-y" flavors that most of us love.

Sadly, this ain't happening for most of us, including me.

Our primary limitation is lack of a locker. This can be solved with a friendly butcher, and I've seen many places in this country with meat lockers the butcher will let you use for a small fee. I know a couple of zealots who have built home walk-ins, and I salute their enthusiasm. But there are a few other solutions, too.

Got a spare fridge in the garage? You know, the one with all the beer in it? Drink the beer, clean out the fridge with a diluted bleach solution or other antibacterial cleanser, and remove all but the top rack. Quarter your deer, then age the hind legs—minus the shanks—in that fridge by suspending them from the top rack with hooks and twine. If you want to dry-age a backstrap, I highly recommend keeping it on the bone, sawing the spine in front of the pelvis and then at the end of the backstrap, which ends above the shoulder. You will need to saw through ribs to do this. Keep in mind that if you are in an area with chronic wasting disease, you'd want to be sure your deer tested negative.

Why not the rest of the deer? Because while dry-aging a whole animal is nice, it's not necessary. You only get the benefit from dry-aging on parts of the deer you plan to cook medium or rare. If you're cooking it for hours in a stew, the benefits of aging get lost.

A more common option isn't dry-aging, but it will give the meat proper time to rest before butchering. Skin the animal, break it down into big pieces (legs plus body), and keep it over ice in a cooler for at least twenty-four hours (forty-eight hours is standard). Then break the animal down and age the pieces in the fridge in plastic containers for another few days. Only then do you vacuum-seal them.

Melting ice water on meat is to be avoided. The water will likely be about 40°F or even warmer, and it will encourage any bacteria already on the meat to start growing. Water will also wash out the meat itself, making it pale and tasteless. So you need to keep the meat off the melt water. It won't be ruined if it gets a little wet, but it's not ideal. Initially, I use garbage bags or burlap sacks to shield the meat. Then, when I am doing the preliminary aging of the primals (legs, shoulders, etc.), I set them in a large, open plastic container inside the cooler. If you have a big deer, you'll need several coolers going at once.

Why not butcher right away? Because you never want to butcher an animal while it is still stiff with rigor mortis. Doing so will cause what's called "shortening," a process that results in tough meat, especially if you freeze the meat after butchering. The most important thing to remember is that you need to let rigor take its course. Patience.

After the meat has relaxed for a day or two, you can butcher without problems.

Wet-aging is different. Wet-aging is what the supermarket industry does to the meat it sells you. The animal is hung a few days, then butchered, then vacuum-sealed and kept refrigerated for up to a couple of months. After that, the meat will get weirdly sour, and not in a good way. Over this period, wet-aged meat may become more tender than meat that's fresh, but it will never develop the flavor complexity of dry-aging. I do recommend it as an option for roasts and backstrap of old or rutty animals. Simply cut your roast or length of backstrap, pat dry, and vacuum-seal. Keep it in the fridge no warmer than 36°F for a month. Then remove from the bag, dry again, reseal, and freeze.

## Dry-Aging

I dry-age the hind legs (minus the shank) and the bone-on backstrap on every old or large animal I bring home. But be forewarned: if you want to do this too, you will need to commit to aging *at least* ten days, because the flavors you are seeking don't develop before one week.

If you want to age venison the way they age steak in the finest steakhouses, cut the carcass into sub-primals—for example, a whole backstrap (or one sliced in two when it's from a large animal), a long length of chops, a hind leg, or a big roast. Why? Because you get better yield and more evenly distributed moisture loss this way, leading to better flavors in the long run. *And you must leave any fat cap on.* This is vital. The fat protects the meat. You will trim much of it off later, but you need it now.

OK, go back to your fridge. (Ideally, you're using the spare beer fridge in the garage, because aging meat smells funky and because the meat can pick up odors from all the other food in the refrigerator, and vice versa.) Set the fridge to between 33°F and 38°F. Set the large pieces of venison on a rack. They *should* be elevated for good airflow.

Set a pan of salty water somewhere in the fridge to promote decent humidity. If it evaporates, refill it.

The hard part: You should have a fan in the fridge. I've tried battery-operated fans but have found them to be frustrating. The batteries seem to run out every other day or so, and while you can recharge them, it's a pain. Better to have a little fan with a power cord that you can snake out the side of the fridge and into an outlet. You might need to cut a small notch in the rubber seal on the side of the fridge door to do this.

Now you wait. How long? At least ten days, but honestly, real dry-aged flavor doesn't happen until two weeks; three weeks is even better. You can go longer. I took the backstrap of the deer I shot in the essay on page 150 sixty-one days, but I coated it in melted deer fat, let the fat solidify, then aged it. If you want to age past three weeks, you'll need this fat cap, which will help prevent the meat from desiccating too much.

One thing about aging venison: You can't truly get that funky-cheesy flavor of well-aged beef, because that comes from the fat, especially the marbled fat within the steaks. It can be done with bison, however.

When the meat is ready, trim off the gnarly, often moldy outside of the venison. Don't worry; mold is normal. Usually, you will need to slice off less than a quarter inch or so. See why you don't want to do this with small deer? Too much meat loss.

A few final tips:

- The older the animal, the longer the hang time and the longer the aging process. This goes for both does and bucks. Shoot a matron cow elk and you will want to hang and age it as long as a bull.
- Artificial tenderizers like pineapple or papaya juice don't work. All they do is attack the surface of meat, making it mushy. Aging works from within.

### Dry-Aging Fridges

**I have one, and I love it. It's made by Dry Ager, a German company, and you can dial in a wide range of temperatures and humidity levels with precision. But they are expensive, at a minimum of $1000, and often a lot more than that. So if you have the means, do it. But I can tell you I did fine with the set up I describe below for many years.**

- The so-called dry-aging bags are also useless for true dry-aging. Don't buy them.
- Keep your meat in darkness. Sunlight oxidizes fat, especially venison fat, which is much higher in omega-3 fatty acids; these oxidize faster than typical beef fat.
- You can use the leathery trim you cut off in broth or stock, if it is not moldy.

You *can* age pre-frozen meat, since freezing simply puts the enzymes that make the magic happen into suspended animation. But keep in mind that aging improves the water-holding properties of the meat, and since you lose moisture when you freeze meat (the water in the cells turns to ice, breaks the cell walls, and then, when you defrost, those cells leak fluid), aging it before you freeze will keep your venison juicier when you cook it. Nevertheless, butchers age meat that's been pre-frozen all the time. Just don't age on both ends of the process (don't age, then freeze, then age again). Butcher and age then freeze, or butcher and freeze then age. Don't age twice.

## Deer Processor Tips

One of the reasons I wrote this book a decade ago was to give you the knowledge and skills needed to free yourself from dependence on meat processors. I'd heard so many horror stories, and I still do. I surveyed hundreds of fellow hunters, for whom processors run the gamut from "national treasure" to "we should burn that place down." Community reputation is a solid place to start. Is it an active meat market, where people come all year long? Are they known for their sausages, jerky, and other value-added products?

Another key that you have a good processor is the cut sheet. Do they offer you one? If not, eh, maybe they're not so great. A cut sheet, where they give you options for how your deer or elk is processed, shows flexibility and skill. I've seen deer cut sheets so rich in options they look like beef cuts, offered alongside the shop's dizzying array of possible sausages. That's a sign of a great processor.

But in general, especially in the South, you get what you get. You can always ask for pork or beef fat in a particular ratio—typically 10 to 20 percent—for your ground meat, and you can almost always get your backstraps back whole, which is what I recommend. You can often convince them to give you your shanks whole, too. Do this.

And you can also ask for specific cuts. The worst they can say is no, and in many cases, they will respect you more for wanting decent cuts on your animal rather than forty-five pounds of snack sticks (although I do know hunters who kill so many deer they can spare one for snack sticks).

If it's a band-saw operation where they love making the dreaded leg "steak," ask them for boneless hind leg roasts. Often times, they'll do it, but sometimes they charge extra. Pay them. It's worth it.

You'll see "tenderized" a lot. This can mean one of three things: the meat was beaten up with a meat tenderizer mallet, run through a "cuber" for cube steak, or stabbed a zillion times with a Jaccard. Generally speaking, these procedures tenderize tougher cuts enough so you can cook them as if they were a steak. And they do make a decent country-fried steak (page 134), but I wouldn't serve them to a date.

## BUTCHERING YOUR OWN DEER

For many of us, the time spent butchering our own animals is a vital period of transition; in the act of butchering, we make the shift from hunter to cook. It's a quiet time during which to focus on the animal, sharp knife in hand, and to think about your plans for this creature you've laid low for your nourishment. Butchery is an intensely personal business—you cut up an animal in exactly the sort of pieces that you intend to cook in the days, weeks, and months ahead.

Chops are my favorite example. On most whitetail deer, chops are so small and thin as to be worse than useless; they get you all excited when you break them out of the freezer, only to dash your hopes as you watch them go from lovely to leathery in seconds in the pan. In these cases, the answer is to cut long rib roasts, the way they do with lamb, so that you have many chops, all attached, which you can then cook as a whole, slicing them into pretty, individual chops before you serve. Oddly, I have yet to see a professional butcher do this for a deer, for reasons known only to them.

A while back, I asked readers of *Hunter Angler Gardener Cook* whether they butcher their own deer (or elk, antelope, or moose) or take them to a processor or butcher. Of the more than three hundred answers I received, only nine people said they use a butcher exclusively, and several of those nine knew the butcher personally. A few more noted that using a professional butcher is a convenience when they are hunting outside their home state or province, and a few more said that they'd take a few deer to a processor, especially when the plan was to give the meat to others, but they'd always butcher the "important" deer themselves.

This was wonderful to hear. I've always likened the process of butchering to opening up a present. This might sound odd to those who've never done it. But the practiced dismantling of a deer, elk, or antelope is strangely calming and exciting at the same time. It's lovely to move your knife in such a way that a perfect holiday roast comes off the hind leg, a single muscle ready for roasting. And yet there are always surprises. Maybe you've shot an elk, an animal large enough to collect the hanger steak from; I know this was downright thrilling for me, after so many little deer that had come before. I love hanger steak in beef, that slab of meat that hangs between the upper and lower body cavity (basically the diaphragm). But you need a big beast to get a usable hanger steak, and an elk is just about big enough.

There is also the warm sense of satisfaction that comes from knowing that you know how to break down a deer and that you did it well. What's more, you know that you alone touched the meat that you

## CLEANING DEER TRIPE

OK, this one is for the gastronauts among you. If you like beef or lamb tripe, you will like deer tripe, which is thinner and more tender than either. First, cut the big stomach away from the other ones; deer have multiple stomachs, as do all ruminants. Unless you're dealing with an elk or moose, the other stomachs are too small to bother with.

Now slice open the stomach and stand back. A tsunami of stinky green ick will flow out like vegetal lava. Yay. Now hose off the stomach as best you can. A good spray jet works for this.

You'll notice that the inside looks disturbingly like brownish-grayish-green terry cloth. Hose this *thoroughly* and set it aside until you are ready to work on it.

When you're ready to continue preparing the tripe, cut the stomach into large pieces that will lay flat. Sprinkle coarse salt on one side and scrub vigorously with a scrub brush to make sure you get every last bit of stray greenery out. Do the same for the other side. Rinse off the pieces.

Now put the pieces in a nonreactive (*not* aluminum or copper), lidded container and cover with water. Add two tablespoons of hydrogen peroxide and mix well. It will fizz alarmingly. Why do this? Hydrogen peroxide will both kill bacteria and slightly bleach the tripe. Soak the pieces in this solution in the fridge for one hour.

Now rinse again. Finally, use a paring knife to scrape away the terry cloth–looking stuff. It will zip off easily in some places and stick in others. Slice off any ugly looking bits.

You now have tripe ready for cooking (Venison Tripe Neapolitan Style, page 276) or for freezing.

plan to feed yourself, your friends, and your family. If there are any food safety issues, you have only yourself to blame. This is a responsibility many people are more than willing to accept.

Now, to be sure, I have nothing against professional butchers. Many are true artisans who work magic on a carcass. But the most common complaint I heard from readers when I asked about outsourcing the processing of their game was the instances of bad butchery they'd encountered—sloppy, callous, and careless. Bone fragments in steaks. Burger ground with no extra fat or with a type of fat the hunter specifically asked not to have included. Missing tenderloins (this happens a lot, apparently). The aforementioned micro-chops. Not getting your own deer back (borderline criminal, in my opinion). And most of all, stupid cuts, the infamous leg steak chief among them.

What the hell is a "leg steak," anyway? You may know what I mean: that horrid "steak" that's been cut with a bandsaw right through a deer's hind leg? It is an abomination. It's three to five separate muscles (depending on where it's been cut), barely attached to each other by membrane, with a disk of sliced femur in the center. Surrounding each of those muscles is a skein of silverskin that, in most cases, is so strong you could lash up your snowshoes with it. When you cook this thing, the silverskin contracts, making the whole piece of meat curl. The separate muscles try to fall away from each other—and sometimes do—and there is so much surface area relative to mass on the thing that it's virtually impossible to cook medium-rare, as a decent steak ought to be. And even if you manage to succeed in this feat, that silverskin will not have broken down, and it will resist all but the sharpest knives; your teeth will be no match for it. Revolting.

And yet I've seen this cut of meat all across the country. Even weirder, I've seen "chops" of backstrap, with both sides of the loin and tenderloin still attached to a sliver of vertebrae. Bizarre.

All of this leads a great many people to home butchery. But how to go about it? How even to get started?

First, you need some tools, both physical and mental. Learning how to butcher a deer from a book isn't ideal, though there are whole books devoted to the task. And while I will give you instructions on how I butcher, you could do worse than pick up copies of Al Cambronne's *Gut It, Cut It, Cook It*, as well as John J. Mettler Jr.'s classic *Basic Butchering of Livestock & Game*. Philip Hasheider's *The Complete Book of Butchering, Smoking, Cooking and Sausage Making* is worth reading too. If you're looking for good information about gutting a deer in the field, Cambronne's book and Jackson Landers's *Hunting Deer for Food* are great sources. None of these guys butcher large animals the way I do, but they're all skilled at the task.

Now you need some implements of deconstruction. I'm hesitant to suggest too many brand names here, as models change over time and often become obsolete. But a few companies do have innovative products that might become standard down the road; those I'll mention by name.

## At Home

Once you get home, you need an area in which to work. I use my little kitchen. Turning the family kitchen over to butchering may not be possible for everyone, and I know many people who set up stations in their garages, complete with stainless steel tables and special sinks. I'll tell you that once you get the hang of it, you won't wreck your kitchen too badly. And besides, it'll be a great excuse for a deep clean afterward.

You'll want lots of cheap, white kitchen towels (so you can bleach them later) and large plastic tubs, both of which are available at your local supermarket. Have several rolls of paper towels around too.

If you haven't done so already, you'll need to quarter your deer. I use a pair of boning knives for most of this work as well as for the fine work that follows. My go-to tool is an ancient, stiff-bladed Old Hickory boning knife. I like a stiff blade for most uses because it feels more substantial somehow. That said, I switch to a flexible boning knife when I remove the backstraps and silverskin because the bend in the blade helps me extract as much meat—or in the case of silverskin removal, to save as much—as possible. Flexible blades also tend to be thinner, which helps a lot.

I can do almost all my butchery with those two knives, plus my regular chef's knife. The only other tool I need is a saw of some sort. I used to use a regular hacksaw, but I've graduated to a proper cordless Sawzall. I use the saw only for ribs and front leg shanks. Everything else I can do with a knife. Keep in mind that I don't cut chops, so I don't need the saw for that.

Keeping your knives sharp is a must. Invest in a good sharpener, or, if you are really serious, a set of Japanese water stones in various grits (one 1000 grit stone and one 6000 grit makes a good, all-purpose set). A sharpening steel is essential too, for honing the blade and realigning the micro-serrations at the edge. That's what I use each day to keep my blades lightning sharp.

## Getting to It

I'm going to assume you have a dead, gutted, skinned deer in your kitchen or work area. Once again, this is how *I* butcher a deer. It's a method that works for me, and it's very similar to what the French call "seam butchery," which respects the natural seams between muscle groups. American butchers tend to ignore these seams and cut things seemingly willy-nilly (thus the "leg steak.") Ready? Here we go.

## Offal

Start with the offal, the wobbly bits. These are probably sitting in a plastic bag in your fridge or cooler. Mostly, I'm talking about the heart, liver, kidneys, and tongue. Tripe (stomach) we just dealt with above (see sidebar on page 43).

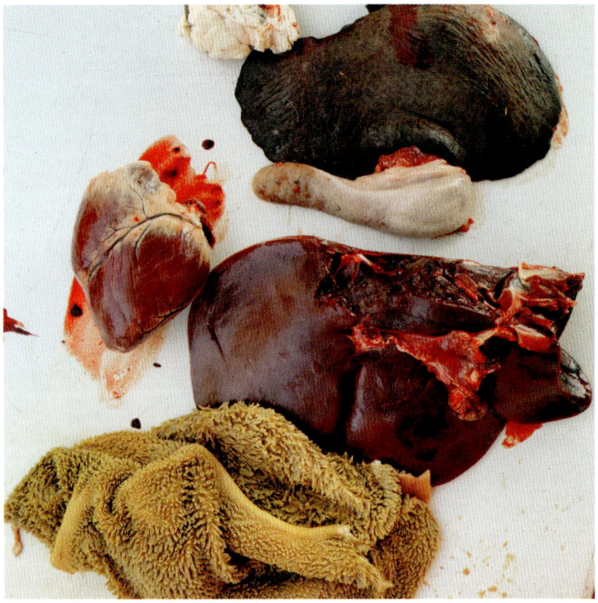

Fresh deer offal

Wash all the various bits under cold water and pat them dry. Slice the top off the heart, above the ring of fat; this is mostly veiny and arterial stuff, anyway. Rinse out any blood clots, and you're done for now. If you want to make heart cutlets, see my recipes for Jägerschnitzel (page 132) or Grilled Heart with Peppers (page 254).

Pull the fat off the outside of the kidneys. Find the gossamer membrane surrounding the kidney and pull it off (it's like the finest cellophane). Wash the kidneys thoroughly. You're good for now.

With both liver and kidneys, you can soak them in a brine that has a ratio of ¼ cup kosher salt to 1 quart water overnight. I do this before a milk soak (see page 253). I like to soak liver and kidneys in milk for a day before storing. This removes even more of the musky, gamey flavor from these organs than does the brine. Mind you, I am no wuss when it comes to gamey flavors, but deer livers and kidneys can get a stink on them something fierce.

When you're ready to store these organs, rinse off the milk and pat dry. Cut out any weird connective tissue, and cut the liver into portions that you might eat in one sitting; I like one-pound pieces.

The tongue is easy. Just rinse and dry, and you're ready to store.

## Primal Cuts

### LEGS

Put the deer on its back, and with your off hand, push one front leg away from the ribs. Using a stiff boning knife, slice into this gap to free the leg. You'll see a cobwebby substance between the leg and the body—this is the connective-tissue membrane that separates things. It's what you always want to keep in view during this whole process, as these membranes demarcate the seams between muscle groups. Keep slicing upward until you find the white cartilage of the animal's shoulder. Try not to slice right through this (as can so often happen) so that you can keep the shoulder whole. Slip the knife under the cartilage, leaving a fair bit of meat on the body attached to the ribs; you'll get to this in a bit. Free the front leg. You'll notice that the front legs of all big game animals aren't attached to the body by a bone. Our own front "legs" (our arms) are attached by our collarbone (the only game animal I know of with a collarbone is a squirrel. Neat, eh?) Do the other front leg the same way.

If it's not cold out, I like to have a cooler with ice close at hand. I'll put the various primal parts into plastic tubs set in the cooler to keep them cold while I work. A fridge works, or if it's cold, leave them on the table while you work.

With the front legs removed, move to the back legs. All game animals have their back legs attached by a ball-and-socket joint. Again, with the deer on its back, feel around for where the ball-and-socket joint ought to be—in the middle of the pelvic bone you probably sawed through in the field.

Use your knife to slice downward along the pelvic bone until you find the joint. When you do, give a good strong yank downward on the leg with one hand while anchoring the pelvis with the other. Your goal is to pop the ball out of the socket. When you do, stop and look at the back end of the ham. You'll notice that it comes up, over, and around the pelvis. This is the rump. Use your knife to free the leg from the pelvis, keeping in mind that it's not one straight cut. If you've ever seen a nice country ham or a whole prosciutto, you may remember that the meat on the outer side of the ball joint (the joint's exposed in a ham) is higher than the inner side. Aim to replicate this. It takes a bit of practice, but all is not lost if you are sloppy here; the meat in this area is excellent for stew or for sausage if for some reason the larger cuts couldn't be kept whole.

Do this for both legs. Move each one to the cooler or fridge.

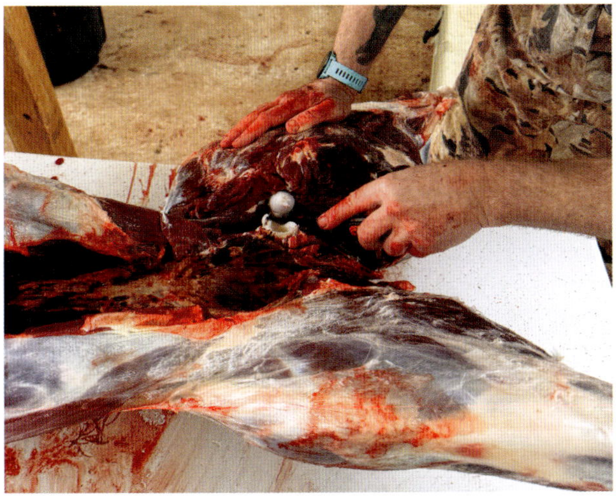

The key to removing the hind leg is to find the ball-and-socket joint.

## BACKSTRAPS AND TENDERLOINS

Now you're left with a (probably) headless torso. If you have the head still attached, sever it where it meets the neck by cutting with a knife all the way around until you can see bone. Twist forcefully until the head comes free. You can also saw it off. You can save doe heads to make Mexican Barbacoa (page 97) so long as your animal doesn't have CWD.

At this point, you have several options for how to proceed, but I like to move on to the backstraps from here.

The backstraps are the loins of the deer, akin to the ribeye in beef. They run along the outside of the entire spine in two thick bands of muscle. You will want to slice them off whole so that you get two pieces, one on each side of the spine. Use a flexible knife for this so you can slide it along the bumpy road of the vertebrae. I move the carcass so the animal is on its side, with its back facing me. Using the knife, start slicing right behind the neck, then cut along the backbone back toward the pelvis. You want to press the blade against the backbone as you cut so you don't miss any meat. As you slice, tap the point of the blade on the lateral flange of the vertebrae that anchors the rest of the backstrap meat. Doing this ensures that you are cutting all the way down. Slice to the pelvis.

Now, using the ribs as your guide, free the backstrap from the spine. As you slice, keep the blade anchored on the ribs so you don't miss any meat, and tap the point of the blade on the vertical flange of the backbone. The backstrap should pull away nicely. Do this for both sides.

Underneath the backstraps are the tenderloins, little torpedoes of meat that are the most tender parts of the animal. You can just pull them off, or you can slice them off the same way you did the backstraps.

### NECK

For the neck, you can do one of three things: You can hack off as much meat as possible and use it in the grinder; you can saw it off whole and use it as a bone-in pot roast, a nice option with small deer; or you can bone the whole neck and use that as a pot roast (this is what I do most often—see Polish Pot Roast with a Venison Neck, page 90). I'm sorry to say that there is no magical shortcut method for boning a neck. With all those weird angles from the vertebrae, you just have to work at it with a small knife in short strokes (I use a paring knife for this). I love how Mettler puts it in his *Basic Butchering of Livestock & Game*: "using your ingenuity . . . " Yeah, that's about it. Figure this one out. There is no easy way.

Whistlers from a large buck deer

That said, it's no biggie if things are a little ragged. If you use the neck as a pot roast, you'll want to roll it and truss it anyway, or braise it long enough that it falls apart and then shred the meat.

On a very large deer, elk, or moose, you can get two fun steaks (called whistlers) off the twin muscles guarding the windpipe and esophagus. They look like a tenderloin but are not as tender. Nevertheless, cooked whole and sliced into medallions, they are very nice. On smaller deer, I use these pieces of meat for stew or stir-fry.

### BRISKET OR BREAST

I happen to love the old recipes that call for "breast of venison," a good description for what is essentially the brisket. To keep the "breast" whole, I never split the sternum when I gut a deer; I reach up under the ribs to grab the heart, lungs, and windpipe. Once the carcass is ready for butchering, you'll see the brisket cupping either side of the front of the sternum. It's a flat piece of meat we call the brisket in beef, but alas, unlike beef brisket, the brisket from venison is usually not fatty. It makes a fantastic pot roast or braise, though, so I like to keep it in one piece. It is easily removed from the ribs with a short, sharp knife. If you are butchering a bovid like bison, nilgai, or oryx, absolutely keep any fat you can find on that brisket!

### FLANKS AND RIBS

By now, the carcass is looking a little worn. Most of the goodies are gone, except for the flanks and ribs. The flanks can be great eating in larger animals, where you can separate the various layers of meat from the fat and connective tissue. And if you have an elk or a moose, you can nab a strip of flank-like meat on the *inside* of the ribs—that's the skirt steak, the best piece of meat on the animal, in my opinion. But it's only available as a steak on bigger animals.

A skirt steak from a nilgai

On deer and antelope, your best bet is to slice it off in as big a piece as you can manage and grind it.

If you plan to cut ribs to eat, you'll want to leave all the meat from the flank that sits above the ribs. If you don't have this in mind, you can easily slice this off, resulting in ribs without much meat on them.

If you do want to cut ribs, use a saw to cut them off right where you sliced off the backstrap. Now you'll want to remove, at the very least, the ridge of bone on the bottom of the ribs. If you don't do this, the ribs get unwieldy. I prefer to cut short ribs about six to eight inches wide—deer ribs are best treated like beef short ribs rather than pork spare ribs. That leaves a few inches of waste underneath, where that ridge of bone is. I just use a knife to cut out any usable meat from that part; that goes in the grinder.

If you don't feel like making ribs, use a knife to cut out all the usable meat from between and over the ribs. This meat is good for the grinder.

There, you've finished the rough cut! Time to clean up and have a beer and some lunch before you get set for the fine work.

## Fine Work

You now have a deer (or elk, or moose, or other venison) broken down into some primal cuts. You can, of course, cook some of these as is, especially if you have small animals like whitetail does, axis or roe deer, or an antelope. But for the most part, you will want to do some extra trimming and slicing to get your animal into more useful pieces.

Much of the work has already been done. The ribs need no more treatment after you've sawed them off to the length and width you want. The neck roast is done, too. Flank steaks need to be separated from the various layers of connective tissue and fat. The tenderloins are also ready to eat. Everything else needs some tending.

### SHANKS

Let's start with the shanks, the last bits of meat on the legs, akin to your calf. To remove the front leg shanks, you'll need your saw. Whether you keep your shanks whole or cut them in cross sections depends on size. Most deer have small enough shanks to cook whole; the size of your Dutch oven or other heavy pot will determine this, as shanks need to be braised. Sometimes, shanks are a little too long for the pot. In such cases, saw them to fit, taking off the narrow end, not the top where it attaches to the leg. Elk, moose, and really big deer have shanks that

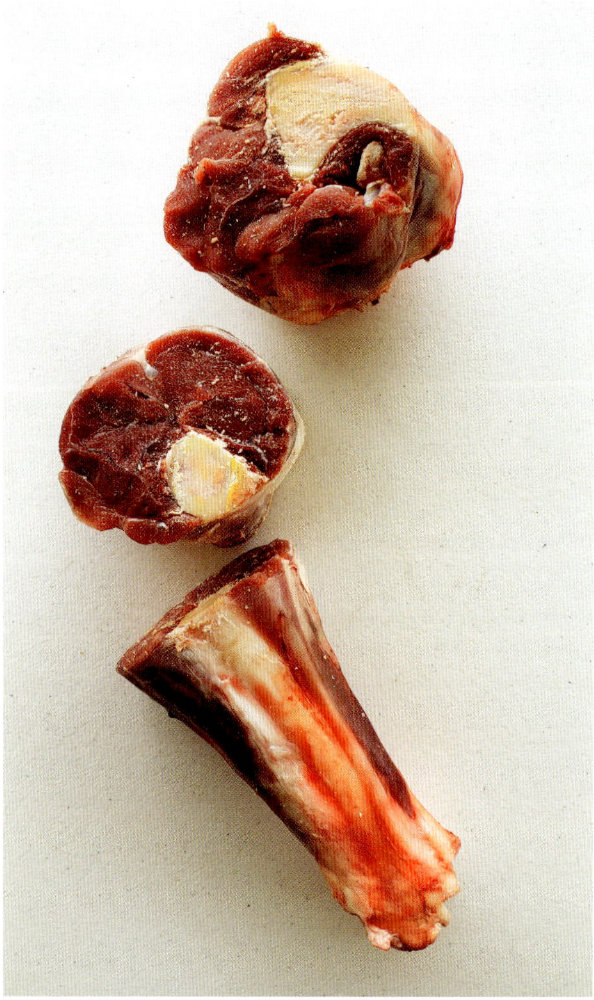

Portioning shanks from a large deer

are much too large for the pot. Saw these into thick (two- to four-inch) cross sections for braises and for Italian Osso Buco (page 232).

Hind shanks you can remove with any knife, because the joint is clean. The foreleg shanks have something like a kneecap that sticks up high, so I saw them. To saw off a shank, find where it bends, then use your knife to cut the meat down to that level; you don't want to saw meat. Saw through the bone, and you're good to go. It helps if you have another person hold the shank steady while you saw, but I do it solo all the time.

To saw your cross sections, do the same thing: Use your knife to slice down to the bone, then saw.

## FRONT LEGS

Front legs are something of a quandary. Unless you're dealing with an elk, moose, or really big deer, there's no real point breaking down the front leg into its constituent muscle groups—there's too much connective tissue in the front legs to make the effort worthwhile. My advice: Just slice off all the meat you can and use the good bits for stews and braises and the gnarly bits for the grinder. Front legs are the main source of my sausage and burger meat.

Now, if the deer is small or you have a doe antelope or some such, you can braise the front leg whole (minus the shank) until all that connective tissue melts. To my mind, this is the best thing to do with this part of the animal. When contemplating this, keep in mind the dimensions of your cookware: If a shoulder can fit into something with a lid or something you can cover with foil, you can braise it whole. Whole braised shoulder is one of my favorites (Braised Shoulder of Venison, page 85).

If you're dealing with an elk or moose, however, the front legs will indeed be large enough to portion out into whole muscle cuts. In general, the front shoulder and leg will be the chuck on a beef, and you can wrangle a few nice roasts from it in moose and elk.

The primo cut from the front leg is the flat iron steak (called the "butler's steak" in Britain, and the "oyster" steak in Australia). This is the blade roast, sliced in half horizontally to remove a thick, nasty band of connective tissue that runs down the middle. You get four flat irons per animal, two from

## How to Cut a Flat Iron Steak

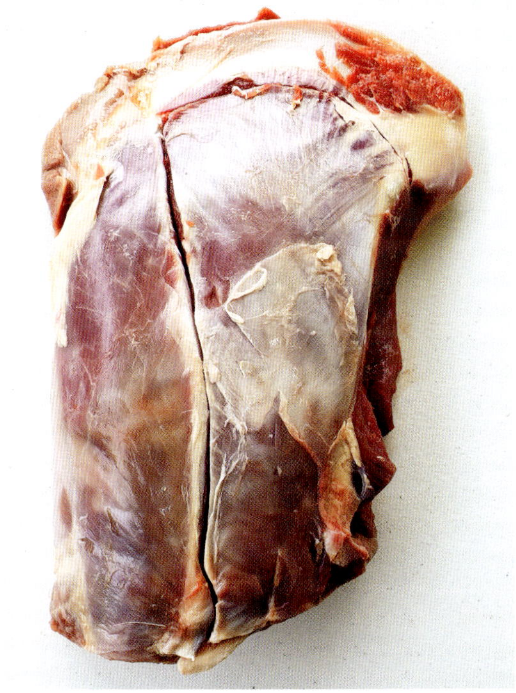

each blade. And of course, you can then portion these smaller if you want. You find the blade roast nestled on the outside part of the shoulder blade. You'll notice that the shoulder blades have a strong ridge of bone in the middle of them. The blade roast is the triangular muscle tucked into the wider half of the shoulder blade. You can get a similar steak from the narrower side of the shoulder blade, too.

Remember that these steaks are quite small in deer, although if you brought home a big bruiser buck, it would be worth it.

Keep the bones in the front leg for stock and broth.

## BACKSTRAPS

A common misconception is that backstraps are all one lovely piece of meat. The fact is that there are several muscles running through the backstrap, each separated by connective tissue strong enough to mess things up when you cook it. You need to separate those muscles to get to the good stuff.

Start with the fat cap. Honestly, as much as I love to work with venison fat, I usually pull this off. Why? Because there's a thick layer of silverskin between the fat and the meat. In a boneless steak or roast, this tends to fall partly away from the meat during cooking, making it tough to properly cook that side of the meat. It's a different story if you've cut chops; the fat cap stays on better when you have the bone on the chop. Think about doing this with big, fat deer like a nice muley buck and definitely with elk and moose. You could also take this route with smaller deer if you cut longer sections of chops, like the lamb racks you see in the store.

Most often, I break the backstrap down into boneless lengths of loin. To start, you need to remove the "chain" from the loin. This is a strip of meat that runs alongside the main loin, separated by

Ideal portions for a backstrap. Save those center cuts for date night!

connective tissue. It's shaped like a very long, skinny triangle and is widest at the end of the backstrap that was closest to the shoulder. You should be able to pull this off if you follow the natural seam of the meat. Use the chain for sausage or burger.

Now the only thing you need to do is carefully slice the silverskin off the loin. For this I use my sharpest, thinnest blade, which is either a flexible blade boning knife or a fish fillet knife, depending on which is sharpest at the moment.

Why not medallions? Fair question. Here's why: Unless you have a very thick and wide steak, the mass-to-surface-area ratio is all wrong. Think about a typical backstrap steak, which is about four inches across. Most butchers cut these less than an inch thick. Sear that in a pan and you've seared the two largest halves of the piece of meat. Yes, you get a nice area of crust, but cooking it this way makes it a lot tougher to control the doneness. You go from just right to overcooked in the time it takes to get your sear on. Many a backstrap steak has been ruined because of this.

Better to cut lengths of backstrap and sear the outside, cooking the whole thing until it's done to your liking, and then slice them into steaks when serving. Doing it this way makes it easier to control the internal temperature. See page 114 for a further discussion of medallions vs. lengths of loin.

### HIND LEGS

This is where seam butchery comes into play. On small deer, I find that it's best to just roast the whole haunch—this makes one helluva party dinner. But more often, I take the leg apart the way it was put together: muscle group by muscle group.

The first thing you do is remove as many layers of silverskin as you can from the outside of the leg. These get in the way. You can pull a lot of it off, slicing where it sticks to the meat. Try to get most of it off, but you need not be too worried about it at this point. I toss all silverskin into the stockpot, where it adds collagen.

Now you're ready to rock. Just so you know, the top of the hind leg, the rump, is the toughest part to separate into a cohesive roast, unless you're dealing with a large animal, and even then you are basically slicing off a big ole' hunk at the top of the leg. This is where I most often get my best stew meat.

Starting the process is the hardest part, and the only part during which you're cutting through muscle instead of alongside it. Turn the hind leg so the ball joint is facing up; this is the inner side of the leg. Trace where the femur goes from that ball joint down to the "knee." That's your line. Slice down along this line, tapping the point of your knife on the femur the whole way down toward the "knee."

From here, you debone the leg exactly as you'd do with a leg of lamb. You have the bone slightly exposed from your first cut. Use the last inch or so of your knife blade to carefully free the bone from the muscles. Use short strokes, and think about "freeing the meat" rather than cutting or slicing. Work your way around the bone until it's attached only at the "knee." Free the femur by cutting through the soft cartilage where it meets the knee.

Save the femur for soup or for marrow (more on marrow on page 251).

Now you have a big lump of meat. How to separate it? Take a look: You will see seams of connective tissue here and there. Put your knife down for a moment and start working your fingers into those seams. You'll see that they pull apart fairly easily. They stay together with that same cobwebby substance that holds the front leg onto the body. You'll see that in some places, the connections are too tough for you to pull them apart without ripping

## Portioning a Hind Leg

1. Remove the femur first.
2. Use your fingers to separate the leg into roasts. Only use the knife when needed.

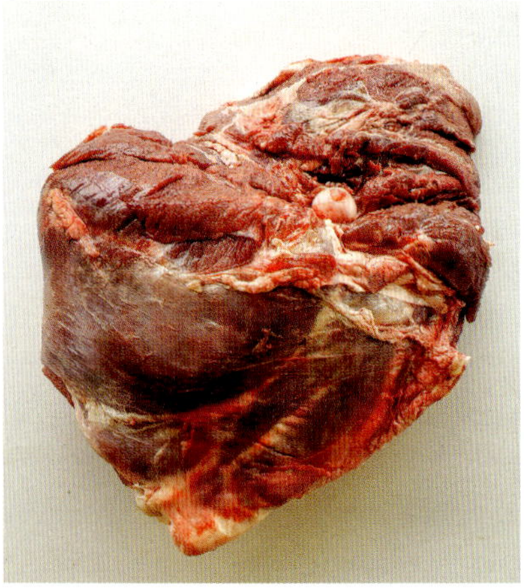

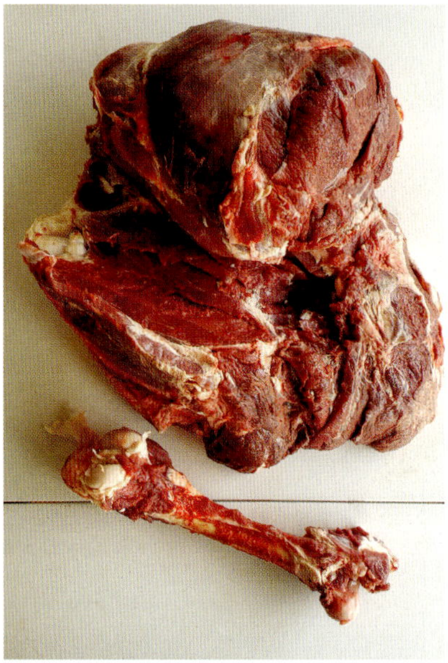

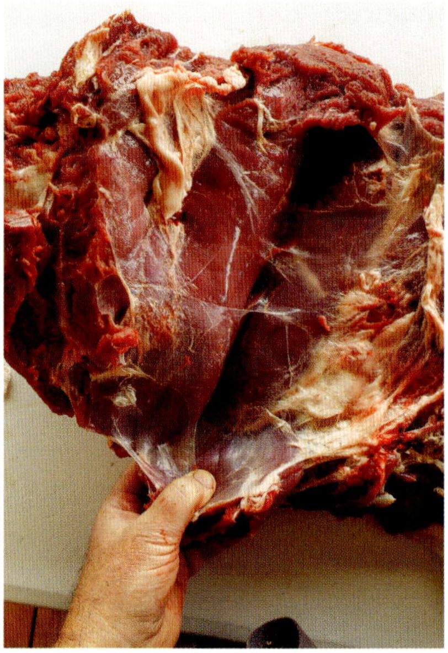

the muscle. That's where you use your sharp boning knife. Again, always think about "freeing" the various muscle groups from each other (rather than "cutting them apart") and you'll get most of the leg separated into nice, big roasts, plus a few oddly shaped smaller muscles that are great as stew meat.

As you proceed in this way, three main roasts will begin to appear. One is the sirloin tip, which I call the "football roast" (because it looks like a football). The other two are the top and bottom rounds, two other rectangular roasts with a strong grain to them that will guide you.

Attached to one of the rectangular roasts is a nifty little cylinder of meat that looks an awful lot like a tenderloin. This is the eye round, or "hidden tenderloin." It's not as tender as the real tenderloin, but it's definitely steak-worthy. Removing it is the one hard part of separating the leg; the connective tissue that attaches the eye round to the larger roasts is tight. Just take your time and work that edge and you'll be fine.

Once you get the main roasts out, you'll want to trim the edges. The football roast is firmly attached to the "knee," so you'll need to slice the end off there; use the trim and the knee in broth-making. The rectangular roasts tend to be more trapezoidal; square the edges off them too and use the trim for stew meat. Finally, trim off the silverskin.

In really big beasts, you will want to cut these primary roasts into manageable pieces; the football roast on a moose can weigh more than ten pounds, and an elk's is often close to that. Unless you plan to feed a crowd, cut the large roast into big cross sections. Keep them thick, as this is the one roast on the hind leg that comprises several muscles.

The other roasts are single muscles, and so if you want, you can cut them across the grain into steaks. I find that cutting the steaks about one to two inches thick or so gives me the best results. Usually, however, I keep the roasts whole, unless they're from a very large deer. A whole muscle roast from a typical deer is a nice size for a family meal.

### THE REST

You'll have lots of scraps and trim left over. The hunks of sinew-free meat should be stored as stew meat, while the gnarlier stuff should go into the grinder for burger and sausage (more on that on page 282).

There you have it: a whole deer, broken down into the sorts of pieces you'll most likely want to cut. As I said earlier, there are several ways to butcher a deer, but this is mine. I find it works well for a home butcher with normal equipment and space.

## STORING VENISON

Storage is a critical issue for a deer hunter. After all, unless you're shooting the tiny whitetails of the South and hosting a barbecue after the hunt, most of us will find ourselves with more venison than we can reasonably eat in a week. In the old days, that meant some serious salting, drying, pickling, and, more recently, canning. All of those methods are great, but freezing beats them all. It's the only way to eat "fresh" venison months after you put the deer on the ground.

Later in this book you'll see methods and recipes for drying venison, mostly as jerky (Chipotle Jerky, page 294) or Mexican Carne Seca (page 293), and salting venison the Nordic way (Icelandic Venison "Gravlax," page 325). Here we'll cover refrigeration and freezing.

Once you have the deer cut into pieces—primals or finished cuts—you will want to age it a bit in the fridge. I do this in large plastic containers with

# FREEZER ESSENTIALS

## How to Thaw Meat Fast

Here's a restaurant trick: The fastest way to thaw any frozen food is in a big pot of *cold* water. Sounds counterintuitive, but it works. Dropped into a bowl of cool tap water, the frozen thing acts like an ice cube, chilling the water as it thaws and thus inhibiting bacterial growth. Never use hot or warm water, which can cook the outside of your meat before the center has thawed, which can definitely encourage bacteria.

You do need to use vacuum-sealed meat for this trick, however. Meat wrapped in butcher paper will get soggy. I've seen people improvise by unwrapping the frozen meat and putting it in a sealable plastic bag, but these tend to leak, and you need to get all the air out or the meat will float, thawing unevenly.

Want to thaw even faster? Set the pot in the sink and run cold water into it in a slow, steady stream. This moving water will thaw even a big venison roast in less than thirty minutes. Either way, fast or slow, the meat should be cooked as soon as possible after it has thawed.

## Dealing with Freezer Burn

If you don't use a vacuum sealer or if the seal breaks on a vac-sealed frozen package, sooner or later you will encounter the dreaded freezer burn. Freezer burn happens when the ultra-cold, ultra-dry air in the freezer comes in contact with meat or fish for an extended period of time. There's nothing harmful about it, but no one wants to eat freezer-burned meat.

Simply slice off the freezer-burned portions of the meat, use them in stock or broth or feed them to the cat or dog, and cook the rest. And next time, seal your meat better.

## Don't Refreeze Uncooked Meat

Why? Primarily because of meat quality, but there is also a potential health risk.

The most important reason for the taboo on refreezing uncooked meat is best explained by the renowned food scientist Harold McGee, who wrote in his *On Food and Cooking*:

> *The intercellular spaces [in meat], which are often large and which contain some water but very little else, freeze first, and then draw water out of the cells by osmosis. This in turn increases the concentration of dissolved substances within the cell, which further lowers the freezing point. Parts of the cell interior do not freeze at all.*

Put simply, freezing damages meat. And when you thaw it, that damage manifests itself as the blood-like fluid that seeps out of the meat. It's not blood but rather cell fluid weeping from the damaged cells. The meat's still fine, just not as good as fresh.

If you put that same piece of meat through the whole freezing and thawing process again, you'll notice it. The meat will be even dryer and mushier than once-thawed meat.

This will be especially noticeable if all you have is a regular stand-up freezer and not a deep freeze. This is because the longer it takes to freeze meat, the larger the ice crystals that will form within its cell walls. The larger the ice crystals, the more damage done. This is why commercial processors use blast freezers, which can achieve temperatures as low as −100°F, freezing the meat so fast that the ice crystals formed are tiny, and meat damage minimal. Your home freezer won't get much colder than about 0°F, and even a top-of-the-line home chest freezer won't get colder than −25°F; most only hit −10°F.

Depending on how you thawed the meat in the first place, you might also be exposing yourself to some nasty bugs. If you've thawed the meat from freezer to refrigerator, you're good— everything's stayed cold enough. But if you thawed it on the counter, which you should never do anyway, there's a distinct chance that the exterior will be covered in bacterial nasties. If you then refreeze that meat and then thaw it one more time, as soon as the temperature rises to about 45°F, the bacteria will become active again and will now have even more cell wall fluid to feast on. This is not good.

Cooking meat alters its cell structure, so it's OK to refreeze meat once you cook it. I often make venison sausages from frozen meat, but I will then hot smoke or poach them so they're fully cooked before I refreeze them.

paper towels set underneath the meat to soak up the juices that slowly seep from the meat. Aging in this way will concentrate the flavor of the venison and tenderize it a bit, without developing the hard rind of dry-aged meat. I find that letting the meat sit in the fridge for up to a week helps its flavor. You can skip this step if you're short on space.

Generally, seven to ten days is about as long as you want any piece of fresh venison to sit around in the fridge. After that, things start to get funky, and the meat can oxidize and turn grayish. You can extend this to a month if the venison's been vacuum-sealed; see wet-aging on page 39.

Freezing is the real long-term solution. And while there are other methods of packing meat for freezing, few beat the vacuum sealer. Vacuum-sealing before freezing will radically change how you look at fish and game storage. By sucking out all the air from the package, you prevent freezer burn and moisture loss and thus triple the effective life of the meat in the deep freeze. I once thawed a six-year-old antelope roast that I'd lost in the bottom of the freezer; because the seal had never broken on the vacuum package, it was perfectly fine.

There are two kinds of vacuum sealers: suction and chamber. Suction-style sealers are fine for most of our purposes. But be aware that the bags for these sealers are relatively expensive (keeping you supplied with these is how they make their money) and that the suction method is inferior to the chamber method.

Restaurants and serious processors all use chamber sealers, which create a vacuum in the entire chamber holding the bag rather than sucking air out of the bag directly. The difference is twofold. First, chamber sealers allow you to seal moist foods, such as a liver, without seepage. Second, chamber sealers seal much tighter than suction sealers, compressing the food to form an almost indestructible seal. Suction sealers have a tendency to "break seal," and if you notice this in your freezer, you must either reseal immediately or thaw and eat.

The downside of chamber sealers is their expense. A good unit is never less than $550, whereas a top-of-the-line suction type costs closer to $425. I use an oil-cooled VacMaster chamber sealer and swear by it. The bags don't break seal, they're cheap and heavy duty, and the machine hasn't failed me even after years of heavy use.

Not all venison bits fit into the vacuum bags. With oddly shaped pieces like big shanks and whole haunches, I use a two-step process. First, I wrap the meat in plastic wrap, often several layers. Around this I wrap butcher's freezer paper—the kind with one waxed side—and tape it down. That will keep the meat in good shape for about six months or so.

A final word on freezing venison: Buy a chest freezer. If you're going to the trouble of killing a deer or an elk or a moose every year, you'll want the extra space. Chances are that most of you reading this already have at least one chest freezer, but it's worth stating, nonetheless. Other than mere issues of space, which are serious if you're an elk or moose hunter or if you kill multiple deer a year, there is the temperature factor. Chest freezers keep meat much colder, often –10°F or colder, whereas a regular kitchen freezer holds 0°F at best, and often closer to 10°F.

## Canning Venison

To be honest, I don't can venison by itself; its smell reminds me too much of dog food when I open the can. I do, however, can ready-to-eat meals like spaghetti sauce or stew, and these come in handy when I'm too busy to cook during the week. Like canned stock, it loses some quality, but you trade that for convenience.

So how to do it? First, you absolutely must have a pressure canner. *You cannot safely can meats with the standard boiling-water bath.* Standard boiling-water baths don't get hot enough to kill the nasty bacteria that are potentially lurking in your soup. When you hear reports of people getting sick from home-canned venison, you can be fairly certain that the cause was improper canning methods, usually from the use of the boiling-water bath. Take this caution to heart; it could save you and your family much grief.

## CANNING VENISON: RAW OR COOKED?

You can pack cold chunks of venison into jars and use the pressure-canning process to cook it, or you can pre-brown your meat and then pack it in. Or—and this is what I do—you make something with your venison and then can that.

I find this to be 100 percent more useful. I am never in need of random hunks of shelf-stable cooked venison on a Tuesday night, but I do find myself wanting a quick spaghetti with meat sauce or some stew or even barbacoa.

Starting with just meat, you'll want to add chunks of meat, a little salt, and not much else, for the raw-pack method.

For the hot-pack method, I would grill, smoke, or sear the meat to get some nice Maillard action going on, then pack into jars, covering with homemade venison broth or water. You must leave one inch of headspace in the jar, or even a tad more. Use a butter knife to poke around to remove air bubbles.

In either case, dampen a paper towel with a little bit of vinegar and wipe the rims. You don't want them wet, but you want no trace residue of fat on them. That can break your seal.

Hand-seal your jars and place in the pressure canner. I like the water to go about a quarter of the way up the sides of the jars. Seal your canner according to its directions—mine requires a slick of oil around the rim of the canner—vent for seven minutes or as required, then start the pressure going.

You'll want 10 PSI up to about 1,000 feet in elevation, or 15 PSI above 1,000 feet—unless you have a canner you can dial in, in which case it's 12 PSI from 2,000 to 4,000 feet, with an extra PSI for each 2,000 feet above that. I use a weighted gauge canner.

Whether you raw-pack or hot-pack, you'll need seventy-five minutes for pints and ninety minutes for quarts. Don't short this time. It's important.

Much of this information is gleaned from personal experience, various state cooperative extensions, and the National Center for Home Preservation.

In short: Be patient!

Once your time has elapsed, turn the heat off and go do something else. You want the temperature and pressure to decline naturally. Decompressing and opening the canner too soon can cause the jars to break seal and spray the contents all over your canner. Ask me how I know.

Only after the pressure gauge is all the way at the bottom and the canner has rested for at least an hour, even two hours, should you open the canner. The insides will still be plenty hot, so set the jars on a cutting board to rest overnight before putting into the pantry. They'll keep more than a year that way.

## CANNING VENISON BETTER

OK, that's basic canned venison. To up your game, make ready-to-eat meals in a jar.

The process is to can in quarts or pints—quarts are smarter—starting with hot stew, following all the guidelines of your individual canner in terms of venting and pressure.

Here are some recipes that can be pressure-canned, some as is, some with only minor modifications, which I'll get into in a moment.

**BASIC VENISON BROTH** (page 73)
Easy peasy, and with a pressure-canning time of only twenty-five minutes.

**BELGIAN VENISON CARBONNADE** (page 162)
Can be canned as is.

**VENISON CHILI** (page 188)
If you are using beans, parcook them first.

**KENTUCKY BURGOO** (page 164)
Can also be pressure-canned as is.

**HUNGARIAN PÖRKÖLT** (goulash) (page 178)
Can be canned, although you'll need to make the dumplings when you want to eat it.

## CANNING DOS AND DON'TS

It is generally fine to freestyle ingredients when pressure-canning venison, with the following exceptions.

- No dairy! Dairy products are not safe for pressure-canning. Add them when you're ready to eat the stew or sauce.
- And no eggs. Eggs in a stew or sauce disqualify it from pressure-canning. This isn't normally an issue, because who puts eggs in a venison stew?
- No flour thickeners, like a roux. That leaves out pressure-canned gumbo. You could in theory make the whole rest of the gumbo and then add the roux at the end, though.
- No pasta, rice, and other starchy grains. Apparently, they interfere with the heat transfer of your canning, and in theory, they can be unsafe. Beans are OK, though. But you'll want to half-cook dry beans before adding to the stew you're going to can.

## TIMING IS EVERYTHING

You may want to cook really tough things, like venison neck or shank meat, an hour or so on the stovetop first. Add long-cooking vegetables like carrots and potatoes for the final ten minutes, and then anything more tender raw. Then be sure to bring your entire stew to a boil before ladling it into jars.

Also remember that some things shouldn't be canned, like fresh herbs. Add them when you're ready to eat.

Another pro tip with beans: You can add fully cooked beans to pressure canned venison, so long as they're bathing in something acidic, like tomato or tomatillo. This prevents them from dissolving.

The following spaghetti sauce is by far the most common thing I pressure-can with big game.

> "Only the trees and the deer shed their foliage each year and replace it more magnificently."
>
> – FELIX SALTEN

# SPAGHETTI SAUCE FOR CANNED VENISON

This is my tried-and-true spaghetti sauce recipe, one I've been making for more than thirty years, with various meats. Any ground meat will work. And of course you need not pressure-can this—it's good as is.

**MAKES ▶** 4 quarts

**PREP TIME ▶** 45 minutes

**COOK TIME ▶** 90 minutes

¼ cup olive oil
2½ pounds ground venison
1 large yellow onion, minced
6 cloves garlic, minced
One 6-ounce can tomato paste
1 cup red wine
½ teaspoon red pepper flakes
2 tablespoons dried oregano
¼ cup minced fresh parsley
Two 28-ounce cans crushed tomatoes
1 quart stock (venison or beef)
Salt, black pepper and sugar to taste

Four 1-quart canning jars

Sauté the venison in a large Dutch oven or similar pot over medium-high heat. If your ground venison is already cut with fat, you might only need a splash of olive oil. You'll need the whole ¼ cup if there is no fat in your ground venison.

Once the meat browns, add the onion, stir, and cook for about 8 minutes, stirring often. Stir in the garlic and cook another minute or two. Stir in the tomato paste and mix. Let this cook a couple of minutes. You want it to turn brick red.

Stir in the wine and add the red pepper flakes and herbs. Boil the wine down by half, then add the crushed tomatoes and the stock. Bring this to a solid simmer and cook it down for about 30 minutes. Add salt, pepper, and sugar to taste. I do like a hefty pinch of sugar, but no more than that.

While the sauce is cooking down, get your pressure canner ready. Set out clean quart jars with new lids. Moisten a piece of paper towel with a little vinegar and set aside; this will be used to remove trace oil around the rim after transferring.

Using a jar funnel to keep your rims clean, ladle the hot sauce into the jars, leaving 1 inch of headspace or a touch more. Don't overfill. Clean the rims with the vinegar-moistened paper towel, hand-seal the lids, and set the jars in the canner. If you have extra sauce, put it in the fridge to eat that week.

Seal the canner according to its directions, vent (mine takes 7 minutes to vent), then set the weight on the vent or set the gauge. Turn up the heat until you get to the pressure you need, normally 10 PSI for sea level to 1,000 feet. Turn the heat to medium so the weight jiggles about three times per minute. Set the timer for 70 minutes.

When the time has elapsed, turn off the heat and leave the canner alone for at least one hour; two hours is better. You want the pressure to return to normal slowly, and you want the temperature to drop significantly. Carefully open the canner. Wait until all the jar lids have popped. Remove the jars to a cutting board and leave them overnight.

Label and store in a cool, dry place for up to two years.

# The White Coyote

Chest heaving, my pulse thumped in my ears as I crested the ridge. For several seconds, I could do nothing but stand, hands on my thighs, breathing like a bellows. Slowly, things began to focus. I stood on a great slab of weathered granite, a chunk of mountain rock exposed to the Sierra Nevada's harsh elements for eons. Great fissures ran through it, cracks from a hundred thousand winters' worth of heaving and thawing and freezing. In front of me yawned a gigantic gap between ridges, Devil's Peak on the mountain beyond looking like a Roman nose stuck atop a forested face.

Soft rain coated the world. My breath sent out smoke signals, my lungs calling for more oxygen. The birds, of course, took no notice of me and continued about the business of being birds. Flocks of tiny juncos flitted about like gray butterflies. Nuthatches, high in the pines, droned on and on—*yank yank yank yank*. Northern flickers did their best impression of hawks, while Steller's jays chattered in that scratchy, metallic voice they're so known for. Beneath it all, a low, constant roar—the sound of traffic on Interstate 80, which split the gap more than 1,500 feet below me. The twin white ribbons of roadway seemed so alien up here, an intrusion on the wild world.

This was where Joe Navari and I had decided to hunt deer.

Joe and I hunt, fish, and forage a lot together. Joe's short but powerfully built—"mountain stock" is how he puts it—with the vise-grip fingers of a professional deckhand, although he's an archaeologist by training. He has a shock of dark, curly hair and a full beard that has a tendency to run wild across his face. In his more feral moments, Joe can bear a striking resemblance to Grog from the old comic strip *B.C.*, but mostly he looks like Dionysus or Pan. And like Pan, Joe is relentlessly amiable, so slow to anger that I'd hate to see what it would take to get him there.

Joe had hunted this spot before. In fact, he shot the biggest buck of his life just below where we stood, a gigantic mule deer with six tines on one side of its antlers, four on the other—a buck that would be right at home on one of those slick hunting shows. We were headed to Clark's Rock, where our host, Clark Blanchard, had shot an equally impressive muley that same year. It was Opening Day for California's dreaded D Zone, a hunting area stretching from Mount Lassen in the north to Mount Whitney in the south that happens to be one of the hardest places in America in which to kill a deer. So far, on this day, it was proving itself to be so.

Habit has a way of gripping us. We succeed at a thing, and when called upon to do that thing again, we repeat the steps that brought us success in the past. This is why Joe and I were atop a mountain in the rain and unseasonable cold, looking for the Phantoms of the Sierra. But Joe knows full well that the deer up here cannot be patterned. This is not Midwestern farm country, and these are not whitetail deer. Food is scarce at 7,000 feet, and predators plentiful. I saw the tracks of coyotes, bobcats, and bears that day. These deer, living near the crest of the Sierra Nevada, can number fewer than ten per square mile. Compare that to the East, where deer densities of a hundred per square mile are not unheard of. Here, you find a deer—any legal deer—and you shoot it. Even a young buck can be a trophy in this country.

Joe and I would have paid a fair dollar to get a chance at even a young buck at this point. We'd hunted hard since dawn, and here it was close to 5 p.m. We'd seen exactly five deer so far, a tiny buck with a fork on one antler and a spike on the other that never gave us a shot and a group of four as we were driving out for lunch. One of those four was a forked horn, but it never presented a shot. Our hunting companions, Oggie and Stu, who had been hunting at the base of the mountain all day, had had similar luck.

Now, Clark, Joe, and I had climbed the mountain again, to see if we might get lucky that evening. The hunt had started well. Just as we neared the top of the ridge, Joe and Clark spotted two adult deer just ahead of us; we had no idea whether they were bucks or does. The deer had heard us coming and sauntered through a grove of Jeffrey pines and down the side of the ridge, out of sight. Joe decided to track them and went off down to the next bench below us. Clark went up to his rock to see if he could spot something. I decided to creep around this mountaintop, hoping to either spot a buck before the buck saw me or, more likely, to bother the deer just enough so that he'd get up and walk a few paces to see what I was.

Creeping about in the rain is a helluva lot easier than the hunting I'd done earlier this season in the dry forests of California's Coastal Range. Yet it still wasn't a walk on pillows. Sierra winters are legendary, and we were not far from where the Donner Party ended up munching on each other back in 1847. Trees that survive grow arthritic, stunted, and wind-chiseled. For many trees, winter is dying time. Their skeletons litter the ground, some as wide as I am tall, others just bunches of kindling, ready to snap when found by a misplaced foot fall. Someone once said that when a leaf falls in a forest, the bear smells it, the eagle sees it, and the deer hears it. Every time I took a wrong step and heard that crunch, I heard my chances of seeing a buck diminish.

Finally, I found a spot to wait out the dusk. I sat underneath a red pine with an open view of a brush-choked ravine before me. Spruces and pines dotted the area, but it was largely open. Perhaps an avalanche had cleared it some years before. We'd checked this spot earlier in the day and had seen deer trails latticed through the manzanita and buckbrush. Joe said he'd seen the telltale oval of flattened grass—deer beds—there the year before. Seemed as likely a spot for a buck as any. So I sat.

Always the roar of the interstate. Its omnipresence offered protection to us all, hunter and hunted alike. It muffled some of my missteps and certainly prevented my imperfect ears from hearing any deer I'd failed to spot earlier that day. But now, sitting still, I began to hear, actually hear, for the first time. The roar faded, and the birdsong returned. I could finally hear the subtle chipping of the juncos. What did they say to each other? I realized that a particular snapping sound we'd been hearing all day was not in fact an animal—it was the sound of pine cones hitting the forest floor. I learned that pine squirrels make a certain set of noises that are different from the frenetic rustlings of the smaller lodgepole chipmunks.

And then I heard something else entirely. Not a pine cone. Not a rodent. Not Joe or Clark or any other human being. I heard the sound of an animal walking up the draw toward me. I adjusted my grip on my Remington 700, my old Dodge Dart of a rifle that suits me just fine. If this creature should be a legal buck, and should it make a mistake and show itself, I was confident I could make this shot.

A glimpse of white. A deer? No, a fox. No. Too large, ears too long. Coyote. Then it walked into the open, ambling as carefree as you might be walking down a city street looking for an ice cream shop. He wasn't an icy white like an Arctic fox or an albino, more ivory-silver-gray. I'd never seen a white coyote before. Shooting it was out of the question, even though it would have been legal and this coyote was within range. It seemed wrong.

About fifty yards away, the coyote stopped. Maybe he saw my blaze orange hat. Maybe he caught my wind. Regardless, he (she?) looked right at me and cocked his head. Silently, I wondered how he was doing, where he was going. He must have wondered the same. We stood there, two fellow predators, for a long moment. Then he ambled along on his way. I watched him go.

The sun fell soon after. No deer appeared. But sitting there, absorbing the wild world for a few hours, reminded me that deer hunting is not just about putting meat in the freezer, and it's certainly not about the size of the buck's antlers. It's about shedding your synthetic self just long enough to see the world as the deer, and the coyote, and the pine squirrel, and the jay see it. To be accepted back into the company of your fellow animals, to take your role as one among equals. If only for a while. Killing a buck may be the goal of deer hunting, but it's not the point.

– Part Two –

# DEER TO TABLE

The first thing you need to know when you have some venison to cook is that the *whole world cooks it*. That means that you can use venison as a substitute for beef, lamb, or goat in pretty much any recipe. In fact, many of the most common meat-based preparations, including curries, stir-fries, soups, stews, braises, meat pies, pasta sauces, and Mexican moles and salsas, originated with venison of some sort and only later evolved to include domesticated meat. No matter where you live on this planet, at least one thing binds us all: a storied tradition of hunting and eating venison.

# MARINADES, STOCKS, AND BROTH

## MARINADES: WHY, HOW, AND WHEN

"What marinade do you use?" is perhaps the most common question I get when people ask me about cooking venison. Truth is, I don't always use a marinade—a fine piece of backstrap needs little more than fire, salt, and maybe some black pepper. But marinades have a place in venison cookery. You'll just want to develop a good sense of when it's better to break out your favorite marinade and when it's better just to make it a sauce you serve at the end.

### Why Marinate?

Marinades are acid-based (or occasionally enzyme-based) liquids or loose pastes that are used to infuse meat (or vegetables) with flavor while at the same time tenderizing them. At least that's the theory.

Bathing venison, or any other meat, in an acidic sauce (or with certain fruit juices, like those from papaya or pineapple) will indeed break down some of the muscle tissue on the outer surface of the meat. The acid or fruit enzymes denature the proteins (essentially modifying their molecular structure), making them a bit mushy, but which we register as tenderness when we eat it. What's more, you should know that marinades cannot penetrate meats the same way that salt-based brines do. According to most food scientists, a marinade penetrates a piece of meat no deeper than an eighth of an inch, even after several days.

The bottom line: Not only don't acidic marinades truly tenderize meat, those with pineapple or papaya juices make the meat mushy. I can hear you saying, "But when I marinate venison roasts, they are absolutely more tender than when I don't!" And you're right—but not for the reason you may think.

According to the great French food scientist Hervé This, long marinades do have an effect. "The meat is more tender," This told the *Washington Post*. "But it is not the marinade that makes it tender: It is time. If you use an acidic marinade, it will protect the surface from spoilage while the rest of the meat matures. And you know when meat matures, it becomes tender." This is the secret behind the long marinades in German sauerbraten, which can marinate for a week in the fridge.

And marinades do impart flavor onto the meat's surface. Even a few minutes' worth of marinating time will give you some added flavor in the finished dish, because the flavorful liquid soaks into any crevices and cuts in a piece of meat.

Most importantly, marinating meat in an acidic sauce for at least forty minutes has been shown by the American Cancer Society to reduce by up to 90 percent the amount of cancer-causing heterocyclic amines, chemical compounds created when meat is cooked by a direct, open flame, for example, by grilling. This means that a marinade not only improves flavor but can also make that chargrilled piece of venison healthier.

#### WHICH CUTS?

Because marinades can only penetrate a few millimeters into a piece of meat (at best), you'll want to use cuts of venison that aren't too thick. This means backstrap medallions from large deer, elk, or moose, all leg steaks, flank steak, cubes for kebabs, and so on.

Or go the sauerbraten route and marinate a large roast for a week or more. Just remember that the acid in the marinade (don't do this with the enzyme-based marinades!), usually red wine, is just there to protect the meat from spoilage, not to tenderize it. It's the wet-aging of the meat for a week that does the trick.

One thing a marinade will *not* do? Tenderize silverskin and connective tissue. You must trim all this off before marinating, because the silverskin will block the penetration of the marinade.

## How to Marinate

You'll want to marinate your venison in a sealable plastic bag or in a covered, nonreactive container such as glass, stainless steel, enamel, or plastic; aluminum reacts to acidic ingredients and can produce off flavors. Do this in the fridge to slow the growth of any bacteria.

Here's a tip: If you like stir-fries and fajitas, marinate the venison slices before you stir-fry them. You'll get more flavor that way.

When you're ready to cook, take the meat out of the marinade and pat the meat dry with paper towels. Wet meat won't brown.

If you want to use your marinade as a sauce, you can do one of two things: boil your marinade for five minutes before using it, or, if boiling would destroy your marinade (as it would in chimichurri, which relies on raw, fresh herbs), make more than you need and use the extra for the sauce. Do not just reuse the marinade in which you soaked the raw venison—there's a chance, albeit small, that you might get food poisoning.

Here are a few ideas for marinades that need no recipe.

**ITALIAN DRESSING.** The classic. Any sort of oil and vinegar dressing works fine as a marinade.

**BUTTERMILK.** It's acidic all by itself, and it's thick enough to use as the base to a batter or crust, the way you do with buttermilk fried rabbit.

**CITRUS.** Like orange juice or lemon or lime juice. Pretty harsh stuff, but it works if you don't marinate too long. A few hours should do it.

**SODA.** A Southern classic. Marinating in RC Cola or Dr Pepper or whatever is a thing. And it's not terrible. Watch the sugar content, though, as it can burn on the surface of your venison if you're grilling over high heat.

**WORCESTERSHIRE SAUCE.** More of a Northern thing, I like this one a lot. It's a sauce and a marinade all in one. Worcestershire is also a hallmark of western Kentucky BBQ.

**SOY SAUCE.** More of a brine than a marinade, the salt level in soy sauce can be severe, and it will darken your meat dramatically. Use only for an hour or so, or dilute it.

# WHEN YOUR TABLE IS UNDER THE STARS

## Deer Camp Essentials

I am often asked for recipes that can be done in a rough kitchen, either in the field or at deer camp. My advice is always the same: So long as you have a few staples on hand, you can always make a great meal after a long day in the field. Here's what I'd want to see in the cupboards of every deer camp:

- **SALT AND PEPPER** Sounds like a no-brainer, but you'd be surprised how many times I've seen people forget these most basic ingredients. And while you're at it, get kosher or sea salt and one of those built-in pepper grinders in the supermarket spice rack so you can get freshly ground pepper easily.
- **ONIONS AND GARLIC** These staples keep for a long time in the pantry and form the basis for almost every recipe in this book.
- **STOCKS** Yes, homemade stock is better, and you can make shelf-stable stock if you pressure-can it (page 57). But having a few boxes of store-bought chicken and beef broth around will greatly improve your camp cooking.
- **WINE, PORT, AND BRANDY** For obvious reasons, but also to add flavor to sauces and stews.
- **JELLY, HONEY, SYRUP, OR MOLASSES** Venison often benefits from some sweetness.
- **A FEW PACKAGES** of dried chiles and dried mushrooms Every decent supermarket sells them. They're lightweight, and they last for years. A few in a stew make everything better.
- **VINEGAR** Any kind but distilled. A splash brightens any dish.

## Backcountry Essentials

Going even farther into the field? Cooking from an open fire instead of a cabin? Here's a stripped-down set of essentials to tuck into your pack. With the exception of the brandy in a flask, everything can be carried in resealable plastic baggies.

- **SALT AND PEPPER** Even a little salt makes food taste so much better in the wild places of this world. My advice? Nice salt, like good sea salt or smoked salt. It will make things all the more wonderful when it is cold or dreary.
- **GARLIC POWDER** I normally don't love this stuff, but it has a lot of flavor.
- **BOUILLON CUBES** Not great and really salty, but compact and easy to carry.
- **BRANDY IN A FLASK** It gets cold out there!
- **A BIT OF WHITE OR BROWN SUGAR** You'll be craving sweetness after a few days in the open.
- **DRIED CHILES AND DRIED MUSHROOMS** See Deer Camp Essentials. They are lightweight flavor bombs.
- **A BIT OF CITRIC ACID POWDER** I know, this may sound odd. But you'll want something acidic to brighten the flavors of your camp food, and this stuff will do it. Lighter than vinegar and less perishable than citrus, you can find this stuff sold as "fruit fresh" in the canning section of your local supermarket.

# BEER AND WINE WITH VENISON

Talking about pairing wines with food always seems to conjure up images of snooty sommeliers in tuxedos telling me what I can and cannot drink with my dinner. Too often there's a holier-than-thou element to discussions of wine pairings—and even beer pairings—when you broach the topic with food professionals. It need not be so.

Remember, the Prime Directive in all pairings is to drink what you like. Period. End of story. If you love drinking Pabst with your backstrap, go for it. Don't let anyone tell you otherwise. That said, certain pairings can make both the food and the drink taste better.

Part of this pairing stuff is voodoo, admittedly, but there is some method to the madness of matching wine and beer with food. You all know the simplest one: red wines with red meat, white wines with white meat, right? Usually, but not always. Fried food with Champagne is a great example. They work great together. Another good rule is the hotter the weather, the lighter the beer. Budweiser or Labatt's at a backyard barbecue? Yes, please. But I'd rather have something more substantial in winter while eating a venison carbonnade.

Next thing to remember: There is no one true venison wine or beer. Yes, most wine drinkers agree that cabernet sauvignon, Italian Barolos or Barbarescos, Spanish Rioja, or French Côtes du Rhône blends are the best overall wines to drink with venison. But that doesn't mean an easier-drinking zinfandel won't be good—if, say, you're barbecuing venison in summertime.

I often hear skepticism when I talk about beer pairings, but beers are in many ways far more varied than wines. After all, even professionals confuse wine varieties with some frequency. But I can guarantee that you'll never confuse an India pale ale with a Scottish ale. As much as I love the good ole' American and Canadian macro-brews we've been drinking for generations—Hamm's in my new home of St. Paul is a current favorite—there are now legions of fantastic local beers to be had in every corner of the country. Other than the tip about lighter beers for hot weather, here are a few others:

- Malty beers (German bocks, Scottish ales, brown ales, porters, and stouts) with heavier dishes, like stews and roasts. Always great in cold weather.
- Hoppy beers (IPAs, pale ales) with spicy foods like venison curry or fried rice.
- More carbonation with fattier foods; for example, pilsner or lager with chicken-fried venison. These are your hot-weather beers. German weiss beer (white wheat beer) is great here too.

There are a few beer styles you might not want to bring to the dinner table. For example, barley wines and imperial stouts, which are too strong and syrupy for food; most double or triple IPAs, unless you are a major hop-head and the food is ultra spicy; weird fruit beers, such as lambic, which are just hard to match with any food.

Wines and venison are a natural match. Here are a few good guidelines:

- Go for a full-bodied red, such as cabernet sauvignon, from Bordeaux or California, a good French Côtes du Rhône, an Italian Barolo or Barbaresco, or a Spanish Rioja.
- If you want to drink zinfandel with your venison, be sure it's a drier style, such as one from Italy or California's Alexander Valley or Amador County. Avoid most Lodi zins, as they tend to be syrupy.
- In summer, a dry rosé is a good idea, as are some whites: Try a viognier or a roussanne from California, especially with grilled venison or tacos.
- In winter, go even darker. I like mourvèdre or a petit verdot with heavy braises and stews. But my all-time go-to wine for venison is a French Châteauneuf-du-Pape. There's just something about it that works with lots of different dishes.

## STOCK, BROTH, AND GLACE DE VIANDE

Knowing how to make stocks and broths, or, if you're adventurous, French *glace de viande*, are important skills every deer hunter should have. It's one of the easiest ways to get more out of your animals and is a great way to make use of the bones and trim left over after butchering. Beyond utility, the satisfaction of making something you simply cannot buy anywhere, perfectly suited to your own tastes, is worth every moment of the time it takes to prepare it. A house where broth simmers on the stove is a happy one. There are several ways to go about making your own stocks and broths, and I'll walk you through them here.

Most cookbooks put discussions of stock and broth at the end. I think this is in error. After all, you make stocks most often when you butcher your own animals—otherwise you'd need to freeze bulky bones, which can take up a lot of space. Not that you can't, but I find myself making big batches of stock when I've finished the fine work of butchering and am letting the meat rest in the fridge for a few days.

Another reason to put these recipes at the front of the book is because they're used in so many of the recipes that follow. Venison broth (a more fully flavored version of venison stock), and the highly concentrated venison *glace de viande* (which is a heavily reduced stock with added gelatin), will come in handy when you begin to explore the recipes themselves.

That said, you can substitute beef broth or veal stock—even chicken stock, in some cases—for homemade venison stock. But there's something special about using homemade broths that will both elevate your cooking and give you the satisfaction of knowing that you made use of one more bit of the animal you brought home.

Any bones will work for stock, although I always discard the part of the animal that's been destroyed by the bullet, especially if I've been shooting with lead rather than copper. Another caveat is to avoid the backbone, neck, and skull of any animal that had lived in an area with chronic wasting disease (see page 25).

The best stock, hands down, is stock that's been made fresh. The quality of freshly made stock is better than that of frozen stock, although frozen is still good. One step below fresh stock is pressure-canned stock (page 57), which isn't as good as fresh or frozen but which has the significant benefit of being shelf stable and convenient. I use all three depending on the circumstance.

Fresh broth is best for fancy dinners where broth will serve as the star of a dish, say with venison tortellini swimming in your luxurious homemade broth. It will also make a spectacular Venison Risotto (page 111). Frozen broth will be perfectly good for these dishes, and it's also excellent for soups with other things in it, like the Scotch Broth on page 172. Pressure-canned is best for sauces, braising liquid, and thick stews where there are other big flavors, like the Hungarian Pörkölt on page 178.

### A Stock Primer

As well as being a core skill of any good cook, making stock is a labor of love I embrace wholly. Some cooks make stock without vegetables, but I rarely do that. Vegetables add so much to the final flavor of a stock and can transform it from an additive into a full-fledged broth suitable for sipping on cold days. Incidentally, while I use stock and broth interchangeably, technically a stock is a base, and a broth is something you can serve on its own. Generally, a broth is more flavorful and better seasoned than a stock.

My essential stock vegetables: onions or leeks, carrots, celery, bay leaves, and parsley. I will add other herbs as appropriate, most often rosemary and thyme. With venison, I add rosemary and juniper berries. Secret weapon for venison stock: parsnips, whose sweetness brings so much to the party.

The first step in making broth is roasting the bones. I like darker, fuller stocks, and this is what does it. The Vietnamese don't roast their bones when making broth for pho, possibly the world's most perfect soup (Vietnamese Pho, page 176), and I too will occasionally make stock without roasting. But not often. So I roast my deer bones at 400°F for an hour or so, until they're browned and yummy looking.

Next, cram your bones into the stockpot and cover with cold water. Cold water to start and slow heating will help extract the maximum amount of collagen; it's collagen from the joints, cartilage, and skin that builds body in your stock by making it thicker than water. Want to make an even better broth? Go buy a pig's or calf's foot from your local butcher or Asian or Latin market and add it; these cuts have lots of collagen and are a time-honored secret to great broth.

Bring the stock to a boil (gradually!) and skim off any scum that floats to the surface. After the surface is clear, reduce the heat to a bare simmer. You want it to shimmy, not roil, not even bubble too much (some cooks call this "moving water"). A boiled stock will turn cloudy, and the higher temps can extract bitter flavors from the bones. Think steeping tea, not simmering. Let the stock shimmy gently for several hours. How long? From four hours minimum to overnight.

After the meat has infused the water to your liking, add your veggies, coarsely chopped. You don't want to use anything spoiled or rotten, but the ends of things like carrots or parsnips make great stock, as do onion skins, which will help turn the broth a lovely brown. Stir in your vegetables and let the broth simmer for another ninety minutes, or up to two hours (but no more; after this point, those bright flavors you added will muddle and become murky).

Now strain everything out. Set a paper towel into a fine-mesh sieve. Ladle your venison stock through this into a large bowl or plastic bin. Is all of this fuss necessary? Yes. Unless you want a mucky, cloudy stock. And it's more than aesthetics. The impurities are just that—impure—and they add off flavors to your otherwise wonderful brew.

Once your stock is strained, clean the stockpot or pour the strained liquid into another one. Now you can reduce it if you want to. This is also the time to salt the stock. Stock gets saltier the longer you cook it down because salt does not evaporate with the water. So add the salt close to the end, tasting as you go, and you'll know what you're getting. If you're making glace de viande, don't salt at all. Yet.

All this takes time, but not a lot of it is active—and it will make your house smell wonderful. The process is as comforting to me as the reward.

## More than Just Bones

**Great broth is made with meat. But don't think for a second that cooks are tossing backstrap into the pot. What they are doing is collecting trim and odd bits like silverskin, sinewy pieces that are hard to deal with, and in some cases shanks, which are loaded with connective tissue, and using these to enrich their broths. Me? I especially love to add those strips of meat we all cut out between the ribs. It's good meat, with a little connective tissue to add body. I also keep a pile of trim that's too gnarly for the grinder—that too goes into the stockpot.**

# BASIC VENISON BROTH

This is my go-to venison broth that can stand alone as a broth for soup or, if you clarify it later, as a consommé. It's stronger in flavor than store-bought stock, so if you use it as a base for stews or soups, remember that and label your jars accordingly. Making a good stock or broth is an all-day affair. Don't take shortcuts, or your broth will suffer. Relax and let things happen as they will.

**MAKES ▶** About a gallon

**PREP TIME ▶** 10 minutes

**COOK TIME ▶** At least 6 hours

- 4 pounds venison bones and random meaty bits
- Salt
- Silverskin, tendons, cartilaginous pieces from the carcass (optional)
- 1 pig's foot (optional)
- 1 tablespoon crushed juniper berries
- 2 tablespoons fresh rosemary, or 1 tablespoon dry
- 1 tablespoon black pepper, cracked or coarsely ground
- 1 tablespoon dried thyme, or several sprigs fresh
- 4 bay leaves
- 1 large onion or leek, chopped
- 2 large carrots, chopped
- 2 to 4 stalks celery, chopped
- 1 parsnip, chopped (optional)
- About 1½ cups chopped parsley

Arrange the bones and meaty bits in a roasting pan in one layer and salt them. Roast in a 400°F oven until brown, about an hour. If you can stand it, add some extra meat—it makes a better broth. Put the bones in a large stockpot. If you want, saw the bones into large pieces with a hacksaw; this lets you fit more bones into the pot—again, yielding a richer broth. Cover with cold water by an inch or two; add the optional silverskin, cartilage, tendons, and/or pig's foot; and bring to a bare simmer over medium-high heat.

While the water is heating up, add more water to the roasting pan and let it sit for a few minutes to loosen up the browned bits on the bottom. Use a wooden spoon to scrape up those bits and pour it all into the stockpot.

Skim any froth that forms on the surface and simmer very gently for at least four hours; I let it go overnight on the lowest possible heat. You want the broth to steam and burble a little, not roil. Think steeping tea, not a real simmer.

Add the remaining ingredients and simmer for another 90 minutes to two hours.

Using tongs, grab out all the bones and large bits and discard. Set a paper towel in a fine-mesh sieve that is itself set over another large pot or plastic bin. Ladle the venison broth through the paper towel–lined sieve. Discard the dregs in the broth pot, which will be loaded with sediment and other bits.

Add salt to the strained broth to taste and pour into quart jars and freeze (or pressure-can; see page 57). If you freeze, leave at least 1½ inches of space at the top of the jar or the jars will crack when the broth freezes and expands. Use within a year. Fresh stock keeps a week in the fridge.

## Basic Venison Broth Variations

- If you want, you can toss in the onions, carrots and celery when you roast the bones.
- You can add a tablespoon or two of tomato paste to darken and enrich the sauce.
- Adding the skins from yellow onions will give you a nicer, darker color.
- Adding one or two star anise pods adds a warm, exotic flair to the stock. If you do this, don't add juniper berries.
- You can substitute chicken feet for the pig's foot. Hack them into pieces first.

# LIGHT VENISON BROTH

**MAKES ▶** About a gallon

**PREP TIME ▶** 10 minutes

**COOK TIME ▶** At least 6 hours

This is an alternative, "white" broth for lighter soups and stews, where you do not roast the bones. Follow the recipe on page 73 for ingredients, with the following method:

Put the bones, meaty bits, silverskin, tendons, and pig's foot into your stockpot and cover with water. Bring this to a full boil, skimming the froth off the top. When you have the froth mostly skimmed—ideally only a few minutes after it starts boiling—dump everything out, reserving the solids.

Clean the pot, return the solids to it, and cover with cold water. Bring this to a very slow simmer and let it cook—again, the idea is more like steeping tea than simmering—for four hours and up to overnight.

Add the remaining ingredients to the stockpot and let it cook gently for another 90 minutes to two hours.

Strain and store as in the recipe above.

> "A dog forced into the woods won't hunt deer."
>
> —DANISH PROVERB

# VENISON GLACE DE VIANDE

**MAKES ▶** 6 half-pints

**PREP TIME ▶** 10 minutes

**COOK TIME ▶** Overnight

Glace de viande, essentially meat jelly, is a secret ingredient of many professional chefs. It's cooked-down stock that has some added source of gelatin in it. A spoonful here and there makes everything better. Glace freezes well, too.

It takes a long time to make, so make a big batch and freeze it for the rest of the year.

Follow the recipe for Basic Venison Broth (page 73), only in this case, you must add a source of collagen: one or two pig's feet, a veal knuckle, calf's foot, or a pound of chicken feet. Once the stock is done, strain it but do not salt it yet! Follow the method below to finish.

When your basic broth is ready, clean the stockpot and return the broth to it, then set it over *very* low heat on a weak burner. Put the pot a little off-center to the burner, which sets up a circulation pattern that concentrates all the impurities on one side of the pot. This makes them easier to skim off. Let the stock reduce by half or more, very slowly, skimming the surface from time to time. If it's late in the day, you can let it go overnight. Don't rush this.

When you're ready, pour the reduced stock through the same set up you used before—the strainer with the paper towel in it—into a container. Only now do you add salt to taste.

Pour the reduced broth into half-pint glass jars, leaving about a ½-inch headspace or so (glace doesn't expand as much as stock). Set the jars in the fridge to cool for a day.

The next day, if the stock has set up and becomes gelatinous, label the jars and put them into the freezer. They'll keep in the fridge for about ten days, and more than a year in the freezer.

**NOTE:** If your glace has not set up into a gel, reheat it and add more gelling agents: pig's feet, calves' feet, chicken feet, or even a tablespoon or two of Knox gelatin.

# PRIMAL CUTS AND ROASTS

There's something primal about cooking great big hunks or even whole cuts of an animal. A smoky hind leg of venison, a whole backstrap chargrilled, a slow-braised shoulder, or even a whole deer roasting in front of a bed of coals made from the forest where it once lived—all evoke our past the way a burger or a simple venison steak cannot. Big cuts are special and should be reserved for family or parties, and most are best cooked with real fire. These are the cuts of our ancient heritage and should be celebrated.

Primal cuts are the larger hunks of an animal, normally the legs or neck but also whole backstraps, which, when still on the spine, are called saddles. If you have especially small deer, you could even do a baron, which is the saddle plus both hind legs, still attached to the pelvis.

This chapter covers big roasts, whole legs and necks, and long lengths of boneless backstrap. Cooking large pieces of meat does require some special consideration. When you're butchering, keep in mind how large your oven is, or your smoker, or wherever you think you might use to cook your big bits. For example, when I want to cut a whole shoulder of venison to braise or barbecue, I make sure it will fit into my largest roasting pan or my smoker. Otherwise, months down the road, when you finally want to cook the thing, you will be sad.

I generally find that roasts and primal cuts are best cooked slowly, either with fire or in broth. Slow braises are wonderful for the front of the animal, because you get the benefit of all the connective tissue enriching the broth, which you would not get with a regular roast. Fire, especially a smoky fire, is better for the hind legs and whole backstraps. The ultimate image of venison, to my mind, is a hind leg studded with garlic and basted with butter or olive oil, hanging from a string next to an oak fire, with a frying pan set underneath to catch the drippings that will soon become gravy. Heaven.

Sadly, most of us don't have a fireplace in which to do this. But these recipes will give you the tools you need to make something special.

## THE SCIENCE OF CARRYOVER HEAT

One bit of cooking science you should know when roasting large cuts—especially whole legs—is carryover heat. (Note that carryover isn't a factor in slow braises.)

Serious steak lovers know that for the best results, you should take the meat off the heat while it's still a little underdone. They know that as the meat rests, the internal temperature will continue to climb, and the steak continues to cook enough to bring it to perfection when it's served. The same is true with poultry and roasts. This remnant heat is called carryover cooking, and there are a few things you need to know to master it.

Carryover heat is a redistribution of heat throughout a piece of meat. For example, while the center of a roast might be 125°F, the exterior could be 200°F. It is this heat on the exterior that continues to cook the center. The redistribution of the heat, from the outside in, is the carryover.

There's a bit of basic physics involved here, though fear not, no equations will be necessary. Simply put, the larger and denser the piece of meat, the greater the carryover and the more the cooking will continue after removing the meat from the heat source. This is because larger roasts have a lower surface-area-to-volume ratio, so they retain heat better. (This same rule in animals is called Bergmann's rule, and it's why a whitetail from Alberta will normally weigh a lot more than one from Louisiana.) Also, denser foods normally have more water content; venison happens to be denser than beef. Finally, water has a higher capacity to retain heat than fat, so there is more energy in a lean venison roast or steak to continue the cooking than there would be in a comparable piece of beef or lamb.

How to apply this?

First, you need one more bit of meat science: Meats cooked slow and low don't undergo the carryover phenomenon. Only things cooked in very hot situations do. This is why there's no carryover in barbecue. So for a roast, you'll want to cook it slow and low first and then sear it brown. This is called reverse-searing.

For starters, you'll want to cook your roast at 200°F to 225°F until the center hits about 115°F, which can take a couple of hours depending on the size of the roast.

You'll then want to either sear it in a very hot pan or do this: Take the roast out and let it rest while you raise the oven temperature to 475°F or even 500°F. Once the oven hits that temperature, return the roast to the oven to brown the exterior. The advantage here is that you'll have more of a traditional roast, without having to use a second pan. The advantage of searing in the pan is that you'll brown the exterior faster (and you'll have more control to prevent burnt spots), and you'll initiate carryover cooking a bit more, allowing you to bring up the interior of the roast a bit higher. Incidentally, doing the finishing sear on a really hot grill is another great option. I use this method all summer.

Regardless of how you cook your roast or steak, you can expect it to carry over at least a little heat. Bigger roasts carry over more, as do leaner roasts; fat is an insulator. So remember this: If the internal temperature of your meat is close to what you want when you eat it, say 125°F, let it rest uncovered on a cutting board. If the temperature is cooler, say 115°F, tent the roast with foil. Foil can add as much as 10°F to the internal temperature of the finished piece of meat compared to open resting.

How long? For primal cuts, at least ten minutes, and up to thirty minutes for very large roasts.

In any event, it's rare for the internal temperature of even a large venison roast to rise more than 15°F. So if you account for that, you're in good shape.

"The fabled musk deer searches the world over for the source of the scent which comes from itself."

—RAMAKRISHNA

# REVERSE-SEARED VENISON ROAST

This is the master recipe for any venison roast, from a small pronghorn to a moose or bison. It works best with roasts of at least three pounds, and I've done it with a ten-pound elk roast. And to be clear, this is for a "roast beef" style roast, where the meat is cooked medium or medium-rare. It's not a pot roast.

I usually use a smoker to do the main cooking. I love the flavor smoke adds, and that smoke ring is pretty. An oven works fine, too.

The finish here is either on a ragingly hot grill or in an oven set as high as it'll go, ideally 500°F. That gets you a nice crust on the outside. If you're working with a smaller roast, you can use an air fryer at 450°F for 5 to 8 minutes to sear.

It really helps to have a probe thermometer to give you a constant read of the temperature in the thickest part of the roast. You pull the meat when it hits your target.

Exactly when you take your roast out of the fridge depends on how you're going to cook it. If you're smoking it, you'll want to go right from the fridge to the smoker. This extends the smoking time and helps develop a better smoke ring. You won't get a smoke ring in the oven, so in that case, it's best to salt the roast and let it sit on a cutting board for an hour before starting.

I also coat my roasts in a little olive oil and then a sprinkling of cracked black pepper, cumin, and/or coriander before they hit the smoker or oven. Just a little added flavor pop.

No matter how you're doing the slow roast, when the thickest part of your meat hits about 110°F, take it out of the smoker or oven. If you don't have a probe thermometer, err on undercooking your roast, because you can always cook it more. Jack your oven up as high as it'll go, at least 500°F. If your oven won't do that, maybe your grill will. Even 600°F isn't too high here, so a pizza oven is a great idea.

Once your high heat is ready, return the roast to the fire and blast it for about 10 to 15 minutes, a little less if you've got that pizza oven. All you want is a pretty crust on the outside.

Then wait at least 10 minutes; 30 isn't too long for a large roast.

Leftovers make killer "roast beast" sandwiches or steak salads. They're also good chopped in tacos or enchiladas, or for pierogi filling.

The spices I use are what I like. Use what you want, or skip everything but the salt.

*continued*

**SERVES ▶** 8 to 10

**PREP TIME ▶** 15 minutes

**COOK TIME ▶** 2½ hours

**4- to 5-pound venison roast (see headnote)**

**2 tablespoons olive oil**

**Salt**

**2 tablespoons cracked black pepper**

**2 tablespoons ground cumin (optional)**

**1 tablespoon ground coriander (optional)**

Coat the roast with the oil, then massage the salt and spices into it.

If you're using a smoker, get it ready. You want to smoke around 200°F and no hotter than 250°F. Wood choice is up to you. If you're using your oven, set it to 225°F.

Set the roast in the oven or smoker and insert a probe thermometer into its thickest part. With a roast around this size, you'll be shooting for an internal temperature of about 110°F to 120°F. This could take as long as three hours to reach, but normally it takes a couple of hours.

When you hit that temperature, remove the roast and set it on a cutting board. Remove the probe thermometer. Either increase the heat of your oven to at least 500°F—better yet 550°F—or get a grill or pizza oven roaring; 600°F is not too hot.

Return the roast to the hot oven or grill (cover the grill if that's what you are using) and roast for 10 to 15 minutes. If you've hit 600°F, you may need only about 6 minutes. You're looking for a pretty, browned crust.

Remove the roast once again and let it sit on a cutting board. Reinsert the thermometer, ideally in the same hole. Let this sit until the internal temperature hits at least 127°F, and no hotter than 145°F. In terms of time, no less than 10 minutes and up to 30 minutes is fine. Slice and serve.

> "People tend to cook the tender parts of a deer too much, and the tough parts of a deer too little."
>
> — HANK SHAW

# ROAST LEG OF VENISON WITH BAVARIAN DUMPLINGS

This is a variation on Reverse-Seared Venison Roast (page 79). I typically make this dish with a young deer or antelope, preferably a doe or yearling. It will work with larger, older animals, but the connective tissue that separates the various muscles in the leg can be pretty tough—and this recipe isn't going to melt them.

A note on the oil: I love the flavor that roasted squash seed oil brings to venison. You can find it in some stores, but your best bet is to buy squash seed oil online. But any good oil will work—good olive oil, walnut oil, even sesame oil. The point is to use something that adds flavor to the roast.

Serve this with classic trimmings: cranberry sauce, something green, and a comforting starch. Mashed, baked, or roasted potatoes are traditional, but I like German dumplings. Stale bread works great with these dumplings, if you have some lying around.

And should you have leftovers, sliced roast venison is awesome on rye bread sandwiches with some mustard and cheese.

**SERVES ▶** 4 to 8

**PREP TIME ▶** 45 minutes, mostly to let the meat come to room temperature

**COOK TIME ▶** 90 minutes, depending on the size of the roast

**ALTERNATIVE CUT ▶** A hind leg roast from a larger animal

**FOR THE VENISON ROAST**

1 hind leg of venison, shank removed

Salt

12 to 20 cloves garlic, peeled and cut into thick slivers

¼ cup squash seed oil or other flavorful oil

2 tablespoons minced sage

2 tablespoons freshly ground black pepper

About 1 cup red wine, stock, or water

Follow the procedures on page 79 for the venison, prepping your oven or smoker. While it's heating up, take a sharp knife with a narrow point and jab holes all over the leg of venison, tucking a sliver of garlic into each hole. You can use more or less garlic, depending on your taste.

Pat the venison dry, then massage the oil all over it. Sprinkle the sage and the black pepper all over the meat, making sure it gets into any nooks and crannies. Set the leg of venison on a rack in a roasting pan and pour enough wine, stock, or water into the bottom of the roasting pan to moisten the bottom—don't totally cover the bottom or the meat will steam.

Put the venison into the oven or smoker and roast until the center of the meat reaches the temperature you want.

Remove the venison from the oven or smoker, then get ready to sear either over a hot grill or by setting the oven temperature to 500°F or more. Add a little more wine to the bottom of the pan if it's dry; this will limit the amount of smoke you produce while you're searing the outside of the meat. Drizzle the meat with a little more oil.

When the hot oven is ready, set the venison back into the oven and roast until it's nicely browned, about 10 to 20 minutes. Move the meat to a cutting board. If the internal temperature is more than ten degrees below your target, tent the roast loosely with foil. If not, let it rest uncovered. Don't carve it for at least 10 minutes; I wait a full 20 minutes. Carve and serve.

*continued*

### FOR THE BAVARIAN BREAD DUMPLINGS

8 to 10 slices bread, crusts removed (about 10 ounces)

1¼ cups lukewarm milk

3 slices bacon

¼ cup minced onion or shallot

1 tablespoon minced parsley

1 teaspoon salt

1 teaspoon dried marjoram

2 eggs, lightly beaten

### PREPARING THE DUMPLINGS

After you take the venison out of the fridge, break up or chop the stale bread and put it into a bowl. Pour the milk over the bread and let it stand while you're getting the venison ready to roast. If it looks like there isn't enough milk, add a little water.

Fry the bacon in a small skillet and remove when crispy. Eat a piece. Chop the rest fine. Sauté the onion in the bacon fat until it's nice and brown. Mix the bacon and onion in a small bowl and allow to cool. Once it's cool, mix in the parsley and marjoram.

When the venison goes into the oven, set a large pot of salted water on the stove to boil. Once it boils, drop the heat to a simmer.

If there's any milk still in the bread bowl, pour it off. Mix the bacon, onions, parsley, salt, and marjoram with the bread. Make sure to break up any large pieces. Wait until the venison is resting to cook the dumplings.

When it's time, add the beaten eggs and mix to combine. If the batter is too wet to form dumplings, add breadcrumbs a tablespoon at a time until you can roll the batter into a ball with your hands. Make sure your hands are wet when you do this or the batter will stick all over them.

Gently lower each dumpling into the simmering water. Cover the pot. Once they float back to the surface, let them cook for another minute or two, then remove with a slotted spoon. Serve hot with the venison.

"The weather was fine and moderate. The hunters all returned, having killed during their absence three elk, four deer, two porcupines, a fox and a hare."

—MERIWETHER LEWIS

# BRAISED SHOULDER OF VENISON

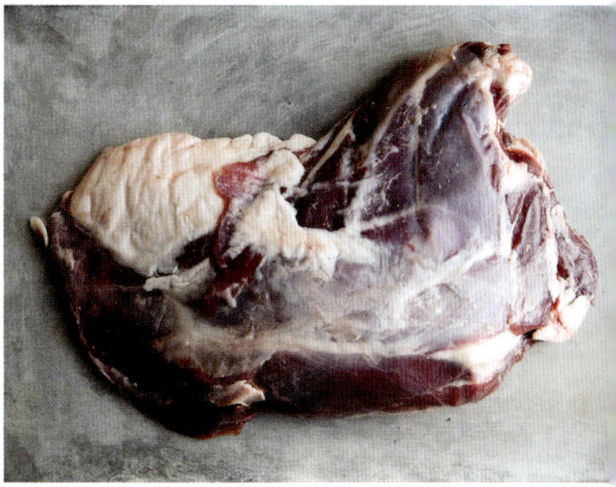

This is one of the few recipes in this book that requires a specific animal: You need to do this with a young deer or antelope, or at least a small one. Older animals will work, but their shoulders tend to be very large, and they will take almost twice as long to become tender. And I can't imagine someone with a pot large enough to roast an entire elk or moose shoulder in.

You have some options for this braise. If you're in the mood for red wine, use it and a dark stock, like Basic Venison Broth (page 73) or regular beef broth. If it's one of those early spring nights when there's still a chill in the air but it's losing its grip, go with white wine and a light stock or chicken broth.

What you drink with this depends on how you make it. If you went red, go with a red wine or a dark, malty beer. If you went white, a dry rosé, riesling, or oaked chardonnay are all good choices, as well as weiss beer or a lager.

**SERVES ▸** 6 to 8

**PREP TIME ▸** 25 minutes

**COOK TIME ▸** 4 hours

**ALTERNATIVE CUTS ▸** Shanks, boneless shoulder roasts, or neck

- 1 bone-in deer shoulder, about 4 to 6 pounds
- Olive oil
- Salt
- 1 bottle red or white wine
- 1 quart stock (see above)
- 3 tablespoons minced rosemary
- 1 tablespoon minced sage
- 1 or 2 sprigs fresh thyme, or 2 teaspoons dried
- 2 bay leaves (optional)
- 12 crushed juniper berries (optional)
- Black pepper

Preheat the oven to 450°F. Coat the shoulder with olive oil and salt it. Set it inside a roasting pan and roast until it browns, 30 to 40 minutes.

When it's nicely browned, take the pan out of the oven and set the meat aside for a moment. Drop the oven temperature to 300°F. Pour the wine into the roasting pan and use a wooden spoon to scrape up any browned bits stuck to the bottom. Add the herbs and a little salt to the liquid. Return the venison shoulder to the roasting pan. The liquid should be about halfway up the side of the shoulder. If it isn't, add the stock and then water if you need to. Cover the roasting pan and braise in the oven for three hours.

Check the shoulder at three hours. You want it almost falling off the bone. It might need another hour or so, depending on the deer's age. When the venison is ready, remove the cover from the roasting pan and increase the heat to 450°F. Roast until a crust forms on the top of the venison, about 15 minutes or so.

Remove the roasting pan from the oven, and gently remove the meat from the pan. Set the meat aside and tent with foil. Taste the remaining braising liquid. If it's to your liking, use that as a sauce. If it's too thin, set the pan over two burners and boil down until it tastes right. I strain the liquid to remove the herbs before serving.

To serve, lift away portions of the venison onto everyone's plate and grind some black pepper over it. Serve with lots of sauce over the meat, alongside wild rice, boiled or mashed potatoes, or dumplings.

# SWEDISH TJÄLKNÖL

Tjälknöl, pronounced something like "shell-knahl," is a Nordic way of cooking frozen meat, usually venison. Known as "frost lump," it involves long, slow cooking, after which you brine the meat for hours before eating it cold, with bread or however you'd like. I first heard about this technique in the excellent cookbook *Fire and Ice: Classic Nordic Cooking*, by Darra Goldstein. It intrigued me, because I'd never thought of the idea of a long, slow roast starting with a cold oven and frozen meat.

The coolest part of making tjälknöl is the long brine soak after the cooking. You can't season a frozen "lump" of meat, so this post-cooking brine makes sense. You can brine for as few as five hours, or up to a whole day. The meat will get saltier the longer you leave it.

Tjälknöl, to me, is something you do at night. After dinner, pull a "lump," a roast from the freezer, unwrap it, and set it on a tray in the oven. Turn the oven on low and make the brine. Then go to bed. It'll be ready by morning, and the brine will have steeped and cooled. Wake up, move the meat to the brine, and go about your day. By dinner, it'll be ready for slicing.

That's it! You can vary the brine as you wish, but I highly recommend the juniper berries.

I serve tjälknöl thinly sliced on rye bread, and a horseradish sour cream makes it all sing. Or you can serve the meat on a charcuterie board, alongside some good mustard and pickles. And tjälknöl sandwiches are fantastic. The meat should keep in the fridge for a week or so—and yes, you can refreeze it. When it thaws again, it'll be ready to eat.

**SERVES ▸** 10

**PREP TIME ▸** 10 minutes

**COOK TIME ▸** 7 hours, not including brine time

- 3- to 5-pound venison roast
- 1 cup kosher salt
- 8 cups water
- 5 bay leaves
- ¼ cup juniper berries, crushed
- 2 tablespoons mustard seeds
- 1 tablespoon white peppercorns, crushed
- 1 tablespoon black peppercorns, crushed
- 3 cloves garlic, crushed

Take the roast out of the freezer and unwrap it. Set it on a tray and put it in the oven. Turn the oven to 175°F. Let this cook undisturbed until the thickest part of the roast reaches about 140°F. Typically, this is between six and twelve hours, depending on the roast. A three-pound roast should take maybe seven to eight hours.

After you set the meat in the oven, make the brine by combining the remaining ingredients in a pot large enough to hold the roast. Bring this to a boil, turn off the heat, and cover the pot. It will cool as the meat cooks.

When the meat is done, set it in the brine and let it steep for at least five hours, and up to a day. It will get saltier the longer it sits.

Remove the roast, rinse quickly in cool water, pat dry, slice and serve.

**NOTE:** My favorite condiment for this is 1 cup of sour cream mixed with as much prepared horseradish as you can stand. I like a little minced dill in there, too.

# TRI-TIP-STYLE VENISON ROAST WITH CHIMICHURRI

Tri-tip is a very West Coast cut of beef, a triangular muscle taken from the bottom of the sirloin at the top of a cow's hind leg; technically, it's known as the tensor fasciae latae. But you need not worry about that, because unless you're dealing with moose or a bull elk, you won't bother isolating this muscle. Mostly, tri-tip is a style of barbecue from Santa Maria, California, basically an indirectly cooked roast. It's a great method of cooking whole-muscle venison roasts from anywhere on the hind leg.

**SERVES ▶** 6 to 8

**PREP TIME ▶** At least 1 hour

**COOK TIME ▶** 1 hour

3- to 5-pound venison roast (see headnote)

**SANTA MARIA RUB**

1 tablespoon kosher salt

1 tablespoon ground black pepper

1 teaspoon garlic powder

1 teaspoon onion powder

1 teaspoon cayenne

**CHIMICHURRI**

2 cloves garlic, minced

1 cup fresh chopped parsley, lightly packed

½ cup fresh chopped mint, lightly packed

1 small hot chile, minced (I use Thai, árbol, or mirasol chiles)

2 to 3 tablespoons freshly squeezed lime juice

Salt and black pepper to taste

½ cup olive oil

Mix together the rub ingredients and massage it into the venison. Let the meat sit at room temperature for an hour, or, alternatively, wrap the roast in plastic and refrigerate overnight.

This roast is best cooked over wood or charcoal, but gas will be OK in a pinch. You need to set up the grill so the heat is only on one side, for example, by piling the charcoal in one corner of the grill. You want to add smoke somehow, ideally from oak, which is traditional for Santa Maria BBQ. Get the grill pretty hot, about 325°F, and set the roast on the side of the grill with no coals. If you've kept a fat cap on the roast, put the fat side up. Cover the grill and roast the venison until the interior hits about 115°F, which will take between 30 minutes and an hour, depending on how hot your grill is and how thick your roast is. Alternatively, smoke the roast at 200°F until it hits that temperature.

When the venison hits the target temperature, move it to the direct side of the coals and sear it until it develops a nice crust, about 3 to 4 minutes per side. Watch for flare-ups from any fat that has not rendered out from the roast. Spray them down with a spray bottle of water.

Remove the venison from the grill and let it rest for 10 to 15 minutes. Slice against the grain and serve with the chimichurri.

There are two ways to make the chimichurri. In a food processor, buzz to combine the garlic, herbs, chile, lime juice, and a little salt. Do not puree. With the motor running, drizzle in the olive oil. Add more salt and black pepper to taste. Let steep for an hour or so before serving. Or you can use the traditional method, which is to mince the garlic, chile, and herbs by hand then pound it all in a mortar and pestle. Slowly add the lime juice, salt, and pepper, pounding all the time, then mix in the olive oil slowly by hand, stirring all the while. Let steep for an hour or so before serving.

# POLISH POT ROAST WITH A VENISON NECK

This is my version of the good ole' pot roast that pretty much everyone ate while growing up. What makes it Polish? Only that I found a similar recipe in a book called *Polish Heritage Cookery* by Robert and Maria Strybel. I like the use of flour and paprika and the overnight wine marinade, each of which adds a layer of flavor to the final dish.

You could, of course, use other cuts for this recipe, such as a shank or shoulder or even a hind leg roast. But a whole neck, boned or bone-in, is the perfect cut. The long, slow simmer melts all that connective tissue and gives you an intensely flavored, yielding piece of meat that can either be torn apart coarsely or sliced thick and served. Note that although a boned-out neck will be sliceable, you won't get clean cuts unless you chill the meat overnight before slicing. Why bother with that, though? Eat it messy.

**SERVES ▸** 4 to 6, depending on the size of the neck

**PREP TIME ▸** Overnight for the marinade

**COOK TIME ▸** 3 to 4 hours, or up to 8 hours for a slow cooker

**ALTERNATIVE CUTS ▸** Shanks, shoulders, ribs

- 1 bottle red wine
- 6 to 10 allspice berries, cracked
- 6 to 10 black peppercorns, cracked
- 3 bay leaves
- 2½- to 4-pound neck roast, boned or bone-in
- 1 cup flour
- 3 tablespoons paprika
- 1 tablespoon cayenne (optional)
- Salt
- ¼ cup lard, bacon fat, or cooking oil
- 2 onions, sliced root to tip
- 2 stalks celery, diced
- 3 carrots, cut into large chunks
- 2 parsnips, cut into large chunks
- 3 Yukon Gold potatoes, cut into chunks
- 1 rutabaga or 2 turnips, peeled and cut into chunks
- Black pepper to taste
- Sour cream, for garnish

Bring the wine, allspice, black peppercorns, and bay leaves to a boil. Turn off the heat and let the marinade cool to room temperature. When it's cool, submerge the venison in the marinade and keep it in the fridge overnight or up to four days. Turn the meat once a day if you're marinating multiple days.

Mix the flour, paprika, and cayenne (if using) in a large bowl or shallow container large enough to hold the neck roast. Pat the meat dry with paper towels and salt it. Coat it in the flour-paprika mixture. Heat the lard in a large Dutch oven or other heavy, lidded pot and brown the meat. With a typical neck roast, you'll need to cut it into two pieces to get it to fit in the pot. Brown one piece and then remove while you brown the other. If you're using a bone-in neck, turn the meat to brown all sides. When the meat has browned, remove it from the pot and set aside for a moment.

Preheat the oven to 325°F. Add the sliced onions to the pot and brown them, stirring occasionally. This should take about 8 minutes. Add 2 cups of the marinade and bring it to a boil. Add the venison back to the pot, along with 2 cups of water. Bring to a simmer, cover the pot, and cook in the oven for 1½ hours.

After 1½ hours have elapsed, add the root vegetables and celery and continue to cook for another 1½ hours, or until the meat is falling apart and the root vegetables are tender.

Remove the meat and set it on a cutting board. Slice coarsely or pull the meat off the bones. Taste the sauce, and add salt if it needs it. Add black pepper to taste and serve with the meat and vegetables, with a dollop of sour cream alongside.

If you're using a slow cooker, brown everything in a pan, move to the slow cooker, cover, and cook on high for three hours before adding the vegetables, then keep cooking until the meat is tender, likely another three hours.

# SAUERBRATEN

**SERVES ▸** 6 to 8

**PREP TIME ▸** 5 days, almost all passive marinating time

**COOK TIME ▸** 5 hours

**ALTERNATIVE CUT ▸** A long length of backstrap, about a foot long or so

3- to 5-pound roast of venison

**FOR THE MARINADE**

1 bottle red wine

½ cup red wine vinegar

2 cups water

1 tablespoon black peppercorns

1 tablespoon juniper berries

1 tablespoon mustard seed

6 to 8 cloves

3 bay leaves

1 tablespoon dried thyme

2 stalks celery, chopped

2 carrots, peeled and chopped

1 medium onion, chopped

**TO FINISH**

¼ cup melted butter or sunflower, pumpkinseed, or walnut oil

8 ginger snap cookies

3 tablespoons butter

2 tablespoons flour

Salt

I think there's a law somewhere that if you write a venison cookbook, you must include a recipe for German sauerbraten. This is a fair and just law, as sauerbraten is one of the great pot roasts of all time. This Teutonic classic comes in as many varieties as there are cooks. I've seen all sorts of variations in the sauce, the cut of meat, and the cooking temperature. At its core, however, sauerbraten involves a large piece of meat that has been marinated a long time and slowly cooked in a vinegar-based marinade, which is then turned into a sauce.

My use of ginger snaps in the sauce comes from the sauerbraten I once ate as a child at a New York restaurant called Lüchows, a bastion of German cooking in the NYC area until it closed in 1982, after operating in the same space for one hundred years. They used ginger snaps in their sauce, and I loved it. Still do.

A word on the marinade. You must boil the marinade before using it for two reasons: first, to burn off much of the alcohol in the wine (otherwise the meat gets a weird metallic taste); and second, the heat extracts more flavor from all the spices you put in it. Let the marinade cool completely before submerging the venison.

Oh, and use an inexpensive wine you might think about drinking on a Wednesday night; nothing fancy. Can you use something other than wine? Yes, but then it's not a sauerbraten. It's a pot roast. Still good, though.

Bring the marinade ingredients—wine, vinegar, water, peppercorns, juniper, mustard, cloves, bay leaves, thyme, celery, carrots, and onion—to a boil and turn off the heat. Allow to cool. Submerge the venison in the marinade and let it sit in the fridge for at least twenty-four hours, and up to five days. Three days is a good length of time. When you're ready to cook, take the roast out of the marinade and salt it. Set it aside for 20 minutes or so.

Preheat the oven to 250°F. Actually, 225°F is a better temperature, but then the roast can take up to eight hours to properly cook; this is what I do at home on weekends. At 250°F, the roast will probably take about five hours to cook. You can go up to 300°F—a typical venison roast will be ready in 3½ hours at this temperature—but you'll get gray, not pink, meat. It will still taste good, though. Another option is to cook sous vide (see sidebar).

Pour the marinade into a Dutch oven or other lidded pot and bring it to a boil. Place the venison inside, cover, and put into the oven. If the venison is not submerged by the marinade, turn the roast over every hour. This is also a good way to test for doneness—you want the roast to be almost falling apart. When the roast is done, take it out of the pot and coat it with some of the melted butter or oil. Reserve the rest of the butter or oil for later. Wrap the roast in foil.

Now make the sauerbraten sauce—and sauerbraten is all about the sauce. Strain the cooking liquid through a fine-mesh sieve into a bowl. Take the ginger snap cookies and pulverize them in a blender. You want it to look like rough cornmeal or coarse flour.

In a medium-size pot, melt the 3 tablespoons of butter over medium-high heat. When the butter is frothing and totally melted, whisk in the flour. Cook until it's the color of coffee-and-cream, stirring often. Slowly whisk in the cooking liquid, one cup at a time. The mixture will turn to clay at first, then loosen into a silky sauce. Taste for salt (it will probably need it) and season to taste.

Whisk in 4 tablespoons of the pulverized ginger snaps. They will not dissolve completely at first, but keep stirring and they will disappear. Taste the sauce. Add another tablespoon of ginger snaps if you want, or add a tablespoon of sugar. The sauce should taste sour, warm (a pumpkin pie sort of spicy warm), and a little zippy and sweet.

To serve, slice the roast into ¼-inch-thick slices. Venison can be dry—it has zero internal fat—so one trick I use is to paint each slice in melted butter or oil before I serve it. You'll need about half a stick of melted butter to do this. Serve with lots of sauce, some braised onions, and either mashed potatoes, egg noodles, Bavarian dumplings (page 84) or spätzle (page 148). A hearty red wine would be an ideal match here, as would a dark, malty beer.

"A hunt based only on the trophies taken falls far short."

— FRED BEAR

## Smoked or Sous Vide Sauerbraten

If you happen to have a smoker or a sous vide water oven, you can pull off a pot roast where the meat is still medium-rare. To do this, marinate as normal, then get the meat ready for the pot—only put it into a sous vide bag or your smoker set to 185°F. Boil the marinade, then let it cool for ten minutes or so before putting it into the bag with the venison. Seal the bag with a vacuum sealer (carefully if you have a suction sealer!) and submerge it in 135°F to 140°F water for eight hours. It will come out a pretty pink, and you'll get a powerful hit of the sauerbraten flavor. Use the marinade in the bag to complete the sauerbraten sauce. You can sear your venison while you're making the sauce if you want, but it's not necessary. For the smoker version, simply smoke the marinated meat until it hits 135°F to 140°F internal temperature and make the sauce as above.

# ITALIAN POT ROAST

**SERVES ▶** 4 to 6

**PREP TIME ▶** 20 minutes

**COOK TIME ▶** 4 hours

**ALTERNATIVE CUTS ▶** Shoulder, shanks, or neck

- 2- to 4-pound venison roast
- Salt
- 2 tablespoons olive oil
- 1 onion
- 1 large carrot
- 1 stalk celery
- A handful of dried mushrooms, crushed (optional)
- 1 tablespoon tomato paste
- 1 cup venison or beef broth
- ½ teaspoon dried thyme
- 1 teaspoon dried oregano or marjoram
- 1 teaspoon chopped rosemary
- 1 bay leaf
- 1 cup red wine
- One 32-ounce can whole, peeled tomatoes
- ½ cup chopped fresh parsley
- Black pepper to taste

This is a pretty classic recipe, with lots of renditions from both native Italians and Italian-Americans. The flavors are similar to osso buco made with shanks (page 117), but this is best done with a shoulder roast from an old animal, a neck roast, or a whole-muscle hind leg roast.

If you have a large piece of meat that you're pot-roasting, you'll want to add a little more tomato, wine, and broth so you have more sauce. After all those hours of slow-cooking, the meat, while tender, can dry out a bit and will need the sauce to keep things moist.

Salt the roast. Heat the olive oil in a Dutch oven or other heavy, lidded pot and brown the roast on all sides. This will take a little while, so take your time. While the roast is browning, coarsely chop the onion, carrot, and celery and put the pieces into a food processor. Pulse until the vegetables are small but not pureed.

When the roast has browned, remove it for now. Add the vegetables and mushrooms (if using) and cook them until the onion is soft and nicely golden, about 6 minutes. As the vegetables cook, use a wooden spoon to scrape up any browned bits that have stuck to the bottom of the pot.

Stir in the tomato paste, then add all the herbs except for the parsley. Nestle the roast back into the pot and pour the wine over the roast. Bring this to a boil and let it cook for a minute or two. Add the juice from the can of tomatoes. As for the tomatoes themselves, take each one and crush and shred it with your fingers, then add to the pot. If the liquids have reached halfway up the sides of the roast, you're good to go. If not, add the stock.

Cover the pot and cook over very low heat until the venison is very tender, about three to five hours, depending on the roast's size and how old the animal was.

Gently remove the roast and set it on a cutting board. Taste the sauce and add salt and black pepper to taste. Stir in the parsley and let the residual heat wilt it. Slice the roast and serve with the sauce and grits, polenta, or pasta.

If you're using a slow cooker, brown everything in a pan, move to the slow cooker, cover, and cook on high until the meat is tender, five to seven hours.

# WHOLE GRILLED BACKSTRAP

Grilling meat is one of the basic skills every cook needs to have. This is especially true with venison, which is so lean that you have very little leeway between perfect and overdone—and overcooked venison is gray, dry, and livery. You can grill any venison steak, but whole backstrap or loin is a better cut for fast grilling. With a whole loin, you grill the sides and then, when you cut into it, you get to see that pink perfection.

Start with a piece of backstrap that's at least ten inches long, which is usually about one pound. Depending on how wide it is, this will feed two to four people. Note that this works best with small or medium-size deer or pronghorn.

I like to serve the venison with a side salad like potato, macaroni, or bean salad, plus maybe some tomatoes and basil, corn on the cob, dinner rolls—you get the idea. Nothing overly fancy.

**SERVES ▸** 4

**PREP TIME ▸** 30 minutes

**COOK TIME ▸** 20 minutes

1- to $1\frac{1}{2}$-pound piece of venison loin, or elk/moose tenderloin

Olive oil

Salt

Your favorite BBQ sauce, or the following mixture:

Zest and juice of 4 lemons or limes

1 tablespoon ground black pepper

$\frac{1}{4}$ cup minced parsley or cilantro

Coat the venison loin in oil and salt. Set aside for 30 minutes at room temperature.

Get your grill hot, clean the grates, and lay the venison on the grill, fat cap facing down if you've left the fat on your deer. Keep the grill cover open. Let this cook for 5 to 8 minutes without moving, depending on how hot your grill is and how thick your venison loin is. You want a good sear, with good grill marks, on that side of the meat. If you left the fat cap on, keep an eye out for flare-ups; douse flare-ups with a spray bottle of water.

Flip the venison and repeat on the other side. Paint the side you seared with BBQ sauce, if using. (Note: If you're going with the citrus-pepper-herb combo, wait until the end to use it.)

Do the finger test to check for doneness (see page 113). If the venison needs more time, turn it to the sides that have not had direct exposure to the grill and cook for 2 or 3 more minutes, checking all the way. Paint those sides with BBQ sauce, too.

When the meat has been cooked to your liking, take it off the fire and let it rest for 10 minutes, fat cap facing up if there is one. (If the meat's still a little underdone, tent it loosely with foil.) If you're using the citrus mixture instead of BBQ sauce, roll the meat in the sauce before it rests.

To serve, slice into medallions and serve with BBQ sauce or the extra citrus sauce on the side.

# MEXICAN BARBACOA

This is perhaps my favorite recipe for a deer's front shoulder. Mexican barbacoa, a mildly spicy, long-braised variant on barbecue, works perfectly with the tough, sinewy front legs of a deer. The meat cooks very slowly, and all that connective tissue dissolves into the broth, making everything richer and a little slick. Keeps your lips shiny.

Barbacoa is more warming than *picante*. Yes, there are chipotles en adobo in it, but not so many that your head blows off (chipotles en adobo can be bought in any Latin market and in some "regular" supermarkets; note that the recipe calls for canned, not fresh, chipotles). The cloves are a stronger element, as are the cumin and bay. If you want to test this recipe before making it, go to your nearest Chipotle restaurant and try their barbacoa: This recipe is virtually identical.

Serve it in tacos, burritos, or tostadas or over rice. And be sure to have at least a few of the traditional accompaniments, like cilantro, crumbled queso seco (a feta-like Mexican cheese), chopped onions, sour cream, fresh or pickled chiles, avocados—basically, anything that works on a taco.

Still not convinced? Well, barbacoa may be in the Top Five Easiest Recipes in this book. It's literally a Crock-Pot-it-and-go dish. Minimal chopping, and the only thing you need to do as a cook is to shred the meat. Stupid crazy easy. Try it and you will not be sad.

No front shoulder? You can also use shanks, roasts, neck, or even the head of the animal; barbacoa is traditionally done with a cow's head, after all.

Note: The single biggest mistake readers made in the first edition of this book was to misread "2 to 4 canned chipotles" as "2 to 4 CANS of chipotles." Yikes! You just want a few chiles, people.

**SERVES ▸** 6 to 8

**PREP TIME ▸** 15 minutes

**COOK TIME ▸** 3 hours, more or less

- 2 to 3 pounds venison, from the shoulder, neck, or legs
- 2 to 4 chipotles en adobo (use canned chipotles rather than dried)
- 1 red onion, chopped
- 5 cloves garlic, chopped
- 2 bay leaves
- 1 teaspoon smoked paprika (optional)
- 1 teaspoon ground cumin
- 1 teaspoon ground cloves
- 1 tablespoon kosher salt
- ½ cup freshly squeezed lime juice
- ½ cup cider vinegar
- 1 quart stock (beef or venison)

**TO FINISH**

- ¼ cup lard or vegetable oil
- Smoked salt (optional)
- Cilantro, shredded cheese, sour cream, avocados, and hot sauce, for garnish

Put everything in a slow cooker or Dutch oven and cook, covered, until the meat falls off the bone, which will be between two hours (for a young deer) and six hours (if you have a very old animal). If you use a slow cooker, set it to "high." If you use a regular pot, put it into the oven set to 300°F. If you're using a pressure cooker, cook it at high pressure for 80 minutes, then let it vent naturally.

Pull all the meat from the bones and shred with forks or your fingers. Stir in the lard, and add smoked salt to taste. You want the lard or oil to coat the shreds of meat. Pour over some of the juices from the pot and put the meat in a pan for the table. Serve with tacos, in a burrito, or on a bun.

# DZIK DE VENADO (YUCATÁN VENISON)

**SERVES ▸** 8 to 10

**PREP TIME ▸** 30 minutes

**COOK TIME ▸** 3 hours

### BRAISE

2 to 3 pounds venison, from the shoulder or legs

1 red onion, chopped

5 cloves garlic, chopped

2 bay leaves

1 teaspoon ground cumin

1 teaspoon ground cloves

1 tablespoon kosher salt

1 quart stock (beef or venison)

Salt

### TO FINISH

¼ cup freshly squeezed lime juice

½ cup orange juice

2 tablespoons minced green onion or chives

1 cup chopped red onion

2 diced plum tomatoes (only if they are in season)

½ cup chopped radishes

½ cup chopped cilantro

1 to 3 minced habaneros

Pickled red onion and sliced radishes for garnish

Dzik de Venado, a traditional venison dish of the Yucatán, is similar to Mexican Barbacoa (page 97), but you then toss the shredded venison with radishes, chiles, cilantro, and sour orange juice (or a combination of orange and lime juice) into a salpicón, a mashup of barbacoa, cochinita pibil, and ceviche.

To pickle the onions, slice them thinly from root to tip and soak them in lime juice while the venison is cooking.

Put all the ingredients for the braise into a pot and mix together. Bring to a boil and then simmer gently until the venison begins to fall apart. When it's tender, shred it with two forks and toss it with the salad ingredients. Garnish with the onion and radishes.

Serve with tostadas or corn tortillas.

# VENISON BIRRIA

Birria has been having a moment in the United States, but it is a cornerstone of the cuisine of the Mexican state of Jalisco—where many of the Mexican immigrants living in my former home of Sacramento come from. I've eaten a lot of birria. Really good birria.

What follows is me trying my best to give you a rendition of birria that is worthy of the name. Birria is like barbacoa, but you eat it either in a bowl, often in its broth, or shredded on tortillas for birria tacos.

Traditionally, birria is made with goat, but you can use many meats, and venison birria is especially good. You want to use the neck or front shoulder or shanks here, because they have a lot of connective tissue that, when cooked slow and low, melts and makes the meat silky.

You make the adobo for your birria and slather it on the meat the day before. This matters. Then, you wrap the meat in leaves—maguey leaves to be traditional, but I use banana leaves—nestle it in a pot, then seal the pot you're using. Put the whole shebang in a low oven for most of the day, crack the seal, and have at it.

An ideal setup would be to use the whole front shoulder or neck of a small deer or pronghorn, cut to fit into a Dutch oven. Wrap the marinated meat in banana leaves, which you can buy in any Asian or Latin market, stuff it all into the Dutch oven, put the lid on, and seal it with fresh masa, the corn dough you use to make tortillas. A good, accessible alternate leaf would be collards; they're sturdy enough to not dissolve in the long cooking process. If you absolutely can't find leaves, use foil instead.

The dough seal does keep all the moisture locked in, so use flour and water if you don't have masa and water. It doesn't matter. Just jam it all around where the lid meets the pot. You'll need to crack it off when you're ready.

When will your birria be ready? Hard to say. But as a general rule, err on the side of cooking it more, not less. Birria cooked twelve hours will still be good, even if it got tender at eight hours. Don't even think about cracking the seal in less than four hours.

Your reward is that aroma that's been sealed in, lots of amazing broth, and meat that falls apart, practically begging to be slathered on a fresh corn tortilla.

Birria tacos are so good that you'll want to top them only with fresh cilantro and chopped white onions soaked in lime juice. Hot sauce is the only other thing you should consider adding, and that's to each eater's taste.

Once made, your birria will keep a week in the fridge. Reheat it slowly in its broth for weekday lunches.

*continued*

**SERVES ▸** 8 to 12

**PREP TIME ▸** 30 minutes

**COOK TIME ▸** 8 hours, more or less

## Birria Tacos

I know you want birria tacos. So here they are. You'll need corn tortillas, and lots of shredded, melty cheese—even the "Mexican blend" in the supermarket is good, although I'd use queso Chihuahua or Oaxaca.

Get a comal or flat-top hot over medium-high heat. Dip a corn tortilla in the hot, fatty cooking liquid from the birria, then load up half of the tortilla with shredded birria and cheese. Fold it over and sear on the comal until the cheese melts and you have some awesome char marks on the tortilla.

To serve, open them up a little and add the onions, lime, and cilantro.

Stem and seed the dried chiles, then pour boiling water over them. Let them soften while you chop the other vegetables.

Get a comal or cast-iron pan hot, and lay the tomatoes and onion cut side down. Scatter the garlic cloves around the edge of the pan. Let them blacken a bit, which should take about 6 to 10 minutes. Turn the garlic cloves after about 5 minutes. Use a metal spatula to turn the onion and tomatoes, scraping up all the blackened and browned bits. Move those bits to the blender.

While this is happening, toast the cumin, black peppercorns, and cloves in a dry pan until you can smell them. Grind them in a spice grinder and put the powder into the blender. Put the salt, bay leaves, and oregano into the blender, too.

When the vegetables are nicely charred, put them into the blender. Tear the chiles into pieces and add them to the blender, along with a healthy glug of soaking water. Puree this, adding the beer and vinegar as you go. You want it smooth.

Coat the meat with this sauce, put it all into a covered container, and let it sit overnight, or at the very least for an hour.

When you're ready to cook, preheat the oven to 275°F. Line a heavy, lidded pot like a Dutch oven with the banana leaves and put the meat into the center. Add the remaining marinade. Wrap the meat up as best you can with the leaves, then put the lid on.

Mix the masa or flour with water until you have a clay-like paste. Jam it all around the seal between the lid and the pot and put the pot in the oven. Let it cook for at least four hours before checking, no matter what. I don't check until eight hours have passed. You want the meat to be falling apart.

When you're ready, move the meat to a large bowl and pour all the broth over it. Pull the meat into largish pieces and give everyone some. Let them make their own tacos as they wish or completely shred the meat and make tacos. Garnish with the cilantro and chopped onion soaked in lime juice.

**NOTES:** You can cook the meat in a pressure cooker, like an Instant Pot, on high pressure for 90 minutes, venting naturally afterward.

**4 pounds shoulder, shanks, or neck roast**

### FOR THE ADOBO

**12 dried guajillo or ancho chiles, about 4 ounces**

**2 pounds Roma tomatoes, sliced in half**

**1 white onion, sliced in half**

**1 head garlic, separated but not peeled**

**2 teaspoons cumin seeds**

**2 tablespoons black peppercorns**

**4 to 6 whole cloves**

**1 tablespoon salt**

**3 bay leaves**

**1 tablespoon dried Mexican oregano**

**1 cup Mexican beer (I use Negro Modelo or Bohemia)**

**¼ cup pineapple vinegar or cider vinegar**

### TO FINISH

**Banana leaves**

**1 cup corn masa or flour (to seal the pot)**

**Cilantro, lime wedges, and chopped white onion, for garnish**

**Corn tortillas**

# VENISON CONFIT

Confit is an old French method of preserving meats, usually duck. Basically, you salt a piece of meat then cook it very slowly in fat. The idea is that poaching the meat in fat for hours and hours will not only give you meltingly tender meat, but it will be bathed in fat, keeping otherwise dry meats silky.

It's perfect for venison. Shoulder, neck, or hind leg roasts—even shanks—are excellent cooked this way. And since it's salted, the finished meat will also keep for more than a week in the fridge.

The easiest way to make this recipe is with a vacuum sealer and a large pot. You salt the meat down, pat it dry, and then put it into a vacuum bag with some fat and herbs. Then you cook it very slowly in hot water. Note that I said "hot," not simmering or boiling water. You want the heat to be at a steam, not a simmer, about 170°F. A big pot of water is the easiest thing to use for this because water holds its temperature well. A sous vide water oven is perfectly designed for this task.

If you don't have a vacuum sealer, you can of course do this the old-school way: Submerge the venison in lard, butter, or duck fat and cook in a 180°F oven all day. This requires a lot of fat, so I rarely do it this way. But it works.

When you're done, shred the meat and eat it in all sorts of ways. My favorite? Either as a taco filling or like pulled pork barbecue, with my favorite mustard-based South Carolina–style BBQ sauce (see sidebar) and some coleslaw.

**SERVES ▶** 4 to 6

**PREP TIME ▶** 24 to 72 hours, passive curing time

**COOK TIME ▶** 6 to 12 hours

**ALTERNATIVE CUTS ▶** Shoulder, shanks, neck, or ribs

**FOR THE BRINE**

¼ cup sugar
½ cup kosher salt
2 teaspoons dried thyme or rosemary
2 bay leaves
4 cloves garlic, smashed
10 juniper berries, crushed (optional)

2- to 4-pound venison roast
1 cup unsalted butter, lard, or duck fat
3 sprigs fresh thyme
3 sprigs fresh rosemary
2 bay leaves

Put all the brine ingredients into a pot with two quarts of water and bring to the steaming point—just enough to dissolve everything. Let this come to room temperature, then chill it. When the brine is cold, submerge the venison in it and store it in the fridge for twenty-four to seventy-two hours. The longer you brine the meat, the saltier it will get. A five-pound roast will need an extra day.

Take the venison out of the brine; discard the brine. Pat the meat dry and, if you have time, let it air dry uncovered in the fridge for an hour or two, or up to forty-eight hours if you put it into a covered container. When you're ready to cook the venison, seal it in a vacuum bag with the lard and the herbs. If you happen to have a sous vide water oven, cook it at 165°F for as long as twenty-four hours, and at least ten hours. Most of you won't have a sous vide machine, however, so instead, fill your largest pot with water and heat it to a bare simmer, about 170°F. Drop the bag with the venison in it and hold the water temperature at the steaming point—do not let it simmer, let alone boil—for about six hours.

*continued*

## South Carolina BBQ Sauce

This mustard-based sauce goes well with pretty much everything from poultry to pork to venison, and even full-flavored fish like amberjack, tuna, and king mackerel.

4 tablespoons butter
1 medium onion, grated on a box grater
½ cup yellow "ballpark" mustard
½ cup cider vinegar
½ cup brown sugar
1 heaping tablespoon powdered mustard
Hot sauce to taste
Salt to taste

Heat the butter in a small pot and cook the grated onion over medium heat for 4 to 5 minutes, until soft but not browned. Add the remaining ingredients, stir, and let this cook over very low heat for 20 minutes. You can puree it in a blender if you want a smooth sauce. Once made, this BBQ sauce will keep in the fridge for a month or more.

How you serve your confit is up to you. You can shred and eat it on the spot. Or shred and mix it into a salad, with pasta, spätzle, on a burger bun, in a taco . . . you get the point. But even better? Before you eat your confit, shred it coarsely and put it under the broiler until one side gets a little charred. That bit of char and caramelized goodness makes a good dish great.

"You can't eat antlers."

— NORTH AMERICAN HUNTING SAYING

# MARINATED VENISON KEBABS

Kebabs are perhaps the best summertime preparation for meat from the hind legs of the deer. And after all, who doesn't love to eat a good kebab? There's a certain jazz-like quality to them: You can vary the veggies to suit your preference, and you can marinate the kebabs in anything from a vivid green herb sauce to Italian dressing to teriyaki. Or try this marinade, a mixture of red wine vinegar and harissa, which is to North Africa what ketchup is to North America.

Harissa is a condiment whose main flavors are chiles and caraway. And while it's supposed to be spicy, it's not supposed to be blow-your-head-off spicy. You'll note in my recipe below that most of the chiles are milder varieties like poblano, pasilla, and ancho. If you're not into hot food, go easy on the hot ones like the cascabels or Aleppo. You can buy harissa in many markets, too.

I like to serve these kebabs with something simple, like grilled potatoes or bread, or, if I'm feeling like a low-carb day, coleslaw.

**SERVES ▸** 4

**PREP TIME ▸** 24 hours, almost all of it marinating time in the fridge

**COOK TIME ▸** 15 minutes

**FOR THE HARISSA**

8 dried mild chiles (guajillo, ancho, pasilla, or New Mexican)

4 to 8 dried hot chiles (Aleppo, if you can get them)

1 teaspoon caraway seeds

½ teaspoon coriander seeds

½ teaspoon cumin seeds

1 teaspoon dried mint

¼ cup olive oil

2 teaspoons kosher salt

4 to 6 cloves garlic, mashed and minced

Freshly squeezed lemon juice

**FOR THE KEBABS**

2 pounds venison, trimmed of sinew and cut into 1½- to 2-inch chunks

¼ to ⅓ cup harissa (see above)

¼ cup red wine vinegar

Various vegetables cut to the size of the venison, such as mushrooms, onions, bell peppers, or zucchini

Salt

If you're making your own harissa, start by removing the stems and seeds from the dried chiles. Tear the chiles into pieces and pour enough hot water over them to barely cover. Weigh the chiles down with a small plate or something similar and let the chiles soak for an hour or two, until they're soft.

Once the chiles are soft, put them and the remaining harissa ingredients into a blender or food processor and process into a paste—it can be smooth or rough, depending on how you like it. You might need a little bit of the soaking water to loosen things up. You can make the harissa days or even weeks in advance and store it in the refrigerator; it lasts for months that way.

To marinate the venison, mix the harissa and the red wine vinegar into a slurry in a bowl. Massage the marinade into the venison and pour the whole shebang into a lidded container. Refrigerate for at least a few hours, and as long as two days.

When you're ready to cook, remove the venison from the marinade. Cut the various vegetables into pieces roughly the size of the venison. Carefully skewer them onto two skewers; doing this makes it much easier to turn the kebabs. I say carefully because you want to watch out for the pointy ends; I've stabbed myself a couple times when I got distracted. When you've made all your skewers, salt everything and put them back into the fridge.

*continued*

Get your grill nice and hot. Make sure the grill grates are clean by scouring with a brush. When your grill is ready, soak a paper towel in some vegetable oil, grab it with a pair of tongs, and wipe down the grates. Lay the skewers on the grill so they are not touching. Grill for 6 to 10 minutes on the top and bottom of the skewers, plus another 1 to 2 minutes on each side to "kiss" the edges. Use the finger test for doneness (page 113) to determine how well-cooked you want your venison.

Let the kebabs rest for 5 minutes, then pull the meat off the skewers and serve.

# A KEBAB PRIMER

The real key to great kebabs is how you cook them. If you follow these general directions, you'll make a better kebab, no matter what meat or marinade you're using.

Cut the meat into chunks no smaller than 1½ inches and not much bigger than 2½ inches. Too big and the outside gets charred before the inside cooks. Too small and you get shoe leather in a hurry.

Trim out all silverskin and connective tissue. Grilling will tighten up these tissues and leave you chewing and chewing and chewing . . .

Vegetables need to be about the same size as the meat. Otherwise they won't cook properly.

Use bamboo or metal skewers. If using metal skewers, freeze them first. Metal conducts heat, which can cook your kebabs from the inside. It's much harder to get a medium-rare kebab with a metal skewer.

Use two skewers instead of one. Yes, it's harder to set them up, but you'll have a far easier time turning them with two skewers. Meat and especially veggies tend to spin when you only have one skewer.

Leave a little space between everything on the skewers. If you pack the skewers, the space where one item meets another will take a long time to cook.

Start with cold meat! Doing this is insurance against overcooking the center of the venison.

Hot fire, open grill. Don't be tempted to close your grill. That creates an oven effect that can overcook your meat in no time. Better to have a really hot fire on one part of the grill and a cooler section off to one side in case things get too hot too fast. Remember, kebabs are supposed to be cooked over open fire with no cover.

Follow those general rules and you'll be in business.

# VENISON PIEROGIS

Pierogis are one of the world's many filled dumplings, addictive and homey. Eastern European in origin, pierogis are serious comfort food in the Midwest, Pennsylvania, and upstate New York. True to form, Casey Barber, a colleague of mine from Pittsburgh, was the inspiration for this recipe. Her book *Pierogi Love* is a must-have if you like these little bundles of happiness. Her original recipe calls for beef short ribs, but I substituted venison here. And I made a few changes to the filling, too.

You can, of course, use leftover braised meat from any of the recipes in this chapter. Obviously, the best choice would be the Polish Pot Roast with a Venison Neck on page 90.

**SERVES ▶** 4 to 6

**PREP TIME ▶** 4 hours, most to braise the venison

**COOK TIME ▶** 15 minutes

**FOR THE FILLING**

3 tablespoons butter, lard, or the cooking oil of your choice

2 pounds venison shoulder, shank meat, or neck meat

Salt and black pepper

2 stalks celery, chopped

1 onion, chopped

1 carrot, chopped

A handful of dried mushrooms

2 cloves garlic, chopped

1 tablespoon tomato paste

1 teaspoon caraway seed

2 tablespoons Worcestershire sauce

One 12-ounce bottle of dark malty beer, such as stout, porter, or a brown ale

1½ cups stock (venison or beef), divided

1 tablespoon cornstarch (optional)

**FOR THE DOUGH**

2 large eggs, divided

½ cup sour cream (4 ounces)

3 tablespoons melted butter (unsalted)

1 teaspoon salt

1 cup all-purpose flour (4¼ ounces)

1 cup dark rye flour or pumpernickel flour (3¾ ounces)

Heat the butter in a heavy, lidded pot large enough to hold the venison. Salt the meat and brown it on all sides. Don't crowd the pot; do this in batches if need be. As the venison browns, remove it from the pot and set aside.

Add the vegetables and garlic and cook over medium heat until they begin to brown on the edges, about 10 to 15 minutes. Stir in the tomato paste and caraway seeds, then add the Worcestershire sauce, beer, and about ½ cup of stock. Return the meat to the pot and add more stock until it comes halfway up the sides of the meat. Cover the pot and simmer gently over medium-low heat until the meat is very tender. This could be anywhere from 90 minutes to three hours, depending on how old your animal was.

When the meat is ready, shred it coarsely. Put 1 cup of this meat into a food processor and add 2 tablespoons of cooking liquid. Pulse until coarsely ground.

Depending on what sort of cuts you use, you may have extra meat. You can eat the rest of the meat as a cook's snack, use it to fill dumplings, or drop it into soup. Strain the cooking liquid and reserve it to make gravy later. All of this can be done up to a day or two before you make the pierogis.

### MAKE THE DOUGH

To make the dough, mix one egg, the sour cream, and melted butter into one bowl and the remaining dry ingredients into another bowl. Stir the wet into the dry, then knead until the dough comes together—this should only take a minute or three. Cover the dough and let it rest for 15 minutes.

Cut the dough in half. Cover one half while you work with the other. Roll the dough into a snake and cut it into twelve pieces. Roll each piece into a ball and set aside, covered. Repeat with the second half of the dough.

*continued*

Ideally, you have a tortilla press; they're cheap and available online or in any Mexican market. It makes the process of forming all sorts of dumpling wrappers (and, of course, tortillas) so much easier that it's worth the $20. If you have one, line the press with cut pieces of a plastic bag (like a produce bag), and press each ball of dough into a flat disk.

If you don't have a tortilla press, flatten each ball of dough with your hands, keeping it as round as possible. Finish rolling out the wrappers out on a well-floured surface with a rolling pin. You want them as thin as possible, like ⅛ inch. Alternately, you can roll out the whole batch of dough and cut out 3-inch circles with a cookie cutter.

Beat the remaining egg for the dough with some water to make an egg wash. Get out a baking sheet and either line it with parchment paper or dust it with semolina flour or cornmeal.

Fill each circle with about a heaping tablespoon of the venison. Using your finger, swipe a little bit of the egg wash along the edge of the dough circle, then fold the dough over the filling to make a half-moon. Seal the dumplings with your fingers and set them on the baking sheet.

When you're done, you have a choice: fry your pierogis or boil them. If you boil them, get a large pot of water boiling and add enough salt to make the water taste a little salty. Boil the pierogis until they float, then boil a minute or two more. If you fry them, get a wide frying pan and add 3 or 4 tablespoons of your favorite fat—lard and butter are mine—and fry the pierogis over medium-high heat in one layer until nicely browned, about 2 minutes.

You can eat them all this way, with sour cream and caramelized onions, or you can make a gravy with your cooking liquid by heating it up to steaming, then adding the cornstarch. To do this without clumping, mix the cornstarch with about 1 tablespoon of water to make a slurry, then stir it into the hot liquid. Keep stirring, and bring the gravy to a boil. That will set the cornstarch. Drop the heat back to a simmer and you're ready.

"A wounded deer leaps highest"

—EMILY DICKINSON

# VENISON RISOTTO

This is a versatile meat-and-tomato-based risotto that works with any sort of red meat. I'm including it in the Primal Cuts and Roasts chapter because this an ideal use for leftover braised meats; leftovers from the Italian Pot Roast (page 94), the Braised Shoulder of Venison (page 85), or the Polish Pot Roast (page 90) would be the best.

**SERVES** ▸ 4 to 6

**PREP TIME** ▸ 20 minutes

**COOK TIME** ▸ 35 minutes

2 tablespoons butter, beef tallow, or olive oil

1 cup minced white or yellow onion

2 cloves garlic, minced

1 cup arborio or carnaroli rice

1½ cups chopped or shredded braised venison (see headnote for options)

Salt

1 tablespoon tomato paste

1 to 2 teaspoons minced fresh sage

½ cup red wine

4 cups stock (venison or beef)

½ cup finely grated pecorino or Parmesan cheese

Black pepper to taste

Heat the butter or beef tallow in a medium pot over medium-high heat. When it's hot, add the onion and sauté until translucent, about 4 minutes.

Add the garlic and rice and sauté another 2 or 3 minutes, stirring often. Stir in the chopped or shredded braised meat, add a little salt and then the tomato paste. Stir this to combine and let it cook 1 minute.

Add the sage and red wine. It will spatter. Stir constantly until the wine cooks almost away, then add 1 cup of the stock. Stir this for about 30 seconds, then drop the heat to medium and let it cook, stirring occasionally.

When the liquid has mostly cooked away, add another 1 cup of stock and stir that for 30 seconds, then let it cook down again, stirring occasionally, Repeat this process until the rice is tender. You will need all 4 cups, and possibly more if the rice is old. Use water in that case. You want the rice to be tender but not mushy.

Stir in the grated cheese and black pepper, as well as another tablespoon of butter or fat if you want. Serve at once.

**VARIATIONS:** I prefer to use leftover braised meat for this risotto (see headnote), but you have options if that's not available to you.

- You can cut some clean, tender venison like backstrap or sinew-free hind leg meat into small dice and add this along with the last cup of stock when you are cooking the rice.
- Or you can add ½ pound of ground venison in the beginning, with the rice. Cook this until the meat has nicely browned. The end result will be a bit different from this recipe, but it'll still be good.

# BACKSTRAPS, LOINS, AND TENDERLOINS

Whether you call it the backstrap, loin, or ribeye, this, along with the coveted tenderloin, is for most people the money cut on a big game animal. Lightly cooked tenderloin is often the celebratory meal after a successful hunt, and rare is the hunter who will share this coveted morsel with anyone other than, maybe—*maybe*—their spouse or partner. Poorly cooking these cuts disrespects the animal; although, sadly, I see it all too often. This chapter will help you perfect your methods for cooking venison steaks large and small.

The backstrap, or loin, is the equivalent of a ribeye in beef. The tenderloin, which is all too often confused with backstraps, is underneath the loin, analogous to the filet mignon in beef. Both cuts are extremely tender and are best suited to fast, hot cooking.

Generally speaking, cook these cuts only to rare or medium, like a beef steak. An exception to this is with stir-fries, where the meat is normally fully cooked inside. Cooking backstraps, chops, and tenderloins is pretty much the same as cooking a beef steak. If you can do that, you can cook venison steak. But cooking a steak properly does require some skill, and you do need to know a little about carryover heat (see page 77) and resting meat, and you should have the finger test for doneness memorized. Let's start with that.

## THE FINGER TEST FOR DONENESS

The fastest and most effective way to test for doneness is the finger test. Open your right hand loosely. Take the tip of the index finger of your left hand and press down on the fleshy area of your right hand where your thumb connects with the rest of your palm, making sure your right hand is relaxed. That's what raw meat feels like.

Now touch the tip of the index finger of your right hand to the tip of your right thumb. With your left hand, press that fleshy part at the base of the thumb again: It should feel a little less squishy. That's how medium-rare meat feels.

Move back one finger on your right hand so you're touching the tip of your middle finger to your thumb. With your left hand, touch the fleshy part of your right thumb once more. This is medium.

One more finger back (to the ring finger on your right hand) and you get to medium-well. Not so good for red meat. Finally, touch your pinky to your thumb and feel the base. Rock hard, right? That's well-done, which means you just made cat food from your venison steak, although I'm reasonably certain even the cat won't eat it.

Remember, once the meat is resting, carryover heat will continue to cook it. So I always take meat off the heat a little before it is where I want it, which is on the rare side of medium. Once it has finished resting, the meat is perfectly cooked.

## Meat Temperature Chart

Many people have an intuitive notion of when meat is rare, medium, or well-done. But if you are using a thermometer, here are some temperature readings to help you make those determinations. Keep in mind that these temperatures are measured at the center of a piece of meat *after* resting.

- Rare: 125°F
- Medium-rare: 130°F
- Medium: 140°F
- Medium-well: 150°F
- Well-done: 160°F

## TO REST OR NOT TO REST?

It's conventional wisdom that after you cook meats, you let them rest a bit on a cutting board before you serve. And in general, this is a good idea, as it can help many kinds of meat retain a bit more moisture.

But not always. First of all, you should know that some water loss is inevitable; it's part of how meat cooks. You'll lose moisture no matter what you do, mostly through evaporation in the oven and while the meat is resting. And you'll lose more moisture by tenting meat with foil than by leaving it uncovered, which sounds odd. But think about it. Tented meat stays hotter and cooks longer while it's resting, steaming more, which equals more water loss. Ever look at the underside of your foil? Coated with condensation from your meat.

Interestingly, in steaks that are cooked rare, the final meat temperature of 125°F or thereabouts is barely high enough to cook the connective tissue or collagen in the meat. This means that the utility of the resting step is limited. If you or your butcher have done the job right, there should be no connective tissue in your venison backstrap at all (yet another reason why the infamous "leg steak" is an abomination; see page 44). In practice, this means you need not rest a venison steak that's been cooked rare. Medium is another story, since the 140°F temperature of medium-cooked meat is hot enough to affect the collagen within the meat—again, if there's any in your steak.

What advantage do you gain by not resting a rare steak? The "bark"—the crispy crust on the exterior of the meat—will stay crispy and bacon-y. If you rest it, that bark will soften.

What happens if you slice into some venison and you get a juice tsunami?

Fear not. First of all, I'm hoping you have a cutting board with gutters to catch the juices. If not, tip the board into a bowl as you work. Keep slicing, and arrange the slices on a platter. Pour all the juices into a bowl and season with a little salt, a splash of olive oil, some vinegar or citrus, and a few chopped herbs of your choice; parsley, chives, and marjoram match nicely with venison. Bam! Instant dressing for your steak or roast. What's more, the meat will reabsorb some of that juice.

## WHICH ONE: LOINS, STEAKS, OR CHOPS?

How you get your backstrap determines how you cook it. If you have the option, you want to prep your backstraps in lengths that you'll cook whole, which will be cut into individual medallions before serving (remember, backstrap and tenderloins are very easy to overcook). The exception to this is backstraps of elk or moose, which are large enough to be sliced into proper steaks first and then cooked. For me, on a typical deer, that means lengths of loin weighing about one to two pounds. Why do this? Because when you cook a length of backstrap, it's a lot easier to cook it to a perfect medium-rare, or whatever temperature you prefer. Then, when you serve, you slice the length of loin into perfectly cooked medallions.

But many butchers don't give you lengths of backstrap, although most will give them to you if you remember to ask before they start on your deer. Many of you reading this have chops or boneless medallions in your freezer right now—and pretty much all commercially available venison (like the stuff you can buy at Whole Foods) will be medallions. What's the difference?

Cooking individual chops and medallions is trickier because of the greater surface-area-to-mass ratio of each piece of meat. Think for a moment about a chop or a medallion that's been cut from a length of backstrap: If you cook it, you will do so on the cut side, the widest, largest part of the medallion. The medallion will cook very fast, going from rare to medium to overcooked in minutes or seconds, depending on how thick it is. What's more, you don't get that lovely sight of perfectly cooked meat when you serve it because the perfectly cooked part is inside the medallion or chop. On the other hand, you get more bark. It's a trade-off.

If you have medallions from a typical deer, they should be roughly an inch thick and three inches wide. In this case, you'll want to take your meat out of the fridge fifteen minutes before you start cooking instead of the thirty minutes I call for in most of these recipes. Unlike a length of backstrap, which you want at room temperature before cooking, you want the interior of smaller medallions to still be cool—an insurance policy against overcooking.

For larger animals, this equation changes. In the case of elk, moose, really big deer, caribou, or red deer, medallions or chops are preferred, since the loin is so wide in diameter that it becomes much harder to cook a length properly; the distance between the edge of the loin and its center is too great. It can be done, but you need to have the meat out at room temperature for about an hour, and you will likely need to finish the loin in the oven. Easier to do full-on steaks or chops. Just be sure to make them at least 1 inch thick; I prefer at least 1½ inches. Two inches is even better. After all, this is the ribeye of an elk or moose, a luxury cut that ought to be celebrated.

All of these recipes can be done with backstrap from any big game animal. They are centered around master recipes for tenderloin, loin (backstrap), cutlets, and stir-fries. After that are a grab bag of great recipes that are best done with loin or tenderloin.

"You run like a herd of luminous deer,
and I am dark; I am forest."

— RAINER MARIA RILKE

# SMOKED BACKSTRAP

Smoked venison backstrap is something you need in your life. Sliced thin and served in a sandwich, or as is with any number of sauces—or au natural—this is one of my favorite ways to celebrate a successful hunt.

First thing to remember is that you don't smoke venison the way you smoke pork. The secret is to smoke the meat only to medium-rare or medium, no more.

You can use curing salt here—if you do, use Insta Cure No. 1—but I rarely do. It's not needed in this case. If you do want to use it, you'll want to weigh out 0.25% (one quarter of 1 percent) of curing salt compared to the weight of the meat; to be clear, that's one quarter of one percent.

Get the smoker going and have it at the target temperature before you add the meat. To get the best smoke ring on your smoked venison backstrap, you'll want to move it right from the fridge to the smoker. Take the meat out of the plastic bag and briefly rinse it, then pat dry with paper towels.

A bit of science: A smoke ring will develop only until the meat hits about 140°F. The slower this happens, the thicker the ring. Now, with this method, you'll be pulling the meat before 140°F, so it will have been working on that smoke ring the whole time.

I like to insert a probe thermometer into the backstrap so I know when to pull it. However you do it, pull the meat when it hits 130°F to 140°F, or medium-rare. I prefer the low end of this scale. At 185°F, that normally takes about three to four hours—a good long smoke for a tender cut of meat.

How to eat your smoked venison backstrap? Any way you like. I prefer to slice it thin and eat it with sandwiches. The sauce you see in the picture is cilantro and roasted Hatch chiles pureed with mayo, black pepper, and smoked salt. Damn sight better than regular mayo, no?

**SERVES ▸** 4 to 6

**PREP TIME ▸** 10 minutes

**COOK TIME ▸** 4 hours, not including cure time

2 pounds venison loin, in one piece

Salt (see headnote)

Weigh the meat in grams. Weigh out 1.5 percent of that weight in salt; you can go as high as 2 percent. Massage the salt into the meat. Vacuum seal the meat and set it in the fridge for two days, longer if you're using elk or moose or something else thick. You cannot leave this too long—it won't get too salty, so you can leave the meat in the fridge for a week if you wanted to.

Get your smoker going; wood choice is yours. Try to keep it below 200°F. When it's ready, rinse the meat, then pat it dry with paper towels. If you have a probe thermometer, insert it into the thickest part of the backstrap. Smoke until it reaches about 135°F, which should take between two and four hours. Slice and eat.

# PAN-SEARED TENDERLOIN

This is the master recipe for cooking a tenderloin of any big game animal, along with a simple pan sauce you can use with all sorts of meats. Tenderloins are always soft, even when overcooked. This can confuse cooks using the finger test for doneness (page 113), because a well-done deer tenderloin will feel like it's only medium. This is why it's better to pay attention to time and temperature.

A meal of venison tenderloin is ultra special, because the tenderloins even on a large deer will still only feed two. The ones pictured were from a 240-pound mature buck. So you want to keep things simple. Deer tenderloin is a perfect date-night meal.

First, salt thine loins. Salting beforehand seasons the meat—the salt will penetrate—removes a little moisture, concentrates flavor, and is an extra food-safety step for meat sitting around at room temperature. I take the meat out of the fridge, salt it, and let it come to room temperature for around 20 to 30 minutes.

You'll want only a little bit of a high smoke-point oil to pan sear. Too much oil or fat limits the sear. I use about 2 tablespoons of grapeseed, avocado, safflower or canola oil for this.

Once the meat is at room temperature and your oil is ripping hot, it should require only about 6 minutes to sear a venison tenderloin—they tend to be kinda-sorta triangular in cross section, so I end up searing 2 minutes on each major side.

Move the meat to a cutting board, grind black pepper over it, and let it rest 5 to 8 minutes. This is when you make your pan sauce.

**SERVES ▸** 2

**PREP TIME ▸** 15 minutes

**COOK TIME ▸** 10 minutes

12 ounces venison tenderloin (both tenderloins from a deer)

Salt

2 tablespoons safflower oil (see headnote for alternate oils)

Freshly ground black pepper

**FOR THE PAN SAUCE**

1 tablespoon safflower oil

1 shallot, minced

½ cup red wine

1 cup venison or beef stock

Salt

2 tablespoon butter, divided

Salt the meat and set aside while you mince the shallot for the pan sauce or make whatever side dishes you have planned.

When you're ready to cook the tenderloins, heat the safflower oil in a pan that will hold the meat—remember, they contract when they hit the heat—over high heat. Turn your stove fan on high and pat the meat dry with paper towels.

Set the tenderloins in the pan. They'll contract immediately. Let them sear hard for 2 minutes, then turn to another side of the meat. Do this once or twice more, depending on how done you like your tenderloin. It's OK to sear a side more than once if you need to. Move the meat to a cutting board and grind black pepper over it.

*continued*

Add the extra safflower oil to the pan, then the shallots, and sauté until the shallots brown a little. Use a wooden spoon to move the shallots over any browned bits in the pan to lift them off the metal.

Add the red wine and let this boil for a few seconds, then add the stock. Sprinkle a little salt over the boiling sauce. Let this boil down for a few minutes, until the whole surface of the pan is covered in bubbles and the wooden spoon leaves a trail when dragged through the center of the pan. Turn off the heat.

Swirl in 1 tablespoon of the butter until it incorporates, then the other. Slice the venison into medallions and pour over the sauce. Serve at once.

**NOTES:** Keep in mind that this method also works for the tenderloins of pronghorn and caribou. For elk and moose, you'll want to increase the cook time about 1 minute per side, so about 3 to 4 minutes total extra time.

## PAN SAUCE JAZZ

This chapter has several recipes for simply seared venison backstrap with specific sauces. But they all follow the same principles, and once you know these principles, you can improvise a pan sauce with whatever you have around. Here are the keys to a perfect pan sauce for four people.

Once you've finished cooking the venison, you'll want to have about 2 tablespoons of fat in the pan. In some cases, you will need to drain off fat to arrive at that amount.

With the pan over medium-high heat, add about 2 tablespoons of minced shallot or onion to the fat and sauté for a minute or so.

Add about 1 cup of low-sodium stock (any kind), or ¼ cup of glace de viande (page 75).

Add a shot glass of hard liquor (brandy, whisky, ouzo, or the like) or a glass of wine, then add a heaping tablespoon or two of something sweet, such as jelly, jam, syrup, honey, or molasses. If you don't drink alcohol, substitute fruit juice or a nice vinegar for the liquor.

Mix, bring to a boil, and boil furiously until the mixture reduces by half or more. Finish by removing the pan from the heat, seasoning the sauce with salt, and then swirling in 2 tablespoons of unsalted butter.

# VENISON STEAK WITH CHERRY TOMATOES

The crux of this dish is venison loin or tenderloin, cooked simply, with the freshest produce of early summer. My vegetable suggestions are just that: if you happen to find some wonderful corn, or fennel, or carrots, or greens, by all means mix and match.

You don't *have* to spend the hour slow-cooking the cherry tomatoes if you want to make this a lightning quick weeknight meal; you can toss them in at the last minute. Drying the tomatoes like this concentrates their flavor, however, and it's worth the effort if you have the time for it.

**SERVES ▸** 4

**PREP TIME ▸** 30 minutes

**COOK TIME ▸** 1 hour, mostly to cook the cherry tomatoes

1½ pounds cherry tomatoes, sliced in half

Olive oil

Salt

1 to 2 pounds venison loin or tenderloin

1 or 2 small yellow zucchini, coarsely chopped (optional)

3 cloves garlic, sliced very thin

1 cup fresh fava beans, peas, or shelling beans

¼ cup chicken broth

1 teaspoon minced fresh rosemary, or ½ teaspoon minced dried

3 tablespoons minced fresh parsley

Black pepper to taste

Coat the halved cherry tomatoes in some oil and salt them. Place them, cut side up, on a baking sheet and put into the oven at 250°F; no need to preheat. If you have a convection oven, turn the fan on. Or, you can put the tomatoes on a rack in your dehydrator and set it to 145°F. It will take longer for the tomatoes to get semi-dry, but it won't heat up your kitchen. Cook the tomatoes until they're about half dried, about 45 minutes to one hour in the oven, a bit longer in a dehydrator. Keep an eye on the tomatoes every 20 minutes or so, as different tomatoes and different ovens will give you different results.

About 30 minutes before the tomatoes are ready, take the venison out of the fridge and salt it. Depending on whether you are using tenderloin or loin, follow the cooking method detailed in the Pan-Seared Tenderloin (page 119) or Steak Diane recipes (page 122).

When the meat is ready to rest, add the zucchini to the pan, if using, and toss to coat with oil. Sprinkle with salt and add another tablespoon of olive oil if things look too dry. Sauté over high heat, tossing and stirring, until the zucchini begins to brown a bit, about 4 to 5 minutes. Add the garlic, beans, and broth and let it boil furiously until almost gone.

Add the tomatoes, rosemary, and the parsley and toss to combine. Cook for about 30 seconds and turn off the heat. Grind some black pepper over everything. Add to the pan any juices that have collected on the cutting board from the venison.

Serve with bread, potatoes, or rice.

# STEAK DIANE

**SERVES ▸** 2, can be doubled

**PREP TIME ▸** 30 minutes

**COOK TIME ▸** 12 minutes

This is the master recipe for cooking venison loins, and it's a good one. Steak Diane may be the most beloved recipe in this book. This dish was already passé when I first began going to restaurants as a boy in the 1970s. Its heyday in America was in the 1950s and 1960s, when French cooking was all the rage (thanks, Julia!). Most people who remember this dish remember it as beef filet mignon with a piquant sauce of mustard, Worcestershire sauce, demi-glace, cream, and shallots, all flambéed at the table with cognac. Ritzy, eh? My version of steak Diane is a little less flamboyant, and it hearkens back to the dish's roots. Diane, you see, is really Diana, the Roman goddess of the hunt. And Sauce Diane, at least in its proto-form, was first mentioned by Escoffier in his *Le Guide Culinaire* back in 1907. And it was a sauce not for beef but for venison.

It's a classic for a reason. This sauce is so good that you must have lots of bread around to sop it up. If you don't, you'll find yourself licking the plate, and that's not very polite. Steak Diane is absolutely a date-night dish, but it's also so easy to make that you can whip it up on a Wednesday night. So I suppose if you have a Wednesday night date, it would be perfect.

- ½ to 1 pound venison piece backstrap
- Salt
- 2 tablespoons unsalted butter
- 1 shallot or ¼ cup onion, minced
- 2 cloves garlic, minced
- ¼ cup brandy
- ½ cup venison stock or beef broth
- 2 tablespoons Worcestershire sauce
- 1 tablespoon mustard
- 2 teaspoons tomato paste
- ¼ cup (or so) heavy cream, enough to turn the sauce the color of coffee with cream
- Minced herbs, for garnish (basil, parsley, chives, etc.)

Bring the venison loin out of the fridge, salt it, and let it come to room temperature, about 30 minutes.

Heat the butter in a large sauté pan over medium-high heat for about 90 seconds. Pat the venison dry with a paper towel and sear it on all sides. Turn the heat to medium so the butter doesn't scorch. Take your time; it should take about 8 to 10 minutes or so to get a nice brown crust on the venison without overcooking the center. Use the finger test for doneness (see page 113) to get the venison where you like it. Remove the meat and let it rest.

Add the shallot to the sauté pan and cook for 1 minute, then add the garlic and cook for another 30 seconds or so. Don't let the garlic burn. Deglaze the pan with the brandy, scraping off any stuck-on bits in the pan with a wooden spoon. Let the brandy cook down almost to a glaze, then add the venison stock, Worcestershire sauce, mustard, and tomato paste and stir to combine. Let this boil down until a wooden spoon dragged across the pan leaves a trail behind it that does not fill in for a second or so. This should take about 3 minutes on high heat.

Turn off the heat and let the boiling subside. Stir in the cream until the sauce is as light as you like. Don't let the sauce boil again or it could break.

Slice the venison into thick medallions. If you find you have not cooked it enough, let the meat swim in the sauce for a few moments to heat through. If the venison is to your liking, pour some sauce on a plate and top with the meat. Garnish with some chopped herbs. Chives are traditional, but basil and parsley are also nice. Serve with a big red wine such as cabernet sauvignon, Barolo, petit verdot, or Graciano.

**VARIATION:** While not traditional, powdered wild mushrooms, like porcini, make the absolute best seasoning for a piece of backstrap while it rests. Take the meat out of the pan, dust thoroughly with the porcini powder, and let it rest.

You can buy dried mushrooms in most supermarkets, or you can buy porcini powder online or gather your own.

# VENISON WITH CUMBERLAND SAUCE

This is to Britain what Diane is to France. A classic. Cumberland sauce, which hinges on the tart-and-sweet red currant, is perhaps the oldest wild game sauce still commonly made today. It dates from at least the 1700s, and it's been modified only slightly since then. It has persisted so long in our kitchens because it's a perfect balance of sweet, spicy, savory. and salty.

One thing that makes this recipe shine is *glace de viande* (page 75), which adds so much to the flavor. But fear not. If you don't have *glace de viande*, use regular, low-sodium stock boiled down by half. Be very careful about adding any other salt to the sauce, though, as the boiled-down stock can get very salty.

What goes well with Cumberland on the plate? I like simple mashed potatoes, but boiled or baked potatoes are just as good. Polenta or fried hominy would be excellent, as would any other mashed root vegetable. Or go simple and serve it with a green salad and some nice, crusty bread.

**SERVES** ▸ 4

**PREP TIME** ▸ 30 minutes

**COOK TIME** ▸ 15 minutes

**FOR THE VENISON**

1- to 2-pound venison backstrap, in one piece

Salt

3 tablespoons unsalted butter, lard, or cooking oil

**FOR THE CUMBERLAND SAUCE**

1 shallot or ¼ cup minced onion

½ cup Port wine

1 cup regular stock, boiled down to ½ cup

A pinch of salt

½ teaspoon mustard powder

¼ teaspoon cayenne

Zest of 1 lemon or orange

¼ cup red currant, cranberry, or lingonberry jelly (not jam)

Freshly ground black pepper

Depending on whether you're using tenderloin or loin, follow the cooking method detailed in the Pan-Seared Tenderloin (page 119) or Steak Diane recipes (page 122).

When your meat has come out of the pan, make sure there's at least 1 tablespoon of butter or oil in it. If not, add more. Sauté the shallot over medium-high heat for 90 seconds, until it softens. Don't let it burn.

Add the Port wine and use a wooden spoon to scrape up any browned bits stuck to the pan. Let this boil furiously until it's reduced by half. Add the glace (or stock), the salt, mustard, cayenne, and citrus zest and let this boil for a minute or two. Stir in the red currant jelly and the black pepper. Let all this boil down until it's thick but still pourable. You can strain it if you want a more refined sauce.

Slice the venison into medallions. Pour any juices that have come out of the meat into the sauce and stir to combine. Serve the sauce either over the meat or alongside it.

# ICELANDIC VENISON WITH BLUEBERRY SAUCE

**SERVES ▸** 2, can be doubled

**PREP TIME ▸** 30 minutes

**COOK TIME ▸** 25 minutes

Venison and blueberries, or huckleberries if you live in the West, is an ancient and well-respected combination—that I'd disliked for years. Every version I had was just too cloying for my tastes. And then I read a quirky little book on, of all things, the food of Iceland. *Icelandic Food & Cookery*, by Nanna Rögnvaldardóttir, has a version of this dish, done with lamb, that was the first one I'd seen that wasn't obviously sweet. Her use of mushrooms in a berry sauce was also unusual. So I studied the recipe, made a few changes, and gave it a go.

I'm glad I did. This dish is a knockout. I serve this alongside some Irish colcannon, which is a fancy name for mashed potatoes with a green thing mixed in. I used nettles, but any green will do. Spinach would be easiest, but kale is pretty traditional in Ireland, and the Icelanders eat it, too.

As for the mushrooms, I used some dried morels. Any good, dried mushroom will do. You'll want the mushroom soaking water, so don't use fresh mushrooms here. Port wine can be a nicer kick in the sauce than red wine, but it's strong; if you use Port instead of red wine, use only ¼ cup. Finally, remember that this is a savory sauce, despite the blueberries (or huckleberries).

I served this with a good Spanish red wine, but any full-bodied red will work, or if you are a beer drinker, a malty Scottish ale or porter is the ticket.

- Venison tenderloins, or ¾ pound venison backstrap
- Salt
- 5 tablespoons clarified butter, regular unsalted butter, lard, duck fat, or vegetable oil, divided
- 1 small onion, peeled, halved, and sliced root to tip
- 1 clove garlic, minced
- ¾ ounce dried mushrooms, reconstituted in 1 cup hot water
- ½ cup red wine or Port
- ½ cup venison stock or beef stock
- ½ cup blueberries or huckleberries, fresh or thawed
- Black pepper to taste
- Malt or cider vinegar, to taste
- Sugar (optional)
- 1 teaspoon fresh rosemary, minced

**FOR THE COLCANNON**

- 2 large potatoes, peeled and diced
- Salt
- 2 to 3 tablespoons unsalted butter
- 1 to 2 heaping tablespoons sour cream or heavy cream
- 1 cup chopped, cooked green vegetables (spinach, kale, nettles, etc.)

Take the venison out of the fridge and salt it. Let it set on the cutting board while you rehydrate the mushrooms and boil the potatoes for the colcannon.

Put the diced potatoes into a pot of salted water and bring to a boil. Simmer until tender. Drain the potatoes and put them back in the pot. Turn the heat to low under the pot and let the potatoes steam for a few seconds.

Beat in the butter, sour cream, and chopped vegetables. You want nice mashed potatoes with green streaks. Add salt to taste, cover the pot, turn off the heat, and set aside.

Get a large sauté pan and put 2 tablespoons of unsalted butter into it. Turn the heat to high, and when the butter is hot, add the sliced onion. Sauté over medium-high heat until browned along the edges, about 4 to 5 minutes. Turn off the heat, remove the onions, and set aside.

Wipe the pan with a paper towel. Pat the venison dry and put the rest of the butter into the pan. Set it over high heat until the butter is very hot, but not smoking. Depending on whether you are using tenderloin or loin, follow the cooking method detailed in the Pan-Seared Tenderloin (page 119) or Steak Diane recipes (page 122).

When the venison is done, move it to rest on a cutting board.

Return the onions to the pan, add the garlic and mushrooms, and sauté over medium-high heat for 2 to 3 minutes, stirring often. Sprinkle some salt over everything and add the wine.

Boil this down until it's almost gone, using a wooden spoon to stir up any browned bits on the bottom of the pan. Add the stock and mushroom soaking water (strain the water if there is any debris in it) and boil this down by two-thirds.

Add the huckleberries or blueberries and cook another minute or two. Add black pepper, salt, and vinegar to taste. If you want it sweet, add some sugar now; start with a teaspoon or two until you get things as sweet as you'd like. Garnish with the rosemary.

# VENISON WITH CARAMELIZED ONIONS AND MUSHROOMS

**SERVES ▶** 4

**PREP TIME ▶** 20 minutes

**COOK TIME ▶** 45 minutes

This recipe is a little like the Venison with Morel Sauce on page 130, but this is more of an autumn recipe, using fall mushrooms and caramelized onions as an accompaniment rather than a sauce. I think you'll like both recipes.

I like to make this with the larger steaks from elk, bison, caribou, or moose, but of course it will work with regular venison backstrap.

Hen-of-the-woods mushrooms, *Grifola frondosa*, are very common east of the Great Plains, emerging in the fall with the autumn rains. They're large, grayish, meaty mushrooms that grow at the base of trees. If you're not into foraging for your own mushrooms, hen-of-the-woods is widely available in bigger supermarkets, where they are often called by their Japanese name, *maitake*; these mushrooms are farmed. But no biggie if you can't get them, as regular button or cremini mushrooms work fine. The porcini powder in which I roll the venison, made by blitzing dried porcini in a coffee grinder, adds a lot of flavor, but if you skip it, I won't be mad at you.

I will, however, be mad at you if you don't caramelize your onions. It's what makes this dish. Follow my instructions below and you'll be fine. Just take your time. Caramelizing onions takes a while; just go with it. And they keep for days in the fridge.

I'd serve this with potatoes of some kind, good bread—black pumpernickel is especially good—or polenta. You'll want a nice red wine too, or maybe a pale ale or Scottish ale.

4 tablespoons unsalted butter, divided, plus more for searing the mushrooms

3 onions, sliced from root to tip

Salt

1 teaspoon dried thyme

2 teaspoons honey (optional)

1- to 2-pound venison backstrap, preferably in one piece

Porcini powder (optional)

½ pound fresh mushrooms, sliced (ideally hen-of-the-woods, a.k.a. maitake)

3 tablespoons fresh chopped parsley

Dandelion leaves, for garnish (optional)

---

Start by caramelizing the onions. Heat 2 tablespoons of the butter in a large sauté pan over medium-high heat. When it's hot, add the onions and toss to coat. Cover the onions, turn down the heat, and cook slowly, stirring once in a while. You're looking for them to slowly soften and brown, not scorch on the edges. After 10 minutes or so, they'll start to get soft. Sprinkle salt over them and let them cook some more. When they're starting to brown, add the thyme and honey, if using. Cook until they're a nice brown. Remove and set aside. The onions can be made in advance.

While the onions are cooking, take the venison out of the fridge and salt it. Let it come to room temperature while you're cooking the onions; this is especially important if you're using elk or moose backstrap, which is thick and will take time to warm thoroughly to room temperature.

When the onions are done, wipe out the pan and add the remaining butter. Pat the venison dry with a paper towel and sear it over medium-high heat, turning it to make sure all sides are browned. Use the finger test for doneness (page 113) to determine when to take it out of the pan. Let the meat rest on a cutting board. If you have some porcini powder, roll the venison in it as it rests.

While the venison is resting, put the mushrooms in the pan and turn the heat to high. Sear the mushrooms until they release their water; this might not happen with hen-of-the-woods. When the water has almost boiled away, or when the mushrooms begin to brown, add some more butter and sauté hard until the mushrooms are nicely browned. Salt them as they cook.

Once the mushrooms are ready, turn the heat down to medium-low and add back the caramelized onions and the parsley, and toss to combine. Heat through and put some on everyone's plate. Add the dandelion leaves if you are using them. Slice the venison into medallions and serve.

# VENISON WITH MOREL SAUCE

I don't know what percentage of deer hunters also hunt morel mushrooms, but it has to be more than half. So venison with morels is a natural pairing. The only hitch is that you need to tuck away some backstrap or tenderloin from the fall until spring. Of course, you can make this recipe with dried morels from the previous spring, too.

If you're making this with dried morels, as I sometimes do, you'll need about 1 ounce, a big handful. Pour boiling water over them and soak while you let the venison come to room temperature. Remove, squeeze out excess water, and chop. Save 1 cup of the water and strain it through a paper towel. Now, when it comes time to put the mushrooms in the pan, instead of the fresh morels, you'll add the chopped, reconstituted morels plus the water.

I did include an early version of this dish in my first book, ***Hunt, Gather, Cook***, but this rendition is streamlined and improved.

**SERVES ▸** 4

**PREP TIME ▸** 30 minutes

**COOK TIME ▸** 20 minutes

1½ to 2 pounds venison steaks or boneless backstrap

Salt

2 tablespoons canola oil, grapeseed oil, or lard

**FOR THE SAUCE**

2 cups chopped fresh morels, about 12 ounces (see headnote for dried)

1 cup minced onion

3 tablespoons butter, lard, or duck fat

1 tablespoon flour

½ cup Port or red wine

1 cup glace de viande (page 75), or 2 cups venison or beef stock, boiled down by half

Black pepper to taste

Depending on whether you're using tenderloin or loin, follow the cooking method detailed in the Pan-Seared Tenderloin (page 119) or Steak Diane recipes (page 122).

When the meat comes out of the pan, add the morels and onion. They'll sizzle for a moment, then the morels will begin to release their water. Let almost all this water boil away before adding the butter. Toss the mushrooms and onion to coat with the butter. Sear this hard for a couple of minutes without disturbing—you want to get some browning. Sprinkle the flour over the mushrooms and stir it in. Add the Port (it might flame up as the alcohol burns off) and use a wooden spoon to scrape up any browned bits on the bottom of the pan. Let the Port almost boil away, then add the glace or stock.

Boil this down a minute or three until the sauce comes together. Pour any juices from the venison that have accumulated on the cutting board into the sauce. Add black pepper and salt to taste to the sauce and serve with the venison.

# VENISON STROGANOFF

**SERVES ▸** 4

**PREP TIME ▸** 20 minutes

**COOK TIME ▸** 20 minutes

This one is a classic. I mean, who hasn't eaten beef stroganoff? I've seen (and eaten) so many versions of it that I've lost track. They've ranged from horrible—cream of mushroom soup and hamburger—to sublime renditions done with care and with great ingredients. I think you'll find this recipe to be among the latter.

Stroganoff has traditionally been made with quality meat, sliced thin. With venison, thinly sliced pieces of loin mixed with mushrooms, shallots, dill, and sour cream are the ticket. This is filling, easy-to-eat, cool-weather food of the first order.

What to eat it with? Historically it's been French fries, believe it or not. But here in America, stroganoff is almost always served with egg noodles. I went with Austrian spätzle, which are a lot like egg noodles. You can do whatever, but I like the way the stroganoff matches with the little spätzle dumplings. Spätzle makers are cheap and easily available online.

Make the spätzle first. These can be made up to a day ahead and stored in the fridge. Mix all the ingredients except the heavy cream together in a bowl. Thin the sticky dough with the heavy cream into a batter that is a bit like thick pancake batter. I use a spätzle maker to make my spätzle, but you can either use a colander with wide holes or flick the dough/batter off a cutting board with a knife.

Get a kettle of salty water going over high heat. Once it boils, make the spätzle. Boil them hard until they float, then 1 minute more. Skim off with a slotted spoon or a spider skimmer. Move them to a baking sheet. When they're all made, toss them with a little oil so they don't stick together.

To make the stroganoff, salt the venison and let it sit on the cutting board for 20 minutes or so. I do this while I make the spätzle. Get 2 tablespoons butter in a large sauté pan good and hot over medium-high heat. Pat the venison dry and sear all sides in the butter. Cook it until it's rare to medium-rare. If you don't know how to determine this, use the finger test for doneness (page 113). When the meat is ready, move it to a cutting board and let it rest.

Add the mushrooms to the pan and turn the heat to high. Soon they'll give up their water, and when they do, use a wooden spoon to scrape up any browned bits from the bottom of the pan. When most of the water has boiled away, add the rest of the butter to the pan along with the shallots and sauté everything for 3 to 5 minutes, stirring often. Add the garlic, toss and cook over high heat for another 3 minutes or so. Sprinkle some salt over everything.

Add the Madeira and toss to combine. Let this boil down furiously. While it's doing so, grate some nutmeg over the mixture. When the Madeira is mostly gone, turn the heat down to low. Slice the venison thinly and return it and any juices that have collected on the cutting board to the pan. Stir to combine and add most of the chopped fresh dill.

Stir in the sour cream and turn off the heat. Stir to combine and let it heat through, using the heat in the pan. Don't let this boil, or even simmer, or Very Bad Things will happen. Think nasty and curdled. To serve, spread out over the spätzle and top with any remaining dill.

**FOR THE STROGANOFF**

1½ pounds venison backstrap, in one piece

4 tablespoons butter, divided

¼ pound sliced cremini or button mushrooms

¼ pound sliced shiitake mushrooms

2 large shallots, minced

2 cloves garlic, minced

¼ cup Madeira wine (or white wine)

1 teaspoon ground nutmeg

Salt

2 tablespoons chopped fresh dill, plus more for garnish

1 cup sour cream, at room temperature

Heavy cream, to loosen sauce (optional)

**FOR THE SPÄTZLE**

2 cups flour

¼ teaspoon nutmeg

¼ teaspoon black or white pepper

1 to 2 teaspoons salt

1 egg, lightly beaten

½ cup sour cream

Up to ¾ cup heavy cream

# JÄGERSCHNITZEL

Consider this the master recipe for making venison cutlets.

Jägerschnitzel means "hunter's cutlets" in German, and like Steak Diane, the dish was originally made with venison. A classic jägerschnitzel is a thin cutlet of meat served with a mushroom gravy. Potatoes—boiled, mashed, or in a salad—are the traditional side dish. It's an unapologetically meaty meal. The only green thing allowed is a garnish of parsley, chives, or chervil. Maybe.

This is an ideal recipe for venison loin or venison heart. Yes, venison heart. You open up the heart, trim away any vein-y stuff, then pound the heart thin, the same way you would with any other meat (instructions are on page 252). It is absolutely delicious. Try it. You'll thank me later. You can also do this with a leg steak, but make sure there's no sinew in it.

What mushrooms to use? Historically, you would use regular button mushrooms or chanterelles. I say use anything you want, but use several varieties together if you can. I like those "chef's sampler" packs you can get in the store. This is a great dish to have memorized, as it's perfect for a cold night in camp after hunting.

**SERVES ▸** 4

**PREP TIME ▸** 20 minutes

**COOK TIME ▸** 10 minutes

4 venison medallions, or 2 venison hearts

Salt (smoked salt, if you have some)

About 1 cup rye or all-purpose flour

½ cup bacon fat, lard, butter, or cooking oil

1 pound fresh mushrooms, cleaned and coarsely chopped

½ yellow onion, coarsely chopped

¼ cup red wine

1 cup venison or beef stock

A pinch of celery seed (optional)

A pinch of caraway seed (optional)

2 to 3 tablespoons sour cream

Black pepper to taste

Parsley, chives, or chervil, for garnish

If you're using venison hearts, follow the directions on page 252 to flatten them out. Place the venison medallions or flattened hearts between two pieces of plastic wrap and pound with a rubber mallet, wine bottle, or dedicated meat mallet until the meat is ¼ inch thick or less. Do this firmly, but don't wail on the meat or you will tear it. Trim the cutlets if you want. Dust the schnitzels with the rye flour in a wide, shallow container.

Heat the oven to 175°F and put a baking sheet in it. Place a cooling rack in the baking sheet.

Put the bacon fat in a large sauté pan and heat it until a little bit of flour sizzles instantly when it hits the oil. Shake off any excess flour from the schnitzels and put as many as will fit into your pan. Fry until nicely browned, about 2 minutes, then flip and cook another 2 minutes. Remove and put on the baking sheet in the oven while you do the rest.

When you're done, pour off all but about 3 tablespoons of the fat. Add the mushrooms and the onion and toss to coat. Stir-fry everything over high until the mushrooms and onions begin to brown, about 3 minutes.

Pour in the wine and boil it furiously for a minute, then add the stock and spices (if using) and boil this down by half, about 4 or 5 minutes. When the sauce has thickened a bit (the stray flour from cooking the schnitzel will do this), turn off the heat, and when the sauce stops boiling, stir in the sour cream. Add salt and black pepper to taste. Top with the sauce and garnish with the herbs.

# COUNTRY-FRIED VENISON STEAK

**SERVES ▶** 4

**PREP TIME ▶** 15 minutes

**COOK TIME ▶** 30 minutes, if you have the caramelized onions premade

**ALTERNATIVE CUT ▶** Sinew-free hind leg meat

This is the American descendent of jägerschnitzel. You'll find it all over the South and especially around Texas and Oklahoma. I learned about this version of country-fried steak from a Mississippi chef, John Currence of City Grocery. Currence's book, *Pickles, Pigs & Whiskey*, is one of my all-time favorite Southern cookbooks, and a version of this recipe is in that book.

Note that because you're pounding the meat, you don't need backstrap here, although it still makes the best cutlet. I will also use leg steaks that have been stripped of all connective tissue.

I like this with grits, mashed potatoes, or hash browns.

If you're going to add the caramelized onions to the gravy, you'll need to make them first. It can even be done several days in advance, and you can keep the caramelized onions in the fridge; it's always a good idea to have some handy, anyway.

Heat 3 tablespoons of the butter in a frying pan over medium-high heat and cook the onions. Toss to coat with the oil and sprinkle the salt over them, then the thyme. As soon as you see some brown edges, turn the heat down to medium-low and cover the pan. Cook, stirring occasionally, until the onions are totally brown. This can take 30 minutes or so. Add a dollop of honey and cook another 10 minutes. Turn off the heat, remove the onions and reserve, then wipe out the pan.

Heat the oven to "warm" and set a cooling rack on top of a baking sheet inside.

Put the venison medallions between two pieces of plastic wrap and pound them thin with a meat mallet, rubber mallet, or empty wine bottle. How thin? Your choice. At least ¼ inch, and as thin as ⅛ inch. Salt the meat and set it aside.

Set up a breading station. Get three large, shallow bowls. In one goes the seasoned flour. In the next goes the eggs, cream, some salt, black pepper, and a few dashes of Tabasco. In the third goes the breadcrumbs.

Heat enough peanut oil to come up ¼ inch along the sides of a cast-iron or other heavy frying pan. Heat it over high heat until a tiny bit of flour sizzles instantly when flicked into it. You're looking for 350°F. While the oil is heating up, dredge the venison cutlets in the flour, then the egg mixture, then the breadcrumbs. Fry the venison for about 2 minutes per side, until they're golden brown. Remove each to the baking sheet in the warm oven while you finish the rest.

When the venison is done, pour off all but about 3 tablespoons of the oil. Heat it over medium-high heat. Mix in the flour and cook this, stirring almost constantly, until it turns the color of coffee with cream, about 5 to 10 minutes. Slowly pour in the broth with one hand while you whisk the gravy with the other. It will sizzle and seize up, but keep pouring the broth in slowly until it is incorporated. Stir in the caramelized onions and simmer the gravy for a few minutes. Add the cream, mix, and add salt, black pepper, and a touch of Tabasco to taste. Give everyone some cutlets and pour the gravy overtop.

**FOR THE CARAMELIZED ONIONS (OPTIONAL)**

3 tablespoons butter or lard

1 large onion, sliced thin from root to tip

A pinch of salt

1 teaspoon dried thyme

1 tablespoon honey

**FOR THE VENISON**

4 venison medallions

Salt

2 cups seasoned flour (add salt, black pepper, cayenne, and garlic powder to the flour, or use a commercial "fish fry")

3 eggs, lightly beaten

½ cup heavy cream

Black pepper

Tabasco sauce

3 cups breadcrumbs

Peanut oil or lard

**FOR THE GRAVY**

¼ cup flour

1 cup dark broth, beef or venison (page 73)

¼ cup cream

Salt

Black pepper

Tabasco sauce

# BASIC VENISON STIR-FRY

**SERVES** ▶ 4

**PREP TIME** ▶ 20 minutes

**COOK TIME** ▶ 5 minutes

Consider this a master recipe for any stir-fry you might want to throw together on a work night. The most important thing is to remember the ingredients and their proportions for the velvet marinade. Everything else is your choice.

When making any stir-fry, the work is in the chopping, so do everything before you heat up the wok. Speaking of which, if you like Chinese food, you ought to own a wok. A wok can get very hot very fast and uses less oil to do the job. But a large sauté pan will work in a pinch. Also make sure to use your most powerful burner for stir-frying.

Slice the venison into thin slivers of about ¼ inch or less and anywhere from 1 to 3 inches long. Mix with the marinade and set aside while you cut all the other ingredients. Slice the chiles if fresh, or break them up if dried.

Heat the peanut oil in the wok or a large, heavy pot until it reaches 275°F to 300°F. Don't let it get too hot. Add about a third of the venison to the hot oil and use a chopstick or butter knife to separate the meat slices the second they hit the hot oil. Let them sizzle for 30 seconds to 1 minute. Remove with a Chinese spider skimmer or a slotted spoon. Set aside and cook the remaining venison one-third at a time.

Pour out all but about 3 tablespoons of the oil. Save the oil for the next time you cook Chinese food.

Heat the remaining oil over high heat on your hottest burner. The moment it begins to smoke, add the chiles and bell pepper and stir-fry for 90 seconds. Add the garlic and cook another 30 seconds. Add the venison and stir-fry 90 seconds.

Add the cilantro and soy sauce and stir-fry a final 30 seconds, until the cilantro wilts. Turn off the heat and stir in the sesame oil. Serve at once with steamed rice.

**FOR THE MARINADE**

2 tablespoons Shaoxing wine or dry sherry

½ teaspoon salt

3 tablespoons soy sauce

1 tablespoon potato or cornstarch, mixed with 2 tablespoons water

**FOR THE STIR-FRY**

1 pound venison, trimmed of all fat and sinew

1½ cups peanut or other high-heat cooking oil

1 to 4 hot chiles, fresh or dried

1 red or yellow bell pepper, sliced

3 cloves garlic, slivered

1 bunch cilantro, coarsely chopped

1 tablespoon soy sauce

2 teaspoons sesame oil

## Velveting Meat, Chinese Style

Ever wonder why the meat in Chinese food is so different from anything you make at home? That no matter what you do, your homemade stir-fry doesn't taste like what you buy at your neighborhood restaurant? Chances are the reason is that they're velveting their meat and you're not. Velveting is a Chinese trick that will make any wild game meat tender and juicy. Learn this technique and your homemade Chinese food will shine.

Velveting is the process of coating the meat with a delicate layer of ingredients, usually involving some sort of starch or egg, and then stir-frying it. It's not so much a batter as it is a gossamer layer of protection for lean meat.

I've velveted everything from venison to rabbit to duck to pheasant, and the trick works on any meat. It's a great way to highlight venison leg meat, but it's best with lean, tender meat such as venison loin.

There are lots of ways to velvet meat. Some are über-simple: Marinate it in soy sauce, cooking wine, and corn starch and proceed to the stir-frying. This works pretty well. A better way, however, is to "pass through" the coated meat in reasonably hot oil. It is the same idea as double-frying French fries. A 60-second bath in 275°F oil sets the velvet coating and helps the meat hold up better under the ferocious heat of a proper stir-fry.

The downside is that you need to use a couple of cups of oil. But you can strain and save the oil for several uses, so it's not that bad.

The result will give you that "ah ha!" moment when you realize that you have cracked one of the secrets of Chinese cooking. No matter what you include in your stir-fry, if you do this velveting trick, you will be overjoyed with the texture of the meat. Give it a go. You'll see.

# CHINESE TANGERINE VENISON

**SERVES ▶** 4

**PREP TIME ▶** 45 minutes

**COOK TIME ▶** 10 minutes

**FOR THE MARINADE**

2 egg whites

¼ cup Shaoxing wine or dry sherry

2 tablespoons peanut or other cooking oil

½ cup corn or potato starch

**FOR THE SAUCE**

¼ cup venison or beef stock

3 tablespoons tangerine soaking water

2 tablespoons soy sauce

2 tablespoons Shaoxing wine, dry sherry, or dry white wine

2 tablespoons rice or cider vinegar

1 tablespoon sesame oil

1 to 3 tablespoons sugar

2 teaspoons corn or potato starch

½ teaspoon salt

½ teaspoon white pepper

This recipe is the origin of the ubiquitous "orange" chicken or beef you see all over Americanized Chinese restaurants. But where that dish is all about a puffy batter and a cloyingly sweet sauce, the real version is all about tang, heat, and crunch. It has only a touch of sweetness, although you could sweeten it more if you wanted to, and there are enough chiles to make you notice. There's something more too: The tangerine peels are ever so slightly bitter, which adds a layer of complexity to the dish.

Dried tangerine peel is pretty easy to come by. You or your kids are probably addicted to those little mandarins, variously labeled as "Cuties" or "Halos." That's the tangerine I'm talking about. Peel a few, let them dry on the counter for a few days, and you're good to go (though the Chinese prefer to use peels that are at least a year old). Dried peels will keep in a glass jar in the pantry forever.

This recipe is best done with backstrap, but you can use any lean, sinew-free part of the animal. But if you do use tougher cuts, take a tip from the Chinese and marinate it in baking soda overnight first. Sprinkle about 2 teaspoons of baking soda over the thinly sliced meat, toss to combine and store in the fridge overnight. The next day, rinse off the meat, pat it dry, and proceed with the recipe. This process will tenderize tough cuts nicely.

A word on the Sichuan peppercorns: These little dried red buds are floral and wonderful to eat, but they also have the effect of numbing your mouth. A few are nice. Too many, and you'll think your mouth is in shock. Start with a small bit and work your way into it.

As with all stir-fries, you need to have everything in place before you start, as it will all come together very fast.

This recipe works best with a wok. If you don't have one, you will need more oil to fry the venison in. Don't worry; you can strain and reuse the oil several times.

**FOR THE STIR-FRY**

1 pound venison, sliced into bite-size pieces, ⅛ inch thick

Dried peel of 1 or 2 thin-skinned tangerines (mandarins are best)

2 cups peanut or other cooking oil (see headnote)

2 to 6 dried hot chiles, chopped (Tsien Tsin, Thai, árbol, or cayenne)

4 cloves garlic, minced

One 2-inch piece of ginger, peeled and minced

6 green onions, sliced into 1-inch pieces, green and white parts separated

2 teaspoons crushed Sichuan peppercorns (optional)

Put the sliced venison pieces into a large bowl. Add the egg whites and use your hands to massage the meat with the egg whites, making sure each piece is coated. Add the wine and oil and do the same thing. Finally, add the cornstarch and mix to coat. It'll be a gloopy mess, but that's OK. Put the meat in the refrigerator for 30 minutes while you do the rest of the prep.

Place the tangerine peels into a bowl and pour hot water over them. Cover the bowl. In another bowl, mix all the ingredients for the sauce together (except for the tangerine water, which you'll add in a bit). Slice the tangerine peel into thin slivers and set aside. The peels will still be a little hard, but that's OK. When you've sliced the tangerine peels, add 3 tablespoons of the soaking water to the sauce.

When you're ready to start, heat the oil in a wok or heavy, deep pan to about 350°F. Set a baking sheet or similar container nearby and have ready a Chinese strainer or slotted spoon and either a chopstick or butter knife. Put about half of the venison in the hot oil and immediately use the chopstick to separate all the pieces, which will want to stick together. Fry over high heat until the venison turns golden brown and crispy, about 6 minutes. Remove with the strainer and set in the baking sheet to drain. Repeat the process with the other half of the venison

Drain off all but about 3 tablespoons of the oil (you can reuse it). Add the chiles to the hot oil and stir-fry until they turn fragrant, about 30 seconds. Add the ginger and the white parts of the green onions and stir-fry 1 minute. Add the garlic and tangerine slivers and stir-fry for 30 seconds. Add the venison back to the wok and toss everything to combine.

Stir the sauce vigorously (the cornstarch will have settled on the bottom of the bowl). Pour it into the wok and toss to combine. Allow this to boil and thicken for 1 minute, then add the green parts of the green onions. Toss to combine. Add the Sichuan peppercorns, if using. Serve at once with steamed rice.

# VIETNAMESE SHAKING VENISON

I am indebted to my colleague Jenny Nguyen of the website *Food for Hunters* for inspiring me to make this insanely good Vietnamese dish. Nguyen is of Vietnamese descent and grew up with the beef version of this dish. Shaking beef, *bo luc lac,* originated during the time of the French occupation of Vietnam, and the shaking refers to how you cook the dish by shaking the pan to toss and mix the ingredients. One day, Jenny decided to make *nai luc lac,* shaking venison, and it worked wonderfully. What you see below is my own take on her recipe.

I use backstrap for this recipe, but you could use leg meat that is absolutely free of silverskin or connective tissue. This is so good you will want to make more than you think you need.

**SERVES ▶** 2 ravenous people, or 4 normal ones

**PREP TIME ▶** 20 minutes, not including marinating time

**COOK TIME ▶** 15 minutes

1- to 1½-pound venison backstrap or tenderloin
½ teaspoon black pepper
1½ teaspoons sugar
2 cloves garlic, minced
2 tablespoons oyster sauce
2 teaspoons fish sauce (optional)
1 tablespoon soy sauce
4 tablespoons lard or vegetable oil
1 medium red onion, sliced thin
1 to 3 hot chiles, such as Thai, serrano, árbol, or cayenne
2 bunches watercress or arugula
2 tablespoons rice or cider vinegar
Salt and black pepper

Cut the venison into ½- to 1-inch chunks. Make sure it has no silverskin at all. Mix the chunks with the black pepper, sugar, garlic, oyster sauce, fish sauce (if using), and soy sauce. Let this marinate at least one hour, and up to a day.

When you're ready to cook, put 2 tablespoons of lard or oil in a wok or large sauté pan and get it ripping hot. When it smokes, add the onion and stir-fry until it begins to brown around the edges, about 2 minutes. Add the hot chiles and stir-fry for 30 seconds. Remove the vegetables from the pan and set aside. Wipe out the wok.

Add the remaining lard or oil and get this hot over high heat. Add about half the venison in one layer in the wok and let it sear for 1 minute without moving. Shake the pan to move the pieces. Use tongs to make sure an unseared side is facing down, and sear without touching for another minute (at this point things are smoking pretty well, so have your stove fan on high). Repeat this one or two more times, depending on how well-done you like your venison. When you're ready, turn off the heat, add the onion and chiles back to the wok, and toss to combine.

Mix the watercress with the vinegar and add a little salt and pepper. Top with the venison and serve either solo as an appetizer or with rice for a main course.

# SOUVLAKI

**SERVES ▸** 4

**PREP TIME ▸** 2 hours marinating time, at least

**COOK TIME ▸** 15 minutes

Souvlaki was one of my go-to lunches when I lived back East. A staple of any decent Greek diner (a redundant term in New Jersey), you'd also see good souvlaki at the "roach coaches" all over town, and especially on street corners in Manhattan. (A roach coach is what everyone used to call a "food truck." It was a rougher time.) Souvlaki is grilled pieces of meat on a pita with cucumbers, onions, tomatoes, and "special sauce," which was either some sort of tomato-based red sauce that I've yet to decipher, or the more typical tzatziki, which is a yogurt-cucumber-dill-garlic sauce. Greek mayo. Basically this is a Greek taco. Really good, super fun to eat.

Making this dish is straightforward, but you do need to remember one thing: Your grill or flat-top or frying pan or whatever needs to be really hot. The reason is that the meat is in small pieces so it needs to cook fast in order not to dry out. Blasting it with the grill cover open will get you there. But keep an eye on your venison, as it can go from rare to medium to "aw crap, I wrecked it" in about 2 minutes. Remember, it's better to have nice, tender meat than pretty grill marks on the outside—this is a sandwich, after all. You can't see the grill marks, but you can tell if the meat's overcooked.

There are a bunch of make-ahead steps here, so if you're pressed for time, you can make the tzatziki sauce up to a few days ahead, and you can marinate the meat a full day ahead of time, too.

If you're using wooden skewers, be sure to soak them in water for an hour, otherwise they'll burn on the grill.

### FOR THE MARINADE

1½ pounds venison backstrap or hind leg meat, cut into 1-inch chunks

½ cup olive oil

¼ cup freshly squeezed lemon juice

Zest of 1 lemon

2 tablespoons dried oregano

2 teaspoons dried thyme

2 teaspoons black pepper

### FOR THE TZATZIKI SAUCE

2 tablespoons olive oil

2 tablespoons freshly squeezed juice

7 ounces Greek yogurt

½ cup diced cucumber, peeled and seeded

1 tablespoon dill

2 cloves garlic, minced

Salt and black pepper to taste

### ACCOMPANIMENTS

Tomatoes

Cucumbers

Red onions

Lemon wedges

Pita breads

Skewers

When you're cutting your venison, make sure it's free of all silverskin and sinew. This will make the meat easier to eat in the pita. Cut the meat into 1-inch chunks—remember, you're going to eat this as a sandwich of sorts, not as a big kebab. Add the meat and all the marinade ingredients to a sealable plastic bag, mix, and put into the fridge for at least two hours, and up to a full day ahead.

Meanwhile, make the tzatziki sauce by mixing all those ingredients together. Keep that in the fridge until you are ready to serve. This can be done a day in advance.

Chop all your accompaniments: tomatoes, cucumbers, lemons, and red onion. If eating raw red onion isn't your cup of tea, soak the sliced onion in lemon juice or white wine vinegar while the meat is marinating. This quick pickle will pull the harshness right out of the onions.

When you're ready, get your grill very hot. Make sure the grill grates are clean. Salt the venison liberally and skewer the venison pieces together; this is not how I normally do meat skewers, but jamming them all together helps keep these small pieces of meat from overcooking. Lay the skewers on the hot grill and cook them with the grill cover open until they're medium, about 4 minutes per side, depending on how hot your grill is. I use the finger test for doneness (see page 113) to determine when to pull the meat off. Keep it on the skewers while you take it to the table.

To serve, lay everything out and let people make their own little pita sandwiches. Serve with a nice light Greek red wine, a dry rosé, or a crisp beer or three.

# ETHIOPIAN TIBS

Tibs is the unusual name for an Ethiopian dish that's a hybrid stir-fry and stew. It comes together in an instant, is meaty and rich, and can be spicy. Served with bread, rice, or, more properly, *injera* flatbread, it was and is my favorite Ethiopian dish. Many years ago, I worked in an Ethiopian restaurant where I always made this dish with lamb, but it's great with venison.

This dish is super easy to make, but you do need a few unusual ingredients and spices, and you need to have everything set to go before you start cooking because it comes together quickly.

First, you must get yourself some Ethiopian berbere. It comes as either a spice mixture or a paste. You can buy it online or in fancy supermarkets, or you can make it yourself. You'll also need clarified butter, although tibs tastes more authentic if you make your own niter kebbeh, an Ethiopian spiced butter (see below). Of the many spices listed in the ingredients, the most important is the fenugreek.

I know it sounds like a lot for a simple plate of food, but if you do this, you'll not be sorry. The flavors are exotic, mesmerizing, and addictive. And once you have the basic ingredients, they all last for months. So you can make it again. And again.

**SERVES ▶** 4

**PREP TIME ▶** 20 minutes

**COOK TIME ▶** 10 minutes

### FOR THE TIBS

- 1 large red onion, sliced thin (about 2 cups)
- ¼ cup niter kebbeh (spiced butter, see below) or clarified butter (ghee)
- 2 pounds venison, cut into bite-size pieces
- 2 tablespoons berbere powder
- 1 teaspoon ground fenugreek
- ½ teaspoon cardamom (optional)
- ½ teaspoon ground ginger
- ¼ teaspoon cumin
- ¼ teaspoon ground cloves
- 1 teaspoon black pepper
- 3 or 4 cloves garlic, sliced thinly
- 1 to 5 green chiles, such as jalapeños or serranos, sliced thin
- 2 cups whole, peeled tomatoes, broken into bits
- ½ cup red wine

### FOR THE ETHIOPIAN SPICED BUTTER (makes about 2 cups)

- 12 to 15 cardamom pods, crushed
- 2 or 3 whole cloves
- 1 cinnamon stick
- 1 pound unsalted butter
- 2 shallots, minced (about ¼ cup)
- 2 cloves garlic, minced
- 2 tablespoons minced fresh ginger
- 1 tablespoon dried oregano
- ½ teaspoon ground turmeric
- 1 teaspoon ground fenugreek

Get the sauté pan or wok very hot. Stir-fry the onions without the butter for a few minutes, until they char a little on the outside. Add the spiced butter and the venison. Stir-fry hot and fast until the outside of the meat is brown but the inside of the meat is still very rare. You need to do this on as hot a burner as you have.

The moment the meat has browned, add the berbere, fenugreek, cardamom (if using), ginger, cumin, cloves, black pepper, garlic, and chiles. Stir-fry another 30 seconds or so, then add the tomatoes and the wine. Toss to combine and let this cook for a minute or two. Serve at once with bread, rice, or *injera*.

### TO MAKE THE ETHIOPIAN SPICED BUTTER

Toast the cardamom, cloves, and cinnamon in a dry pan over medium heat until they're aromatic. Cut the butter into cubes. Toss everything into a heavy pot and turn the heat on low. Let this come to a bare simmer and cook for at least 30 minutes. We cooked ours for at least an hour. It's vital that the milk solids don't burn. If they do, you've ruined the butter. Watch for browning, and as soon as you see it, remove from the heat.

Strain through a cheesecloth and store in a clean glass jar. It'll last six months in the fridge, at least a week on the counter, and forever in the freezer.

# VENISON TARTARE

**SERVES ▶** 4

**PREP TIME ▶** 20 minutes

Tartare is the "trust fall" of the culinary world: raw meat and a raw egg yolk. If your ingredients aren't impeccable, things can go very, very wrong. But done right, this is at once a primal and an exciting appetizer.

Tartare is all about texture. Raw meat has a savory slipperiness that causes many people to argue within themselves. It seems so wrong, almost dangerous, yet something deep within urges you to take another bite. It's our inner Australopithecine talking. Beyond the meat, the silky richness of the broken yolk acts as a sauce, flecks of herbs or other flavors sparkle here and there, and the decided crunch of raw shallot punctuates each bite.

Some people, notably Wisconsinites, seem to like their tartare ground. I don't. I prefer it minced, which I think has a better texture. Use a large, very sharp chef's knife to mince the venison. Take your time and don't chop it like you would herbs or it'll get all stringy. If you're going to make this recipe for more than four people, my advice is to cut the venison into manageable pieces first, then keep them all in the fridge. Mince one piece at a time and then return it to the refrigerator; this keeps everything cold.

After that, it's all a question of seasonings. Mine are woodsy, with juniper and caraway. The garnish is wood sorrel, which tastes lemony; it's a hat tip to Chef Rene Redzepi of Denmark, who uses wood sorrel in his tartare.

Any species of venison will work, as will any cut of meat that's free of fat and sinew. Backstrap is best, I find, but I also like using the heart.

I use some esoteric ingredients here, but there are easy substitutions for most of them—but not all. You do need the juniper berries, which you can find in many supermarkets or buy online. Or, if you have Eastern red cedar in your neighborhood, that's actually a juniper; harvest these berries when they're deep bluish purple. The other key ingredient here is smoked salt. Any finely ground smoked salt will work.

If you want to use quail eggs here, as I do, look for them at farmer's markets or Asian markets.

Serve this on crackers or in little bowls with crackers alongside. Remember, a little tartare goes a long way.

Soak the minced shallot in the vinegar in a small bowl. Toast the juniper berries, caraway seeds, and peppercorns in a small pan over medium-high heat (shaking often to prevent them from burning) until they're fragrant, about 2 minutes. Move the spices to a grinder or mortar and pestle and grind to a coarse powder.

Mince the venison with a sharp knife. I prefer to cut it into ⅛-inch dice or smaller. If you're not terribly skilled with a chef's knife, partially freeze the meat, which will make it easier to dice small. Put the minced venison in a bowl and sprinkle over the ground spices. Drain the shallots and add them to the bowl. Add the smoked salt and mix the tartare together. Add more salt to taste.

To serve, give everyone some tartare and make a little depression in the center. Separate the egg yolks from the white and discard the whites (or use in another recipe). Put the yolks in the little depression. Garnish with the wood sorrel or lemon zest.

1 shallot, minced (about 1 heaping tablespoon)

3 tablespoons red wine vinegar

1 heaping teaspoon juniper berries (about 6 berries)

1 level teaspoon caraway seeds

1 teaspoon black peppercorns

½ to ¾ pound venison

½ teaspoon smoked salt

4 egg yolks (quail egg yolks are cool if you have them)

Wood sorrel, or grated lemon zest, for garnish

## Eating Raw Venison

I know what you're thinking: No way I'd eat raw venison! It's not a crazy concern. But here's what you need to know to eat raw venison as safely as possible:

- Shoot straight. Seriously. If you've gut-shot the animal, think twice about making it into tartare or carpaccio. *E. coli*, both the nasty O157 variety and the nasty-but-nonlethal O103 strain, have been found in venison (and all other ruminants). It mostly lives in the digestive tract. So if you break that tract and get gut gunk all over the inside of your deer, you'd better cook it thoroughly.
- Cut cleanly. This is an extension of Rule No. 1. If you break the guts while eviscerating the animal, it's nearly as bad as gut-shooting it.
- Freeze your venison first. This should kill any larval parasites that might be in the venison, as well as tapeworm and *Toxoplasma gondii* (which causes toxoplasmosis), which are known to exist in deer. Freezing the meat below 0°F (some sources recommend −4°F) for at least two days will go a long way toward making any raw meat safer to eat.
- Avoid any possible cross-contamination. Your venison might be perfectly fine, but if you have a dirty cutting board or knife or even hands, you can wreck the whole thing. Sanitation is very important when preparing and serving raw food.
- Keep it cool. Just as sushi should be served cold, so should tartare. Work quickly, and keep the venison in the fridge when you are not cutting or mixing it.

Even so, this is not a 100% risk-free recipe. But then again, neither is a trip to your neighborhood sushi bar. Or your breakfast. You're far more likely to get salmonella from eggs than you are to get sick from raw venison, if you follow the steps above. Needless to say, your egg needs to be of the finest quality to use for tartare.

# Buck Hunting

*Okay, okay, I won't shoot him.*

I rarely say this when hunting deer. In fact, the number of times I have consciously passed up on what I consider a good buck can be counted on less than one hand. Oh who am I kidding? I've never passed up what I consider a good buck.

Until the 2024 season in Oklahoma. This story is my first journey into North American "trophy" hunting and what it means to probably 98 percent of hunters in the US and Canada.

Let's start with my buck history. For almost the first decade of my deer-hunting life, I shot only does. I remember vividly seeing what to me was the biggest deer on earth saunter by us at close range near Miles City, Montana, on a day when my friend Tim and I held only doe tags. It was the first time I'd seen a serious buck in real life. I was thirty-two.

The first buck I ever shot was Spork the Deer, an ancient Columbia blacktail deer the ranch owner wanted dead because over the years, his antlers had degenerated into a fork and a spike . . . really a spear (see page 244). I cleaned the skull for a European-style mount and then Katrina, sister to Holly, painted it beautifully in red and gold. He guards my collection of Mexican cookbooks now.

I shot a few forked horns here and there subsequently, but the first truly nice deer I killed was a Coues deer, a sort of tiny, desert white-tailed deer that lives in the Sonoran Desert. This deer I shot with the aid of my friend John Stallone, who lent me his rifle, tricked out for long-range shooting. I killed that deer across a canyon at 525 yards. He guards my collection of British, German, and Scandinavian cookbooks.

That was 2017. I still haven't killed anything more than a forked horn mule deer, but when we started hosting white-tailed deer hunts in western Oklahoma at my friend Larry Robinson's lodge, I started seeing a lot of nice bucks. One year, Larry said I could shoot one. We sat in the blind together, and sure enough, on that first day, a decent deer walked out. "You want him?" Larry asked. You bet! *Blam!* Dead deer.

A couple of years later, Larry had a mission for me: to kill a geriatric buck that had nice antlers but was so old he might not survive even Oklahoma's mild winters. How will I know which deer he is? "You'll know," Larry said.

The next morning, as daylight gathered across a huge wheat field, I saw deer. Lots of does, a couple little bucks . . . and one really big one. He was lumbering along, eating a bit. He looked tired. And he had great big antlers. Had to be him, so exactly seven minutes into that year's deer season, I killed him. He scored 150, which in whitetail deer terms is pretty good.

This deer was interesting. Old. Tougher. A bit rutty, which is to say the meat was dark, without fat, and while not stinky, certainly more . . . deery than the little does I'd spent my adulthood slaying.

The next year, I wanted to try for another decent buck. Larry likes me to kill the old ones because their antlers are on the decline. It's a bit like our own strength and vigor as humans. The older we get, the less robust we are. Declining antler growth is a visible sign of this. Paying customers get a shot at the true giants. I'm perfectly OK with this.

First day, all I saw was a funny little six point, which in Oklahoma terms is a tall forked horn with prominent eye guard antlers. But he was a legal buck. No, I told myself. I wanted to shoot a mature deer, or another grandpa, regardless of headgear. I let him pass and killed a little doe instead.

Second day, I sat with Jake, one of the guides. It turned out to be a good thing. Before dawn, he spotted a gigantic deer with all sorts of antlers sticking out all over—definitely something well north of fourteen points. We named him Megatron. But he never gave me a shot, gone before legal shooting light. A few more young bucks wandered around.

And then a very nice buck started walking right at us! He was big and healthy, and his antlers were impressive. This was the guy. But Jake said no. This deer was too healthy, too vigorous. Too young. He was maybe four years old, tops. Deer can live to seven or more in this part of Oklahoma. Gah.

That evening, we hunted the same spot. Again, this deer showed up, right at sunset. No go. But a nearby blind had a number of huge deer milling around, and the hunter was only doe hunting. Right at the end of legal shooting time (thirty minutes after sundown), they wandered our way. So we ended the night hopeful.

Next morning, Jake and I were pumped. It just felt right. And it was the penultimate day of the rifle season, so time was running short. Funny thing about white-tailed deer. They're creatures of habit. Unlike blacktail deer, which are the mafia dons of the deer world, never taking the same route twice (and speaking in hushed tones into their hooves), whitetails give zero effs. They'll pound a trail in the prairie like cattle. We figured those big deer would be around.

I love that moment before the morning begins, when all is still night. (To be fair, I hate getting up for it unless there's a good reason.) We watched shooting stars flash and satellites blink across the night sky. Orion the Hunter watched over us, as did Venus, the morning star.

Slowly, like water seeping over parched ground, the light oozed into the world. At first, nothing. Then a sound, a scuffle, a hoof step. Another few minutes, and dark shapes milled about. Another few minutes, and we could tell the bucks from the does. Again, lots of teeny bucks in the field. No Megatron. No big bucks at all.

Sunrise was close, and to the east we heard *Crack! Crack-a-tack-a-crack!* Antlers! Two bucks fighting! We carefully swung toward the sun and soon saw three big bucks, including my no-shoot-'em nemesis. He had just finished wrestling with a much larger deer, but he appeared to have won.

The larger deer was massive, but he looked tired. His face lacked the sharp black-and-white definition around the nose that marks a younger whitetail. This was him. This was the grandpa I'd been looking for.

Just then, the sun broke the horizon. *Crap!* It immediately became almost impossible to look through my scope. Jake had eyes on the old man, but the three bucks were milling around. I was under orders not to shoot my nemesis, and I'll be perfectly honest: I had no real idea what any of their antlers looked like, just that there were lots of them. I didn't want to mess up and shoot the "wrong" deer.

Finally, Jake and I were both on Grandpa. "Ready?" he asked. By way of answer, I shot the buck through the neck at 220 yards. He fell dead on the spot. I suppose I should have waited until Jake could have videoed the kill, but I'm not a huge fan of that anyway.

My nemesis stood off, then walked away with the other younger buck. He would survive this deer season. In the end, I passed on that deer three times. Three times I had a dandy buck in my crosshairs but held off. I've never done that before. As we walked back to get the truck, I told Jake that at the very least, I get to name him: Big Bank Hank.

Maybe I'll see you next year, Hank. Maybe not.

This whole process opened up in a personal way a world I'd only known through reflective light: American trophy hunting. Several of the guides knew exactly which buck they wanted to kill or wanted a client to kill. Most notable is The General, who had reached Turdy Point Buck status in camp. He survived hunting season.

One thing to remember: In the overwhelming majority of cases, the hunter who waits and ultimately kills an older buck, one with large antlers, is also eating that deer. It's no different from me killing does or forked horns. We're all eating what we kill.

This is not well understood by many nonhunters. The fiction is that the hunter takes only the trophy, the antlers, and leaves the meat to rot. Not only is this a literal crime, but it happens so rarely that it becomes a topic of conversation among hunters. "Yeah, hear about that guy last year who 'ditch cleaned' a 180-class buck. He got pinched."

I've lost count of the conversations I've had with hunters about the intricacies of cooking and prepping big bucks since I started writing publicly about wild game in 2007. Yes, older deer are different. Yes, a buck in rut will not be as good eating as the same buck before the rut. But that's all detail.

The larger point is that the deer is getting eaten. I frankly don't care if someone grinds it all into burger or snack sticks. I mean yeah, there are waaaay better things to do with an animal like that. But if that's how the hunter will feed the ones he or she loves, so be it.

I wonder how many people would oppose something called "culling," which is what I do with Larry by targeting the oldest bucks. Or even "selective harvest," which sounds weird to my ears, but hey, it's better than "trophy hunting." That phrase evokes feelings of waste, of toxic testosterone. And make no mistake. Both exist.

But they are not the norm. The fact that I have gleaned so much knowledge from so many hunters over so many years about how to go about making these older animals better at the table is heartwarming. It means that the majority of hunters are viewing both the antlers and the meat as their trophy. One just lasts longer.

As for Grandpa? I'm putting him through his paces, dry-aging the hindquarter and a huge saddle of backstrap, the latter coated in deer tallow to protect it from too much moisture loss. I'll report back on my findings. But win, lose, or draw, he's gettin' et. Nose to tail. Because that's what we do around here.

# SOUPS AND STEWS

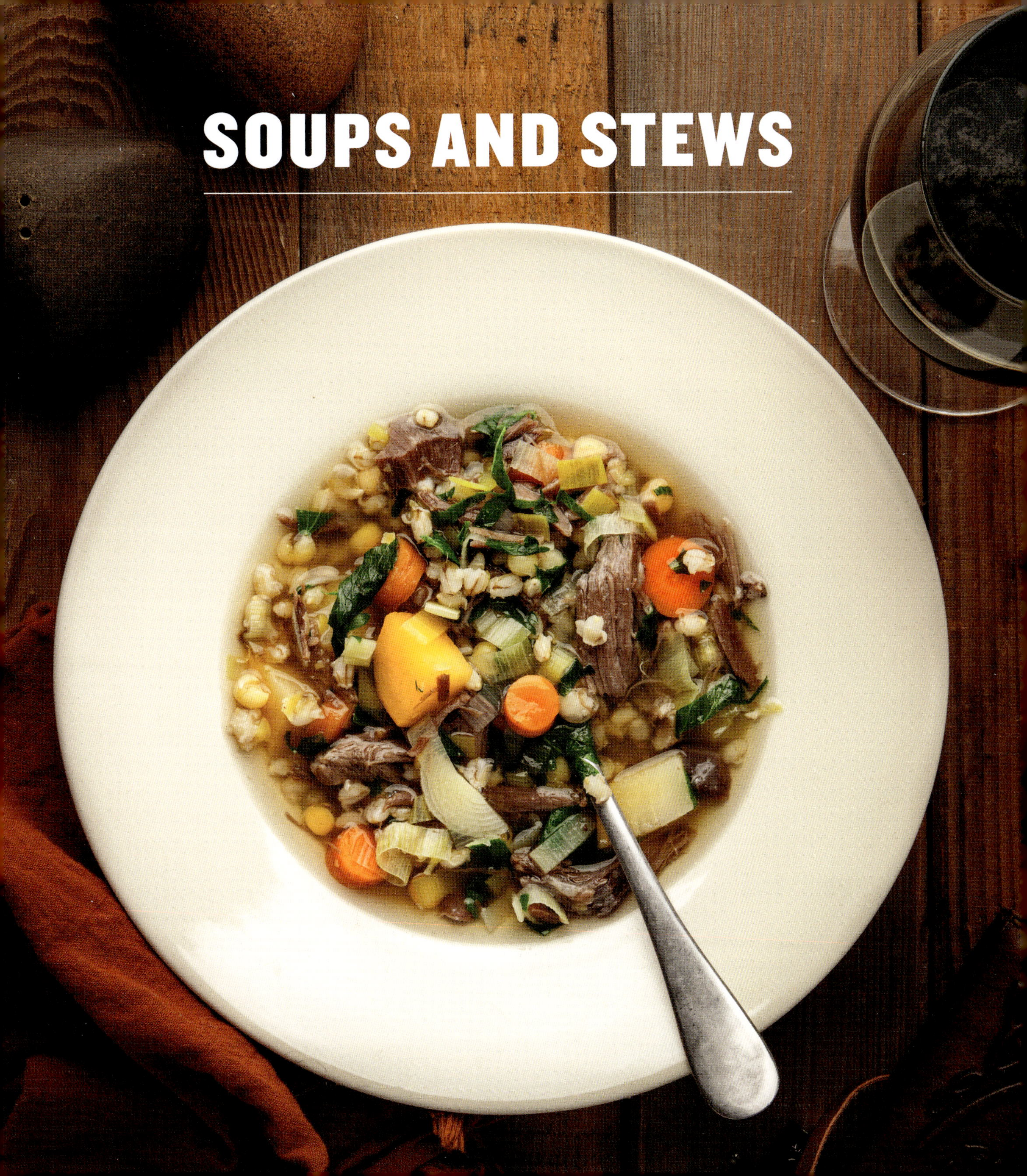

Soups and stews are, at their core, amalgamations of good things to eat, cooked just so in one big pot. Some are simply collections of ingredients tossed in at once and simmered, but the finest soups and stews are built like houses, with foundations, structure, and lots of delicate touches added at precisely the right moment. A stew such as this needs nothing other than good crusty bread to accompany it.

## SOUPS VS. STEWS

Put simply, soups are bowls of goodness where the broth itself is the star and the things in it play backup. Broth is equally important in a stew, but stews tend to be heartier and are all about the things floating around in it. Most of the recipes in this chapter are stews, but there are a few soups here, such as Scotch Broth (page 172) and Pozole Rojo (page 156), as well as a wonderful soup in the chapter on the wobbly bits that relies on a clear, dark, venison broth with marrow dumplings (page 278).

Most of these recipes are very easy, but almost all require time. They are intended to be made on a weekend, a day off, or a holiday. The good news is that all stews are better in the couple of days after they're made, so make a pot and eat it for lunches or easy dinners during the week. A few, notably the Massaman Curry (page 166) and the Vietnamese Pho (page 176), can be done in a hurry if you're using premade curry paste or premade broth. But for the most part, relax and enjoy the process. Making soup is comforting, nourishing, and will perfume your house all day.

# CAJUN SAUCE PIQUANTE

Cajun sauce piquante is about as thick as a gumbo and very tomatoey, usually served with an island of white rice in the center and lots of diced meat floating around. It is spicy but not blow-your-head-off spicy. I've never eaten anything like it. Gumbo meets chili. Venison sauce piquante is a thing in Cajun Country, and here is my homage to a specialty I first ate in Houma at a place called Bayou Delight.

What's unique about a sauce piquante is that the meat is diced small. This works great for venison, which has a tendency to become dry in stews. Always serve this with white rice. And remember, like all good stews, this one is better the day after it's made.

**SERVES** ▶ 6 to 8

**PREP TIME** ▶ 15 minutes

**COOK TIME** ▶ 3 hours

⅔ cup peanut oil or lard
¾ cup all-purpose flour
2 cups chopped onion
1 cup chopped celery
1 cup chopped green pepper
5 cloves garlic
Salt
1 tablespoon Cajun seasoning, or more to taste
One 6-ounce can tomato paste
3 pounds venison, diced small
1 cup red wine
One 28-ounce can tomato puree or crushed tomatoes
2 bay leaves
Salt
Hot sauce
Black pepper
Chopped green onions or parsley, for garnish

In a large, heavy pot, heat the peanut oil over medium-high heat for a minute or two. Stir in the flour, then turn the heat down to medium. Cook this roux, stirring often, until it turns the color of peanut butter, at which point you'll need to stir it almost constantly to prevent it from burning. Keep cooking the roux until it turns the color of milk chocolate, about 15 to 20 minutes.

While the roux is cooking, bring six cups of water in another pot to a boil, then drop it to a simmer.

When the roux is ready, add "the trinity"—onions, celery, and green pepper—and stir to combine. Turn the heat to medium-high and cook, stirring often, until everything is soft. Sprinkle in some salt. Stir in the garlic, Cajun seasoning, and tomato paste. Drop the heat to medium. Cook, stirring occasionally, for 3 minutes.

Stir in the venison, then add the red wine, the can of crushed tomatoes, and the hot water. Add the bay leaves and bring everything to a gentle simmer, about 180°F. Add salt and hot sauce to taste. Simmer very gently until the meat is tender, two hours or more.

When the sauce piquante is ready, add any more salt, black pepper, hot sauce, and/or Cajun seasoning you want, then serve it with white rice and lots of green onions or parsley. Make sure you have hot sauce at the table. I use Tabasco, but use whatever variety you prefer.

If you use a slow cooker, move everything from the pan to the slow cooker after you make the roux, add the "trinity," and then the tomato paste. Then cook on low for six to eight hours.

# ROCKY MOUNTAIN ELK STEW

**SERVES ▸** 8 to 10

**PREP TIME ▸** 30 minutes

**COOK TIME ▸** 3 hours

When it came time to create an elk stew, my mind immediately went to the Rocky Mountains, home of most of the world's elk. So this recipe is an ode to the Rockies, from Canada down to New Mexico. Pretty much every ingredient in this elk stew is something significant to a state or province in or around the Rocky Mountains: green chiles, great northern beans, wheat berries, porcini mushrooms, greens, and root vegetables.

This stew works equally well with any meat—deer, pronghorn, bison, beef, sheep will all be great. You could even use pork if you wanted to. I like to use big chunks of neck or front shoulder meat, sliced across the grain. They may look gnarly at first, but after several hours in the pot, that connective tissue melts and you get a nice stew. Shank chunks work for this too.

Although the recipe calls for roasted chilis, feel free to use frozen or canned green chiles.

Take your time with the browning step for both the meat and onions. This is the foundation of the stew's flavor.

Note that there are a lot of optional ingredients; I like them a lot, but you can skip them if you prefer. If you have the starchy optional things, like the wheat berries and beans, you won't need anything else. If you skip them, serve this with crusty bread.

- 4 tablespoons butter, canola oil, or sunflower oil, divided
- 2 to 3 pounds stew meat
- Salt
- ½ cup flour
- 1 large yellow onion, chopped
- 5 roasted peppers (Hatch, Anaheim, poblano), seeded and chopped
- 1 quart elk, venison, or beef stock
- 4 cloves garlic, minced
- 1 ounce dried porcini, crushed (or some other dried mushroom)
- 1 pint Belgian beer (or another malty beer)
- 2 large carrots, peeled and cut into chunks
- 1 tablespoon fresh sage, minced

**OPTIONAL INGREDIENTS**

- 1 parsnip, peeled and cut into chunks
- 1 cup corn kernels
- 1 cup cooked barley or wheat berries
- One 15-ounce can great northern beans
- 3 cups chopped greens, like spinach, nettles, or chard

Heat 2 tablespoons of the butter or oil in a large soup pot with a lid over medium-high heat. Salt the stew meat, then dust in the flour. Brown the meat in batches, making sure they do not touch each other. Remove the meat to a bowl as it browns and reserve.

When all the meat is nicely browned, add the remaining oil and the chopped onion. Stir and brown this too.

While this is happening, put two of the roasted chiles into a blender with the stock and puree.

Add the garlic and stir to combine. Return the meat to the pot, along with any juices that have collected in the bowl. Pour the contents of the blender into the pot. Crush the dried mushrooms in your hands and add to the pot. Fill the blender bowl again with water and pour that into the pot. Finally, add the beer. Bring all this to a simmer, add salt to taste, partially cover the pot, and let this cook gently at about 180°F.

If you're using dried beans, wheat berries, or barley, now is the time to cook them. If you're using canned beans, wait.

After about two hours, add the carrots and the sage, as well as the parsnip, if using. When they are tender, about 40 minutes or so later, add the remaining green chiles and any of the other optional ingredients you happen to be using. Let the greens wilt, taste for salt and black pepper, and serve.

**NOTES:** If you can't find dried mushrooms, use ½ pound of fresh ones, chop them, and add with the onions. If you're using a slow cooker, move everything to it after browning the meat, onions, and garlic. Cook on low for six to eight hours, adding the greens in the last 10 minutes.

# POZOLE ROJO

Pozole is a classic Mexican soup that relies heavily on dried chiles, some form of meat, and hominy corn. Any combination of ancho, mulato, negro, pasilla, or guajillo chiles will work. None are terribly spicy, and all are easily found in any Latin market; anchos are often found in regular supermarkets these days. You could use dried red Hatch or other New Mexican chiles, but they're a little spicy, so only use six chiles.

Hominy in this context is a giant corn kernel that has been nixtamalized, an ancient process that opens up the whole array of nutrients in the corn. It has a distinctive flavor—it tastes like corn tortillas smell—and is indispensable in a true pozole. Hominy is also easily found in Latin markets dried or in cans.

The fun of pozole is its interactivity. The soup itself is pretty basic, but everyone at the table gets to put on whichever toppings they want; it's very much like eating Vietnamese Pho (page 176). The stew will keep for more than a week in the fridge once you've made it.

**SERVES ▸** 6 to 8

**PREP TIME ▸** 30 minutes

**COOK TIME ▸** 3 hours

**FOR THE POZOLE**

4 ancho chiles
2 mulato or chile negro chiles
3 guajillo chiles
6 cloves garlic, chopped
3 tablespoons lard or cooking oil
2 pounds venison, cut into 4- to 5-inch hunks
5 cups water
2 teaspoons Mexican oregano
2 teaspoons ground cumin
Two 28- to 32-ounce cans white hominy
Salt

**FOR THE TOPPINGS**

Hot sauce
⅓ head cabbage, shredded
1 sliced radish per person
2 diced avocados
Chopped cilantro
1 red onion, chopped
Lime wedges, preferably Key limes

Tear the dried chiles into a couple of large pieces. Discard the stems and seeds. Heat a comal or other heavy frying pan (cast iron is best) over high heat and toast the dried chiles until they're fragrant and start popping, which takes only a few seconds. Watch carefully and do not let the chiles burn; they'll become bitter. When they're all toasted, put the chiles in a bowl. Cover the chiles with hot water and place a smaller bowl or plate on them to weigh them down. Soak for 30 minutes.

When the chiles are soft, chop coarsely and then put into a blender with the garlic cloves and enough of the soaking water to let the blades run. Puree until smooth.

Heat the lard in a large, lidded pot. Pat the venison chunks dry with a paper towel and brown them. Don't crowd the pot; do it in batches, if need be. Take your time with this step.

When the meat is browned, add a little water to the pot so you can scrape up any browned bits on the bottom with a wooden spoon. When that's done, add the chile puree and the rest of the water. Bring to a simmer, about 180°F. Add the oregano, cumin, and salt to taste. Return the venison to the pot and simmer gently until the meat is tender.

Once the meat is ready, remove it to a plate or pan to cool. Rinse the hominy under cold running water, then add it to the soup. Shred the meat with two forks and return it to the soup. Ladle some pozole into everyone's bowls and let them choose which toppings they want.

If you're using a slow cooker, move everything to it after browning the meat. Cook six to eight hours on low, adding the rinsed canned hominy in the final 90 minutes.

# UKRAINIAN BORSCHT

This version of borscht, hearty and slightly tart, seems to contain pretty much everything in a typical Eastern European produce aisle. Borscht in America is a polarizing dish. Some think that its vivid crimson color means it's sweet. It's not. This is a rich vegetable soup based on meat broth with some meat in it—in this case, venison. The red of the beets is for show, although you certainly can taste them in the stew. Use any cut of venison here. Roasts, stew meat, neck, shanks, and shoulder are all fine.

**SERVES ▸** 4 to 6

**PREP TIME ▸** 15 minutes

**COOK TIME ▸** 2½ hours

1½ pounds venison, cut into 1-inch chunks
1 quart venison or beef stock
½ ounce dried mushrooms
Salt
3 beets, about 1 pound
2 tablespoons unsalted butter
1 onion, sliced from root to tip
1 large carrot, cut into ¼-inch slices
1 large parsley root or parsnip, cut into ¼-inch slices
1 small celery root, diced (optional)
2 tablespoons tomato paste
1 large potato, peeled and diced
⅓ head cabbage, coarsely shredded (about 2 cups)
Juice of 2 lemons, or 2 to 3 tablespoons red wine vinegar
2 tablespoons chopped parsley
1 tablespoon chopped dill
Black pepper
Sour cream, for garnish

Preheat the oven to 375°F.

In a large Dutch oven or other heavy, lidded pot, barely cover the venison with water and bring to a boil. Immediately turn off the heat, drain the water, and reserve the venison. This removes any scum that might otherwise rise to the surface of your broth. Return the venison to the pot and add the stock and 1 quart of water. Bring to a gentle simmer, at about 180°F, and add salt to taste. Crumble the dried mushrooms into the soup, cover, and let it cook gently while you turn to the rest of the soup.

As soon as you put the lid on the soup, move to the beets. Coat them in oil and wrap loosely in foil. Roast in the oven for 60 to 90 minutes, until reasonably tender. Remove from the oven and let the beets cool enough to handle. (If you have latex or nitrile gloves, put them on. Beets stain.) Peel the beets and then shave them on a coarse box grater.

Heat the butter in a sauté pan. When it's hot, add the sliced onion and sauté over high heat until the edges brown, about 6 minutes. Drop the heat to medium-high and add the beets, carrot, parsley root, and celery root (if using). Cook for 10 minutes, stirring often.

Stir in the tomato paste, adding a ladle or two of the simmering soup to help blend everything and to scrape up any browned bits on the bottom of the sauté pan. Turn off the heat.

When the venison is tender, add the diced potatoes to the soup pot and simmer for 10 minutes. Add the cabbage and simmer another 10 minutes. Add the contents of the sauté pan to the soup and cook another 5 minutes.

When the potatoes are ready, add the lemon juice or vinegar, parsley, dill, and a healthy grinding of black pepper. Serve with a dollop of sour cream in the middle of the soup.

# BELGIAN VENISON CARBONNADE

**SERVES ▸** 4 to 6

**PREP TIME ▸** 15 minutes

**COOK TIME ▸** 3 hours

Belgian carbonnade flamande is one of the few dishes from that little country to gain wide renown. Cousin to the more famous French beef Bourguignon, this is a sort of hybrid stew-braise that relies on beer, not wine. It's hard to say when this dish was invented, but I'd guess sometime in the Middle Ages because it relies on a little bit of sweet-and-sour that is characteristic of that era of cooking.

Regardless of its history, carbonnade is a damn good dish to make with any cut of venison—stew meat, shoulder, neck, or shank. You can eat this dish in one of two ways: as a full-on stew or as a braise you eat with a knife and fork alongside a starch and a vegetable—the "stew" here becomes the sauce. Either way, you're in for a treat.

What does it taste like? I use the hard-working, sinewy cuts of meat, because when they finally do get tender, they get super silky and nice. But it's the sauce/gravy/stew that makes this dish: dark and rich, with a very European version of that magic combination of sweet-spicy-sour-salty from mustard, cider vinegar, and a little bit of red currant jelly mixed in (you can use brown sugar if you can't find red currant jelly).

The beer matters here. Make this with a real Belgian abbey ale and you'll understand why this is such a famous dish. Make it with Budweiser and you might wonder what all the fuss is about. The mustard is also important, although not as important as the beer. Try to get a mustard like Dijon, not one with turmeric added for extra yellow. You don't need color here, you need flavor. As for the mushrooms, I use dried morels or porcini. Any good dried mushroom will do.

Like all stews, this one is even better the next day, and it reheats beautifully—perfect to make on a Sunday for lunches or quick dinners during the week.

- 3 pounds shank, shoulder, neck, or stew meat
- ¼ cup duck fat or unsalted butter
- Salt
- 3 onions, peeled and sliced root to tip
- 1 ounce dried mushrooms, rehydrated in 1 cup warm water and chopped
- 2 teaspoons dried thyme
- 2 tablespoons mustard (Dijon is best)
- 3 to 4 tablespoons flour
- 1 cup venison or beef broth
- 1 or 2 bottles of beer (Belgian abbey ale is traditional)
- 1 heaping tablespoon red currant jelly or brown sugar
- 2 tablespoons cider vinegar
- Black pepper
- Chopped parsley, for garnish

---

If you're using elk shanks, cut the shank off the bone in large pieces, about 2 to 4 inches across; same thing if you're using shoulder meat. If you're using venison shanks, you can leave them whole if they fit into your pot.

Heat the duck fat or butter in a large Dutch oven or other heavy-lidded pot over medium-high heat. Pat the meat dry and brown it on all sides. Salt them as they cook. You might need to do this in batches. Remove the pieces as they brown and set aside in a bowl.

When all the meat has browned, add the sliced onions and mix. Turn the heat down to medium and cook the onions until they're nicely browned and soft, which can take a solid 20 minutes. About halfway through, salt the onions and add the chopped mushrooms and thyme.

When the onions are ready, return the meat and all juices from the bowl into the pot. Mix in the mustard, then add enough flour to dust everything in the pot.

Stir in the mushroom soaking water (strain it if there is debris in it), the venison broth, and at least one bottle of the Belgian beer. You want the meat to be barely covered. Pour in more beer, if need be. Bring to a simmer, about 180°F, add salt to taste, cover, and cook slowly until the meat is tender, from two to four hours depending on the age and cut of the animal.

Once the meat is tender, whisk in the red currant jelly and vinegar, and add black pepper to taste. Garnish with the chopped parsley. Serve with spätzle, egg noodles, or potatoes.

If you're using a slow cooker, move everything to it after browning the meat and onions. Cook on low for six to eight hours, add the jelly, vinegar, and pepper in the last 10 minutes.

# KENTUCKY BURGOO

**SERVES ▸** 6 to 10

**PREP TIME ▸** 30 minutes

**COOK TIME ▸** 3 hours, or more if your game is old and tough

3 tablespoons vegetable oil
1 or 2 squirrels or rabbits, cut into serving pieces
2 to 3 pounds venison, cut into 3- to 4-inch pieces
3 to 5 pheasant legs/thighs (bone-in)
1 green bell pepper, chopped
1 large onion, chopped
2 carrots, chopped
2 stalks celery, chopped
5 cloves garlic, chopped
1 quart pheasant or chicken stock
1 quart beef or game stock
One 28-ounce can crushed tomatoes
¼ cup Worcestershire sauce
2 large potatoes
1 bag frozen corn (about 1 pound)
1 bag frozen lima beans (about 14 ounces) or canned black-eyed peas
Black pepper
Salt
Tabasco or other hot sauce

Every region of the United States has its big, burly stew, from gumbo to chili to cioppino. This is burgoo, a Kentucky classic, done with a menagerie of wild game: pheasant, squirrel, and venison. This is a stew thick enough to stand your spoon in. How you get there is more a matter of personal taste. There are as many versions of burgoo as there are cooks throughout the Greater Burgoo Diaspora, which is basically Kentucky, southern Illinois, and Indiana, as well as parts of the Ohio River Valley.

When you cook this stew, don't mess around: Make enough for leftovers. A particularly grand burgoo party written up in the *New York Times* in 1897 included "400 pounds of beef, six dozen chickens, four dozen rabbits, thirty cans of tomatoes, twenty dozen cans of corn, fifteen bushels of potatoes, and five bushels of onions." My recipe is a bit more modest, but it will still get you through a few lunches at work.

Don't worry if you don't have squirrel, venison, and pheasant on hand all at once. The only true rule in burgoo seems to be that you need at least three different meats, so let your imagination wander. Chicken is obvious, as is pork. But lamb, rabbit, hare, other game birds, duck, muskrat, whatever is in this stew, they'll all get hammered into submission regardless.

---

Pour the oil into a large Dutch oven or soup pot and set the heat to medium-high. Working in batches, brown all the meats. Don't crowd the pan, or the meat will not brown. Salt the meat as it cooks. As they brown, move the various meats to a bowl.

Add the green pepper, onions, carrots, and celery to the pot and turn the heat to high. Cook the vegetables until they're well-browned; you might need to add a little more oil to the pot. When the vegetables have browned, add the garlic and cook for 1 minute. Add back the meats, along with the chicken and beef stocks and the tomatoes. Stir to combine and add salt to taste. Bring to a simmer, cover, reduce the heat, and simmer gently for two hours, at about 180°F.

Fish out the meat pieces. Strip the pheasant and squirrel off the bone. Tear the large pieces of venison into bite-size pieces. The reason you did not do this right at the start is that venison will stay moister when it's cooked in larger pieces. Return all the meat to the pot and return the stew to simmer.

Peel and cut the potatoes into chunks about the same size as the meat pieces. Add them to the stew and simmer until they're tender. Add the Worcestershire sauce, mix, and taste for salt. Add more Worcestershire sauce to taste if needed.

Finally, add the corn and lima beans. Mix and cook for at least 10 minutes, or longer if you'd like. Serve with cornbread and a bottle of hot sauce on the side.

If you're using a slow cooker, move everything to it after browning the meat and vegetables. Cook on low for six to eight hours.

## Another Way to Brown Meats

For every recipe that calls for you to brown meats before stewing or braising, I'll normally ask you to brown them in some sort of fat or oil in the pot they'll ultimately cook in. But there's another way, one we use in restaurants or when cooking giant batches. You can cut the meat into pieces, coat with a little oil and salt, and then roast them in a very hot oven, turning them once or twice. I do this on big baking sheets or roasting pans at about 450°F. Make sure the oven is preheated and your meats are loosely set in one layer in the pan—don't pack everything close together. This way, the meats will brown, not steam.

# MASSAMAN CURRY

Thai-style massaman curry is a great curry for people who don't normally like curry. It's a solid meat-and-potatoes meal that doesn't taste as exotic as it really is. And if you use a premade curry paste, available online or in many decent supermarkets, you can make this in the time it takes to cook the potatoes.

There are many versions of massaman curry. Mine is an adaptation of a recipe I found in what may be the first Thai cookbook in English, Jennifer Brennan's *The Original Thai Cookbook*, published in 1981. And since Brennan first wrote that book, the ingredients required to make a good Thai curry from scratch have become pretty easy to find: galangal and turmeric (both relatives of ginger), lemongrass, coconut milk, and fish sauce. So I've included a recipe for homemade curry paste, but the premade curry pastes are quite good.

Because this curry does not stew for hours and hours, you need to treat the venison or other meat in a special way. First, make sure the meat is completely free of all silverskin or connective tissue. Second, drop it into the curry maybe 5 minutes before you serve—just enough time for the chunks of meat to cook through yet still be pink inside. If you cut it into thin strips, put the meat in as you serve; the curry's carryover heat will cook it through like a Vietnamese pho (page 176).

**SERVES ▸** 4

**PREP TIME ▸** 10 minutes, more if you're making homemade curry paste

**COOK TIME ▸** 30 minutes

**FOR THE CURRY PASTE**

- 1 tablespoon lard or vegetable oil
- ½ cup onion, minced
- 8 cloves garlic, minced
- 7 to 10 dried hot chiles, Thai, Tabasco, or piquin
- 6 cloves
- One 2-inch cinnamon stick
- 12 cardamom seeds, or ½ teaspoon ground
- ½ teaspoon ground nutmeg
- 4 bay leaves, crushed fine
- 1 teaspoon salt
- 1 tablespoon minced galangal, fresh or pickled
- One 2-inch piece of fresh turmeric, or 2 teaspoons powdered
- 1 stalk lemongrass, minced

**FOR THE CURRY**

- 1 tablespoon lard or vegetable oil
- 1 large onion, sliced
- 1 pound potatoes, peeled and cut into 2-inch chunks
- One 14-ounce can coconut milk
- 3 tablespoons fish sauce or 2 tablespoons soy sauce
- One 2-inch cinnamon stick
- 4 tablespoons yellow curry paste (homemade or store-bought)
- 2 pounds venison, trimmed of fat and silverskin and cut into 1-inch cubes
- Chives, Thai basil, or cilantro for garnish

If you're making your own curry paste, heat the lard and sauté the onion and garlic until soft and translucent. Let cool a bit and put into a bowl. While the onions are cooking, grind the chiles, cloves, cinnamon, cardamom, nutmeg, bay leaves, and salt into a powder. Put the spice mix into a sturdy bowl or mortar and pestle with the onions and garlic. Add the galangal, turmeric, and lemongrass and mix everything. Pound everything into a rough paste and set aside.

In a large sauté pan or wok, heat the other tablespoon of lard or vegetable oil and sear the onions over high heat. Toss to combine, then don't move the onions for a minute or two—you want some char on them. Toss again and let sear one more time.

Add the potatoes, coconut milk, fish sauce, cinnamon, and enough water to barely cover the potatoes. Mix in the curry paste 1 tablespoon at a time, stopping when it's spicy enough for you. Cover and simmer, at about 180°F, until the potatoes are tender, about 20 minutes. When the potatoes are tender, mix in the venison and cook gently for 5 more minutes. Serve at once with chives, Thai basil, or cilantro, and a cold beer.

# VINDALOO

**SERVES ▶** 4 to 6

**PREP TIME ▶** 30 minutes

**COOK TIME ▶** 2 hours

**FOR THE CURRY PASTE**

4 cloves garlic, chopped

2 tablespoons chopped fresh ginger

2 to 8 red chiles, fresh or dried (serrano, cayenne, or árbol are good choices)

2 teaspoons ground cumin

2 teaspoons ground coriander

2 teaspoons turmeric

1½ teaspoons ground fenugreek (optional)

¼ cup malt vinegar

¼ cup water

**FOR THE MARINADE**

1 teaspoon salt

1 teaspoon sugar

½ teaspoon ground cardamom

½ teaspoon ground cloves

1 teaspoon black pepper

1 tablespoon chopped fresh ginger

¼ cup malt vinegar

¼ cup water

**FOR THE VINDALOO**

1½ pounds venison stew meat

¼ cup peanut oil

1 large onion, sliced root to tip

Salt

1 tablespoon tomato paste (optional)

1 pound small potatoes, cut into chunks

Cilantro, for garnish

Originally a lamb dish from the western Indian state of Goa, vindaloo is a stalwart of Indian menus all over the world. It's a sharp, spicy stew that will make you grab your beer and a spoonful of raita, that Indian yogurt and cucumber sauce that seems to make the heat all better, at least for a moment.

Traditional vindaloo doesn't have tomato or potato in it, but I like both. This version is closer to what you'd get in an Indian restaurant in America.

Blend all the ingredients for the marinade in a blender, then pour into a non-reactive container or sealable plastic bag with the venison and marinate in the fridge for at least an hour, and up to a day.

Blend all the curry paste ingredients in the same blender; no need to clean it beforehand. Spoon out the paste and set aside. Don't clean the blender yet.

Heat a deep sauté pan or wide pot over medium-high heat. Add the peanut oil. When it's hot, sear the onions until they brown at the edges, about 6 to 8 minutes. Salt them as they cook. Mix in the curry paste and bring to a boil. Stir in the tomato paste, if using. Pour about a quart of water into the blender, swishing it around to capture all the leftover good stuff.

Mix the venison and the marinade into the sauté pan and let this cook a minute or so. Pour in the spicy water from the blender. Cover the pan and let this simmer gently, at about 180°F, until the venison is tender, anywhere from two to three hours. Remove the lid from the pan, add the potatoes, and cook uncovered until the potatoes are tender, about 20 minutes. Garnish with cilantro and serve with long-grain rice.

If you're using a slow cooker, move everything to it after browning the onions. Cook on low for six to eight hours, adding the potatoes in the last two hours.

# STIFADO

Stifado is the chili of Greece. Everyone's got their own version, from beef to lamb to rabbit to venison. Stifado tastes like the Orient, in its classical sense. It must have been quite the treat when it was invented, most likely in the Middle Ages when Greece was under Venetian rule. Any combination of sweetness with exotic spices such as cinnamon and allspice in an otherwise savory dish fairly screams fourteenth century.

Stifado uses a lot of olive oil, which keeps the venison moist as it slowly cooks until it's about to fall apart. The spices give the stew zing without heat, and the tomatoes, which are a post-1492 addition, add a bit more sweetness and needed acidity.

You'll want either a nice Greek red wine, a lager beer, or ouzo with a glass of water as a chaser to go along with this stew. And don't forget to have lots of good crusty bread around, too.

**SERVES ▶** 4 to 6

**PREP TIME ▶** 30 minutes

**COOK TIME ▶** 90 minutes

- 1 to 2 pounds venison, cut into bite-size pieces
- Kosher salt
- ¼ cup olive oil
- 2 large red onions, sliced about ¼-inch thick, root to tip
- 5 cloves garlic, chopped
- 4 bay leaves
- 1 tablespoon dried oregano
- 10 allspice berries
- 1 cinnamon stick
- 2 tablespoons tomato paste
- 4 large tomatoes, grated, or one 14-ounce can crushed tomatoes
- 1 cup sweet red wine, such as mavrodaphne or Port
- 1 to 4 tablespoons red wine vinegar, to taste
- 1 quart venison or beef stock
- Freshly ground black pepper

Salt the venison and set it aside, then chop the vegetables.

Heat the olive oil in a Dutch oven or other heavy, lidded pot. Pat the venison dry with paper towels and brown it in batches, making sure to not crowd the pot. Remove the pieces as they brown and set aside.

Sauté the onions for 8 to 10 minutes over medium-high heat until they begin to brown. Add the garlic and sauté for another minute. Sprinkle with salt. Do not let the garlic burn.

Pour in a little water and use a wooden spoon to scrape up any browned bits on the bottom of the pot. Add the bay leaves, oregano, allspice berries, and cinnamon stick to the pot. Mix in the tomato paste, then the canned or grated tomatoes, sweet wine, 1 tablespoon of vinegar, and stock. Return the venison to the pot. Cover and bring to a simmer, about 180°F. Cook slowly for 90 minutes, then check. The meat may need to cook for as much as one additional hour.

When the venison is tender, add salt, black pepper and more red wine vinegar to taste.

If you're using a slow cooker, move everything to it after browning the meat, onions, and garlic. Cook on low for six to eight hours.

If you have some really good olive oil, drizzle a bit over everything right when you serve.

# GHANAIAN PALAVA

This stew, or something very much like it, is found all over West Africa, but my version is Ghanaian. I took for my inspiration several African cookbooks I own, but I leaned most heavily on Zoe Adjonyoh's excellent *Zoe's Ghana Kitchen*, which I highly recommend.

At its core, palava sauce is something of a curry, with meat and lots of greens. It can be as spicy as you want it to be, in both senses of the word. At the very least, you'll want some chile in there, ideally Scotch bonnets or their more easily found cousin, the habanero.

I also use some ingredients not easily found other than online, such as grains of Selim, also known as hwentia. You can buy hwentia online, or leave it out. It adds a certain floral aroma to the stew you won't get otherwise, but it's not absolutely necessary.

What is vital for palava sauce is another unusual ingredient, agushi, or egusi. Agushi is ground melon seeds. Like hwentia, you can buy agushi online, but you don't need to. Most supermarkets, and even a lot of convenience stores, carry pepitas, those green pumpkin seeds. Use those and grind them at home. They'll get you close.

You can use whatever greens you'd like. I used *Atriplex hortensis*, orache, but spinach or chard also work. Pretty much any leafy green thing will work; just know that collards take longer to cook than spinach.

Finally, it is traditional to add ground dried shrimp to palava sauce. It adds a savory note and doesn't make the dish fishy-shrimpy at all. Most Asian or Latin markets carry dried shrimp, but you can skip this too. I'd recommend a few splashes of Asian fish sauce or Worcestershire as a substitute.

**SERVES ▶** 6

**PREP TIME ▶** 30 minutes

**COOK TIME ▶** 2 hours

**FOR THE SPICY TOMATO SAUCE**

1 white or yellow onion, chopped

3 cloves garlic

2 tablespoons minced fresh ginger

2 cups tomato puree, preferably fire-roasted

1 to 4 habanero peppers, chopped

Salt

**FOR THE STEW**

3 tablespoons red palm oil, lard, or vegetable oil

1 large white or yellow onion, chopped

2 pounds venison, diced

3 cloves garlic, minced

2 tablespoons minced fresh ginger

½ teaspoon ground nutmeg

½ teaspoon cinnamon

½ teaspoon dried thyme

1 teaspoon curry powder

1 tablespoon ground coriander

4 hwentia (grains of Selim), crushed (optional)

Salt

1 to 2 tablespoons ground dried shrimp or fish sauce

1 cup agushi or ground pepitas (see headnote)

½ pound chopped greens

First make the tomato sauce by pureeing everything in a blender. My advice is to add half a habanero first, puree, then see how you like it. (I like it with the full four.) Set the sauce aside for now.

In a soup pot, heat the palm oil over medium heat and cook the onions, stirring occasionally, for 10 minutes. Stir in the venison and cook another 5 minutes, then add the garlic, ginger, and all the spices. Stir, cover the pot, and turn the heat to low. Let this cook gently for 20 minutes, stirring once or twice.

Now pour in enough water to cover everything, bring it to a simmer, about 180°F, and add salt to taste. If you're using the ground dried shrimp, add it now. Cook gently with the lid on until the venison is tender, anywhere from 45 minutes to two hours.

Stir in the tomato sauce, cover the pot, and let this simmer 20 minutes. Stir in the agushi and the greens. The stew will seize up a little, so keep stirring until the greens wilt. Cook only until they're tender. Add more salt if you want. Serve with simple steamed rice.

If you're using a slow cooker, move everything to it after browning the meat, onions, garlic, and spices. Cook on low for six to eight hours, adding greens in the last 10 minutes and the agushi or ground pepitas right at the end.

# SCOTCH BROTH

This is a traditional Scotch broth, a simple lamb and barley soup with carrots, turnips, and other wintry things for which I substitute venison for lamb. Venison is still widely eaten in the United Kingdom, and Scotland is home to one of the largest remaining herds of red deer (they're like our elk) left in Europe. So it seems appropriate.

My special ingredient? Nettles. Blanched and chopped, nettles, a wild vegetable adored by both Irish and Scots cooks, add a vivid spring green to the soup. If you can't get nettles, use spinach or any other leafy green.

There is one vital key to my version of this soup: Never ever let this soup boil. If you do, the soup will still be OK, but you'll wonder what all the fuss is about. Keeping the venison cooking below a simmer—about 170°F—breaks down the connective tissue of the meat but keeps the venison tender and still pretty pink. If the soup boils, the meat will tighten up and turn gray.

The recipe keeps in the fridge for up to a week, although the barley will swell over time. It's best eaten the day after it's made.

**SERVES ▸** 6 to 8

**PREP TIME ▸** 30 minutes

**COOK TIME ▸** 3 hours 35 minutes

**ALTERNATIVE CUTS ▸** Shoulder, neck, or shanks

- 1 quart venison or beef broth
- 2 quarts water
- 2 pounds venison stew meat
- Salt
- 1 medium yellow onion, sliced
- 2 or 3 turnips, peeled and cut into chunks
- 5 or 6 small carrots, peeled and trimmed
- 2 stalks celery, chopped
- 1 cup barley
- 1 cup blanched and chopped nettles or spinach
- Black pepper to taste

Pour the broth and water into a large pot and bring it to a full boil. Add the venison chunks. The heat will drop. Let it. You'll notice scum collecting on the surface of the soup; skim it off. Let the venison cook below a simmer, at about 165°F, for 20 minutes, then fish out the venison pieces and put them in a bowl. I then pour the broth through a paper towel set in a sieve over another pot or large bowl. This strains out all the scum. If you skip this step, your soup will be cloudy but still perfectly edible. I just like clear soup.

Add salt to this new broth and return it and the premade venison stock with the venison chunks to the heat, only this time, do not let it even simmer. Cover the pot and set it on low heat. You're shooting for about 160°F to 175°F. Cook the meat this way until tender, which will take two to three hours.

After two hours have passed, add all the vegetables and the barley, cover, and cook for another hour or so, or until the barley is tender.

Stir in the chopped nettles, add some black pepper, and heat this through, about 5 minutes. Serve at once with a dark ale or red wine.

# CHILINDRÓN

Chilindrón is a Spanish stew dominated by roasted red peppers, paprika, and onions. Most recipes also call for rosemary, olive oil, garlic, some tomatoes, good stock, and wine. It's rich, woodsy, and bright, a perfect combination of the "red foods" many of us crave, like spaghetti sauce and chili (think about the colors in your favorite foods, and you'll find many of them are reddish), with the slightly austere, piney flavors that mark European wild game cooking. I love this stew so much that it's become a standard I repeat on a regular basis.

**SERVES ▸** 8

**PREP TIME ▸** 20 minutes

**COOK TIME ▸** 2 hours

- A large handful of dried mushrooms (optional)
- 3 pounds venison stew meat, neck, shank, or shoulder, cut into bite-sized pieces
- ¼ cup olive oil
- 2 large onions, sliced root to tip in half-moons
- 1 whole head garlic, chopped
- ½ cup diced cured meat such as bacon, pancetta, or ham
- 2 cups red or white wine
- 1 cup crushed tomatoes
- One 15-ounce jar or 5 roasted red sweet peppers, chopped
- 2 tablespoons sweet paprika
- 1 tablespoon hot paprika
- Venison or beef stock (optional)
- 1 tablespoon chopped fresh rosemary
- 4 bay leaves
- ½ cup chopped fresh parsley
- Salt and black pepper

If using, put the mushrooms in a container large enough to hold them and pour hot water over them. Cover and set aside.

Salt the meat and set aside for 20 minutes at room temperature. Use this time to chop the vegetables.

Pat the meat dry and pour the olive oil into a large Dutch oven or other heavy pot that has a lid. Heat the pot over medium-high heat. Brown the meat on all sides in batches. Don't overcrowd the pot. Set the meat aside in a bowl when browned. Take your time and do this right. Add more oil if needed.

When the meat is browned, add the onions and stir to bring some of the browned bits up off the bottom of the pan. Sprinkle the onions with a little salt. Cook until they begin to brown, then add the garlic, the cured meat, and the mushrooms. Cook until fragrant, then add the meat back to the pot and mix.

Pour in the wine and turn the heat up to high. Stir and boil furiously until the wine is half gone. Turn the heat back down to medium and add the tomatoes, the roasted red peppers, and all the spices and herbs (except the parsley). Stir. The level of liquid should be about two-thirds of the way up the sides of the meat. If it is low, add the venison stock. I typically need about 2 cups.

Cover and cook at a bare simmer—barely bubbling, so about 175°F—until done. How long is that? Depends on the meat. Rarely is any venison done within 90 minutes, and old animals can take three hours or more to get tender. Use your judgment.

Right before serving, test for salt and add some if needed. Add black pepper and the parsley and stir. Serve with mashed potatoes, rice, polenta, or bread. Simple sautéed greens are a good accompaniment. A big red wine is also a must, ideally something Spanish, like a Rioja.

# VIETNAMESE PHO

**SERVES ▸** 8 to 10

**PREP TIME ▸** 3 hours

**COOK TIME ▸** 30 minutes

### FOR THE BROTH

- 3 to 5 pounds venison bones or scraggly meat
- 1 pig's foot or calf's foot
- 2 sliced onions
- 1 tablespoon coriander seed
- 6 cloves
- 1 tablespoon fennel seed
- 5 star anise pods
- 10 cardamom pods
- One 6-inch piece of ginger, sliced
- ¼ cup fish sauce
- 3 tablespoons sugar
- 1 tablespoon salt

Pho is quite possibly the best soup in the world. Typically made with beef broth, venison broth is an excellent stand-in. In that soup, you get a host of meats, ranging from thinly shaved tender meat to meatballs to slow-cooked fatty brisket—even tendon and tripe make an appearance.

Everything hinges on the broth, which is sweet-smelling from ginger, star anise, and other spices. It's a special broth in that you don't roast the bones; pho broth must be light. Also, it needs body, which is why it's traditionally made with knuckle bones. Give the broth all day to simmer and you'll be rewarded. You can make it ahead, and it freezes well—you can even pressure-can it if you want (page 57).

Once you have the broth, pho comes together quickly. Have everything set out beforehand and bring it all together quickly.

To make the broth, put all the bones and meat into a large stock pot, cover with water by one inch, and bring to a boil. Skim the scum that rises to the top, then turn the heat down to a bare simmer. Don't let it boil from here on in.

While the water is coming to a boil, toast the coriander, cloves, fennel seed, cardamom, and star anise in a dry frying pan until fragrant. Stir often to keep it from burning.

Once the water in the stockpot is pretty much scum-free, add the onion, ginger, toasted spices, fish sauce, sugar, and salt and stir. Move the pot off the center of the burner a little and simmer at about 175 to 180°F for two to three hours. Moving the pot a little off to the side allows you to periodically skim the top. You want to remove most of the fat this way. When the broth is ready, turn off the heat and discard all the solids. Ladle the broth through a paper towel placed in a fine-mesh strainer that's set over a large bowl. Discard the last dregs of the broth, which will have sediment in it.

If you want to be fancy, cool the broth now, and once it's been refrigerated for a while, pick off the fat cap that may form.

To serve, heat the broth gently (do not let it boil) with the sliced 4-inch piece of ginger and the sliced onions. Cook until the onions are wilted, about 10 minutes. Taste and add salt if you need to. If you're using the meatballs and leftover roast venison, add them now.

Set out an array of condiments: bean sprouts, herbs, sliced chiles, fish sauce, hot sauce, or hoisin sauce. This is traditional, although you can improvise if needed. The one thing you must have, however, is fresh herbs.

Boil water, salt it, and cook the noodles. Traditional pho noodles (available at Asian stores) are best, but if you absolutely can't find them, spaghetti will work. When the noodles are done, gather up portions and put them in serving bowls.

Lay the thinly sliced venison on the noodles. Pick the ginger out of the broth, then pour some broth over the noodles and venison. Be sure to give everyone some onions, leftover vension, and meatballs, if using. Serve at once. Let everyone add whatever condiments they want.

**NOTE:** The broth can be made in an Instant Pot, after you blanch the bones. Pressure cook for 90 minutes to two hours on high, then let the pressure release naturally.

**TO ASSEMBLE**

One 4-inch piece of ginger, peeled and sliced

2 thinly sliced onions

Salt

¼ pound venison backstrap, sliced as thinly as possible

A few Japanese teriyaki meatballs (page 202) (optional)

Some leftover venison pot roast (page 90) (optional)

½ pound bean sprouts

A large bunch of cilantro or Asian basil

4 hot chiles, thinly sliced

Fish sauce, to taste

2 pounds Vietnamese rice noodles (spaghetti will work in a pinch)

"Every morning in Africa, a gazelle wakes up. It knows it must run faster than the fastest lion or it will be killed. Every morning a lion wakes up. It knows it must outrun the slowest gazelle or it will starve to death. It doesn't matter whether you are a lion or a gazelle . . . when the sun comes up, you'd better be running."

—SOURCE UNCERTAIN

# HUNGARIAN PÖRKÖLT

Making an authentic Hungarian dish is like running a gauntlet. There's no single "authentic" pörkölt—a cousin to the more well-known (and soupier) Hungarian goulash (gulyás)—as every Hungarian cook makes it their own way. Tomatoes? Green peppers? Verboten in some recipes, required in others. Sour cream? Typically only allowed as a tableside condiment, if at all (although there is a dish, paprikás, that includes sour cream mixed into the stew itself and is usually done with chicken). Vegetables? Sometimes, and most often carrots, parsnips, and potatoes, which are in an actual gulyás. Wine? Only with venison, apparently. Stock? A little. Beans? Hell no! After no small amount of research, the only constants I can determine are paprika and onions. Lots of onions and lots of paprika. More than you think you'd need.

What to serve with your pörkölt is also variable. Mashed, boiled, or smashed potatoes are all common, as is spätzle. This, I think, is an Austrian touch (those of you who remember your history might recall that there was once this thing called the Austro-Hungarian Empire). So here we have the Hungarian version of Austrian spätzle, called *nokedli*.

You will want fresh paprika for this recipe. The stuff that has likely been sitting around in your pantry since the Pleistocene won't cut it. Paprika needs to be bright red and smell wonderful. Oh, and don't freak out about the huge amount of onions. They cook down.

**SERVES** ▶ 6 to 8

**PREP TIME** ▶ 30 minutes

**COOK TIME** ▶ 3 hours

**ALTERNATIVE CUTS** ▶ Shoulder, neck, or shanks

**FOR THE NOKEDLI DUMPLINGS**

2 cups flour
1 teaspoon salt
4 eggs, beaten
A little water or milk

**FOR THE PÖRKÖLT**

¼ cup lard, bacon fat, or sunflower oil
2 pounds venison stew meat, cut into 3- to 4-inch hunks
Salt
5 cups chopped onions
2 teaspoons caraway seed
¼ cup sweet paprika (Hungarian if at all possible)
2 teaspoons hot paprika
1 teaspoon dried marjoram
1 cup crushed tomatoes
2 cups venison or beef stock
1 cup red wine

Heat the lard or bacon fat over medium-high heat in a large Dutch oven or stewpot and brown the venison in batches. Salt the venison as it cooks. It will take 20 minutes or so for all the meat to brown. Remove the venison as it browns and set aside.

Add all the onions and caraway seeds and turn the heat to medium. Sauté the onions, stirring often, until they are browned. This will take a solid 30 minutes if you do it right. I cover the pot about halfway in. Add the venison back, then all the other ingredients. Mix and bring to a simmer, at about 180°F. Cover and cook over low heat for two hours, or until the meat wants to fall apart.

When the meat is ready, make the nokedli dumplings by mixing all the ingredients in a bowl until you have a thick batter. Get a large pot of water boiling and add enough salt to make it salty. Push the batter through a spätzle maker or a colander with large holes into the boiling water. Boil the nokedli dumplings until they float, then 1 minute more. Drain and set aside.

Use a pair of forks or a potato masher to shred the meat in the pot. Add salt if needed. Serve the pörkölt alongside the dumplings with some sour cream at the table to mix in.

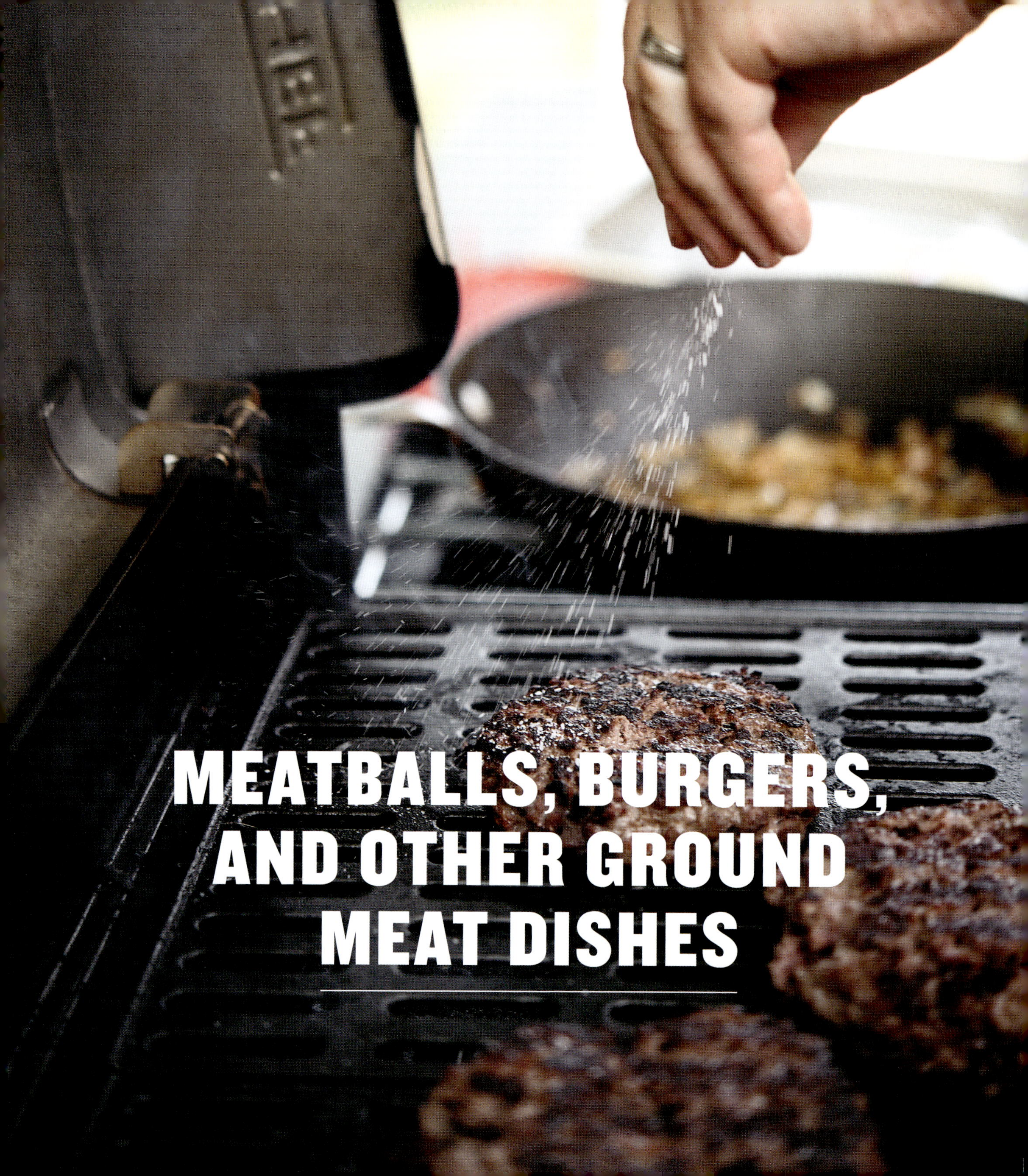

# MEATBALLS, BURGERS, AND OTHER GROUND MEAT DISHES

Burger, that catchword for those endless pounds of ground deer or elk or moose you get when you bring your animal home from the butcher, is often the last bit left in the freezer. What's more, "burger" can be something of a mystery meat. Was there fat ground in with your venison? Was it ground coarsely or fine? *Is it even from your deer?* Better to grind your own meat to suit your own needs. Meatballs are best ground one way, burgers another. Most of the time, you want to add fat. But not always. And if you do add fat, which fat? I'll walk you through the nuances of the grind. Follow my lead, and you might find that your ground meat is the first to get eaten, not the last.

You should also know that ground venison behaves differently from beef because it's leaner and often lacks fat. Most recipes in this chapter assume 10 to 20 percent added fat unless otherwise noted.

## A DISCOURSE ON VENISON BURGERS

It has occurred to me that the single most consistent ingredient in the Great American Hamburger is testosterone. The chest-thumping that surrounds the making and cooking of burgers is matched only by that of chili in winter or barbecue in the South. This is especially true of men who have grown up eating wretched fast-food patties or had mothers who made, as comedian Eddie Murphy so memorably put it, "brontosaurus burgers." There's something validating about being able to rectify a childhood wrong, as a bad burger seems to be in America.

Ideas about the "perfect burger recipe" are as varied as there are minds to contemplate such weighty matters. I've seen complicated equations involving exact percentages of this cut of meat or that one, including such horrors as including hanger steak or skirt steak in a burger. These are noble cuts, not something to be ground into a Wednesday gut filler. Might as well grind a ribeye. And yes, I'm certain that at least one person reading this has done so.

Meat-to-fat ratio is a big area of contention, too. So is the timeless debate over whether to salt the meat as you make the patty or just salt the outside. A few errant souls even add things to the meat itself, which to purists is anathema. To flip once or many times? Toast the bun or no?

And then there's the Toppings War. Cheese or no cheese? Cooked or raw onions? Is it nobler to use hothouse tomatoes on your burger in winter or not to do so, and by opposing this outrageous arrow against seasonality, end the debate forever? (Sorry, Hamlet.)

Here's where I stand:

1. All burgers, venison or no, need fat. Period. My preferred ratio is 80 percent meat, 20 percent pork fat. Beef fat is OK, and lamb fat would be my third choice, although I don't love it.

2. Grind your own, if possible. This is the secret to virtually every great burger joint's meat. Grinding your own takes less than ten minutes (unless you're feeding an army) and gives you control over texture and composition. And in the world of venison burgers, this is what I've come to like best: venison meat from the shoulder, ribs, neck, or hind leg, ground with bacon ends. If you've never tried this, do it. It's amazing. What's more, I vary my grind. (Exact proportions are in the recipe below.) Why? Because it makes the burger taste more interesting.

## When to Skip the Fat

I include fat in almost all my grind. But there are a few instances where you not only can get away with 100 percent meat, but your final dish will be better that way. Here are three places where you might want to skip the fat:

- **GROUND MEAT JERKY.** Fat will go rancid far faster than meat. So if you make ground meat jerky, like my Pemmican-Style Ground Meat Jerky on page 296, it will last longer if you don't have added fat. The jerky stays moist because of all the dried berries in it.
- **SPAGHETTI, CHILI, AND TACO MEAT.** All are great with added fat, but when you use 100 percent meat, you can alter the fat to match the dish—for example, olive oil with a spaghetti sauce or lard with taco meat. Nothing wrong with using ground meat that has fat included, but you can get a better result when you match the fat to the dish.
- **BASE MEAT FOR SAUSAGE.** You get a better bind on sausage and salami when you mix the ground meat and salt and let it sit in the fridge overnight. The presence of fat hinders this process, so if you have a lot of 100 percent ground meat, you can go right into the binding process, skipping the initial grind.

3. “Gently patties must you make, young padawan.” So sayeth Yoda. These aren’t meatballs, folks. Think of a burger as you would a crab cake, which is supposed to just barely hold together. It’s a fine line between perfect and too crumbly, but a dense, packed patty is depressing and somehow un-American.

4. Salt only the outside of the burger, right before you cook or even when you flip the patty. This one matters. Salt denatures proteins, which is why sausage binds so well and, incidentally, has a very different texture from a good burger. Add salt to the meat mixture and you have a sausage patty, not a hamburger. And yes, people have done experiments proving this. (As for my bacon ends, which contain salt, I use them only when I grind and cook, not when I grind lots of burger in advance and freeze it.)

5. Grilled burgers are only better when there’s wood or charcoal involved. Yes, I cook burgers over gas grills and they are nice, but not qualitatively better than those done in a pan inside. Unless, of course, you add smoke chips to your gas grill. Meat + woodsmoke = awesome.

6. Flip once, or several times. It apparently doesn’t matter in the final judgment. And again, yes, people have done experiments proving this. I flip only once because I want a hard crust on the outside of the burger, which I find helps hold it together.

7. Rest thine burgers. It’s the little-known Twelfth Commandment, lost in the making of Mel Brooks’s classic film *History of the World Part I.* Why? Remember the original name of a hamburger: hamburger steak. You rest steaks, right? Right? Please tell me you do.

8. Let all else be free. Let your burger freak flag fly when it comes to toppings. Just let the meat be the star, OK?

These steps make—for me—the perfect burger. I do like other sorts of burgers. But this is my Once and Future.

“And, gallant Stag! to make thy praises known,
Another monument shall here be raised;
Three several pillars, each a rough-hewn stone,
And planted where thy hoofs the turf have grazed.”

— WILLIAM WORDSWORTH

# A BASIC VENISON BURGER

**K**eep in mind that what's important here is the technique and the grind, not so much my additional ingredients. Of course, I love my venison burgers like this, so I'm biased. But so long as you follow general guidelines on toppings—mix something rich (cheese) with something sharp (tomato) and something slightly bitter or cleansing (lettuce or sorrel leaves) and a touch of sweet (ketchup)—you'll be in good shape.

I know many of you get your venison pre-ground from the butcher shop. Go ahead and use what you've got for now, but next time make sure that (a) the butcher grinds your venison with pork fat and/or (b) ask for more stew meat so you can grind the meat yourself.

**SERVES ▸** 4

**PREP TIME ▸** 20 minutes, more if you grind your own meat

**COOK TIME ▸** 10 minutes

1½ pounds venison meat

½ pound bacon ends or regular bacon, coarsely chopped

3 tablespoons butter, lard, beef tallow, or vegetable oil

1 large or 2 medium onions, sliced thin

Salt (smoked salt if you have it)

Freshly ground black pepper

Slices of cheese of your choice

Burger buns

Something green, like Bibb lettuce, arugula, sorrel, or spinach

Condiment of your choice (ketchup, mustard, remoulade, mayo, etc.)

Slices of fresh tomato (summer), or canned fire-roasted peppers (winter)

Make sure the meat and bacon are very cold. Cut the venison into chunks that will fit into your grinder. Do the same for the bacon. Mix the two together roughly so you can add a bit of each into the grinder as you go. Grind one-third of the mixture coarsely and the rest with the fine die, or just use one die.

Make between four and six patties, depending on how large you want your burgers. I like smaller burgers. Form the patties with only as much force as absolutely needed—you want the patties to hold together loosely. Make them about ½- to 1-inch thick. Use your thumb to press an indentation into the center of each patty. This prevents the burgers from turning spherical when you cook them. Set the burgers aside.

Heat the butter in a frying pan over medium-high heat. When it's good and hot, add the sliced onion and cook until it's done to your liking. Some people like juicy onion with a little char on the edges; others prefer to go the full caramelized onion route. When finished, put the onions in a bowl so you can have them ready.

I prefer grilled burgers, so I'll go through that method. Heat your grill (charcoal, wood, gas) on high, and be sure to scrape down the grates with a brush. Only salt your burgers right before you cook them, and if you're salt-sensitive, you might not need to with these because of the bacon. Place the patties on the grill and cook them without disturbing them with the grill cover open for 3 to 5 minutes, depending on how well-done you like your burgers. Flip and cook for the same amount on the other side. I prefer 3 minutes per side with a really hot grill.

*continued*

When you flip the burgers, grind some black pepper over them, then spoon a little caramelized onion on each one if you'd like. With about 90 seconds to go on the second side, lay the cheese on top of the onions and cover the grill until the burger's ready. If you like toasted buns, toast them on the grill in the last 90 seconds. When everything's done, move the burgers and buns to a sheet tray or plate so the meat can rest for 5 minutes while you build the burgers.

You can do this any way you want, but I start with a green thing (sorrel leaf), then some ketchup or mayo or whatever, then the burger patty that has the onions and cheese already on it, topped with a slice of tomato (or roasted red pepper), and finally some more of whatever condiment I happen to be using. My method is how I do things; you can do anything you'd like.

# VENISON SMASHBURGERS

Usually it is considered a sin to mash your burger patties with a spatula while you cook them. This allows the juices to escape and can break apart your burger, which will make you sad. But as in all things in life, there is an exception to this rule: the smashburger.

Now the headliner in a successful chain of fast-food burger joints, this was the standard way many greasy-spoon diners made burgers decades ago. You get a juicy burger with a great crust that cooks in a couple of minutes.

There are some tricks to doing this successfully. First, you need finely ground venison. Second, that meat needs to be fatty—I prefer a full 20 percent fat content in my burger for this. And the pressing is important too. When you smash your burger, hold it down for 20 to 30 seconds, then slide off whatever you squashed the meat with; if you lift, chances are you'll break your burger.

Needless to say, my toppings are standard, and you can vary them at will. Use your imagination.

**SERVES ▸** 4, and can be scaled up

**PREP TIME ▸** 20 minutes

**COOK TIME ▸** 20 minutes

1 to 1½ pounds finely ground venison (must have fat in the grind)

3 tablespoons vegetable oil, lard, or clarified butter, divided

Salt

Black pepper

Cheese (optional)

**TO SERVE**

Burger buns

Sliced tomato

Lettuce

Ketchup

Form the meat into four to six equally sized "hockey pucks" and set aside. Preheat the oven to 185°F and put a baking sheet inside; this is to collect the finished burgers while you cook the rest.

Get a large frying pan, or even two if you have them, and set them over high heat. I prefer cast iron here, but anything other than nonstick will work; nonstick pans don't do well at high heat. When the pans are hot, put 2 teaspoons of oil or lard in the center of the pan. When it melts, put a puck of meat on the melted fat and use a bacon press or another, smaller pan to squash it down until the patty is between ¼ and ½ inch thick. Err on making them a little thicker until you get it right. Hold this down for 20 to 30 seconds, then remove the press. Salt and pepper the exposed side of the burger.

Turn the heat down to medium-high and cook the burger for 90 seconds. When you see red juice percolating up in the center of the uncooked side, you're ready to rock. Use a metal spatula—the toughest and stiffest one you have—and scrape the burger off the pan. It's likely that it will be sticking in several places.

Flip the burger, salt and pepper the exposed side, and add cheese if you're making cheeseburgers. Cook another 30 seconds for rare and no more than 2 minutes for well-done, then remove and put on the baking sheet in the oven and repeat until you've done all the patties. You might need to scrape down the pan a few times to remove debris that collects and keep adding fat as needed to lubricate the pan. When you're done, build your burger as you wish.

# VENISON CHILI

**SERVES ▸** 8 to 10

**PREP TIME ▸** 1 hour

**COOK TIME ▸** 3 hours

**ALTERNATIVE CUTS ▸** Shoulder, diced hind leg meat, neck, or shanks

Who doesn't love chili? And what hunter doesn't love venison chili? Keep in mind that chili has endless variations: Beans or no beans? Ground meat or chunks? Or no meat at all? Tomato products or no tomato products? Add coffee? Chocolate? Cinnamon? In fact, so far as I can tell, the only things that must be in chili to make it chili are red peppers of some sort, cumin, and onions.

This is my version and I am proud of it. It hinges on ground venison, but I've made it with all kinds of meats, even ground turkey. What makes my chili unique is the huge amount of dried chiles I use. I will typically use 12 to 16 dried chiles of all sorts, reconstituted and then pureed with a cup of weak coffee to make the backbone of the dish. My advice is to use at least four kinds of chiles, and most should be mild. I like a mix of ancho, chipotle, guajillo, chile negro, chile mulato, cascabel, New Mexican, and pasilla chiles. As you get to know these chiles—some are smoky, some hot, some sweet—you can adjust the mix to your taste.

You can find these chiles in any Latin market, and even in many regular supermarkets where there is a Latino population. They're not as hard to find as you might think.

If you use the alternate cuts, you'll need to fish them out and chop them before you serve the chili.

Serve this over rice or with crackers, garnished with cilantro, raw onions, and maybe some Mexican queso seco, Jack cheese, or American cheddar.

- 1 pound pinto, brown, or kidney beans
- 16 to 20 dried chiles (ancho, guajillo, pasilla, cascabel, mirasol, or mulato)
- 1 cup weak coffee
- ½ pound bacon or Mexican chorizo
- 2 to 3 pounds ground venison
- 1 large onion, diced
- 6 to 8 cloves garlic, chopped
- 2 tablespoons paprika
- 2 tablespoons cumin
- 1 tablespoon ground coriander
- At least 2 tablespoons salt
- 2 tablespoons tomato paste
- 2 large tomatoes, peeled, seeded, and chopped, or 1 small can
- 3 tablespoons molasses
- Beef or venison broth (have a quart ready)
- Cilantro and shredded cheese, for garnish

Soak the beans in water overnight. If you forget to do this the night before, pour boiling water over the beans and soak for two to four hours. Break up and seed the chiles, and cover with hot water. (If your hands are sensitive, wear gloves while doing this.) Let stand for 20 to 30 minutes. Grind to a thick puree, adding about 1 cup of the soaking water and the coffee.

Chop the bacon and fry over medium heat in a Dutch oven or other large, lidded, ovenproof pot. Once the bacon is crispy, remove it and set aside.

Add the ground meat and brown over high heat. You want the highest heat on your most powerful burner here, otherwise the meat will want to steam and stew and not brown. Stir occasionally.

Once all the meat is browned, add onion to the pot and cook for 6 to 8 minutes, stirring often. Add the garlic, stir, and cook for 1 minute. Add the beans, paprika, cumin, coriander, and salt, stirring to combine.

Add chile puree and tomato paste and stir to combine. Add the chopped tomatoes, molasses, and enough beef broth to cover everything—you want it loose now; it'll cook down. I typically need at least a pint of broth, sometimes a quart.

Stir to combine, cover, and simmer very gently for two to three hours. Check after two hours to see if you need more salt and broth and to see how the beans are doing. When the beans are tender, you're ready. Use the reserved bacon for garnish. Or just eat it.

If you want to use a slow cooker, brown the meat, onions, and garlic, then move everything else to the slow cooker and cook on low for eight hours.

# VENISON LASAGNA

**SERVES ▸** 8 to 10

**PREP TIME ▸** 30 minutes

**COOK TIME ▸** 3 hours

Lasagna was a staple of my childhood in New Jersey. I grew up around a lot of Italians, and everyone's mother or nonna made lasagna for special occasions, like Sunday nights. I've eaten more versions of lasagna than any man has a right to. Even my own decidedly non-Italian mother made a version of the dish. And it was good. Really good. It hinged on Mom's meat sauce, which cooked all day on the stove while I was at school and she was at work. Other than that, it was pretty standard: lotsa meat, lotsa cheese, and those wavy sheet noodles that seem to serve no other purpose. Of course, Mom's lasagna is the best in the world. How could it not be? That's the thing about lasagna. It is one of those classics everyone makes that is so evocative of warm moments in our past. This is a riff off my mother's lasagna.

Lasagna seems like such a commonplace lunch in a cafeteria. But think for a moment: it's loaded with cheese and meat, making it deceptively expensive. For preparation of this dish, I spent handsomely just on the cheese—and I already had pecorino at home. All told, the recipe had 3 pounds of meat and 2 pounds of cheese. This may be a familiar form, but lasagna New Jersey style is festival food, make no mistake.

### FOR THE SAUCE

- 1 pound ground pork or wild boar
- 2 pounds ground venison
- 1 chopped onion
- 1 head garlic, chopped
- Salt
- 1 teaspoon fennel seeds (optional)
- 2 tablespoons dried oregano
- 1/4 cup chopped fresh basil leaves
- 1 cup red wine
- 1 can tomato paste
- One 8-ounce can tomato sauce
- One 28-ounce can crushed tomatoes
- Black pepper

### TO ASSEMBLE

- ½ cup chopped parsley leaves
- One 15-ounce container ricotta cheese
- 1 cup grated pecorino cheese
- 1 pound mozzarella cheese, shredded
- ½ nutmeg, grated, or ½ teaspoon ground
- 12 lasagna noodles

### MAKE THE SAUCE

Brown the meat in a large Dutch oven. Take your time and do this in batches. It could take as long as 20 minutes. Put all the browned meat back in the pot and then add the chopped onions and cook for another 3 to 4 minutes, then add the garlic and cook for another 2 to 3 minutes. Add salt, seasonings—fennel seeds (if using), oregano, basil—and mix.

Mix the wine and tomato paste and pour into the pot. Bring to a boil over high heat, stirring often. Add the tomato sauce and the can of crushed tomatoes and mix again. Bring to a simmer and cook slowly for one to two hours. Add black pepper to taste. This can be done as much as two days ahead of time.

### PREPARE THE LASAGNA

Soak the lasagna noodles in hot water for 15 to 20 minutes. Preheat the oven to 350°F.

Meanwhile, mix the parsley with the ricotta cheese in a bowl. Grate the pecorino and shred the mozzarella. Grate half a nutmeg into the ricotta. If you can't find whole nutmegs, use ½ teaspoon.

To assemble, spread a good amount of the meat on the bottom of a standard 9 by 13-inch casserole pan. Remove the lasagna noodles and lay on the meat sauce. Spread half the ricotta cheese mixture on the noodles, then half the mozzarella cheese, then half the pecorino.

Add another layer of meat sauce—you'll have one final layer after this—then the rest of the noodles. Add the remaining ricotta and mozzarella, plus half of the remaining pecorino. Spread the remaining meat sauce on this, then sprinkle with the last bit of pecorino.

To cook, cover the lasagna with foil; you might want to spray the underside first with nonstick spray so the cheese doesn't stick to it. Bake covered for 25 minutes. Carefully take off the foil and bake for another 25 minutes. Let the lasagna rest for 15 minutes before serving.

# ITALIAN VENISON PASTA CASSEROLE

Adding to the New Jersey Italian American classics, like the lasagna and the meatloaf, this casserole is roughly in the style of baked ziti and loaded with meat, cheese, pasta, and tomato sauce. I like to add some leafy greens, too. If you're looking for a more Midwestern-style hotdish, my Corned Venison Casserole is on page 291.

**SERVES ▸** 8

**PREP TIME ▸** 45 minutes

**COOK TIME ▸** 35 minutes

- 1 pound rigatoni, ziti, or penne pasta
- Salt
- 2 tablespoons olive oil
- 1 pound ground venison
- ½ pound Italian sausage
- 1 large onion, chopped
- 4 cloves garlic, minced
- 2 tablespoons tomato paste
- 1 teaspoon dried oregano
- 1 teaspoon red pepper flakes
- 1 cup red wine
- One 28-ounce can crushed tomatoes
- ¼ pound chopped leafy greens (spinach, lambsquarters, chard, etc.)
- 1 cup ricotta cheese
- ½ pound grated mozzarella cheese
- 1 cup grated pecorino cheese

Boil the pasta in salty water until it starts to soften. You want it tougher than you'd want to eat it but soft enough to bite through. Drain, toss with a little olive oil, and set aside.

Preheat the oven to 375°F and grease a 9 by 13-inch casserole dish.

Heat the olive oil in a large sauté pan over medium-high heat. Add the ground venison and brown it. Salt it as it cooks. If you're using uncased sausage, add it and brown that, too. If you're using cased sausage, slice it into disks and wait to cook it for a moment.

Stir in the chopped onion and cook until it softens, stirring often. Stir in the garlic and cook that for a minute or two, then mix in the tomato paste and the sliced sausage links, if using. Let this cook for a few minutes.

Add the oregano, red pepper flakes, and wine and stir. Everything will thicken as the wine and tomato paste mix. Let this cook for a minute or two, then add the crushed tomatoes. Stir this in with the cooked pasta and the leafy greens and turn off the heat.

Put about half of the mixture into the casserole dish. Dot with about half the ricotta, then sprinkle about half the mozzarella and pecorino over it. Add the rest of the meat-and-pasta mixture, then top with the rest of the cheese. Bake at 375°F for 35 minutes.

# ITALIAN VENISON MEATLOAF

**SERVES ▸** 4 to 6

**PREP TIME ▸** 30 minutes

**COOK TIME ▸** 1 hour 15 minutes

To the question "What's for dinner?," the answer "Meatloaf" struck fear to my very core. To be sure, Mom made lots of good things to eat. But her meatloaf wasn't one of them. I remember it as a desiccated block of unhappy beef, laced with veins of melting cheese of unknown origin. The only thing I could do to choke it down was to submerge each piece in Worcestershire sauce. My fear and loathing of meatloaf endured for many years until one day when I was at a "pork store"—Long Island slang for Italian deli—with a friend ordering lunch. I happen to love meatball sandwiches, and Del Fiore's in Patchogue had some of the best. My friend wanted a meatloaf sandwich instead. I must have wrinkled my nose or something. "What? What's wrong with a meatloaf sandwich?" he asked. "It's nasty," I said, conjuring childhood images that made me shudder visibly. My friend was exasperated. "You do know that all meatloaf is just a big meatball, right? Just try it. Tell you what. I'll order the meatball sandwich, and you order the meatloaf. If you don't like it, we switch. Deal?" Deal.

The sandwiches came, and I immediately noticed something. The meat looked the same, as did the marinara sauce on top. Only the meatloaf sandwich was easier to eat—no meatballs rolling off the back end of the hoagie roll and onto my jeans. I took a bite, and dammit if my friend wasn't right. Meatloaf, at least *this* incarnation of meatloaf, was basically a big slab of the same meatballs I knew and loved. It was a revelation.

Meatloaf is more of an art than a science, and the loaf's final consistency depends on a few things: how much stuff you put into the mix that isn't meat, how thoroughly you work the meat, and what sort of binder you use. I like a meatloaf that will hold together, but loosely—cake-ish, not dense. The recipe method that follows will do that.

A couple of tips. First, when you're chopping the Italian bread, wherever you have a piece with crust, cut it smaller than crustless pieces. I like having the crust in there, though, as it adds texture and flavor. Second, although this recipe calls for marinara sauce, any simple tomato sauce will do, so long as it's not too chunky.

This meatloaf keeps well and is great as a sandwich filling during the week.

Soak the bread cubes in a bowl with the milk for 30 minutes while you chop the vegetables and get everything else ready. Put the coarsely chopped vegetables into a food processor and blitz them until it begins to form something of a paste. This will keep the meatloaf super moist.

Preheat your oven to 375°F. When the bread has softened, squeeze out the excess milk and chop and mash the soaked bread on a cutting board until it too forms something of a paste. Toss it and the vegetable mixture into a large bowl. Add the ground venison, cheese, marinara sauce, parsley, eggs, salt, and oregano and combine. I like to work the meatloaf mix because the bread and vegetable mix will keep it moist and tender. Normally, you don't want to overwork meatball mixes, but this is an exception. It will help the meatloaf bind together better.

Grease a loaf pan. I used a Pyrex 1½-quart pan that's 8½ by 4½ by 2½ inches. Something more or less this size will be fine. Or you can set the mixture on a greased baking sheet and mold it into a loaf. Pack the meat mixture into the pan and bake it until the center reads about 160°F, which will take roughly 1 hour 15 minutes. I put the loaf pan on top of a baking sheet to catch any overflow of fat or tomato sauce.

About 30 minutes before the meatloaf is ready (shoot for the 45-minute mark), paint the top of the loaf with marinara sauce. Have some more sauce warming in a small pot to serve with the finished meatloaf.

Once the loaf is ready, set it on the countertop for 5 to 10 minutes to rest before popping out of the loaf pan. Do this carefully. Slice and serve with sauce.

**1½ cups Italian bread, cubed (see headnote)**

**1 cup milk**

**1 medium carrot, sliced**

**1 small fennel bulb, coarsely chopped**

**1 stalk celery, chopped**

**3 cloves garlic, chopped**

**2 pounds ground venison (see headnote)**

**1 cup grated Italian cheese (parmesan or pecorino)**

**⅓ cup marinara sauce**

**3 eggs**

**¼ cup chopped parsley**

**1 tablespoon kosher salt**

**2 teaspoons dried oregano**

**More marinara sauce, for painting the top and serving**

# VENISON BOLOGNESE SAUCE

A true Bolognese is different from a typical meat sauce: smoother, meatier, mellower, and a lot richer than a typical ragu or sugo. A little goes a long way.

There's a reason that the guardians of this sauce are so strict about what is and what is not an authentic Bolognese. This is a sauce with rules. It's built on a base of onion, carrot, and celery. No garlic. Nor does it have lots of herbs in it. The sauce contains dairy products. Tomato, while present, isn't the star of the sauce. Meat is. And to make a real Bolognese, it must cook a long, long time. Every cook has a personal version. This is mine.

Don't try to make this sauce on a weeknight. It takes a long time to come together, and it's the time spent slowly simmering that makes this sauce special. But fear not: it keeps in the fridge for up to a week, and it freezes very well.

Porcini mushrooms are my first choice here, but any dried mushroom will work. Many deer hunters also pick morels, so use them if you have them. One tip on getting the onion, carrot, and celery minced: chop coarsely, then buzz a few times in a food processor.

**SERVES ▶** 8 to 10

**PREP TIME ▶** 20 minutes

**COOK TIME ▶** 4 hours

- 4 tablespoons unsalted butter
- 1 cup minced onion
- 1 cup minced carrot
- 1 cup minced celery
- Salt
- 1 ounce dried mushrooms, reconstituted in 2 cups hot water and chopped
- One 6-ounce can tomato paste
- 2 pounds ground venison
- 1 cup venison or beef broth or water
- 1 cup white wine
- 1 cup milk
- ½ nutmeg, grated, or ½ teaspoon ground
- Black pepper
- 2 pounds of pasta (tagliatelle, penne, etc.)
- Grated cheese, for garnish

Heat the butter over medium-high heat in a large, heavy pot like a Dutch oven. Add the onion, carrot, and celery and cook gently, without browning, for 5 to 8 minutes, stirring often. Sprinkle a little salt over the vegetables as they cook.

When the vegetables are soft, stir in the chopped mushrooms and tomato paste and allow everything to cook for 3 to 4 minutes, again stirring often. When the tomato paste begins to turn the color of brick, add the ground meat, the mushroom soaking water, and the broth. Bring to a simmer.

Allow this to cook down over medium-low heat. Take your time here and resist the urge to do this over higher heat. Stir from time to time. When the liquid has mostly evaporated, add the wine and repeat the process. When that has mostly evaporated, add the milk, nutmeg, and black pepper and stir. Bring back to a simmer and add salt to taste. Let this cook until it is the consistency you want.

When you add the milk to the sauce, bring a large pot of water to a boil. Add enough salt to make it taste like the sea. Once the Bolognese sauce has thickened, add the pasta and cook until it's al dente.

To serve, put the pasta in a large bowl and add a healthy ladle of sauce. Toss to combine. Give everyone their portion, then top with a small ladle's worth of sauce. Grate the cheese over the top and serve.

# SWEDISH MEATBALLS

**SERVES ▸** 8 to 12

**PREP TIME ▸** 2 hours

**COOK TIME ▸** 45 minutes

This is a version of my mom's recipe for Swedish meatballs, also known as *köttbullar*. Her mother was of Swedish extraction, and while I can't remember her ever making Swedish meatballs, I do have strong memories of Mum making these little balls of yum in the seventies. *Of course* we ate Swedish meatballs in the 1970s—everyone did. They were right next to the fondue. Can't you see the chafing dish, the Sterno, and the meatballs nestled in that slowly congealing-yet-somehow-irresistible gravy? *Groovy, baby, yeah!*

Serve these little meatballs in the sauce over mashed potatoes. A salad or sautéed greens would round things out.

Lingonberry jelly can be tough to find, although the Swedish furniture store IKEA carries it. Red currant jelly is in most supermarkets and makes a good substitute. I've used highbush cranberry jelly, too.

⅔ cup milk
4 slices of stale bread
2½ pounds ground venison
1 grated yellow onion
2 teaspoons kosher salt
2 teaspoons ground allspice
1 teaspoon caraway seeds
1 teaspoon black pepper
2 eggs
1 cup flour
Butter or oil, for frying
1 quart beef or venison stock
½ cup sour cream
½ cup red currant or lingonberry jelly

Pour the milk into a pot and set it on low heat. Remove the crusts from the stale bread and break the rest into pieces. Add it to the pot. It will begin to absorb the milk. When it does, turn off the heat and mash everything into a paste. Let it cool to room temperature.

Add the ground venison, grated onion, salt, and spices to a large bowl. Crack the eggs into the bowl, then pour the bread-milk mixture in. With clean hands, mix everything together. Work the mixture gently—think cake, not bread. When it's mostly combined (you need not get everything perfect), grab a tablespoon and scoop some up. Roll it into a little ball with your palms, not your fingers. Gently roll the meatballs in flour; you'll probably need about 1 cup. Put them onto a baking sheet.

When the meatballs are all made, get a large pan ready; I use a big cast-iron frying pan. Fill it with a little less than a ¼-inch of oil. I use canola oil with a little butter tossed in for flavor. Bring it up to 325°F over medium-high heat; when a bit of flour splashed in the oil immediately sizzles, drop the heat to medium and add the meatballs. Do not crowd them.

You want the oil to come up halfway on the meatballs. Add a little oil if need be; don't worry, you can reuse it for another dish. Fry for 3 to 5 minutes. You're looking for golden brown. Turn only once. The other side will take about 4 minutes. You can also cook them in an air fryer at 375°F for 10 to 12 minutes before finishing in the sauce.

When cooked, set the meatballs on a paper towel or wire rack to drain. They can be used right away, cooled, and then refrigerated for a week or frozen for several months.

### FOR THE SAUCE

Once the meatballs are cooked, drain all but about 4 tablespoons of butter/oil from the pan. Over medium heat, add 4 tablespoons of the flour left over from dusting the meatballs. Stir to make a roux and cook slowly until it turns a nice golden brown. Think coffee with cream.

Add the stock gradually, then turn the heat up to medium-high. Stir to combine and add more stock or some water if need be—you want this thicker than water, thinner than Thanksgiving gravy. Taste for salt and add if needed.

Put the meatballs in the pan, cover, and cook for 10 minutes over medium-low heat.

Add the lingonberry or highbush cranberry jelly to the pan. Let it melt and then mix it in gently. Coat all the meatballs with the sauce. Cover and cook another 10 minutes over very low heat. Add the sour cream and warm through, maybe 3 minutes. Serve over mashed potatoes or with German egg noodles.

# ALBÓNDIGAS AL CHIPOTLE

This is a simple meatball recipe from Mexico that comes together in an hour or so, making it easy enough to do on a work night. I mostly like eating these with rice, but they also make a damn good party appetizer. The only thing even remotely challenging about this recipe is finding the chipotles in adobo, but pretty much every Latin market in America sells it, as do most larger supermarkets. In a pinch, you can buy chipotles in adobo online.

**SERVES ▶** 4 to 6

**PREP TIME ▶** 20 minutes

**COOK TIME ▶** 40 minutes

**FOR THE MEATBALLS**

- 2 pounds ground venison
- 4 cloves garlic, minced
- 2 tablespoons dried mint
- 2 eggs
- 1 cup breadcrumbs
- 2 teaspoons ground cumin
- 2 teaspoons salt
- 1 teaspoon black pepper
- Bacon fat, lard, or other high-heat oil, for frying

**FOR THE SAUCE**

- 2 tablespoons lard, bacon fat, or oil
- 1 onion, minced
- 4 cloves garlic, minced
- 2 cups tomato puree
- 2 cups broth (chicken, beef, venison, whatever)
- 3 to 6 chipotles in adobo, chopped
- 2 teaspoons ground cumin
- 2 teaspoons dried oregano
- Salt to taste

Put all the meatball ingredients, except the bacon fat or lard, together in a large bowl. Mix with your clean hands until the mixture comes together. Don't overwork the mix or the meatballs will get tough. Roll into meatballs of whatever size you want. I like to make them by the tablespoon. If you have the time, let the meatballs sit in the fridge for up to an hour; this helps them stay together.

Brown the meatballs in the bacon fat, lard, or oil. Or you can air-fry them at 400°F for 8 to 10 minutes before adding them to the sauce. Once they're browned, set aside.

If you browned the meatballs in a large enough pan to hold all of them, drain all but about 2 tablespoons of the fat and keep using that pan. Otherwise, get a pot or pan large enough to hold all the meatballs and heat 2 tablespoons of fat in it. Cook the onions in this until soft and browned at the edges, about 10 minutes. Stir from time to time. Add the garlic and cook another minute.

Add the tomato puree, broth, chipotles, and spices and mix. Nestle the meatballs into the sauce and bring to a simmer. Simmer for about 20 to 30 minutes, until the meatballs are cooked through. Eat with rice or by themselves as an appetizer.

# JAPANESE TERIYAKI MEATBALLS

This is a traditional Japanese style of meatball called *niku dango*, and it's damn good. It's basically a teriyaki meatball, normally made with pork. Venison works fine. It's a pretty simple meatball, made "Japanese" with the addition of ginger, green onion, coarse panko breadcrumbs, and soy sauce in the mix. All by itself, it's a nice meatball.

The star of this show is the sauce, which is essentially a homemade teriyaki. Could you use store-bought teriyaki sauce? I suppose you could. But homemade is better. That's all there is to this recipe: easy meatballs glazed with a homemade teriyaki sauce, dusted with sesame seeds. Stick a toothpick in each meatball and you have a great party appetizer. Toss a few on top of some steamed rice and you have an easy weeknight meal. But a fair warning: Make more than you think you'll need. People seem to be unable to control themselves while eating these.

I don't like a super-sweet sauce, so I only have 1 tablespoon of sugar in it; mirin is also sweet (it's a sweet cooking wine, fermented from rice, that you can get in most supermarkets), so that's enough for me. Feel free to double the amount of sugar if you like a sweet teriyaki sauce.

**SERVES ▸** 4 to 6

**PREP TIME ▸** 20 minutes

**COOK TIME ▸** 20 minutes

**FOR THE MEATBALLS**

2 pounds finely ground venison

3 tablespoons minced green onions

1 cup panko breadcrumbs

2 tablespoons soy sauce

½ teaspoon black pepper

2 tablespoons minced fresh ginger

2 eggs

**FOR THE SAUCE**

2 tablespoons sake

½ cup mirin, sweet Japanese cooking wine

1 tablespoon sugar

½ cup soy sauce

2 teaspoons potato or cornstarch

Toasted sesame seeds, for garnish

---

Mix all the meatball ingredients together in a bowl. Mix all the sauce ingredients in another bowl.

Form meatballs anywhere from the size of a walnut to the size of golf ball. For best results, set the meatballs on a baking sheet and put them into the fridge for an hour to firm up. But you can cook the meatballs straight away if you'd like.

Cook the meatballs. You can deep-fry them at 350°F for about 5 minutes; you can poach them in simmering water for about the same amount of time (they're ready when they float); you can bake the meatballs at 400°F for about 20 minutes; or you can cook them in an air fryer at 375°F for 10 to 12 minutes, shaking halfway through.

Glaze the meatballs. Whisk the sauce together so the starch doesn't stick to the bottom of the bowl and pour it into a large sauté pan. Bring it to a boil and add the cooked meatballs. Roll them around in the hot sauce to glaze for 30 seconds or so. Move the meatballs to a serving plate and sprinkle sesame seeds over them. Serve hot as an appetizer or with rice.

# STUFFED JALAPEÑOS

This is a knockout appetizer for a party or barbecue. I prefer jalapeños here, but you can use any sturdy pepper: bell peppers, Anaheim (Hatch), poblanos, or Hungarian wax. Ditto for the sausage; just make sure it's been finely ground.

**SERVES** ▸ 6 to 8

**PREP TIME** ▸ 30 minutes

**COOK TIME** ▸ 20 minutes

**FOR THE TOMATO SAUCE**

8 plum tomatoes

½ white or yellow onion

3 cloves garlic, unpeeled

1 habanero

1 cup chicken or other light stock

Salt

**FOR THE PEPPERS**

16 large jalapeños

1 pound loose sausage, ideally chorizo

½ pound Jack cheese

Dried oregano, for garnish

To make the sauce, start by getting a comal or heavy skillet hot. Slice the tomatoes in half, and cut the half onion into thirds through the root, so the pieces stay together. When the skillet is hot, put the unpeeled garlic cloves, habanero, and onion pieces on the hot iron and arrange the tomato halves around them. Turn each when they are a bit blackened. The tomatoes will take the longest to blacken.

When each vegetable has gotten a good amount of blackening, move it to the cutting board to cool a bit. Peel the garlic and put that in a blender. Slice the habanero in half and remove the seeds and stem, then put that in the blender. Coarsely chop the onions and add them to the blender. Finally, peel the tomatoes and put them in the blender with the stock. Puree. You want the consistency of heavy cream, so add more stock if needed. Add salt to taste.

While the vegetables are charring, roast the peppers. Again, you don't *have* to do this, but it makes for a better end result. To roast the peppers, I arrange them over my gas burners to char and blister. You can get most of the peppers blistered this way, but you'll need to finish them off by holding them with tongs to get any parts of each pepper that are still green. When each pepper is done, put it in a plastic bag to steam. When all the peppers are in the bag, let them steam for a few minutes, then remove the skins. I do this with a butter knife. Resist the urge to rinse the peppers; doing so washes away a ton of flavor.

Use a paring knife to make a slit in each pepper then carefully slice off where the seeds meet the stem. Carefully remove the seeds; it's OK if you have a few seeds still in there, but get most of them.

Cook the sausage in a pan, breaking it up as it cooks. Let it cool enough to work with. Heat the oven to 400°F. Spoon the sausage into the peppers, and stuff in some cheese either before the sausage goes in, after, or both.

Grease a baking sheet and set each finished pepper on it. Bake the peppers for about 10 minutes, or until the cheese has melted. Serve with the tomato sauce, which you can heat up if you'd like (it should still be warm by the time the peppers are ready), garnished with the oregano.

**NOTE:** You can make the sauce up to a few days beforehand, and you can pre-roast the peppers up to a day before.

**AIR FRYER OPTION:** Cook at 375°F for 6 to 8 minutes until the cheese melts.

# MEXICAN PACHOLAS

**A**ccording to Larousse's *Diccionario Enciclopédico de la Gastronomía Mexicana*, the bible of Mexican cuisine, pacholas are a very old dish, possibly pre-Hispanic. I had never heard of these glorious meaty treats until I read my friend Pati Jinich's cookbook *Treasures of the Mexican Table*, which I highly recommend. This is not her recipe, however.

Pacholas are easy to make, and they're definitely kid friendly. They're basically a flattened meatball. And who doesn't like meatballs? Traditionally, you make pacholas on a metate with a metatil, the grinding stone that comes with the metate. I prefer to make pacholas with a tortilla press. You can also simply put the mixture between two pieces of wax paper or plastic wrap and use a rolling pin (or an empty bottle) to make them.

I use ground venison for my pacholas, but any finely ground meat will work.

Serve your pacholas with beans—freshly made or refried—maybe some nice Mexican rice, and a salsa of your choice. The photos show my version with pico de gallo and added cotija cheese.

You can also put the patties in a bun to make a Mexican torta sandwich, maybe with a smear of refried beans and some salsa and shredded lettuce.

**SERVES ▸** 4 to 6

**PREP TIME ▸** 30 minutes

**COOK TIME ▸** 15 minutes

- 1 ounce ancho, pasilla, or guajillo chiles, stems and seeds removed
- 1 white onion, peeled and sliced into quarters
- 3 cloves garlic, unpeeled
- 1 hamburger roll
- ½ cup milk
- 2 pounds ground venison, beef, or other ground meat
- 1 egg, lightly beaten
- 1 teaspoon Mexican oregano
- 1 teaspoon salt
- Black pepper
- Vegetable oil, for frying
- ½ cup flour, for dusting

Put the chiles in a bowl and pour boiling water over them. Cover the bowl while you do other things.

Get a comal or griddle or flat-top or large frying pan very hot and set the quartered onion and the garlic cloves down on them. You want to char them on the cut sides of the onion and whatever sides of the garlic cloves that can touch the pan.

Tear the hamburger roll into pieces and soak it in the milk.

By the time the onion and garlic are nicely charred, your chiles will be soft. Put them in a blender. Remove the bread from the milk and squeeze the excess milk out of it. Put the bread in the blender. Coarsely chop the onion, peel the garlic, and put those into the blender, too. Puree. You'll need to use a wooden spoon or tamper to get this done, because the mix won't be very liquidy. But this needs to be a homogenous puree.

Scrape the contents of the blender into a large bowl, add the ground meat and the egg, the oregano, a hefty pinch of salt—maybe a teaspoon or so—and a few grindings of black pepper. Mix this with your clean hands until it's one cohesive mass. You should be able to pick it up as one big blob of meat.

Clean off your comal or griddle, get it hot, and slick it with vegetable oil. I prefer canola here because it has a high smoke point.

*continued*

Line a tortilla press with plastic wrap. Pull off a piece of the meat mixture about the size of a lime. Shape it into an oval, then carefully press it until the meat is about ⅛ inch thick. You can also do this with a rolling pin or an empty bottle.

Remove the top piece of plastic. Pick up the pachola and carefully remove the other piece of plastic, letting the meat rest in your open hand—this is exactly the move you make when making tortillas. Set the patty on a plate with the flour in it, to dust the outside. Flip to dust the other side.

Carefully set the meat on the hot griddle. If you have a bacon press, set it on top of the meat for 30 seconds, then slide it off. Cook the meat on high heat for about 1 minute per side. I like to put each pachola on a cooling rack set over a baking sheet in an oven set to 200°F while I make the rest.

Once they're all made, serve with beans, rice, and the salsa of your choice.

**NOTES:** If you don't have hamburger rolls lying around, you can use 1 cup of breadcrumbs or crushed saltines. If you use the saltines, you won't need to salt the rest of the mixture.

- If you use breadcrumbs or saltines, add a little water or milk to the blender to help things puree.
- For a gluten-free option, use about 1 cup of prepared masa, either fresh or made from masa harina. If you're using masa harina, make the dough a little too wet.
- If you want it spicier, you can add hotter fresh or dried peppers. One or two chipotles in adobo (from the can) is a nice touch.
- The flour helps the pacholas brown nicely. Gluten-free flour works fine for this.

# POLISH GOLUMPKI

**G***olumpki*—the Polish version of stuffed cabbage—are one of the few Polish dishes I grew up with; a few of my childhood friends were of Polish descent, and their moms would make these. They are packets of comfort and ideal for a big dinner or a potluck. Feel free to play with the filling and the sauce if you want.

**SERVES** ▸ 8, can be doubled

**PREP TIME** ▸ 45 minutes

**COOK TIME** ▸ 2 hours

1 head cabbage

**FOR THE FILLING**

1½ ounces dried mushrooms (any kind)

2 cups chopped onions

2 tablespoons butter

2 cups cooked barley

1½ pounds ground venison

1 tablespoon marjoram

2 teaspoons caraway seeds

1 teaspoon celery seed

2 teaspoons salt

2 eggs, lightly beaten

**FOR THE SAUCE**

1 quart crushed tomatoes

2 to 3 cups mushroom soaking water

2 tablespoons vinegar, or to taste

1 tablespoon Maggi seasoning, or to taste

Salt

Bring a large pot of water to a boil and add 1 tablespoon of salt. Remove the core from the cabbage and discard. Cook the cabbage in boiling water for 10 minutes. Remove it and let it cool, cut side up.

In another pot, cook the barley in salted water until it's about half cooked, about 15 minutes. Drain and reserve.

### TO MAKE THE FILLING

Meanwhile, make the filling. Put the dried mushrooms in a bowl and ladle a little of the hot water you're cooking the cabbage in over them.

Cook the chopped onions in the butter over medium-high heat until they begin to brown. Turn off the heat and move them to a large bowl to cool quickly.

Remove the mushrooms from the soaking water and squeeze excess water out of them. Chop them fine. Strain the soaking water through a paper towel to remove any debris and reserve a couple cups for the sauce.

Add the mushrooms to the bowl with the onions and add the remaining filling ingredients. Mix.

### TO MAKE THE SAUCE

Use the pot you cooked the barley in. Add all the sauce ingredients and bring it to a bare simmer.

### TO MAKE THE GOLUMPKI

Preheat the oven to 350°F. Separate your cabbage leaves. Use the biggest outer leaves to line a heavy, lidded pot like a Dutch oven. Spread some sauce over that.

*continued*

Set a leaf in front of you, main rib closest to you, with the curve of the leaf facing up. Cut the base of the rib out with a knife. Crush the rest of the rib with the palm of your hand.

Spoon some filling onto the leaf, perpendicular to the rib. Compress it a bit. Fold the bottom of the leaf up, then the sides. Fold this over to seal, like a burrito or grape leaf. Set the cabbage roll in the pot. Repeat until you have a full layer in the pot.

Spread some sauce over this first layer, then finish with all the cabbage leaves large enough to make into a roll. Spread the rest of the sauce over this, then top with the smallest leaves. Cover the pot and bake in the oven for 90 minutes. Remove from the oven and let the pot sit for 30 minutes before serving. If you have an Instant Pot, you can cook them at high pressure for 20 minutes, then release the pressure naturally, then let them rest.

**NOTES:** I like to sprinkle some dried marjoram on top of the cabbage rolls. Black pepper is another good option.

"These are the animals you may eat: the ox, the sheep, the goat, the deer, the gazelle, the roe deer, the wild goat, the ibex, the antelope and the mountain sheep. You may eat any animal that has a split hoof divided in two and that chews the cud."

—DEUTERONOMY 14:4-6

# CORNISH PASTIES

**MAKES ▸** About ten 6-inch pasties

**PREP TIME ▸** 3½ hours

**COOK TIME ▸** 50 minutes

Pasties are one of mankind's great convenience foods. Handheld, nourishing, filling, and tasty either hot or cold, they were a mainstay lunch for me when I was in graduate school at the University of Wisconsin. The pasty shop, called Teddywedgers, still stands at the top of State Street, and as of 2023, thirty years after I first ate there, still makes a damn good pasty. This is my rendition of their classic.

True pasty freaks will note that I include the "Scarborough Faire" herbs of parsley, sage, rosemary, and thyme, which are not traditional. They add a lot of flavor and are still very British. If you don't like them, leave them out. If you can't get the fresh stuff, which I prefer, dried is fine—cut the amounts in half.

Incidentally, you can also use ground venison for this recipe, although I prefer diced meat. If you do use ground meat, keep in mind that all my ground venison has fat cut into it. If yours doesn't, put a pat of butter (about 2 teaspoons) on top of the mixture before folding up the pasty.

And finally, if you can't find rutabagas, use turnips; if you can't find either, use all potatoes. My pastry calls for lard and butter, but you can use butter only if you'd rather. The crust is different, but still good.

A word on the vegetables. Since you are only baking the pasties for 45 minutes, be mindful of the size of your pieces. Most good pasties have vegetables that are more sliced than chunked.

**FOR THE PASTRY**

2 teaspoons salt

17½ ounces (500 grams) bread flour, about 4¼ cups

4 ounces (115 grams) lard (see headnote)

4 ounces (115 grams) unsalted butter (1 stick)

6 ounces cold water, about ¾ to 1 cup

Beaten egg, for glazing

**FOR THE FILLING**

1 pound venison, cut into small cubes or ground

½ pound waxy potatoes (like Yukon Gold), peeled and sliced

½ pound rutabaga, peeled and sliced

1 small onion, chopped

Salt

Black pepper

1 teaspoon chopped fresh sage

½ teaspoon chopped fresh rosemary

2 teaspoons chopped fresh parsley

2 teaspoons chopped fresh thyme

Mix the salt with the flour. Rub the lard and butter into the flour until it looks like breadcrumbs or wet sand. Add the water and knead until the dough comes together and becomes elastic. This will take a little longer than you might think, about 6 to 8 minutes, but you need to really knead here to make a strong dough. Cover the dough with plastic wrap and let it rest for at least one hour in the fridge, and up to overnight; this lets the dough relax—rolling it out immediately is virtually impossible—and allows the fats to chill.

About 15 minutes before you want to begin making the pasties, mix all the filling ingredients in a bowl and set aside.

Preheat the oven to 350°F. Roll out the pastry and cut into circles about 6 to 8 inches in diameter; this is a typical size for appetizer plates, which work as a guide. If you don't have enough dough to make ten circles, gather the excess into a ball and roll it out again.

Layer the vegetables and meat in the center of the pastry circles. Brush the outer edge with a little water. Fold the circle over to make a half-moon and press firmly to seal, taking care to push out any air pockets. Push down on the edge of the pasty and using the thumb of one hand and the thumb and forefinger of the other, twist the edge of the pastry over to form a crimp. Do this along the whole outer edge of the pasty and tuck the end corners underneath it.

When you're done, paint the pasties with the beaten egg. Ideally, line your baking pan with a Silpat silicone baking liner or some parchment paper to prevent the pasties from sticking to the pan. Bake for about 45 to 50 minutes until golden brown.

# BRITISH MINCEMEAT PIES

Mincemeat pies are a fun holiday treat that will surprise everyone with how good they are. These are venison mincemeat pies—and yes, long ago, mince pies did indeed have meat in them—made with a Scottish flair.

All mincemeat pies have fruit in them, usually dried. Most use raisins, sultanas, and "currants," which in this context are still raisins. Boring. Use dried berries instead, several kinds if you can. This recipe has dried lingonberries, blueberries, and black currants. Other options that are good are chopped, dried apricots and dried cranberries, blackberries, gooseberries, raspberries, huckleberries, mulberries, or dewberries.

The filling's acidity, fat, and salt content, plus the presence of hard liquor, all help preserve it for weeks, even months. It is said to improve over time, to the point where some cooks make their mincemeat pie filling in October or November for Christmastime.

But yes, you can absolutely make it, let it cool, and fill your pies with the fresh filling, too.

I include a pie crust here, but you can use a store-bought crust if you want. In a perfect world, you'd use a mincemeat pie tin, which you can buy online, but a mini-muffin pan also works. Or you can make your venison mincemeat pie a regular pie in a regular pie pan, which is a thing. Or you can use any small tart pan you happen to have.

Once made, these will keep about a week or so in the fridge, but it's unlikely that any will be left after that long. You can freeze them, too.

To reheat, remember that they're already cooked, so a toaster oven is ideal. Ten to fifteen minutes at 375°F will do. I do like these pies at room temperature but not actually cold.

**SERVES ▸** 12

**PREP TIME ▸** 3 hours 45 minutes

**COOK TIME ▸** 30 minutes

#### FOR THE MINCEMEAT FILLING

125 grams dried lingonberries or cranberries (about 4 ounces)

125 grams dried blueberries or raisins, about 4 ounces

125 grams dried currants or other berries, or dried chopped apricots, about 4 ounces

1 cup brandy, rum, or Scotch

325 grams ground venison, about 12 ounces

Salt

½ cup lard, beef suet, or butter

125 grams brown sugar, about ½ cup

¼ teaspoon ground cinnamon

¼ teaspoon ground clove

¼ teaspoon ground nutmeg or mace

1 baking apple, such as granny smith, peeled, cored, and grated

Zest and juice of 1 lemon

#### TO MAKE THE FILLING

Make the filling first. If possible, soak the berries in the alcohol overnight, then strain off the alcohol to use later. But you can skip this if you're short on time.

Put all the filling ingredients except for the Scotch or brandy in a bowl and mix. Put this in a lidded pot and cook at 225°F for three hours. Pull it out and stir several times as it cools, which helps distribute the fat in the mix. When it's cool, add back the reserved alcohol. This mix can sit in a sterilized Mason jar for a month or so, or you can simply proceed with making pies.

*continued*

### FOR THE DOUGH

Pinch of salt

250 grams all-purpose flour (about 2 cups)

100 grams unsalted butter, diced

25 grams bacon fat (see below)

1 egg

¼ cup cold water

### TO FINISH

1 egg

1 tablespoon milk or cream

Turbinado, brown, or demerara sugar, for dusting

### TO MAKE THE DOUGH

If you're doing this all at once, make the dough while the filling cooks. Mix the salt and flour, then cut the fats into it with a cutter or your fingertips until the mix looks like a coarse meal. This will take a little time.

Mix in the egg and the ice water and work this dough into a nice ball. It's not necessary to be gentle with it like a regular pie dough, because you want the crust on these to be a bit sturdy, so you can pick them up and eat them. Regardless, refrigerate for no less than 20 minutes, and up to a day.

### TO MAKE THE PIES

Preheat your oven to 350°F. Grease a mincemeat pie or muffin tin, then dust it with flour.

Roll the dough out thin, to about ¼ inch or even a little less. Depending on your tin, you'll want to cut out one set of larger circles to fill the bottom of the tin, then another set of smaller ones for tops. You can also cut out stars with a cookie cutter to serve as tops. For my standard mincemeat pie tin, I use a 3-inch cutter for the bottom and a 2-inch for the top. Wine glasses or empty jars are good substitutes for a dedicated cutter.

Beat the egg with the milk or cream to make an egg wash.

Fill each tin with the bottom crust, then fill those with the filling. Paint the rim of a pie, set the top on, then crimp or pinch the edges all around to seal. Move on to the next pie.

When they're all sealed, paint them with the egg wash, then dust them with the turbinado sugar. Use a sharp knife to cut a cross in the center of each pie. Bake for about 30 minutes, or until they're pretty and browned.

Let them sit out of the oven in their tins for about 10 minutes, then move them to a rack to finish cooling. Eat warm or at room temperature.

**NOTES:** Instead of mixing the fats, you can use 125 grams (9 tablespoons) of butter, lard, or Crisco. The dough recipe makes enough for twelve pies in a muffin tin but will be a bit more than you need for a proper mincemeat pie tin. The filling recipe makes a lot, enough for several batches of pies. But since it keeps for weeks in the fridge, you'll want to make lots of these.

# KEFTA KEBABS

This is another party snack based on street food—in this case, from North Africa. Ground meat on a stick makes an appearance all over the Mediterranean and into Persia, and every cook uses a different spice mixture. This one is inspired by Morocco and Tunisia. The herbs and spices play very well together, but if you're short on one, you can leave it out and still be fine.

It is important that you use finely ground venison and that you knead the mixture of meat, onion, and spices so that the kebabs will stay on your skewers. This is not a burger barely holding itself together. Think of this as a caseless sausage on a stick. Serve the kebabs with roasted or grilled vegetables, crusty bread, or rice.

This recipe works best with flat skewers. Many supermarkets sell them, but in a pinch, you can skewer the ground meat with two round bamboo skewers instead of one. That will help you flip them. Don't forget to soak the bamboo in water for an hour first, or the skewers will burn.

**SERVES ▸** 4 to 6

**PREP TIME ▸** 30 minutes

**COOK TIME ▸** 10 minutes

- 1 pound ground venison
- 1 small onion, grated or finely minced
- 2 tablespoons chopped parsley
- 2 tablespoons chopped oil-packed sun-dried tomatoes (optional)
- 2 teaspoons dried mint
- ½ to 1 teaspoon cayenne
- 1 teaspoon ground cumin
- 1 teaspoon salt
- 1 teaspoon black pepper
- ½ teaspoon ground coriander

The easy way to make these is to use finely ground venison and mix together all the ingredients. But I find that you get a better texture and bind if you use coarsely ground venison or even stew meat, mix in everything else, and then grind everything fine. The easy way works, but if you have the time, try double-grinding it. Regardless, let the mixture sit in the fridge for 30 minutes or so to allow the flavors to meld a bit. You can keep the mix in the fridge for up to a day before the herbs start to get sad.

For the skewers, use flat metal skewers if you have them. You can use two bamboo skewers, or, if you happen to have access to a rosemary bush, you can strip off the leaves and use a few stems as skewers—this being ground meat, the flat metal skewers are best. Be sure to soak bamboo skewers or rosemary stems for an hour before you put them on the grill.

When you're ready to cook, build a hot fire. Charcoal is best, but gas is fine. If you don't have a grill, you can broil the skewers. Form the meat onto the skewers into long, skinny sausages. You are looking for any length, but no more than about 3 inches thick. Grill, turning often, until the kebabs are slightly charred, about 4 to 6 minutes.

A good sauce to accompany this dish is tzatziki. I have a recipe for it on page 143.

# SCOTTISH MINCE AND TATTIES

One of Scotland's national dishes, this is easy weeknight comfort food, perfect for ground venison or whatever meat you have handy. Leftovers make a great filling for pasties.

**SERVES** ▸ 4 to 6

**PREP TIME** ▸ 20 minutes

**COOK TIME** ▸ 45 minutes

### FOR THE MINCE

- 3 tablespoons bacon fat, beef drippings, butter, or oil
- 1 large yellow onion, minced
- 1½ pounds ground venison, beef, lamb, or turkey
- Salt
- 2 tablespoons oat flour or regular flour
- 1 rutabaga, peeled and diced
- 1 large, fat carrot, peeled and diced
- 1 teaspoon dried thyme
- 1 teaspoon black pepper
- 2 cups porter or other dark, malty beer
- 2 cups stock, venison or beef
- A few dashes of Maggi seasoning (optional)
- 2 teaspoons Worcestershire sauce

### FOR THE TATTIES

- 2 pounds yellow potatoes, peeled and cut into chunks
- Salt
- ¼ cup butter
- ¼ cup heavy cream
- ½ teaspoon white pepper (optional)

Heat the bacon fat or other cooking oil in a large frying pan over medium-high heat. Sauté the onions until they're nicely browned, about 6 minutes. Stir in the ground meat, salt everything, and brown the meat, which should take another 6 to 10 minutes. This stage is important, as the browning adds a ton of flavor to the finished dish.

Sprinkle the oat flour (or regular flour) over everything and mix. Let this cook a minute or two, then add the remaining ingredients, stirring. Bring this to a rolling boil, then drop the heat to a simmer and let this cook down into a nice gravy. This usually takes about 15 to 20 minutes.

When the onions and meat are cooking, you're ready to make the tatties. Put the potatoes in a pot, cover with water, and bring to a boil. Add a good pinch of salt and simmer until tender.

Drain the potatoes, then return them to the pot. Drop the heat to low. Let the potatoes steam out for about 30 seconds, add the butter, and mash. Keep mashing while adding the cream. Mix in the white pepper, if using, and salt if it needs it.

# SOUTH AFRICAN BOBOTIE

Bobotie, a national dish of South Africa for the better part of four hundred years, is believed to be Indonesian in origin (the Dutch who settled South Africa also colonized Indonesia). It is essentially a curry meatloaf casserole with baked egg.

There are an awful lot of variations on bobotie , but the goal is curry-like, sweet, sour, and savory. I add a little cayenne for balance, but this isn't traditional. You'll note a bunch of alternatives in the ingredient list. The first listed are my preferences, followed by easier-to-find alternates.

This is a one-pot meal, although I like it served alongside rice; a salad is a good accompaniment, too. To drink, I'd go with an IPA or pale ale.

**SERVES ▸** 6 to 8

**PREP TIME ▸** 20 minutes

**COOK TIME ▸** 1 hour

- 3 slices white bread
- 2 cups milk
- 2 large onions, chopped (about 3 cups)
- 3 tablespoons butter
- Salt
- 2 cloves garlic, chopped
- 2 pounds ground venison
- 2 tablespoons mild curry powder
- 2 tablespoons tamarind paste, mango chutney, or peach jam
- 2 teaspoons garam masala (or ½ teaspoon ground clove and 1½ teaspoons ground allspice)
- ⅓ cup chopped cilantro or parsley (loosely packed)
- Cayenne pepper (I use 1 teaspoon)
- 3 tablespoons golden raisins (optional)
- 3 citrus leaves (or bay leaves)
- Juice of a lemon or lime

**FOR THE TOPPING**

- 1 cup heavy cream
- 2 large eggs

Preheat the oven to 325°F. Soak the bread in the milk.

Cook the onions in butter over medium heat until they're soft, about 6 to 8 minutes. Sprinkle some salt over them as they cook. Add the garlic and the venison and brown. Salt this as it cooks, too. Break apart the ground venison as it cooks so it looks like taco meat.

When it's pretty much browned, add the curry powder, tamarind paste, and all the remaining spices and herbs, as well as the raisins if using. Cover the pan, add the lemon or lime juice, and let this cook for a few minutes.

Squeeze the milk out of the bread and mash into the mixture. Turn off the heat. Move the mix into a casserole dish and press it down.

Beat the cream and eggs together and pour over the casserole. Bake for 45 minutes to one hour, until the egg mixture is set and turning golden.

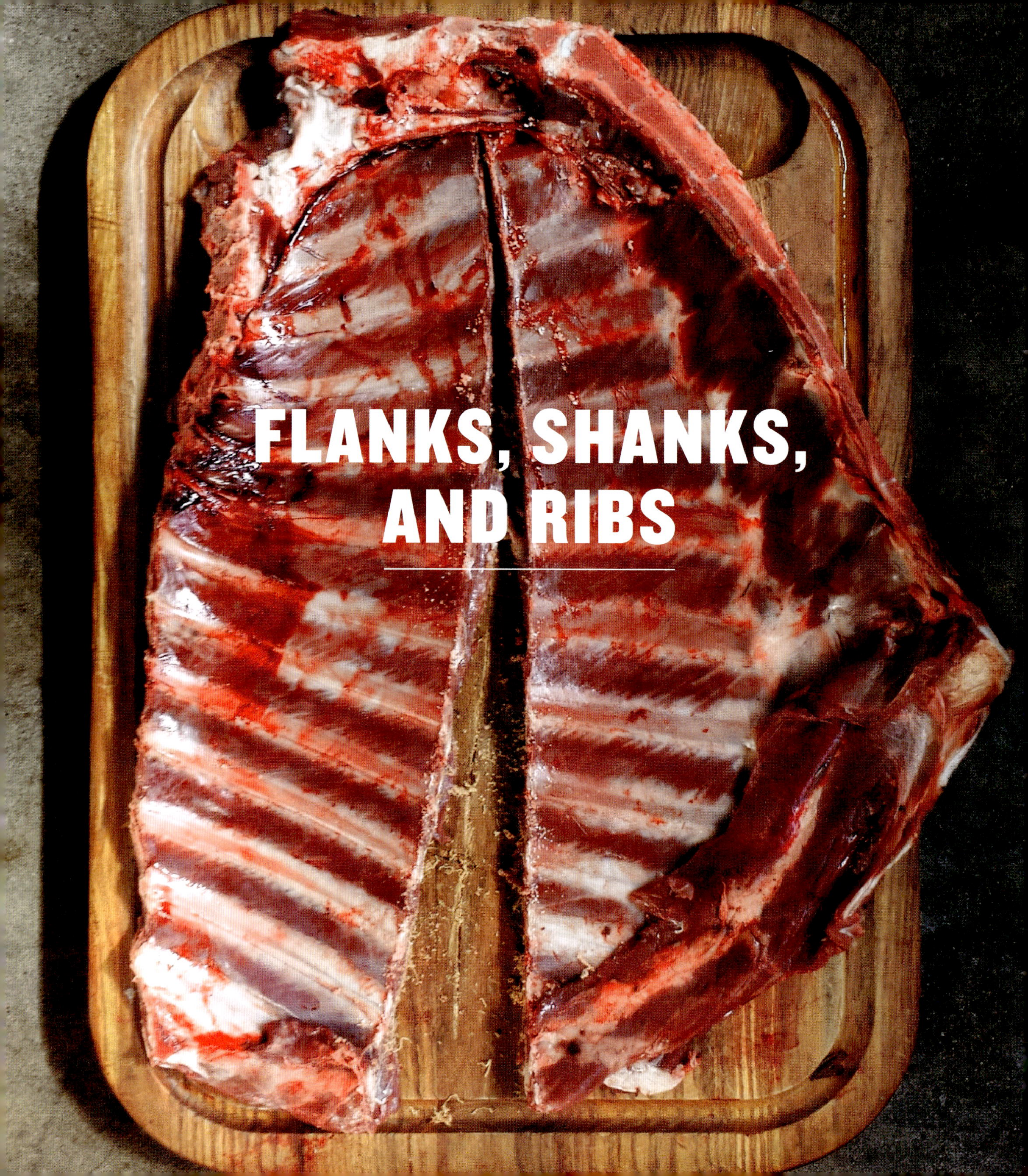

# FLANKS, SHANKS, AND RIBS

Flanks, shanks, and ribs are probably the most underrated cuts on a deer. This is a sad thing. While it's true that ribs on a deer can be tricky, the shanks are every bit as easy to cook as those of lamb, veal, and beef. And enjoying venison flank steak is simply a question of slicing away silverskin with a sharp knife.

Being some of the hardest-working muscles on the animal, shanks are tough and very sinewy. Grinding them is a chore, as anyone who's done it can attest. All that connective tissue gunks up the grinder, forcing you to stop and clean it repeatedly—especially if you're doing this with a giant elk or moose shank. Far better to cook those shanks whole. It will open a whole new world to you, and you will be thankful.

Flank meat and ribs are two other sorely underused cuts on a deer. Both are also often headed to the grinder, and while this is no sin, on larger deer and especially elk, moose, and nilgai, the pure cuts are far more fun to work with than another few pounds of burger. Flank and skirt steaks, cut from the outside and inside of the belly flap, respectively, are taco meat par excellence. Both have a very distinct grain that makes thin slices cut across it meltingly tender. Simple grilled flank with salt, pepper, and lemon is a summertime specialty, although sometimes I'll serve it with chimichurri sauce (page 88) or marinate it for Venison Bulgogi (page 238).

Venison ribs, on the other hand, are fiddly. You can't barbecue them like pork or beef ribs, largely because deer and their cousins are almost always older than their analog in the barnyard. A typical whitetail is two to four years old, and the largest bull elk and moose can be more than a decade old. Beef is normally about eighteen months old when slaughtered, although grass-fed animals tend to be a few months older than that. Hogs are rarely more than a year old, and most of the ribs you find in a supermarket came from pigs that were about four to six months old.

Age does two things: It makes the meat tougher, and it makes it more flavorful. To enjoy the latter, you must deal with the former. The answer is to braise or otherwise parcook your venison ribs before finishing them in another way. Slow, moist, moderate heat gradually breaks down the connective tissue in the ribs and makes them tender enough to enjoy. On large animals, you can follow beef short rib recipes. On deer and antelope, follow recipes for baby back ribs.

How do you get there? The simplest way is to season your ribs and braise them in broth with some herbs and vegetables until they're tender. This takes a few hours. You can also use a pressure cooker. Cover the venison with some water or broth and cook at high pressure for about forty minutes.

## Shanks 101

**Generally speaking, you'll brown and then slow-cook all game shanks the same way. Many of the following recipes are variations on this theme. I prefer a heavy Dutch oven or Le Creuset pot for this, and usually the meat will be tender in somewhere between two and four hours. That said, shanks are good with Crock Pots and pressure cookers, too. If you use a Crock Pot, you'll want it on a simmer setting—often "high"—and add a couple of hours to the cook time. With a pressure cooker, figure on one hour cook time at high pressure, then a natural pressure release of fifteen minutes.**

# GREEK BRAISED VENISON SHANKS

This is a great recipe to make with smallish shanks of any animal, from young deer, antelope, lamb, goats, and pork.

A key to the flavor of the dish is to use a variety of fresh herbs. It brightens up an otherwise moody plate of food. I used a combination of parsley, dill, and the leaves from the center of a bunch of celery. Other options would be fresh oregano or thyme, lovage, savory, or fennel fronds.

There is one modification you'll need to do if you're using game instead of lamb. After you cook your vegetables in the olive oil, you'll need to remove them until the meat is close to being tender. Otherwise, they'll cook into mush. You don't need to do this with lamb shanks.

My inspiration for this recipe is from a wonderful, if little known, cookbook by the great chef Michael Psilakis, called *How to Roast a Lamb*. It's a classic Greek recipe, with sturdy vegetables, lots of herbs, and a little tomato and red wine.

**SERVES ▸** 4

**PREP TIME ▸** 20 minutes

**COOK TIME ▸** 3 hours, or more for an old deer

**ALTERNATIVE CUTS ▸** Shoulder, neck, or ribs

- 4 tablespoons olive oil
- 4 lamb or venison shanks
- Salt
- 2 carrots, peeled and cut into large chunks
- 1 white or yellow onion, thickly sliced
- 3 stalks celery, cut unto large chunks
- 5 cloves garlic, peeled
- 3 tablespoons tomato paste
- ½ cup red wine
- 1 teaspoon dried thyme
- 4 bay leaves
- 2 teaspoons dried oregano
- 2 tablespoons cold butter
- 2 tablespoons chopped fresh parsley
- 2 tablespoons chopped fresh dill
- Black pepper to taste

In a large Dutch oven or other heavy, lidded pot, heat the olive oil over medium-high heat. Salt the shanks, then brown them on all sides except the one with the bone; this helps the shanks hold together better. Preheat the oven to 325°F.

When the shanks are nicely browned, remove them to a bowl. Add the carrots, onion, and celery and sauté until slightly browned, about 6 to 8 minutes. Add the garlic cloves and cook another minute, stirring often. If you're cooking lamb shanks, leave the vegetables in. If you're cooking deer or other wild game shanks, remove the vegetables.

Add the tomato paste, wine, thyme, bay leaves, and oregano to the pot. Mix, and once it thickens, add the water and mix. Add the shanks back in now, along with any juice that has accumulated in the bowl. Cover with more water by just a little, bring to a simmer, and add salt to taste. Cover the pot and let this cook in the oven for 90 minutes.

At this point, lamb shanks will be done. Deer shanks will still need some time, but you can add back the vegetables now. Keep cooking until the meat wants to fall off the bone, anywhere from another 30 minutes to another two hours. It's wild game, so you never know.

When the meat is tender, remove it gently to an ovenproof pan, along with all the vegetables. Turn off the oven and set this pan in the oven to keep warm. Set the pot on a strong burner and boil down the braising liquid. This will take roughly 20 to 30 minutes, so now is a good moment to make rice or mashed potatoes.

When the sauce has reduced and thickened a bit, turn off the heat. When it stops bubbling, add the cold butter a tablespoon at a time, swirling until it disappears. Use this as your sauce for the shanks and vegetables. Top it all with the fresh herbs and black pepper.

# TUNISIAN BRAISED SHANKS

**SERVES ▶** 4

**PREP TIME ▶** 10 minutes

**COOK TIME ▶** 3 hours

**ALTERNATIVE CUTS ▶** Shoulder, neck, or ribs

2 to 4 venison shanks
Salt
1 large onion, chopped
¼ cup butter or olive oil
4 cloves garlic, minced
1 teaspoon ground ginger
1 teaspoon ground cumin
1 teaspoon ground cinnamon
½ teaspoon turmeric
½ teaspoon cayenne pepper
Small pinch saffron (optional)
½ pound peeled chestnuts, cut in half (optional)
One 15-ounce can chickpeas, rinsed (optional)
½ cup chopped dates or chopped dried apricots (optional)
1 tablespoon honey
Cilantro or parsley, for garnish

This is a standard North African tagine (a kind of stew) that features all the hallmark spices of this region's cuisine, as well as the quintessential mix of sweet-and-savory that sets Arab cooking apart. Both are relics of the medieval spice trade, which the Arabs controlled until the Renaissance. If you don't have shanks, use neck meat, shoulder, or even roasts cut into chunks.

You'll notice a lot of optional ingredients; these will allow you to tailor the dish to suit your own tastes. You wouldn't see dates and apricots combined in the same tagine in North Africa, so choose one. Similarly, if you're serving this with a big bowl of couscous or rice, you probably don't need the chestnuts and chickpeas, but they'll definitely add some welcome heft if you're serving this with flatbread.

Preheat the oven to 325°F. Salt the shanks and set aside. Set a Dutch oven or other heavy, lidded pot over medium-low heat and slowly soften the onion in the butter, covering the pot and stirring occasionally. This will take about 10 minutes. Add the garlic and cook another 2 minutes. Add all the spices and mix to combine. Add three cups of water and mix. Bring to a simmer.

Add the shanks, cover the pot, and cook in the oven until the shanks are tender, about two hours. If you're using chestnuts, add them after 1½ hours.

Once the shanks are tender, add the chickpeas and any of the dried fruits you're using and mix in the honey. Put back in the oven and cook another 15 minutes. Serve garnished with cilantro alongside couscous, rice, or flatbreads.

# PORTUGUESE-STYLE VENISON SHANKS

These venison shanks are so tender you could eat them with no teeth, and the sauce is so rich you'll want to save the leftovers for pasta. The basic recipe is one I've adapted from my friend David Leite's *New Portuguese Cuisine,* modified to work with venison.

**SERVES** ▸ 4

**PREP TIME** ▸ 15 minutes

**COOK TIME** ▸ 4 hours

**ALTERNATIVE CUTS** ▸ Shoulder, neck, or ribs

- 4 small or 2 large venison shanks
- Salt
- ¼ pound bacon, thickly cut
- 2 yellow onions, grated on a coarse grater
- 1 head garlic, cloves peeled and coarsely chopped
- 2 cups red wine
- 2 cups beef stock or venison stock
- 1 teaspoon black peppercorns
- 1 teaspoon allspice berries
- 1 teaspoon juniper berries
- 8 cloves
- 1 cinnamon stick
- 1 hot dried chile
- 2 bay leaves
- 2 tablespoons molasses

Salt the shanks and set aside. In a Dutch oven or other heavy, lidded pot, cook the bacon slowly until crispy. Remove when it's done and set aside. When the bacon is done, brown the shanks on all sides except the side with the bone; this helps the shank stay together after long cooking. Take your time on this one, and do this over medium-high heat. Set the shanks aside when they're done.

Preheat the oven to 300°F.

Add the onions and turn the heat up to high. You'll notice that the onions will loosen all the browned bits in the pan; scrape the bits up with a wooden spoon. Sprinkle some salt over the onions and sauté, stirring often, until the onions brown, about 5 minutes. Add the garlic and cook another minute.

Chop the bacon while the onions are cooking and add it to the pot with the garlic. Pour in the wine and bring it to a boil. Add the stock, the spices, molasses, and the shanks, bone side up. Add salt to taste. Cover the pot and cook in the oven for at least two hours, and likely three hours. You want the meat to be almost, but not quite, falling off the bone.

When the meat is ready, remove it gently so it doesn't fall apart and tent it with foil. Fish out the bay leaves, cinnamon stick, and as many cloves, peppercorns, allspice, and juniper berries as you can; it's OK if you don't get them all. Puree the sauce in a blender or pass it through a food mill set on a fine setting. It should be thick. If it's not, boil it down until it is. Pour over the shanks and serve at once with mashed root veggies and something green.

# AUSTRIAN BRAISED ELK SHANKS

I cooked this dish with a large shank from a big Ohio whitetail buck that my friend Joe gave me. For whatever reason, his butcher sliced the shank bones—maybe for osso buco—but not all the way through. I like the effect, because it looks cool on the platter, and it opens up the bones to the marrow, which you can easily scoop out and add to the sauerkraut mixture. Trust me, it's delicious. Smaller shanks work fine, too.

If you can't find squash seed oil, which is dark and tastes vaguely of roasted peanuts, use a high-quality sunflower or walnut oil here. You want an oil with some flavor to it, not just a bland cooking oil.

Serve this with good bread, like a German pumpernickel or a Jewish rye. And even though this is a red-meat dish, I like an Austrian white wine here. German beer is another good alternative, such as a weizenbock, or if the weather's a little warmer, the same hefeweizen you used in the pot.

**SERVES ▶** 4

**PREP TIME ▶** At least 1 hour, or up to overnight for the marinade

**COOK TIME ▶** 3 hours, or more for an old deer

**ALTERNATIVE CUTS ▶** Shoulder, neck, or ribs

- 1 elk shank, or 4 deer shanks
- 2 tablespoons squash seed oil or sunflower oil
- 1 tablespoon, plus 1 teaspoon caraway seeds
- 1 teaspoon garlic powder, or 2 teaspoons minced fresh garlic
- Salt
- 4 slices bacon
- 1 medium onion, chopped
- 2 cups sauerkraut, drained
- 1½ cups coarsely shredded potato
- One 12- to 16-ounce bottle of hefeweizen beer
- 1 cup stock (any kind)
- 1 bay leaf
- 1 teaspoon dried thyme
- Black pepper
- Chopped chives, for garnish

Massage the venison shanks with the squash seed oil, then with 1 tablespoon of caraway seeds, garlic, and enough salt to season the meat. Set this on the counter for at least one hour to come to room temperature; however, the seasonings will penetrate better if you leave this covered in the fridge overnight. When you're ready to cook the shank (or shanks, if using deer), preheat the oven to 475°F; if the shanks were refrigerated, let them come to room temperature while the oven heats. Set the shanks on a rack in a roasting pan and blast them in the oven until nicely browned, about 15 minutes. Remove and set aside for now.

While the oven is heating, cook the bacon in a large pot or Dutch oven (it needs to be able to fit the shanks) over medium-low heat until it's crispy. Remove, chop, and set aside.

Add the onion to the pot and sauté in the bacon fat over medium-high heat until it begins to brown on the edges, about 5 minutes. Add the sauerkraut and shredded potato and mix. Sauté this for a minute or two, then pour in the beer and stock. Mix in the reserved bacon, the bay leaf, thyme, 1 teaspoon of caraway seeds, and a healthy pinch of salt. Bring this to a simmer.

When the venison is ready—out of the hot oven—nestle the shanks into the pot, cover, and cook until meltingly tender. You can do this in two ways: on the stovetop over low heat or in a 300°F oven. Either way, it should take about three hours, or a little longer if you are dealing with an old deer.

You can serve this in one of two ways: as a centerpiece, where everyone pulls off pieces of shank at the table, or with the meat stripped from the bones and served on top of a bed of kraut. Don't forget the marrow in the bones! Scoop it out with a spoon and stir it into the kraut for extra flavor. Add black pepper and chives right before you serve.

# BRAISED VENISON SHANKS WITH GARLIC

This is a recipe specifically designed for a small shank, so you'll need something like it to really appreciate the dish. I prefer to use shanks from young animals, such as yearlings or young does. Shanks from the exotic axis, roe, or fallow deer, or muntjac if you're in the United Kingdom, are perfect. If you make this with large, old animals, the flavors won't work as well.

Serve this with mashed potatoes, polenta, or something else to soak up the sauce, which is so good you'll want to save any leftovers. It's great as a pasta sauce the next day.

**SERVES ▶** 4

**PREP TIME ▶** 10 minutes

**COOK TIME ▶** 2 hours

**ALTERNATIVE CUTS ▶** Shoulder, neck, or ribs

4 small venison shanks
3 tablespoons vegetable oil or butter
Salt
4 heads garlic
¾ cup white wine
½ cup chicken or other light stock
1 teaspoon dried thyme
1 tablespoon chopped fresh rosemary, plus more for garnish
Zest of 1 lemon
2 tablespoons unsalted butter

Take the shanks out of the fridge, coat them in a little oil, and salt them. Preheat the oven to 300°F.

Heat the vegetable oil or butter in a Dutch oven (or other ovenproof pan that will fit all the shanks) and brown the shanks on every side but the one with the "shin," where the bone shows clearly; if you brown this part, the shank is more likely to fall apart before you want it to. Remove the shanks as they brown and set aside.

While the shanks are browning, peel the garlic. Think it's hard to peel four heads of garlic? Try this trick: Separate the cloves and put them in a metal bowl. Cover the bowl with another bowl of the same size and shake them vigorously for about 10 seconds. All the cloves will be peeled.

Put the garlic in the pot and brown a little. Pour in the white wine and scrape up any browned bits from the bottom of the pot with a wooden spoon. Bring this to a boil, then add the chicken stock, thyme, rosemary, and lemon zest. Bring to a simmer and add salt to taste. Return the shanks to the pot and arrange "shin"-side up with the garlic all around them. Cover the pot and cook in the oven until the meat wants to fall off the bone, anywhere from 90 minutes to 2½ hours.

Carefully remove the shanks and arrange on a baking sheet or small roasting pan. Turn the oven to 400°F. Remove about twelve of the nicest garlic cloves and set aside.

Puree the sauce in a blender, swirl in the unsalted butter, and pour the sauce into a small pot to keep warm.

Paint the shanks with some of the sauce and put them in the oven. Paint with sauce every 5 minutes for 15 minutes, or until there is a nice glaze on the shanks. To serve, give everyone some mashed potatoes or polenta and a shank. Pour some sauce over everything and garnish with the roasted garlic cloves and rosemary.

# ITALIAN OSSO BUCO

Osso buco is an Italian classic normally done with cross sections of a calf's shank, but it's a perfect use for big shanks from an elk, a moose, or a huge deer. The easiest way to get these cross sections is by cutting them down to the bone with a knife, then sawing them off with a hacksaw. If you have your animal processed at a butcher shop, ask the butcher to cut you cross sections about 3 to 5 inches thick.

One important tip on dealing with large shanks: Use kitchen twine to tie them tightly while cooking—this keeps them together and compact. Mostly, it's for presentation, but if you skip this step, you run the risk of the shanks falling apart in your sauce. Not always a bad thing.

Dried porcini mushrooms are readily available in supermarkets in little plastic packets, but any dried mushrooms will work, especially morels.

Make this dish when you have a little time, as it will always require at least two hours and probably more. The good news is that it reheats beautifully, so you can make it on a weekend and eat it during the week. You'll also have more sauce than you need—use it for pasta or on polenta or grits for a midweek meal.

Risotto Milanese is the normal accompaniment, but you could substitute polenta or eat some good bread with it. A salad of bitter greens is another good addition.

**SERVES ▸** 4

**PREP TIME ▸** 15 minutes

**COOK TIME ▸** 3 hours or so, depending on the animal

¼ cup olive oil, butter, or bear fat

4 cross-cut shanks

Salt

Flour, for dusting

1 onion, chopped

2 carrots, chopped

2 stalks celery, chopped

½ ounce dried porcini mushrooms (about a handful), chopped

1 cup white wine

1 cup stock (chicken, beef, or game)

One 28-ounce can crushed tomatoes

1 teaspoon dried thyme

1 teaspoon dried oregano

Zest of 1 lemon, cut into large strips, white pith removed

2 bay leaves

¼ cup chopped fresh parsley, for garnish

Preheat the oven to 300°F. Heat the olive oil in a Dutch oven or other large pot set over medium-high heat. Salt the shanks and dust them in the flour to coat. Brown them in the pot. Take your time and get a good browning on them, which should take a solid 10 minutes. Remove and set aside.

Add the onion, carrot, celery, and mushrooms and sauté until slightly browned around the edges, about 6 to 8 minutes. Sprinkle some salt on them as they cook.

Pour in the white wine and use a wooden spoon to scrape up any browned bits on the bottom of the pot. When this comes to a boil, add the stock, crushed tomatoes, thyme, oregano, lemon zest, and bay leaves and bring to a simmer. Return the shanks to the pot and turn to coat with the sauce. Cover the pot and move it to the oven. Cook until tender, between two and four hours, depending on the animal.

Serve on top of risotto or polenta or alongside some bread, garnished with the parsley.

# TAIWANESE "BEEF" NOODLE SOUP

**SERVES ▸** 6 to 8

**PREP TIME ▸** 20 minutes

**COOK TIME ▸** 3 hours

**ALTERNATIVE CUTS ▸** Shoulder, neck, or ribs

Using shanks in a soup is another fantastic way to coax the best out of them. All that connective tissue enriches the broth they cook in, making it silky. Normally you would use beef shank (shin) meat for this, but any shank will work. Deer, lamb, elk, antelope, bear, or wild pig would be good choices. That said, you can make this soup with shoulder or neck meat, too.

A word on the noodles: Actual Chinese noodles make a difference. They're paler and chewier than spaghetti, which would be a reasonable substitute. You can obviously find them at Asian markets, but in many cases, you'll see these noodles in the Asian section of regular markets. Ramen noodles are similar and will work, too.

The way to eat this soup all week is to have lots of broth and shanks cooked on, say, a Sunday. Then, when you want to eat some soup, all you need to do is heat the broth and meat, boil some noodles, and top with the vegetables and herbs. And like most braises, Taiwanese noodle soup is indeed better a day or three after it's made.

The pickled mustard greens are easy to find in an Asian market, but sauerkraut will get you close.

- 2 deer shanks, or 3 to 4 pounds of similar shank meat
- 3 tablespoons lard or peanut oil
- 6 to 8 green onions, white and green parts divided
- 6 cloves garlic, peeled and smashed
- A 4-inch long piece of ginger, peeled and sliced thinly
- 4 star anise pods (optional)
- 1 heaping teaspoon Sichuan peppercorns (optional)
- 2 to 6 dried hot chiles, broken and seeded
- 1 cup Shaoxing wine or dry sherry
- 1 cup soy sauce
- ¼ cup Chinese black bean sauce
- 1 tablespoon sorghum syrup or dark honey (optional)
- 4 baby bok choy heads, leaves separated
- 2 pounds Chinese wheat noodles (see headnote)
- ½ cup chopped cilantro
- 1 cup chopped pickled mustard greens (optional)

Submerge the shanks in water in a large soup pot. Bring this to a boil and let it roll for a couple of minutes. Remove the shanks and toss the water. This process removes some of the scum that floats to the surface and will make a cleaner tasting, clearer broth.

While you're waiting for this to happen, chop all your vegetables. Separate the white parts from the green parts of the green onions. Leave the white parts in large pieces, but finely chop the green parts.

Wipe the pot out and heat up the lard or oil over medium-high heat. Sauté the white parts of the green onions, the garlic, and the ginger for about 1 minute. Add the star anise, Sichuan peppercorns, and chiles and stir to combine. Return the shanks to the pot.

Pour in the Shaoxing wine, soy sauce, bean sauce, and sorghum syrup (or honey), then enough water to cover everything by about 1 inch. Bring this to a simmer, cover the pot, and cook gently until the shanks are tender, up to four hours for a very old deer or moose or elk or whatever.

When the shanks are tender, fish them out. While they're cooling, strain the broth. Pull the meat off the bones and cut it into largish chunks. Discard the bones and any weird, vein-y looking things. Wipe the pot again, then pour in the strained broth and add the shank meat to keep warm. Taste it for salt and add some if needed.

Bring a large pot of water to a boil, salt it, then add the bok choy. Boil the bok choy for about 2 minutes, then remove. Add the noodles.

To serve, when the noodles are done, put some in everyone's bowls. Top with broth and meat, then add some bok choy, the green parts of the chopped green onions, cilantro, and pickled mustard greens. Some people like a bit more heat, so if you have Chinese chile sauce handy, have that at the table.

# GRILLED VENISON TACOS

This is an unusual marinade from Mexicali, in the Mexican state of Baja, that includes soy sauce, an ingredient you might not think of as Mexican but that's been used on that country's Pacific coast since the 1500s.

I prefer to make these tacos with the skirt steaks off large animals like elk, bison, nilgai, or moose or with the flank steak from deer or other smaller animals. You can absolutely do this with backstrap or tenderloin, too.

If you're looking for more taco recipes for venison, I have dozens in my book *Borderlands: Recipes and Stories from the Rio Grande to the Pacific.*

**SERVES ▶** 4 to 6

**PREP TIME ▶** 3 hours, to marinate

**COOK TIME ▶** 15 minutes

**ALTERNATIVE CUTS ▶** Backstrap, tenderloin, or hind leg meat free of connective tissue

**FOR THE MARINADE**

½ cup soy sauce
⅓ cup lager beer
Zest and juice of 2 limes
1 teaspoon ground black pepper
1 teaspoon ground cayenne
1 tablespoon garlic powder

**FOR THE VENISON**

1½ pounds skirt or flank steak, membranes removed (see headnote)
1 white onion, minced
⅓ cup lime juice
Salt
12 flour or corn tortillas
3 tablespoons olive oil
Cilantro, for garnish
Salsa, for serving

---

Mix all the marinade ingredients together and submerge the skirt steak in it, making sure every bit is coated with the marinade. Let this sit in the fridge for at least an hour, and up to overnight, although the longer you marinate, the saltier the meat will get. About four hours is a nice amount of time.

Mix the chopped onion with the lime juice and a pinch of salt. Let this sit at room temperature while you marinate the meat.

When you're ready to grill, get your fire very hot. High heat is vital. Because the meat is so thin, it cooks fast. You want some char, and to give yourself enough time to get it, high heat and cold meat are the keys.

While this is happening, heat up your tortillas on a comal or heavy skillet. Keep them warm in a tortilla warmer or wrapped in kitchen towels.

Remove the steak from the marinade and pat the meat dry with paper towels. Make sure it's dry. Rub oil all over the meat.

Sear the skirt steak on the grill for only about 2 minutes per side, tops. Let it rest for a few minutes before slicing. My trick is to cut the skirt steak across the grain first, then keep chopping until you have little bite-size pieces. Doing this ensures that you'll have tender meat. Serve the skirt steak with cilantro and the quick pickled onions, plus some salsa.

---

**NOTES:** You can make these on a flat-top or large pan. Just be sure to turn your stove fan on high! And don't overload these tacos. Just a few toppings and one salsa is all. This one should be simple.

# VENISON BULGOGI

**SERVES ▸** 4 to 6

**PREP TIME ▸** 24 hours, to marinate

**COOK TIME ▸** 15 minutes

**ALTERNATIVE CUTS ▸** Backstrap, tenderloin, or hind leg meat free of connective tissue

This is a family favorite, an Americanized version of the Korean barbecue classic that is perfect for any sort of flank or skirt steak. The key here is to marinate the meat a long time, up to two days if you have the patience, to get the flavors well-established on the meat. You also want to grill the venison over a very hot fire right from the fridge. Flank is so thin that grilling it cold helps protect the center of the meat from overcooking while you're getting those nice grill marks on the outside.

If you prefer to serve this with the something other than rice, which is traditional, it's good sliced thin on a hoagie roll instead. Either way, you'll want some kimchi or Asian slaw to go with it.

4 green onions, minced
2 tablespoons grated ginger
4 cloves garlic, mashed and chopped
2 tablespoons toasted sesame seeds
2 tablespoons sesame oil
3 tablespoons sugar
2 to 6 hot chiles, minced (Thai, cayenne, serrano, etc.)
1 tablespoon molasses or Asian plum sauce
¼ cup mirin, rice wine, or lemon juice
⅓ cup soy sauce
1 large venison flank steak, or 2 smaller ones

Mix all the ingredients except the venison in a bowl, or go the extra step and buzz them in a blender. Pour into a heavy-duty, sealable plastic bag and add the venison. Seal the bag, put it into a bowl or other container (in case it leaks), and set it in the refrigerator for at least one hour, and up to two days.

When you're ready to cook, remove the venison from the marinade and wipe it dry with a paper towel. Coat the meat with a little more sesame oil or vegetable oil. Bring the marinade to a boil in a small pot and skim any froth that forms. Turn off the heat and use this to baste the venison.

Grill over a very hot fire (charcoal, if possible) with the grill cover open until the meat is medium-rare, about 3 to 5 minutes per side, depending on how thick it is. Baste the venison as it cooks. Do not let it overcook—better for the meat to be a little too rare than too well-done.

Let the venison rest for 5 minutes, then slice very thin against the grain. Serve with white rice and Asian-style slaw.

"The deer are messengers of the gods."

— NARA SHINTO TRADITION

# SMOKED RIBS WITH BOURBON BBQ SAUCE

Yes, you can barbecue deer ribs. The trick is to braise first, then get a good smoke on them. Without this two-step process, the ribs would get a nice smoke ring but would be inedibly tough. Once they're tender, however, you can smoke ribs for a few hours, basting them to keep the meat moist until you want to serve.

What you baste your venison ribs with is your choice. Any mop of vinegar and sugar works, as does any store-bought sauce. I like a bourbon-based barbecue sauce with venison, making these close to Kansas City–style. If you want a Memphis-style rib, press your favorite dry rub onto the meat after it's been braised, then smoke.

I prefer deer ribs here. If you use elk or moose ribs, they will be far larger, and you won't have racks so much as individual ribs, like beef. But this works fine, too.

**SERVES ▸** 4

**PREP TIME ▸** 3 hours to parcook the ribs

**COOK TIME ▸** 2 hours in the smoker, plus optional 10 minutes on the grill

**ALTERNATIVE CUTS ▸** Shoulder, neck, shanks

**FOR THE BRAISE**

4 to 6 pounds of venison ribs

5 cloves garlic, peeled and smashed

1 onion, chopped

3 bay leaves

1 teaspoon dried thyme

Salt

Black pepper

1 cup red wine (optional)

**FOR THE BBQ SAUCE**

¼ cup unsalted butter

1 medium yellow or white onion, chopped

1 chopped chile pepper, such as a serrano

½ cup bourbon or Tennessee whiskey

¼ cup ketchup or tomato sauce

½ cup apple cider vinegar

3 tablespoons Worcestershire sauce

¼ cup molasses

2 tablespoons brown sugar

Salt to taste

Put the ribs and all the braise ingredients in a pot, along with enough water to cover the ribs, and bring to a boil. Add salt to taste. Lower the heat and simmer gently until the ribs are tender but not falling apart, usually about 2½ hours or so. Remove and let cool a bit. You can hold the ribs for a day in the fridge this way.

While the venison ribs are braising, heat the butter in a small pot over medium-high heat. Cook the onion and chile until the onions turn translucent, about 4 minutes or so. Take the pan off the heat and pour in the bourbon. Return to the stove, turn up the heat to medium-high again, and boil down the bourbon for 5 minutes.

Add the ketchup, vinegar, Worcestershire sauce, molasses, and sugar. Mix and simmer gently for 10 minutes. Taste it, and add more salt, brown sugar, or chiles to taste. Cook it another 10 minutes, then turn off the heat and let it cool for an hour while the venison cooks. Puree in a blender until smooth. You can make the sauce up to a week beforehand, as it keeps in the fridge.

When you're ready, get your smoker reasonably hot, about 225°F. Lightly coat the ribs with vegetable oil or butter and smoke them for at least an hour, and up to two hours. They're already cooked—you're just adding smoke here. Paint the ribs with the BBQ sauce every 30 minutes, turning the ribs carefully halfway through.

You can finish the ribs on the grill over high heat with the lid open. Grill for a couple of minutes or so per side—the sugar in the sauce will go from caramelized to burnt quickly.

# BEER-BRAISED SHORT RIBS

The beauty of this recipe is its simplicity. Other than the juniper berries, everything is easy to find. Like my Belgian Venison Carbonnade recipe (page 162), the beer matters a lot here. My preferences, in order, would be Scotch ale or a "wee heavy," an unflavored porter or stout, a brown ale, or a Belgian beer that isn't Stella Artois (usually dark, often very malty). Avoid hoppy beers.

Bison ribs will be the best here, but you could use ribs from elk, moose, bear, nilgai, or oryx. If you use elk or moose ribs, trim most of the fat.

If 4 pounds seems like a lot for six people, remember that most of that weight is bone.

You can roast the garlic up to a few days in advance. And once made, these short ribs will keep a week in the fridge.

**SERVES ▸** 6

**PREP TIME ▸** 1 hour

**COOK TIME ▸** 3 hours

**ALTERNATIVE CUTS ▸** Shoulder, neck, shanks

- 2 heads garlic
- Olive oil, for drizzling
- 4 pounds short ribs
- Salt
- 4 cups sliced yellow onions
- 1 tablespoon flour
- One or two 12-ounce bottles of dark, malty beer (see headnote for styles)
- 1 tablespoon juniper berries (optional)
- 1 tablespoon dried marjoram or lovage
- 2 tablespoons Dijon mustard
- A splash of Worcestershire sauce
- Black pepper

Preheat the oven to 350°F. Slice the top third of the heads of garlic off. Set them in a foil packet. Drizzle some olive oil over the cut tops, then close up the packet. Pop into the oven for one hour. If this is the first thing you do, you'll be mostly done chopping and browning things by the time it's ready.

In a large Dutch oven or other heavy, lidded pot, sear the ribs over medium-high heat, starting with the fattiest side down. This renders fat for browning everything else. If you're using elk or moose ribs or your ribs aren't fatty, add oil or fat. Salt the ribs as they cook. Brown on every side except for the side that's just bone and membrane. Take your time and do this in batches if needed. Set the browned ribs aside.

When all the ribs are done, add the sliced onions, some salt, then brown them. You might need to add more fat or oil. This step can take a solid 10-plus minutes.

When this is done, check the garlic to see if it has browned and softened. If not, wait until the garlic is ready before proceeding. Just turn the heat off the pot.

When you're ready to add the garlic, squeeze it into the pot, stir, and add the flour. Cook this over medium heat for a few minutes. Again, this step takes some time because you want the flour to brown. If you use Wondra flour, you'll save a few minutes.

Once the flour has browned, add some beer to the pot and use a wooden spoon to deglaze it. Stir in the remaining ingredients and return the ribs to the pot. If the level of beer isn't up to the top of the ribs, add some water or stock. Cover the pot and put into the oven, which should still be hot from the garlic. Drop the heat to 300°F and simmer for at least two hours, and in some cases as much as four hours. (Five hours is not unheard of, but it's rare.)

When the ribs are tender, gently remove them to plates. Add salt and black pepper to taste, then spoon sauce over them. Serve with mashed potatoes or other root vegetables, bread, or roasted root vegetables.

# ITALIAN SHORT RIBS

**SERVES** ▸ 4, can be scaled up

**PREP TIME** ▸ 30 minutes

**COOK TIME** ▸ 3 hours

**ALTERNATIVE CUTS** ▸ Shoulder, neck, shanks

This is an adaptation of a wonderful recipe in a wonderful book, Paul Bertolli's *Cooking by Hand*, which would be one of my "stuck on a desert island" cookbooks. It will really only work with ribs cut from a large animal —certainly elk and moose but also bison or the exotic red deer, nilgai, and oryx. You might be able to get away with using a great big deer, but it would have to be a lunker.

You'll want the ribs cut somewhere between 4 and 6 inches long and either in a block of ribs or as individual ribs. Trim any excess fat off the cap of the ribs, but leave some fat remaining. (If you're squeamish about venison fat, don't be. Read all about it on page 21.)

The sauce is an agrodolce, a sweet-and-sour sauce highlighted by balsamic vinegar and saba, which is boiled down grape must. Yeah, I know, you don't have any lying around. Only reason I do is because I grow grapes.

Fortunately, you can get close by boiling down purple grape juice by two-thirds and using that.

The celery, carrots, and onions need to be pretty fine, so I mince them in a food processor. Just make sure they don't become a paste.

---

- 3 cups purple grape juice, or 1 cup saba
- 6 ribs, each about 4 to 6 inches long
- Salt
- 4 slices bacon
- ¼ cup olive oil
- 1 large stalk celery, minced
- 2 carrots, minced
- 2 large onions, minced
- A big handful (or 1 standard package) dried mushrooms
- ¼ cup tomato paste
- 2 cups red wine
- ½ cup balsamic vinegar
- 10 fresh sage leaves, or 1 tablespoon dried and ground
- 1 sprig fresh rosemary, or 1 tablespoon dried
- 1 quart broth (venison or beef)
- Black pepper

Boil down the grape juice to 1 cup in a small pot. Set aside. Take out the ribs and salt them. Preheat the oven to 350°F.

In a large, heavy, lidded pot such as a Dutch oven, fry the bacon over medium heat until crispy. Remove, chop, and set aside.

Pat the ribs dry with a paper towel and brown them in the bacon fat, adding olive oil if you need to. When you brown the ribs, do every side except the one with the bone showing—if you brown this side too, the meat will fall off the bones too soon. When the ribs are browned, remove them to a plate.

Add the minced vegetables and cook over medium heat until they're browned, stirring occasionally. This should take about 8 to 10 minutes. Crumble the dried mushrooms over the vegetables, add the tomato paste, and mix. Cook this another 3 or 4 minutes, stirring often. You want the tomato paste to darken.

At this point you'll notice that the bottom of the pot has a brown residue on it; add the red wine and use a wooden spoon to scrape it all off. Boil the red wine down by half, then add the cooked-down grape juice and the balsamic vinegar. Mix and return the ribs to the pot, bone side up. Pour in any juices that have accumulated with the ribs, too. Add the herbs.

Let this cook down a few minutes, then add the venison broth and mix. Cover the pot and put it in the oven to cook for at least 2½ hours. You want the meat to be thinking about falling off the bone but not there yet. This could take as long as four hours with an old elk or moose.

When the meat is ready, gently remove it from the pot and set aside. Now you have a choice: You can use the braising liquid as is, or you can make it smooth. I prefer it smooth. To do this, you can either push it through the medium plate of a food mill, use a "boat motor" stick blender, or pour everything into a blender and buzz it. I prefer the food mill option. Taste the resulting sauce. If it is to your liking, you're good to go. It might be too thin, however, in which case boil it down until it's like a barbecue sauce. Right before you serve the sauce, add some black pepper.

Coat the ribs in the hot sauce and serve with mashed potatoes or another mashed vegetable; I'm big on mashed celery root with this recipe. To drink, you'll want a big red wine like a Barolo or Bordeaux or a big malty beer. A good Belgian beer like Chimay is a good choice.

# The Legend of Spork

The morning broke clear and chilly, and the fog lay thick in California's Coastal Range valleys near King City, a little cow town in Monterey County. Phillip and I stood high above the fog on a hilltop, searching for deer.

Phillip Loughlin, who's been hunting deer for more than four decades, spotted them first: three does, munching sagebrush on a steep hillside. We watched the does closely, hoping their boyfriends would be near.

This arid hillside is the southernmost range of the Columbian blacktail deer. Spot-and-stalk hunting is the rule. No tree stands in the Coastal Range, no scent attractants, grunt calls, antler rattling, or even camouflage. Wear a tan shirt or jacket and some sturdy jeans or Carhartts and you're fine. But you must have a good pair of boots, a better set of binoculars, a rifle that will shoot a long way, and the stamina to climb mountains.

Soon enough, the does' boyfriends showed up—or rather, boyfriend. The buck was obviously the sultan of this particular harem. He was grayer than the young does and the yearling buck who was tagging along with them. Bigger too—about 140 pounds. Coastal Range blacktails don't grow terribly large. Nor do Coastal Range blacktails grow gigantic antlers. This one was only a 2 by 3: a fork on one side, three points on the other. Not a shooter if you were some big-time TV hunter but a decent young buck for this part of the world.

Maybe too good. The owner of this particular ranch had let me hunt blacktail deer in return for catering a big dove shoot he held on Labor Day. But I couldn't shoot just any legal deer. It seems the previous owner of the ranch had shot too many deer on it, leaving a motley assortment of bucks in charge of the place. One was a gigantic forked horn I had originally been charged with assassinating, but that plan got changed at the last minute. Phillip and I were looking for a decent buck but one that would probably not become grand enough for a high-dollar hunt down the road.

Phillip kept glassing the Sultan. "I can shoot him now, if you want," I said. I had the buck steady in my crosshairs at a little more than 250 yards. He was just grazing. Broadside shot. "I don't know," Phillip said. "He's branching," meaning the buck was developing that classic set of antlers most hunters desire. So we let him go and went looking for one of the Motley Crew. But none of its members showed themselves, and we drove back toward the ranch house—only to see the Sultan and his harem not forty yards above us on the hillside, still grazing. There's so little hunting pressure for blacktails on this ranch, they didn't care about the vehicle. This was an all-time gimme shot. Phillip hesitated; this was too good. But we held off. It was the first morning, and we wanted to find an older, weirder buck to cull.

It was at lunch when Sam, one of the ranch's resident hunting guides, told us about this crazy old deer in the front of the property: It had a gnarly spike on one side of his head and a fork on the other. A genetic oddity, as this was apparently a mature, dominant buck in the area. Phillip named him Spork, as in spike-and-fork.

Immediately, we knew we had to kill Spork. Big deer, weird antlers, hard to find. Sam had not seen the deer since it was in velvet this past spring.

That evening, we went up Bulldozer Canyon, where Spork had last been seen. It's a classic Coastal Range canyon, steep and slippery. Everything here was once the bottom of the ocean, and the white, talc-like limestone is studded with fossilized seashells. The rock itself is weak, and it disintegrates into a slippery gravel that is extraordinarily difficult to climb on.

But climb we did, all the way to the top of the ridge into the pines. My heart was pounding like a jackhammer as we trudged up, reminding me that I'm not in in the kind of shape I used to be. We picked along the ridge looking for a good spot to sit down and wait, a place where we could see the whole canyon and yet not be seen. We found a perfect spot in between an old oak and a pine tree.

As soon as we settled down, we saw the signs all around us. This was Spork's lair.

Deer scat was everywhere, including a pile still black and shiny. It was cold and hard, though, which was good. It meant Spork had left, probably in the morning. How did we know it wasn't a doe hangout? Nearly every tree in the vicinity had been rubbed with his antlers, a sign of territoriality.

So we sat and waited. A herd of wild pigs wandered through, making lots of noise. Pigs are far more similar to humans than to deer; they'll march through the wilds as if they own the place. Marching pigs sound very different from the soft touch of a deer walking, which sounds like falling leaves if you're not listening very carefully.

Waiting there, the world closed in around us. The ripples we made walking into the place receded, and we began to absorb it all. My eyes are only so-so, but my hearing is better than most. Phillip is an expert spotter of game. In this heightened state, we hoped we wouldn't be fooled by any movement. The sun began to fall behind the opposite ridge. "Won't be long now," Phillip said.

He was right. Out stepped a nice blacktail doe. She began eating leaves off a bush, as calm as can be. Then Spork appeared. Phillip stared at the buck through his binoculars. "That's him! That's Spork!" I got ready to shoot, my heart fluttering again. I immediately realized that the syndrome known as buck fever is real. I've shot many does before, but I had only shot one other buck—and that was an antelope. At this stage in my hunting career, I had never shot a buck deer before, and I had to will myself to not look at the antlers.

I got my .270 ready, looked through the crosshairs, and saw him . . . sitting down, with his ass facing us, at absolutely the worst angle possible. As if he knew, the bastard. The only remotely achievable shot would be to his neck, but I've shot deer in the neck before and it can be iffy.

"Relax, he'll get up and follow his lady friend soon enough," Phillip said. So we waited. And waited. And waited. The doe got more than a hundred yards away from Spork, but he still just sat there. Light was fading fast. He wasn't going to stand up before shooting light ended. Shit.

"OK, ready now," Phillip said. I readied. He called out his best impression of a bleating doe. "Beeap!" Spork looked at us but didn't move. Phillip did it again. This time Spork didn't even bother looking in our direction. Light was almost gone. Phillip stood up. Spork looked but stayed in his semi-recumbent position.

Finally, Phillip started waving his arms around and twirling his hat in the air. At last, Spork took an interest. But in a bad way. I had him in my crosshairs at one instant, but in another he had leapt up the hillside and trotted away. No shot. At the same moment, I was thinking that if Spork were a mule deer, he'd stop and look back at us. He did. Broadside.

Time slowed. In less than a second, I got Spork back in my crosshairs, put them on his heart, felt my own heart pound, pulled the trigger—and realized I could see brush between Spork and my scope. CRACK! It was done, a copper bullet was in the air, and I knew before it hit him that I had done Spork a grave injustice.

He jumped and dashed over the edge of the ridge and into a thicket of pin oaks, juniper, and thornbushes.

"I don't feel good about that shot," I said.

We rushed over to where I thought I hit Spork, looking for blood. Its color would help us figure out exactly where I'd hit him. Lurid red blood is a heart shot. That same color with little flecks of foam is a lung shot. Liver blood is darker, as is muscle blood. I looked around the zone while Phillip followed Spork's tracks.

No blood. Not a drop. Anywhere. We couldn't hear Spork in the brush. Light was fading. "Go down that hillside and see if you see him laid up under a bush or something," Phillip said. "And keep your rifle ready in case he pops out in front of you. I'll swing around and meet you at the bottom of the ridge."

Down I went. Fell is more like it. The hillside was so steep it was all I could do not to fall ass over tea kettle on the slippery gravel. I tried as best I could to stay semiquiet, but I definitely made a racket. About twenty yards down, my stomach began churning: This is very thick brush. It's dark. We're not going to find this deer. Oh my God.

I passed a spot that looked like Spork had run into, and I crept into the bush. I squatted, stock still, and listened. Nothing. I remembered that spot and continued down the hill, hoping to see Phillip at the bottom.

What I saw was a fence. I was in a corner of a fence, with nothing but more rocky gravel in front of me for a quarter mile. Now it was truly dark. I shouldered my rifle and realized that I needed to get out of here before I got lost. But after another heart-hammering climb up the gravel, I realized the distressing truth. I was lost. Phillip was nowhere. There was no way I was going back up that Hill of Death, but I figured I could find the road and walk back from there.

The trail turned, and I found myself in a place I didn't recognize. The stars were the only light. It was at that moment that it struck me that I could be spending the night here. Wandering around in the pitch dark is a terrible idea, especially in a place where you can turn your ankle easily. I did have my day pack with me, which had water and several of the fig cakes I bring with me on trips like this. But no flashlight. Stupid.

After a few minutes, however, the panic response ended, and I realized that I knew where I could find the road, even if I needed to bushwhack my way to it. So I turned around and eventually found my way back. I can honestly say I was scared, for at least a little while. But as Phillip said later, every true deer hunter has gotten lost, if only for a short time like I'd done. It's a rite of passage.

That night, we replayed the shot over and over, and the total lack of blood made us wonder if I'd even hit Spork at all. Phillip said he'd looked hit, but he'd never seen a hit deer not drop any blood. Was it the copper ammo? Was it the brush I'd hit, which deflected the bullet? Either way, we needed to go back to that spot and search in the morning.

When we reached the ridge in the morning, it was confirmed: no blood. We began to think we'd see Spork looking at us on the ridge. For two hours, we blanketed that area, looking for sign. As the sun began to warm, we finally headed up the Hill of Death. This hill is so steep and so slippery, we had to grab onto the fence with one hand—avoiding the strands of barbed wire—and haul ourselves upward.

At last we came to the spot I'd thought Spork had gone down. Phillip picked up his tracks and crept into the bush. For twenty minutes, he followed sign, moving slowly, looking for blood. "I think Spork is off running around somewhere," Phillip said. "Meet me at the top of the hill."

I had not gone ten steps when he called out. "Wait! I found him."

Spork was dead. And my first reaction had been right. I shot him in the gut, and he had bled to death internally overnight. It would have been a grim death, and I began to feel nauseous again about how it all had happened. But competing with that emotion was the elation that we had indeed found him. Bad shot or no, we had closure. We had done our job and had not just left him in the bush and gone off to shoot another deer, perhaps the Sultan.

Now we had to haul Spork, which Phillip estimated at four years old and about 140 pounds, up the Hill of Death. It almost killed me, but I suppose I deserve even harsher penance for doing Spork the injustice of a slow death.

When we cut him open, much of the meat was tainted. My heart sank even lower. Spork had lain on his left side when he died, so all that meat was ruined. Writing this now, it sounds more tragic than it felt at the time. At that moment, I was still just happy we'd found him and been able to save half the meat. I'm still confronted by such a mix of emotions about this hunt that they've all crashed into themselves, leaving a dull uncertainty.

I'm no longer a virgin buck hunter. Thanks to Phillip, I learned so much on this hunt, and I finally understand why buck hunters feel such a strong urge to head into the woods every year. Bucks are far harder to kill than does, and to hunt a particular buck is tougher still. There is definitely an element of a duel that develops, and it's not just a testosterone-soaked, manly-man thing. On my way home, I stopped at a convenience store for some water. I moved Spork's head (I intended to save the skull) from the bed of my pickup to the back seat, not wanting to force everyone who passes by to see a dead deer.

A young woman of about twenty saw me do it. "Hey," she called out. "Is that a deer head?"

Oh no. "Uh, yeah. It is."

"Can I see it?"

Huh? "You bet. It's a weird deer. Old, with only a fork and a spike on it."

She admired it. "That buck's got a lot of character. I've been chasing a 4x4 on our property for five years. He always slips me. But I'm hoping to get him this year."

I smiled. She smiled. I said, "Go get him! And good luck to you."

"Thanks! Can't wait to get out there this weekend!"

As I drove off, I understood.

# THE WOBBLY BITS

Heart, liver, kidneys. Tongue, heads, brains, even tripe and the euphemistically named "lights," which are lungs. Collectively, all this is known as the "fifth quarter" of an animal—those parts the English have named "the wobbly bits" and that you'll see in markets labeled less euphonically as "variety meats." I'm talking about offal, the inner parts and extremities of animals in general and big game animals specifically, a collection of meats that, for the most part, I love dearly.

Why, when I have access to backstraps galore, lovely roasts, and the holy tenderloin, do I enjoy these so much? Because making these cuts taste wonderful is a true act of cooking. It's the culinary equivalent of alchemy. Sometimes it's as simple as properly cooked liver smothered in onions and studded with chopped crispy bacon. Sometimes it's long-simmered tongue or fire-grilled slices of heart. Rarely do you need any technical skill to make the wobbly bits taste nice. But you do need some information first. Walk with me as I show you how.

I used to think that no one else but me loved the "fifth quarter" on a deer. Having no preconceived notions about what is and isn't good to eat on a deer, I worked my way through the liver, heart, kidneys, tongue, and even marrow bones as though I were a kid opening up presents on Christmas morning. Each offered something new and exciting, a new texture, a new flavor, a new challenge in the kitchen.

Then I began reading other venison cookbooks and talking to other deer hunters, and I soon learned that eating venison offal wasn't as universal as I'd thought. For a time, I really did think I was something of an anomaly in the hunting world.

But after my first book was published in 2011 and I began to drive across the country, talking to folks all the way, I was overjoyed to learn that, far from being loathed, many of these bits and bobbles within what's unceremoniously called "the gutpile" are treasured symbols of a successful hunt: liver and onions on the evening of the hunt, heart pot roast at deer camp, grilled heart on toast for breakfast. The reason I'd not heard so much about eating venison offal was because it's most often eaten simply, and soon after the deer has hit the ground.

To honor that, I do have a few dead-simple recipes in this chapter for deer camp, and I'd be remiss to not include my version of liver and onions (Deer Camp Liver and Onions, page 259). But the reason I was so jazzed about eating venison offal remains as strong today as it was when I shot my first deer almost three decades ago: Hearts, livers, kidneys, and the like all offer something different from the ocean of red meat on the rest of the animal. Cooking them often requires patience, and sometimes, it requires legitimate cooking skill. But when it comes together, I feel I've created something grand from something that many consider inedible.

What follows are my favorite recipes for the wobbly bits from deer, antelope, elk, moose, and the like. Virtually all of them work with any of these animals, although I vastly prefer the dainty little kidneys on deer to the monstrous kidneys on moose and elk, although they're both perfectly edible. Conversely, extracting marrow from the femur of deer is fiddly, but it's child's play with elk and moose. And should you get your hands on bison? Heaven.

But before we get to the recipes, you'll need to know a few tips and techniques to get the most out of your wobbly bits.

## What, Exactly, Are We Talking About?

When I refer to offal (and all its euphemisms), I'm specifically talking about heart, liver, kidneys, tongue, marrow, caul fat (the lacy membranous skein of fat that encircles all the lower organs), stomach (tripe), and head/cheeks.

The fascinating thing about these bits is that they're all edible, and all have historic recipes associated with them, if not for venison per se then for their kitchen cousins, the sheep and the cow. In England, the whole lot is known as umbles, and if this has a familiar ring to it, that's because "to eat humble pie" refers to a real pie made from the innards of deer; the rest of the animal was reserved for the lords. As it happens, umble pie can be very, very good; its echo today is British steak and kidney pie.

I have recipes in this book for all of these parts except the brains. I'm not a fan of brains, and with chronic wasting disease so prevalent in many parts of the country, eating deer brains may be dangerous.

## Are These Parts Safe?

In a word, yes—with a few caveats. Deer aren't normally heavily parasitized, but it can happen. Livers are one location for potential wee beasties, so look over the liver before saving it. If it has weird striations, whitish flecks, or wormy looking things in it, toss the liver. Most liver parasites are visible.

If you feel like working with the stomachs of deer to make haggis or tripe, understand that ruminants use bacteria to help them digest. Most of these bacteria are not harmful (although many are stinky), but still, you don't want to mess around if you're making tripe. I use a diluted solution of hydrogen peroxide to cleanse my deer tripe (see page 43).

Of most concern in terms of food safety is the issue of chronic wasting disease. There's a full examination of CWD as it pertains to cooking venison on page 25, but for this chapter, our particular focus is the marrow and head of the animal. If you live in an area with CWD, don't eat these parts. While there's no evidence linking CWD to humans, if it were to jump species—which can happen with this sort of ailment—it would most likely be from people eating brains, spinal tissue, or marrow. Fortunately, CWD doesn't exist in most of the West, nor does it exist among pronghorn, bison, nilgai, oryx, or caribou.

## In the Field

In the field, you need to be ready to collect your wobbly bits before you put an animal on the ground. Offal is very perishable, and it tends to get dirtier than the rest of the meat. Be prepared, and you'll be better off. I always bring a few items in my pack for this job:

- **SEVERAL SEALABLE PLASTIC BAGS.** I keep each bit in a separate bag.
- **PAPER TOWELS.** Wiping off excess blood is important. It can give the organ an off taste if left on too long. I also like to rest the innards on paper towels on the grass to cool off before I put them into bags.
- **WATER.** In addition to carrying water for drinking, it's important in the field to have water to rinse off the bloody innards. I'd avoid rinsing in a stream because of the possibility of the meat picking up giardia or other waterborne disease. Many organs are best served lightly cooked, and you want to be careful. Snow is fine to use, too.
- **A COOLER WITH ICE (IF IT'S ABOVE FREEZING OUT).** I keep this in the truck, but it's important to chill down the innards as fast as possible. They need to get cold faster than the rest of the animal.

## At Home

When you get home, you need to do some prep work before you can store your various bits. Rinse everything under cold water, and carefully pick off anything that might have attached itself to the organs; caul fat especially seems to pick up debris. For hearts, try to wash out any blood clots in the arteries before you vacuum-seal them.

Once they're all rinsed, you can vacuum-seal tongues and hearts straight away.

For the liver, trim off any membranes and connective tissue and discard, then slice the liver into portions you might eat at one sitting before sealing and freezing. See below for my method to make this often unpleasantly strong meat milder and more accessible.

Kidneys come encased in hard fat. I rarely eat this fat, as it's very waxy in deer. But it can be rendered to use as waterproofing if you want (see page 23). Keep the kidneys whole until you process them (see below).

All the best marrow is in the femur on the hind legs. If you have access to a bandsaw, you can cut the bones canoe-style (lengthwise), which exposes a lot of marrow and is easier to cook. If you don't have one, use a hacksaw to cut off both ends of the femur to leave the shaft. Cut into three- or four-inch cylinders. For regular deer, which are too small to do the marrow bone cylinders, saw off the ends of the femur and use a chopstick or dowel to push out the marrow. Soak the marrow in the same weak brine as you would soak the liver for twenty-four hours in the fridge; this draws out blood. Use this marrow for the German Marrow Dumplings (page 278). If you're not serving it straight away, seal and freeze.

If you've saved the caul fat, rinse, gently fold it into smallish squares, and vacuum-seal it.

Heads don't store well, so if you're going to use one, my advice is to use it fresh. You could make either a traditional head cheese with it or make the Scottish Powsowdie recipe on page 260.

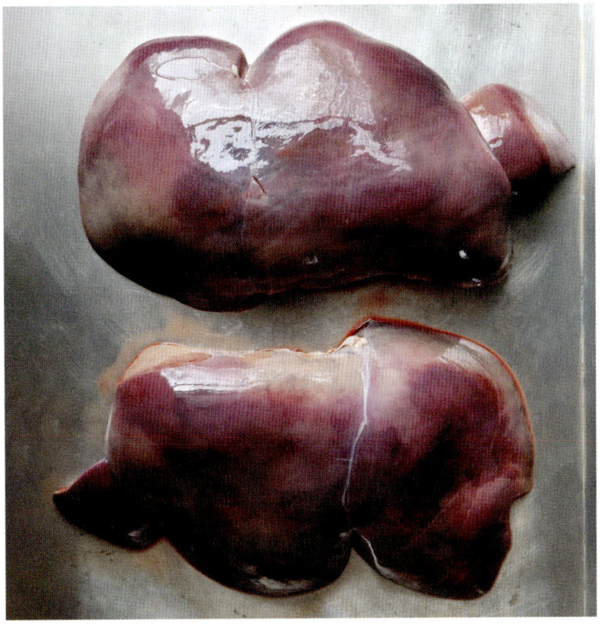

## Prepping Hearts

The easiest way to prep a deer heart is to slice off the top, which consists mostly of veins and arteries, hollow it out, stuff something nice inside, and bake. But to me, that's not a very good way to eat a heart. Better to unroll it like a scroll and cook it that way.

To do this, start by trimming off any visible fat on the outside of the heart. Look at the top of the heart. See all the gaps and holes? Use them as a guide to slice the heart into several thick cutlets. You'll get one nice cutlet, then two slightly thicker ones.

Carefully cut away all the vein-y bits from the inside of the heart; they look like cobwebs sticking to its inner walls. You should have two to four nice, clean hunks of meat. If you're dealing with an elk or moose heart, note that they'll be quite large—close to four pounds in moose.

From here you can pound the heart flat to make Jägerschnitzel (page 132) or Grilled Heart with Peppers (page 254), or you can cut it into chunks for Peruvian Anticuchos de Corazón (page 257).

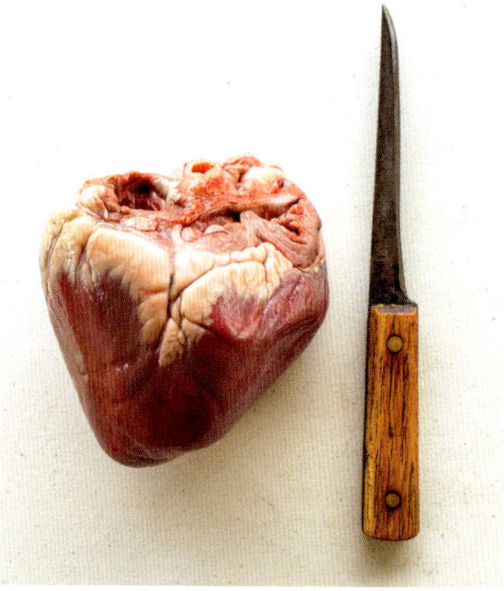
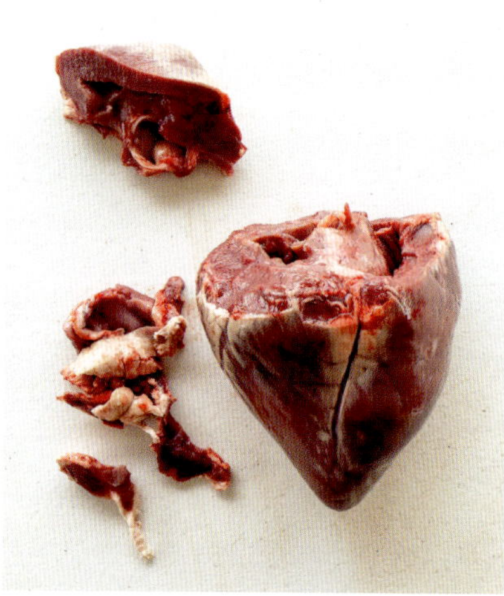
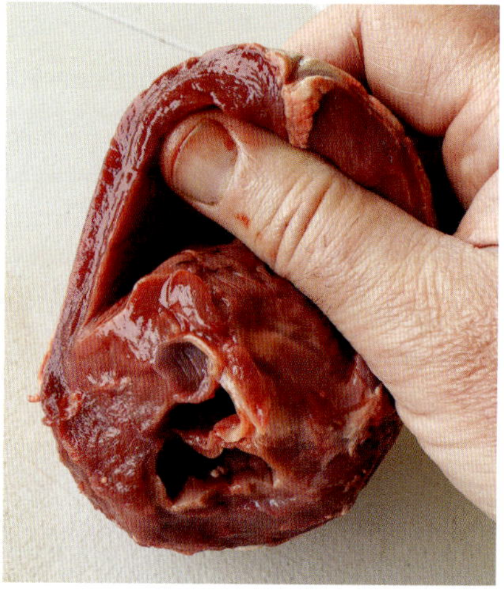
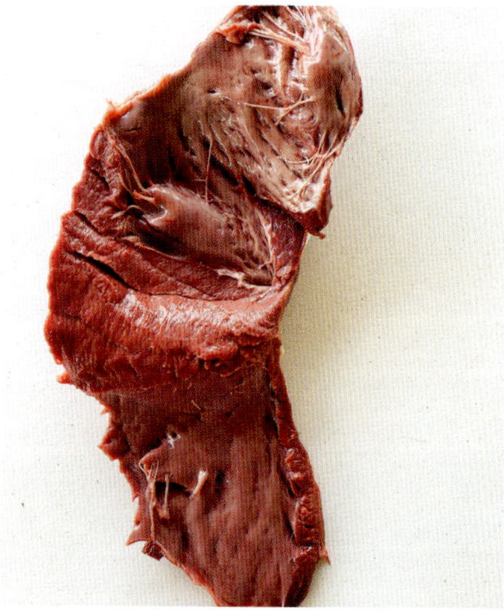

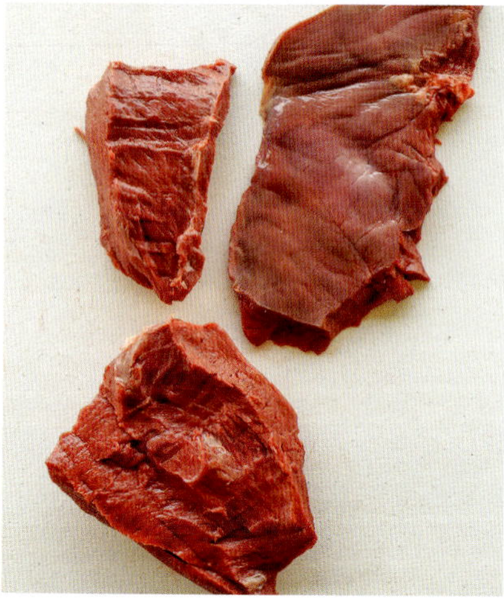

## Liver and Kidney Soak

Many people recoil at livers and kidneys because, well, they stink. But there's an easy way to prep these organs so they'll be almost as mild as calf's liver. Start by dissolving ¼ cup of kosher salt in 1 quart of water. Soak prepped livers or kidneys in the fridge overnight in this.

After the brining, rinse off the organs and soak in milk (I normally use 2 percent milk, but I don't think it matters) for up to two days in the refrigerator. This also seems to pull out blood, and the resulting liver or kidneys, which I rinse once more before cooking further, are *much, much* milder in flavor.

Of course, if you like your liver and kidney straight up, you do you.

## Prepping Kidneys

Kidneys can be cooked whole, but most people like them better cleaned and sliced in half or chunked.

The first thing you need to do is pinch the gossamer membrane on the outside of the kidney and slip it off. It's so thin you might not think it's there, but it's so strong that when it contracts on hitting the heat, it will disfigure your kidney. Er, not *your* kidney, the deer's.

Now slice the kidney lengthwise, to preserve its shape. You'll see a lot of white stuff in the center. I like to snip this out with kitchen shears as best I can. You can slice it out with a knife, but kidneys are slippery things, and shears seem to work better.

Soak your kidneys as above.

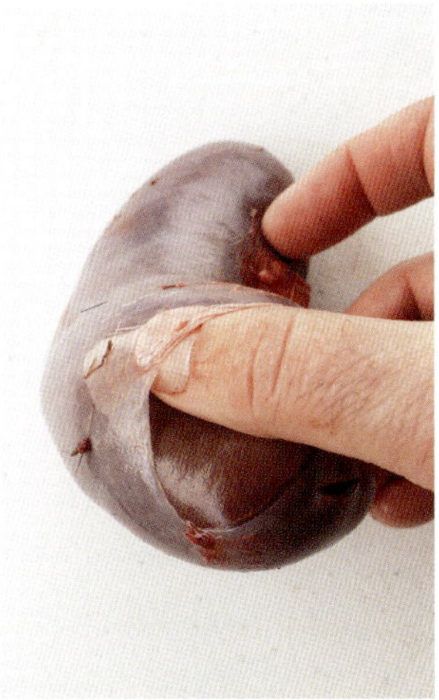

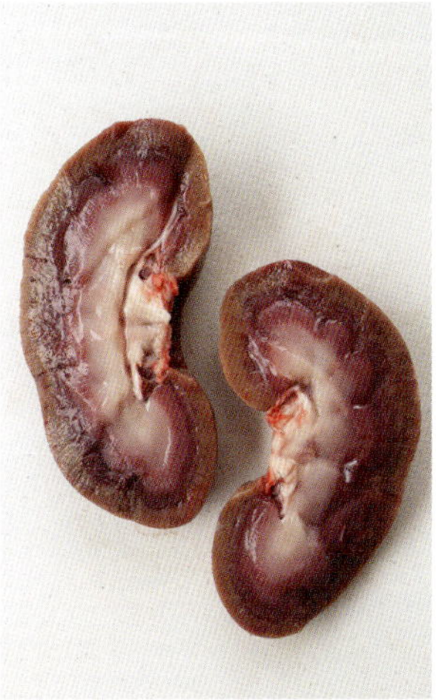

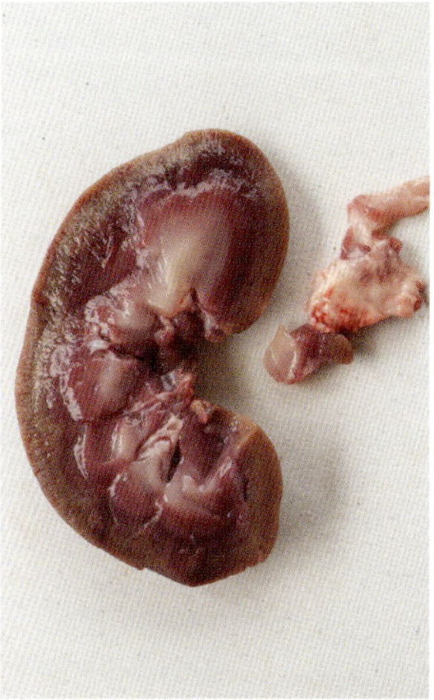

# GRILLED HEART WITH PEPPERS

**SERVES ▸** 2 to 6, depending on the heart

**PREP TIME ▸** 30 minutes, plus up to a day for marinating

**COOK TIME ▸** 15 minutes

**ALTERNATIVE CUTS ▸** Backstrap, tenderloin, or hind leg meat free of connective tissue

As much as I love a classic jägerschnitzel done with a deer heart, this is my hands-down favorite way to cook hearts. Marinated and then grilled over very high heat long enough for the center to warm, then sliced thin with some grilled peppers and onions—man oh man, you've got to try it.

With a typical deer heart from a whitetail deer, a blacktail, or a muley, one heart will feed two people. Maybe. A big deer will definitely feed two, an antelope only one. An elk heart or a moose heart will feed up to six.

My final piece of advice: Undercook the hearts a little. For whatever reason, hearts tend to go from pretty pink to icky gray faster than other cuts.

And an overcooked heart is a sad thing. Best to undercook a bit, then let the meat rest for a good 10 minutes.

If all goes well, you'll be rewarded. Grilled hearts have a smoky, charred flavor on the outside, a tang from your marinade, and a dense, firm texture somewhere between ribeye and flank steak. Slice thin and enjoy. Oh, and if you're serving people who might get all squinchy about eating deer heart, don't tell them until after they've demolished their plate.

A tip on the peppers and onions: Cut them into large pieces so they don't fall through your grill grates. For the onions, make sure you keep the stem end attached, which keeps them together on the grill. And cook the skin side of the peppers first—if you get any parts that blacken, the skin peels right off. You want significant blackening here, so keep your grill ragingly hot.

**1 or 2 deer hearts, or 1 elk or moose heart**

**4 tablespoons olive oil, divided**

**1 tablespoon sherry or red wine vinegar**

**1 tablespoon Worcestershire sauce**

**1 teaspoon salt**

**1 teaspoon dried oregano**

**1 teaspoon dried thyme**

**1 teaspoon black pepper**

**3 or 4 colored bell peppers, cut into 2 to 3 pieces each**

**1 large onion, cut into large wedges**

---

Trim the hearts as discussed above. In a large bowl, mix 2 tablespoons of olive oil with the vinegar, Worcestershire sauce, salt, oregano, thyme, and black pepper. Massage the marinade into the meat, put everything into a container that can just about hold everything, and marinate for as little as 30 minutes, or as much as two days.

When you're ready to cook, get your grill hot. Coat the peppers and onion in the rest of the olive oil and salt. Put the veggies on the grill—skin side down for the peppers—and leave them alone with the grill cover open for 8 minutes. Flip everything and put the hearts on the grill. Cook, uncovered, for 5 more minutes. Remove the vegetables and put them in some foil to steam.

Turn the pieces of heart. Keep an eye on them, as small hearts might only need 2 or 3 more minutes, and very large ones might need a few more. If you're using a thermometer, you want to get the meat off the grill when it is 130°F in the center. You can also use the finger test for doneness (page 113).

Tent the hearts loosely with foil and let rest for 5 minutes. Sprinkle with black pepper and good sea salt and slice thin. Serve with the vegetables and some crusty bread.

# PERUVIAN ANTICUCHOS DE CORAZÓN

This is an ancient dish, dating back before European contact with the Inca in the early 1500s. Originally done with llama or whitetail deer (yes, there are whitetails in the Andes), anticuchos are basically marinated kebabs done with heart.

The main ingredient of the marinade is a Peruvian chile paste called *ají panca*. You can find it in good Latin markets or online. But my recipe uses Mexican chipotles, which are way easier to find. Bottom line is you want a thick puree of mildly hot chiles—don't blow your head off with heat here. You can get close with some chipotles in adobo buzzed in a blender with a few preserved red bell peppers.

Normally, anticuchos are a snack or appetizer, not a main meal. But if you have lots of deer hearts, go for it. And yes, you can make these with other parts of the deer.

You should always cook these skewers over charcoal or other open flame, and they are traditionally served with potatoes (also native to the Andes), corn, and hot sauce.

A word on prepping the heart. After cutting it into pieces as described on page 252, you'll want to tenderize it. Mostly I do this with a Jaccard meat tenderizer, which is a nifty handheld device with a handle and lots of sharp, pointy blades. You put the meat on the cutting board and bounce the Jaccard all over the meat, making hundreds of little cuts in it. Works with any tough piece of meat, hearts especially. A Jaccard is cheap too, costing about $20 in any good supermarket or online.

Your other option is to score the heart meat with many thinly spaced, crosshatched cuts from a knife. I don't love this method for anticuchos, but it will work in a pinch. You can also pound the heart into flat cutlets and thread them on the skewers.

**SERVES ▸** 4, as a snack or appetizer

**PREP TIME ▸** 1 hour or longer, to marinate

**COOK TIME ▸** 10 minutes

**ALTERNATIVE CUTS ▸** Backstrap, tenderloin, or hind leg meat free of connective tissue

- 3 roasted red peppers, chopped
- 1 to 4 chipotles in adobo, depending on how hot you want things to be
- 1 tablespoon minced garlic
- ¼ cup red wine vinegar
- 1 tablespoon dried oregano
- ½ cup vegetable oil
- Salt
- 1 teaspoon ground cumin
- 2 to 4 venison hearts, trimmed and cut into 3-inch pieces
- Skewers

Mix all the marinade ingredients together and buzz them into a puree in a food processor or blender. Submerge the heart pieces in the marinade for at least one hour, and up to a day.

Thread the heart pieces on the skewers—this helps you flip them more easily and helps them cook more evenly. Grill over very high heat with the grill cover open until you get a nice char on the outside, about 3 minutes per side. Baste with the marinade as the skewers cook.

# SICHUAN SPICY HEART STIR-FRY

**SERVES ▸** 4

**PREP TIME ▸** 20 minutes

**COOK TIME ▸** 15 minutes

**ALTERNATIVE CUTS ▸** Backstrap, tenderloin, or hind leg meat free of connective tissue

### FOR THE SAUCE

2 teaspoons sugar

2 tablespoons Shaoxing wine or dry sherry

1 tablespoon Chinese black vinegar or malt vinegar

1 tablespoon soy sauce

¼ cup beef broth

2 teaspoons cornstarch

2 teaspoons sesame oil

### FOR THE HEART

1 pound venison heart

2 tablespoons chile bean paste

2 teaspoons minced fresh ginger

2 cloves garlic, sliced thin

4 green onions, sliced into thin discs

4 or 5 small hot chiles, sliced

One 8-ounce can bamboo shoots, sliced into matchsticks

Heart meat works with Chinese stir-fries because it's dense enough to slice into uniform, small pieces and it cooks up quickly. In this case, you're shredding the meat after trimming and tenderizing the heart. Any heart will work here, as will any good piece of venison, so long as it's free of fat and connective tissue.

Most of the ingredients here are easy to find. The bamboo shoots and chile bean paste will be in the Asian or "ethnic" section of your supermarket; I've found them even in many small-town markets.

One word of caution: Don't double this recipe. Stir-fries need really high heat to work, and you kill that if you overload the pan. If you want to make a double batch, set out the ingredients for both batches and do them one after another. That's how they do it in Chinese restaurants.

Start by prepping the heart. Slice off any fat and any vein-y looking bits of the heart first. Slice off large pieces using the chambers of the heart as a guide. Trim any connective tissue; there's often weblike tissue on the interior of the chambers. Now you're left with pure meat. You'll likely have more than the pound you need. Use this for another dish, or make a second batch of this one.

Slice the big pieces crosswise into thin slices—this is pretty easy to do because heart meat is so dense—then tenderize them. Put the heart slabs between two pieces of plastic wrap and pound with a meat mallet or an empty wine bottle or pierce them all over with a Jaccard meat tenderizer. Once the slabs have been tenderized, cut them into thin slivers of about ¼ inch wide. If you've ever had Chinese "shredded" dishes—usually pork, beef, or chicken—this is what you're going for.

To make the dish, mix all the ingredients for the sauce except for the sesame oil in a bowl. Set aside. Put 2 tablespoons of peanut oil (or some other vegetable oil) in a wok and turn the heat to high. When the oil starts smoking, take the wok off the heat and add the chile bean paste and minced ginger to the oil. Put it back on the heat and cook for 30 seconds.

Add the heart, garlic, green onions, chiles, and bamboo shoots and stir-fry for 2 minutes. Pour in the sauce and boil furiously for 2 minutes. Turn off the heat, add the sesame oil, and serve with rice.

# DEER CAMP LIVER AND ONIONS

You pretty much can't do a venison cookbook without liver and onions. To many, this is the first meal after a successful hunt, either that night or for breakfast the following morning. There are a zillion variations on this recipe, but this is the one I like best.

You caramelize the onions, which form a sweet and savory bed for thin slices of liver—I cut them about ¼ to ½ inch thick. Sometimes I dust the liver in flour, sometimes not. Then you fry bacon and sear the liver in the fat. Remember that liver is best cooked medium or even rare. Fully cooked liver, which is gray inside, is nasty, at least to me. Scallions, chives, or some other sort of green onion balances things out, and a little splash of lemon juice brightens things up.

All of the ingredients are easy to have on hand in deer camp. Honey never goes bad, and lemons will keep for more than a month in the fridge. Onions will also last for more than a month in the pantry.

You'll want either hash browns or good bread to go along with this.

**SERVES ▶** 4

**PREP TIME ▶** 10 minutes

**COOK TIME ▶** 30 minutes

¼ pound thick-cut bacon

2 onions, sliced root to tip

Salt

2 tablespoons butter

1 teaspoon fresh or dried thyme

1 tablespoon honey or brown sugar (optional)

8 thin slices of deer liver, prepped (see page 253)

Flour, for dusting

4 green onions or ¼ cup chives, chopped

Black pepper

Zest and juice of 1 lemon (optional)

Fry the bacon in a large frying pan until crispy, then remove it and chop coarsely.

Remove all but about 2 tablespoons of bacon fat from the pan (but save it) and turn the heat to high. When the bacon fat is hot, add the onions. Toss to combine. Salt the onions, cover the pan, and turn the heat to medium-low. Let the onions cook this way, stirring occasionally, for 20 minutes. Add the butter, thyme, and optional honey, stir to combine, and cook another 5 to 10 minutes. If too much liquid forms in the pan, uncover it and it will cook away. Remove the onions from the pan and set aside. Wipe out the pan.

Add another 2 tablespoons of bacon fat. Get the pan very hot. Turn on your stovetop fan, as things will start to smoke. Dust the liver slices with flour and sear them in the bacon fat for no more than 90 seconds per side; I prefer 1 minute per side, which leaves the interior of the liver nice and pink.

Remove the liver and let it rest while you reheat the onions and bacon. Add the green onions or chives, toss to combine, and heat through, about 2 minutes. Give everyone some of the onions and top with the liver slices. Grind some black pepper over everything and garnish with the lemon zest and juice.

# SCOTTISH POWSOWDIE

**SERVES ▸** 8

**PREP TIME ▸** 30 minutes

**COOK TIME ▸** 4 hours

1 pound lamb or deer tongues (see heanotes for alternates)

2 lamb or deer shanks

2 pig's trotters

½ cup dry green peas

Salt

½ pound barley

1 rutabaga, peeled and cut into chunks

2 leeks, white and light green parts, sliced thin

2 stalks celery, chopped

½ cup chopped parsley

Black pepper

Powsowdie is a centuries-old dish, a stew for the poor and middle class that uses humble ingredients, most notably a sheep's head. Yes, an actual sheep's head. You can of course make this with a real sheep's head, which you will most likely find in a halal market in the United States. Or, if you live in a place without chronic wasting disease, definitely make this a deer head stew and use the skinned-out head of a doe or button buck.

Or do what I did and use bits that mimic a whole head: deer or lamb shanks, a couple of deer or lamb tongues, and a pair of hog trotters. This mix includes meat you'd get in the traditional dish, plus the addition of sticky, gelatin-rich trotters, which you can get in most butcher shops and Asian or Latin markets.

Use odd bits if you can because powsowdie is a celebration of no waste, of using bits and bobbles and odds and ends to make something beautiful. And this stew, despite all odds, is beautiful.

There are two striking things about it. First, there's no browning. Everything is all cooked slow and gentle. And there's an added scald-and-clean step, very common in Asian cooking but relatively rare in Europe. More on that below. Second is the use of dry split green peas right at the beginning. The peas completely dissolve and further thicken the stew. Barley, which is eaten as a grain element in the stew, comes later.

Add to this humble things like rutabagas, leeks, celery, carrot if you want it, barley, and parsley and you have something so simple you'll wonder what makes it so good.

The answer is time. Powsowdie is a weekend or day-off stew, as it's best cooked very slowly over the course of a day. You'll also need to do things like debone and mince the trotters if you're using them, pick meat off a head if using that, shred meat off a shank, or peel skin off a tongue.

Serve powsowdie with bannocks, rye bread, or any sturdy loaf and some dark, malty beer or red wine, and cozy up on a dark winter's day knowing you cooked—really cooked—and made something satisfying out of practically nothing.

Put all the meats in a large pot, bring this to a boil, and let it cook for a minute or two. Pour off the water and discard, rinse the meats under cold water, and clean the pot. This process "cleans" the meats and will limit the froth that forms on the actual broth.

Put the meats back in the pot and cover with water by about 2 or 3 inches. Bring to a simmer and skim any froth. Pour in the dry green peas. Add a tablespoon or two of salt and let this simmer gently until everything is tender, which will be about three to four hours.

Remove all the meats carefully. Let them cool on a baking sheet for a bit. If you're using tongues, you'll need to peel the skin off them while they're still warm. If you have trouble, use a paring knife. Discard all the bones from the trotters (there are many) and the shanks. Coarsely shred the shank meat and finely mince the various bits of trotter. Cut the tongues into chunks.

Put all this back in the pot and add the barley, rutabaga, leeks, and celery. Let all this simmer until the barley and rutabaga are tender, about 40 minutes. Adjust the seasonings with salt and black pepper and add the parsley. Serve with bread and beer.

### NOTES

- The stew thickens over time. You might want to reheat it with a bit of broth or water to thin it out. It will also completely set up in the fridge because of the gelatin. Fear not. It liquifies on the stovetop.
- If you lack or don't want to source trotters and tongues, use shoulder or more shanks. I'd also recommend adding into the pot a teaspoon or two of gelatin, mixed first with some of the cooking water.
- If it pleases you, add one or two chopped carrots.
- One nice, but not traditional, addition is to "German" this up with some sour cream and sauerkraut. Add it to taste in your bowl.

# BRITISH MEATBALLS

**SERVES ▸** 4 to 6

**PREP TIME ▸** 25 minutes

**COOK TIME ▸** 50 minutes

This is a British classic, available all over the island in various forms. I include it in this chapter because the meat mixture includes liver, and they're wrapped in caul fat. Incidentally, its traditional name, "faggots," comes from a Middle English term for a bundle of something (usually sticks); in this case, it's meat wrapped in caul fat. In some places, these are also called "savoury ducks."

If you're in a hurry, you can indeed start with ground pork or venison, something meat processors love to give you a lot of if you don't butcher your own deer. You must make sure that the ground meat has some fat in it, otherwise your meatballs will be dry and sad.

The caul fat matters here. Your meatballs will be far better with it than with the thin bacon, but they'll still work with bacon. Most butchers will have caul fat frozen, and even some larger supermarkets, like Whole Foods, should be able to order it for you. Caul fat can be frozen and thawed several times with few ill effects, so you can keep some on hand for whenever you want to make this or its French cousin, *crepinettes.*

Serve this with the traditional mashed potatoes (or rutabagas) and peas. Gravy is a must.

- Caul fat or very thin bacon
- 1 pound venison
- ½ pound bacon ends (or regular bacon)
- ½ pound venison liver
- 1 cup oats or breadcrumbs
- 1 cup minced onion
- 1 teaspoon salt
- 2 teaspoon dried thyme
- 1 tablespoon fresh sage, minced
- ½ teaspoon nutmeg
- 3 tablespoons chopped fresh parsley
- 2 cups venison broth or beef broth

Take the caul fat out if you are using it and soak it in tepid water with a little salt tossed in, maybe a teaspoon. This will help it loosen.

Cut the venison, bacon, and liver into 1-inch chunks and freeze for 30 minutes to an hour, until they're about half-frozen. Grind the oats in a food processor or spice grinder into a coarse meal like coarse cornmeal. Or use breadcrumbs.

When the meat is ready, mix it with the onions and grind on a medium die, 6 mm if you have one, or the "coarse" on a KitchenAid grinder. Put the meat in a bowl and mix with the oats and all the herbs and spices. Preheat the oven to 375°F.

Gently unravel the caul fat into one layer and lay it on a clean work surface. Form balls with the meat mixture a little smaller than a baseball or the size of a small orange. You want them big. Place the ball on the caul fat and slice enough of the caul around it to wrap the ball completely. Arrange the meatballs seam side down in a baking dish. If you can't find caul fat and are using thin bacon, wrap the balls in bacon strips until you have them covered. Repeat until all the meat is used.

Bake uncovered in an oven for 40 to 50 minutes, basting every 10 to 15 minutes with the stock. Serve with mashed potatoes and peas.

# CAJUN BOUDIN BALLS

**SERVES ▶** 6 to 8

**PREP TIME ▶** 20 minutes, to get to the boudin stage. Another 30 minutes to make and bread the balls

**COOK TIME ▶** 2 hours for the boudin, 30 minutes to fry the balls

### FOR THE BOUDIN

⅔ pound venison

¾ pound fatty pork shoulder or "country ribs"

1 pound venison liver

1 onion, chopped (about 1 cup)

3 cloves garlic, minced

1 green bell pepper, chopped

3 stalks celery, chopped

1½ tablespoons Cajun seasoning, divided

½ cup minced parsley

½ cup chopped green onions

5 cups cooked short- or medium-grain rice

1 tablespoon black pepper

1 tablespoon paprika

1 teaspoon cayenne

### FOR THE BALLS

1 cup flour

2 cups breadcrumbs

3 eggs

½ cup milk

Vegetable oil, for deep-frying

Quite possibly the greatest fast food on Planet Earth. I first had boudin balls at a place called the Best Stop in Scott, Louisiana, which is that state's western frontier. Hot fried balls of sausage, seasoning, and rice? Oh my God, so good! I bought a dozen and ate them all the way to Austin, Texas, 372 miles away. This is my version of both the boudin needed to make the balls and the balls themselves. Traditional boudin is with pork and pork liver, but venison and venison liver work great, too.

Keep in mind that you can stuff the boudin into hog casings and smoke it if you want.

Once made, you can eat these cold as a snack or take them out of the fridge, let them come to room temperature, and refry them for a couple minutes to crisp up. Or you can reheat them in a 400°F oven on a baking sheet. If you have lots of leftovers, freeze them on a plate, then put the frozen boudin balls in a freezer bag, where they'll keep for several months.

Cut the venison, pork, and liver into chunks that will fit into a grinder. Put the meats and enough water to cover by about an inch into a pot and bring to a boil. Skim off any scum that floats to the top. Reduce to a simmer and add the onions, garlic, bell peppers, and celery, plus about 1 tablespoon of Cajun seasoning. Simmer for 90 minutes, or until the meats are tender. Drain most of the liquid from the pot (reserving its contents) but keep about 2 cups of the broth. Let the meats cool a bit before proceeding.

Add ½ cup of the parsley and ½ cup of the green onions to the meats and vegetables and grind everything through a coarse die, ideally 8 to 10 mm. Alternatively, you can chop everything by hand. Put the mixture into a mixing bowl. Stir in the rice, remaining Cajun seasoning and other spices, and the rest of the parsley and green onions. Add the broth, ½ cup at a time, and mix thoroughly into a paste. You now have boudin, and you can put this in a casing if you'd like and smoke it. Or make these balls.

To do that, set up a breading station. Put the flour into one large, shallow bowl. You can add a little Cajun seasoning to it if you want, but be careful, as the premade seasoning mixes tend to be very salty. Beat the eggs with the milk and put that into another large, shallow bowl. Finally, put the breadcrumbs into a third bowl.

Form the boudin into little balls—I like them a little larger than a walnut—and dredge in the flour, then the egg wash, then the breadcrumbs. Set them on a baking sheet. If you have time, let them chill in the fridge for up to a few hours before frying them; this helps them hold their shape.

Fry the boudin balls in 350°F oil until golden brown, about 3 to 5 minutes. Do this in batches and keep the balls warm in a 200°F oven while you do the rest. Serve with hot sauce, Cajun remoulade, mustard, or whatever you please.

## Cajun Remoulade

This is a fantastic all-purpose sauce for fried anything. Serve this with the boudin balls as a start.

1¼ cups mayonnaise

¼ cup mustard (Creole mustard if possible)

1 tablespoon sweet paprika

1 to 2 teaspoons Cajun or Creole seasoning

2 teaspoons prepared horseradish

1 teaspoon pickle juice (dill or sweet, your preference)

1 teaspoon hot sauce (preferably Tabasco)

1 large clove garlic, minced and smashed

Mix everything together and serve cold.

# BRAISED ELK CHEEKS

This recipe works with the cheeks of any large animal, from elk to beef and bison and moose. You could also use short ribs or multiple cheeks from smaller animals like deer or pigs, or venison shoulder, neck or shanks.

**SERVES ▸** 4

**PREP TIME ▸** 30 minutes

**COOK TIME ▸** 3 hours

**ALTERNATIVE CUTS ▸** Shoulder, neck, shanks, ribs

**FOR THE MARINADE**

1 bottle red wine

12 black peppercorns, cracked

12 juniper berries, crushed (optional)

3 bay leaves

1 small onion, sliced

**FOR THE BRAISE**

2 to 3 pounds elk cheeks, or see headnotes for alternatives

Salt

3 tablespoons beef fat, lard, butter or oil

2 onions, chopped

2 stalks celery, chopped

2 carrots, sliced thick

1 sprig rosemary

2 tablespoons tomato paste

Bring the marinade to a boil, let it cool to at least room temperature, then submerge the cheeks in it for at least six hours, and up to several days. I prefer a solid twenty-four hours.

When you're ready to make the dish, remove the meat from the marinade and pat it dry. Salt it. Strain the marinade, keeping the liquid and bay leaves.

Heat the beef fat or whatever fat or oil you're using in a Dutch oven or similar heavy, lidded pot set over medium-high heat. Brown the cheeks. Don't crowd the pan; do this in batches if you need to. Remove the meat as it browns and set it aside.

When the meat has browned, add the chopped onions and celery and brown these as well. Turn the oven to 325°F.

Add some of the reserved marinade to the pot and use a wooden spoon to scrape up the browned bits. Return the meat to the pot, along with any juices that collected where they were sitting. Add the carrots, rosemary, the rest of the marinade, and the bay leaves. If the meat isn't totally covered, add enough beef, game, or vegetable stock (or water) to barely cover them. Bring to a simmer and add salt to taste. Cover the pot and put it in the oven. Let this cook at least two hours. It could take more than that, but start checking for tenderness at the two-hour mark.

When the meat is tender, carefully remove it to a pan or plate. Fish out the rosemary and bay leaves and discard. Puree the braising liquid with the tomato paste and add salt if needed.

Coat the meat with the sauce, serve it over mashed potatoes, and pour some more sauce over it all.

**NOTE:** Use leftover meat and sauce for pasta, potatoes, or for a pot pie.

# A LOVELY TONGUE SANDWICH

**SERVES ▶** 4

**PREP TIME ▶** 3 to 5 days, for brining the tongue

**COOK TIME ▶** 3 to 4 hours

This sandwich is kind of a big deal (sort of like Ron Burgundy of *Anchorman* fame). It takes three days to make, so you have to know you want to eat it. I can assure you, you want to eat this sandwich. All that time is spent with the tongues brining in the fridge, so it's not as big a commitment as you might think.

Basically, you corn the tongue like you would any other cut of meat (Corned Venison, page 288), simmer it in a broth for a few hours, peel it, slice, sear, and stuff it in a sandwich. So OK, it's not something you mindlessly make in the morning before hitting the deer stand. It's a dinner sandwich, or one for a nice weekend lunch.

I use deer tongues here, but the chef whose recipe I'm indebted to, April Bloomfield of The Spotted Pig in New York City, uses beef tongue—and beef tongue is not so different from a bison, moose, or elk tongue, although beef tongue does need a bit longer to brine. Oh, and I use a bit of curing salt in my brine because I love that red color and "hammy" flavor you get from it. You can skip it if you want, but the meat will be gray and not red.

The condiments and accompaniments to this sandwich are what I happen to like. Feel free to play around as you want.

4 deer tongues or 1 elk, moose, or bison tongue

**FOR THE BRINE**

- ¼ cup kosher salt
- 1 quart water
- 1 tablespoon black peppercorns, cracked
- 5 to 8 cloves
- 3 bay leaves
- ½ teaspoon Insta Cure No. 1 (optional)

**TO COOK THE TONGUES**

- 1 carrot, chopped
- 2 stalks celery, chopped
- ½ onion, chopped
- 2 bay leaves

**FOR THE HORSERADISH MAYO**

- 4 tablespoons mayonnaise
- 1 tablespoon prepared horseradish
- 1 teaspoon Dijon mustard
- 1 teaspoon lemon juice
- Salt
- Black pepper

**FOR THE SANDWICH**

- Sandwich rolls
- Grilled, caramelized, or raw onions
- Zippy greens like arugula, cress or dandelion greens

Bring the brine ingredients to a boil, then let cool to room temperature; this infuses the flavors into the brine. Submerge the tongues in the brine and refrigerate for three days (five days if you're using moose, elk, or bison tongue). Once brined, you can remove the tongues from the brine and keep in the fridge a few days before you cook them.

Put the tongues, the vegetables, and the herbs in a pot that just about fits them. Cover with water by 1 inch and bring to a boil. Drop the heat to a gentle simmer and cook, covered, until the point of a thin, sharp knife easily pierces the thickest part, about three to five hours.

Remove the tongues (save the broth) and set them on a cutting board to cool. As soon as they're cool enough to work with—about 10 minutes—peel off the skin around the tongues. It should come off easily. Discard. Return the peeled tongues to the broth and allow them to come to room temperature on the stove. At this point, you have corned tongue, which you can keep in the broth in the refrigerator for up to a week.

To make the sandwich, slice the rolls almost all the way through to the other side and dig out a trench on both sides of the bread to accommodate the fillings. You can toast it if you want.

Cut the tongues into ¼-inch slices on the diagonal if you can. Lay down about 2 tablespoons of oil, lard, or bacon fat (bacon fat is best) in a large frying pan and set it over medium-high heat. When the oil is hot, sear the tongue slices. They'll want to stick a little, so use a metal spatula to flip them. They'll need only about 2 minutes per side to crisp. Set them aside.

Mix all the ingredients for the horseradish mayo together, and when it tastes the way you like it, slather it on both sides of the roll.

Add some onions if you like, lots of tongue slices, and the greens. The greens are important because they help cut the richness of the tongue and the mayo. Slice the roll in half and have at it!

# TACOS DE LENGUA

**SERVES ▸** 6 to 8

**PREP TIME ▸** 15 minutes

**COOK TIME ▸** 3 hours

1 elk, moose, or bison tongue or 4 to 6 deer tongues
1 large onion, chopped
5 cloves garlic, peeled and crushed
5 bay leaves
1 tablespoon black peppercorns
2 tablespoons salt
3 tablespoons lard or vegetable oil
Corn tortillas
Salsa (canned or homemade)
Diced avocado (optional)
Cilantro
½ cup white onions, chopped

This is a taco-truck standard in Northern California, where I lived for many years before moving to Minnesota. Typically, it's braised beef tongue chunked and seared on the flat-top then added to corn tortillas with some salsa and lime. Super simple.

I like my tongue sliced thin or shredded, not in big chunks, but it's up to you. I also like a bit more in the way of toppings, and I especially think a fiery salsa verde or roasted chile salsa, plus some fresh avocado, is a perfect balance with the rich, tender tongue meat.

This is beer food—Mexican beer, German lagers . . . hell, Budweiser or Miller are fine here.

Put the tongue in a large pot and cover it with water by 2 inches. Bring to a boil and skim any froth that forms on the water's surface. When it's all gone, drop the heat to a simmer and add the onion, garlic, bay leaves, black peppercorns, and salt. Simmer the tongue until the sharp point of a thin knife pierces it easily, about two to three hours.

Once the tongue is tender, set it on a cutting board to cool somewhat. When it's barely cool enough to handle, peel off the skin and discard. You can do all this up to a week ahead if you want. Just cool the peeled tongue and wrap in plastic wrap. It'll keep in the refrigerator a week.

When you're ready to make the tacos, slice the tongue on the diagonal into ¼-inch slices. Sear them in the lard until they're nicely browned, then chop coarsely. Serve on warm corn tortillas with the salsa, avocado, cilantro, and chopped white onions.

"Let the reindeer decide."

— SÁMI PROVERB

# VENISON AND KIDNEY PIE

A British classic even more famous than the Deviled Kidneys recipe on page 274, this is a similar recipe in that it relies on mustard, Worcestershire sauce, and black pepper for its zip. It bears repeating that you probably won't like this recipe unless you have double-soaked your kidneys as detailed on page 253. And yes, you can skip the kidneys and make this with other bits and bobbles, like heart, liver, pre-skinned tongue, and cheeks.

Once made, this will keep a week in the fridge. I like to reheat it, covered, in the oven at 300°F for about 30 minutes.

**SERVES ▸** 8

**PREP TIME ▸** 30 minutes

**COOK TIME ▸** 3 hours

**FOR THE FILLING**

2 pounds venison shank, shoulder, or neck meat

1 pound venison kidneys

Salt

½ cup flour

¼ cup lard, bacon fat, or butter (or beef drippings)

1 pound fresh mushrooms (any kind), chopped

1 large yellow onion, coarsely chopped

2 cups stout or porter or other dark, malty beer, divided

1 teaspoon dried thyme

4 bay leaves

1 tablespoon chopped parsley stems

1 stalk celery, minced

1 tablespoon minced fresh rosemary (or 1 teaspoon dried)

2 cups venison stock

3 turnips or parsnips, peeled and diced

¼ cup chopped parsley leaves

Worcestershire sauce

Coleman's dry mustard

Black pepper

**FOR THE PIE**

One 17-ounce box puff pastry (I use Pepperidge Farm)

1 egg, lightly beaten

1 tablespoon milk

---

Chop the venison and kidneys into chunks. Salt them and toss in flour. Heat the bacon fat in a large pan and brown the meats. Don't crowd the pan—you might need to do this in batches—and take your time. You want them all nicely browned. Remove the pieces as they brown.

Preheat the oven to 325°F.

Deglaze the pot with the fresh mushrooms and the chopped onion; their moisture will loosen all the browned bits on the bottom of the pan, which you want to scrape up with a wooden spoon. Salt these as they cook, and cook them, stirring occasionally, until they're beginning to brown, about 6 to 8 minutes.

Add 1 cup of the beer to the pot and use it to scrape up any more browned bits from the pot. Add the thyme, bay leaves, parsley stems, celery, and rosemary, along with the rest of the beer and the venison stock. Return the meats to the pot along with any juices in the bowl where you left them.

Cover the pot and cook in the oven for 90 minutes. After 90 minutes, add the parsnips or turnips. Taste for salt and add some if needed. Cover the pot again, return it to the oven, and cook until everything is nice and tender. This could be 30 minutes, could be another couple hours, depending on how old and tough your game was.

Remove the lid and add the chopped parsley leaves, Worcestershire, dry mustard, and black pepper to taste. Let this cool. At this point, the filling can be stored up to a few days before making the pie.

Jack the oven up to 425°F

*continued*

To make the pie, let the puff pastry thaw according to the directions on the box. Press in one sheet of pastry into a standard pie pan and dock it by poking it all over with a fork. Fill the pie generously. The filling should be sorta jellified if it came out of the fridge, and even if you let it cool, it will be very thick. Top with the other sheet of pastry and seal the edges.

Whisk together the beaten egg and milk and paint the whole pie with it. If you have stray bits, make a fun deer or whatever out of them and stick it in the middle; it will adhere because of the egg wash. Paint the decoration, too. Finally cut vents in the pie here and there.

Bake the pie about 45 minutes, or until pretty and browned. Remove and let it rest 10 minutes before serving.

"Life in the open is one of my finest rewards. I enjoy and become completely immersed in the high challenge and increased opportunity to become for a time a part of nature. Deer hunting is a classical exercise in freedom. It is a return to fundamentals that I instinctively feel are basic and right."

—FRED BEAR, ONE OF THE GREATEST ARCHERS OF ALL TIME

# DEVILED KIDNEYS

Deviled kidney is an old British standby, and my version of it owes a lot to one of my culinary inspirations, the great chef Fergus Henderson of St. John in London. A rendition of this recipe done with lamb appears in his excellent book, *The Whole Beast: Nose to Tail Eating.* If only I could cook for Fergus someday.

Most people don't have lots of venison kidneys lying around, so this recipe reflects that. But if you do have, say, eight to ten kidneys, scale up this recipe.

I like to soak kidneys in milk for a day before doing this recipe, as it makes them taste milder. But you can skip this if you want.

I'm a big fan of mushrooms with kidneys—it's a texture thing. I prefer the mighty porcini mushroom here, but any good fresh mushroom will do.

Serve your kidneys on excellent toast. A pale ale or even a porter would be perfect with this, as would a nice red wine.

**SERVES ▶** 2 as a snack, and 1 as a meal

**PREP TIME ▶** 10 minutes

**COOK TIME ▶** 10 minutes

**ALTERNATIVE CUTS ▶** Backstrap, tenderloin, or hind leg meat free of connective tissue

- 2 to 4 deer kidneys
- ½ pound fresh mushrooms, cut into large-ish pieces (optional)
- 6 tablespoons unsalted butter, divided
- ¼ cup flour
- 1 teaspoon cayenne
- 1½ teaspoons dry mustard (Colman's if you can get it)
- 1 teaspoon salt
- 1 teaspoon black pepper
- Worcestershire sauce
- 3 tablespoons stock (chicken, venison or beef)

Clean and trim the kidneys as shown on page 253. Cut each half into three or four pieces. If you're using the mushrooms, sear them in a hot pan with 3 tablespoons of unsalted butter until nicely browned on their edges. Remove them and set aside for the moment.

Mix the flour with the cayenne, mustard, salt, and black pepper and dust the kidneys with it.

Get the pan very hot, then add the remaining 3 tablespoons of butter. Brown the kidneys in the butter. You may need to press them down with a spatula, as they'll want to arch upward. Turn and cook another minute or two. Remove them and cut into pieces you'd like to eat.

Return the kidneys and the mushrooms to the pan, add a big splash of Worcestershire sauce and the stock, and shake the pan to meld everything together. Let this cook for a minute or two.

Remove the kidneys and mushrooms and set them on top of your toast. Boil down the sauce for a few minutes—don't let it boil completely away—then pour it over everything and serve.

# VENISON TRIPE NEAPOLITAN STYLE

Simmered in a spicy Italian red sauce is how I first ate tripe as a kid in the Italian restaurants of New Jersey and Long Island. It's a pretty innocuous way to eat tripe, which essentially takes the role of pasta in a zippy tomato sauce.

Usually, you'll see this done with honeycomb tripe from beef, but the corresponding section of a deer's stomach is tiny, so you'll most often use the rumen, which is sold commercially as "blanket tripe"; it's the large, first stomach. If you feel like cleaning out the honeycomb (for example, the second stomach) of an elk or moose, go for it.

By the time you've cleaned and simmered the tripe, the usable portion from a small doe or buck will feed two people, so keep that in mind. This recipe can be scaled up easily, though.

The odd inclusion of vanilla extract in the initial simmering process is a tip I learned from Chef Mario Batali's cookbook, *Babbo*. The addition removes most of that barnyard odor people hate about tripe.

You need to serve this with good, crusty bread and a light red wine like a Chianti, pinot noir, or grenache. If you're a beer person, lean hoppy here, not malty.

**SERVES ▶** 2

**PREP TIME ▶** 1 hour

**COOK TIME ▶** 2 hours

**FOR THE TRIPE**

Cleaned tripe from 1 deer (see page 43)

A healthy pinch of salt

¼ cup white or cider vinegar

1 teaspoon vanilla extract

**FOR THE SAUCE**

½ cup carrot, coarsely chopped

½ cup celery stalk, coarsely chopped

½ cup onion, coarsely chopped

¼ cup olive oil

3 cloves garlic, minced

1 to 2 teaspoons hot chile flakes

1 tablespoon tomato paste

1 cup white wine

One 28- to 32-ounce can crushed tomatoes

1 or 2 bay leaves

4 to 6 sage leaves, minced

Salt

Black pepper

2 tablespoons chopped parsley or basil

Grated Parmesan or pecorino cheese

Set the tripe in a heavy pot and cover with water by 1 inch. Add the salt, vinegar and vanilla extract. Boil and skim off any foam that forms on the surface. Simmer gently for one hour, until reasonably tender.

After an hour, remove the tripe and set on a baking sheet to cool. If you notice any unsightly brownish-gray bits on the smooth side of the tripe—the one without the terry-cloth texture—scrape them off with a knife. If you're in a hurry, slice the tripe into 2 by ½-inch strips. Or chill the tripe in the fridge overnight and then slice, which makes things easier.

To finish the dish, buzz the carrot, celery, and onion in a food processor until finely chopped. Cook this in a heavy lidded pot with the olive oil over medium heat until the vegetables are soft but not browned, about 5 minutes. Add the garlic and chile flakes and cook another minute.

Mix in the tomato paste. Cook until everything begins to stick to the bottom of the pot, then add the white wine. Scrape up any browned bits on the bottom of the pot with a wooden spoon and let the wine boil for a minute.

Add the crushed tomatoes, bay leaves, sage, and salt. Add the cut-up tripe to the pot and simmer gently until the tripe has the texture of al dente pasta. To serve, add black pepper to taste along with the chopped parsley. Top with the grated cheese and serve with good, crusty bread.

# GERMAN MARROW DUMPLINGS

These are easy to make, thrifty, and wonderful to eat. What's not to love? I prefer to make these with marrow from deer (as opposed to elk or moose) because usually the amount of marrow you get from a typical deer's femurs is just about right for this recipe. But of course, any marrow will do.

If you haven't already done so, first soak your marrow to remove blood (instructions on page 251). If you make this with store-bought marrow, you don't need to do this.

Know that these are dense dumplings that require a fair amount of cooking to lighten up. Don't worry, they won't fall apart.

Serve as a soup course in a larger meal or as a simple weeknight meal with some vegetables and, if you're feeling flush, a simply roasted or grilled piece of meat.

**SERVES ▸** 4

**PREP TIME ▸** 30 minutes

**COOK TIME ▸** 15 minutes

- 2 ounces bone marrow, chopped fine
- 2 ounces flour, about ½ cup
- ½ teaspoon baking powder
- ¾ cup fine breadcrumbs
- 2 teaspoons finely chopped shallot or onion
- 1 tablespoon finely chopped parsley
- ½ teaspoon salt
- ½ teaspoon black pepper
- 1 egg

Get a pot of salted water or broth boiling. Mix all the ingredients together in a large bowl and form into balls about the size of a large hazelnut or small walnut. Move each marrow dumpling into the water or broth and let them cook until they float. When they do, cover the pot and let the dumplings simmer gently over medium-low heat for 7 to 10 minutes. You might need to do this in two batches so you don't overload the pot.

Serve these dumplings in a clear venison or other broth. The Basic Venison Broth on page 73 is a good choice. Garnish with shredded leeks, carrots, or chopped chives or parsley.

> ". . . just as a deer herd lives in mortal fear of its wolves, so does a mountain live in mortal fear of its deer."
>
> —ALDO LEOPOLD, *Thinking Like a Mountain*

# CURING VENISON AND MAKING SAUSAGE

When it comes to culinary artistry, it's hard to top the beauty of a properly cured ham, or the fermented tang of smoked salami, or even that pop—Germans call it *knacken*—of a well-made sausage hot off the grill. Most often called by its French name *charcuterie*, the art and craft of curing meat is something every deer hunter should consider learning. Yes, there are processors out there who do a good job, sometimes even a great job. But mastering this skill allows you to craft everything to your own tastes. The control you have once you know how to make sausage or cure ham is, frankly, empowering. And the look on people's faces when you tell them you made that salami or snack stick or ham is so worth it.

Curing venison and making venison sausages and salami is similar to doing the same thing with pork, but the processes differ slightly, due mostly to the differences in fat content. Venison tends to be lean. Whitetails living around alfalfa fields in the Midwest often have a thick layer of fat, but it's less common to find a fat mule deer or California blacktail. That said, any deer can put on fat, especially in a good acorn year. And in moderation, that fat can be useful, too (see page 21).

## SAUSAGES

Sausages are a mainstay in venison cookery. And let me tell you, if you know how to make your own sausages, you'll never buy them again. Controlling the seasoning, fat content, grind, size, and level of smoke in your links is an act of true creation. It's kind of a rush when it all comes together.

The recipe for Venison Sausage with Sage and Juniper (page 297) is a master recipe. Use that for all the detailed instructions on grinding, mixing, and making links. Beyond that will be recipes that will increase in difficulty, until you get to salami. Salami, or dry-cured sausages, are the pinnacle of the sausage-maker's craft.

### Special Equipment Needed

You'll need some special equipment to make sausages. You can hand-chop or grind meat in a food processor and stuff by hand with a funnel, but unless you're an expert, this results in an inferior sausage and is far more work. At a minimum, you'll need a meat grinder. I use a half-horsepower grinder, which is enough even for medium-size jobs. If you plan on making more than about twenty pounds of sausage at a shot, you might want a bigger grinder.

If you're serious about making sausages, you'll want some extra gear. Here's my setup:

- Hog, sheep, and beef casings, available at butcher shops or online
- A dedicated sausage stuffer. Avoid both the KitchenAid attachment and those cornucopia-shaped stuffers.
- A wooden rack to hang sausages on to dry

When you're beginning, start by making sausage patties, not links. Remember, you can also wrap your sausage meat in blanched cabbage or chard leaves, roll it in bulgur wheat and make Lebanese kibbeh, wrap it in caul fat (available from good butchers, although you might need to order ahead), or stuff it in grape leaves.

If you do plan to stuff your sausages, hog casings are the easiest to buy. Nearly every good butcher has them, and they're inexpensive. Most come heavily salted in plastic tubs and must be soaked in warm

## Why I Measure Salt in Grams

In a word, control. Old-style, traditional recipes use teaspoons and tablespoons for ingredients, and honestly, that's perfectly fine for seasonings like pepper and herbs and garlic. But for salt, it won't work. It's more than a flavor issue. It's one of safety.

Salts are not equally ground. A tablespoon of, say, Morton's kosher salt will not be the same weight of salt that you'd get in a tablespoon of Diamond Crystal salt and definitely won't even be close to a tablespoon of table salt. (For the record, I use Diamond Crystal kosher salt.)

And the difference between 34 grams of salt and 38 grams of salt in a 5-pound batch of sausage is very noticeable—despite the fact that, depending on which brand of salt you use, each could be a couple tablespoons. What's more, when you're curing meats, you need a set percentage of salt to be safe. Normally, it's about 2.5 to 3 percent, including the curing salt. You can't get there accurately with tablespoons.

In terms of the salts used for curing, sodium nitrite and sodium nitrate, you generally want them to be 0.25% (one-quarter of one percent) of the weight of the meat and fat. So in my 5-pound batches, my standard is 6 grams. Hard to reach this precision just scooping out teaspoons. Incidentally, if you put too much nitrite in your meat, it can cause dehydration, nausea, vomiting, and shortness of breath. So get the scale, OK?

water for half an hour or more to reconstitute them. You can also use narrow sheep casings or very wide beef casings, but you may need to special order them from your butcher or buy them online from dealers such as The Sausage Maker or Butcher & Packer. You can buy artificial casings made from edible collagen, but I use them only for Slim Jim–like snack sticks, and only then because they are even narrower than sheep casings.

### Venison Sausage Basics

Venison's leanness can be a problem when you decide to make sausages. If you have a fat deer, you can use its fat to grind with sausages, but that fat is different from pork fat—it can coat your mouth if you use too much (see page 24). A good rule of thumb is to include no more than 35 percent deer fat with your sausage grind. For a five-pound batch of sausages, I typically include no more than half a pound of deer fat and a shade more than half a pound of pork fat along with the lean venison.

Also, if you're going to use deer or elk fat, try to get it from in between muscles, not the fat cap on the outside of the animal, which will be waxier. You can always use fat from pronghorn, bison, nilgai, or oryx.

Pork fat is the primo fat for making any sausage or salami. You can use beef fat, too. Pork fat is softer than beef fat and far more neutral tasting. Add beef fat to a venison sausage and you'll taste it. Add pork fat to a venison sausage and it tastes like venison. Good pork fat can be had in any decent supermarket and in all butcher shops. It's usually cheap, too. Your first choice should be back fat, which is easier to cut and slightly harder than the fat in the shoulder, which is the next best thing. Pork bellies are OK, but there's enough meat in them to influence the flavor of your sausage—not necessarily a bad thing, but you should be aware of it before you toss some bellies into the grinder.

Sausage is traditionally made with the random trim and wobbly bits of an animal. The idea of grinding up a nice roast or, God forbid, the backstrap of an animal, would make an old-school butcher vomit. And while it's true that sausage-making with these luxury cuts is easier—you have far less silverskin and gristly parts to contend with—if you take your time and remove as much silverskin as you can by hand, you can make excellent sausages with the sketchier pieces from the critter. Alternatively, if you plan to triple-grind your meat fine and you have a burly grinder, you can pretty much ignore the silverskin.

And most venison sausages and salami *should* be ground twice, or even three times. When you butcher, you'll be faced again and again with the choice of either discarding some good chunk of meat that's loaded with connective tissue or putting it through the grinder anyway. Put it through the grinder. Start with the coarsest setting, like 10 mm or even a 12 mm, which is really wide. Then go with something like 7 mm or 6 mm, and then, if you want, the fine 4.5 mm or even 3 mm die. Silverskin will gunk up your grinder if you go right to the narrow die, sometimes quickly. You'll know this is happening when the meat and fat that comes out of the grinder begins to smear together instead of coming out looking like meaty spaghetti.

Make sure your venison and fat are *very* cold when you do this. Ideal temperature is around freezing, about 32°F or thereabouts; the salt with the meat will prevent it from freezing solid. Put the meat and fat in the freezer for an hour or so between grindings to be sure. This helps prevent smear, where the fat breaks down and coats the

meat. If this happens, you will never get a good bind on the sausage and it'll be crumbly, like bad cat food.

While you mix the meat, unless you're using the finest dies, you still want to see individual little pieces of fat, like those little marshmallows in a kid's breakfast cereal. I often mix by hand now, and I know by feel when the mix has bound. Your achingly numb hands will feel the mass as one thing, rather than lots of bits of meat. You can pick up an entire five-pound batch, and it will hang together.

Use natural casings to make your sausages. I don't like synthetic casings, except for snack sticks. Thread a whole casing on your sausage stuffer, then make one big coil of sausage at once. After you have big coils, *then* link them. For fresh sausages, I pinch off six- to eight-inch links with my fingers then roll them in opposite directions. I roll the first link away from me, the next link toward me. That helps the links keep their shape while you dry them.

Drying links helps the sausages tighten up in their skins, which improves the texture. I use a wooden clothes-drying rack to hang my sausages, and it works like a charm. Hang your links for a couple of hours at room temperature and then let them sit overnight, uncovered, in the fridge, surrounded by paper towels to soak up any stray moisture. Even better is to let them hang at around 33°F to 40°F overnight. Can you eat them the first day? You bet, but the texture and flavor will improve the second day.

All this work applies equally to salami, which are just dry-cured sausages. You do need to use a different curing salt, in this case Insta Cure No. 2, and it's best to get a bacterial starter culture from a place like The Sausage Maker or Butcher & Packer. Why? You need the good bugs in the starter culture to properly ferment the salami—and yes, salami is a fermented meat product. That's why it's tangy; it's the lactic acid you're tasting. More on this later.

## Advanced Sausage-Making Tips

Once you have several batches of sausages under your belt, you can start thinking more about perfecting your craft. Here are a few advanced tricks and tips I've learned over the years.

When making fresh sausages, use fresh ingredients if possible—fresh herbs, fresh garlic, fresh everything. You'll notice the difference.

When you do use dried spices (seeds like black pepper, fennel, and coriander, for example), toast

them in a dry pan first. It makes them taste stronger, even weeks later. Don't toast dried herbs, though, or you'll burn them.

Stuff your sausage rather loosely when making the initial coil. This gives you more wiggle room to make links. If your initial coil is too taut, you won't be able to twist them enough to keep the whole coil from unraveling. They can (and do) burst when this happens.

Vary the length of your sausage links depending on how rich they are. This is, of course, a matter of opinion, but I think leaner links ought to be long and skinny, and fatty ones shorter and plumper.

The liquid you use to moisten your links matters a lot. The exact same sausage recipe made with red wine will taste different with white wine. Vinegar will change it again, as will water or fruit juice or liqueur; I've added ouzo to a few of my recipes. Put some thought into not only what kind of liquid you want to use but also the quality of it. If you wouldn't drink it, don't use it.

The most important thing to learn is balance. Make enough sausages, and after a while you'll develop an eye for such things as the right amount of spice or herb to not overpower the meat and the ideal length of the links. A good sausage has all its flavor elements in harmony. Savory is easy; so is salty. Sour can come from vinegar, sweet from any number of sources. Herbs need to play well with one another, as do spices.

My final bit of advice: Write everything down. If you don't keep accurate notes, you'll never be able to tinker with your recipes, and, most importantly, you'll never be able to recapture those moments of perfection.

### Vac Vacay

**Once you've finished hanging your cured meats, consider giving them a vacation in a vacuum bag for a week or more. Sealing a salami or cured loin or ham in a vac-bag and storing it in the fridge will help the moisture in the meat equalize, which reduces or even eliminates any case hardening, which is that dark ring around the outside edge of a dry-cured sausage. Case hardening is caused by the meat drying too fast, so the outside dries harder than the center. If it gets too severe, case hardening can destroy your sausage; the dried outer ring forms a barrier to the center, preventing the core of the sausage from drying properly. It then rots from within. This is why we cure meat at high humidities.**

## SALAMI, METTWURST, SAUCISSON

Dry-cured sausages are the most technically advanced level of sausage-making. You'll need extra equipment to make these sausages, and what's more, you'll need patience. None of these recipes can be made in less than two days, and all require long drying times in a special environment.

Whole books have been written about making salami, and I highly recommend *The Art of Making Fermented Sausages* by Stanley and Adam Marianski, *Cooking by Hand* by Paul Bertolli, and *Salumi* by Michael Ruhlman and Brian Polcyn. These books will give you an excellent overall grounding in the ins and outs of making dry-cured salami. What follows is a primer.

## Cures and Bacteria

While salami *can* be made without nitrates or starter bacteria, only experts can make such salami safely. Nitrate, which you will find commercially as Insta Cure or Prague Powder No. 2, and scientifically as sodium nitrate, are important safeguards against botulism and food poisoning. These additives also help the meat bind to itself and give it a pretty red color.

And for those who may recoil at the thought of nitrates in their food, know that the commercial products are extremely safe and are used in precise measurements. Most so-called uncured charcuterie products available in the markets are selling a lie: They *all* include celery juice or celery extract, which is nothing more than nitrite; it's just "natural" nitrite. In fact, you'll ingest more nitrite by eating a plate of celery with blue cheese than you would by gorging yourself on salami and sausages.

Specialized bacterial starters aren't strictly needed so long as you make salami in the right conditions, but again, unless you're an experienced salami-maker, I *highly* recommend using them. These starters inoculate your salami with good bacteria, and these bacteria crowd out and kill any toxic bacteria. They're also vital to getting that distinctive tangy flavor of a good salami. The lactic acid the good bacteria give off is what makes the meat tangy.

You can buy Insta Cure No. 2 at most decent butcher's shops, and you can order it online. Bacterial starters are available online through outlets such as Butcher & Packer and Sausagemaker.com.

### CURING CHAMBER

You'll need to hang your dry-cured sausages in a curing chamber. That chamber needs to be between 45°F and 60°F, with an ideal of 55°F, along with a humidity of 60 to 85 percent If you're blessed with a basement that meets these criteria, you're good to go. Most of us are not, however. So you need to build a chamber.

Many people start with a wine fridge. This is great if you already have one, as they allow you to control temperature and, to some extent, humidity. But if you don't own one already, you can set up an inexpensive curing rig using:

- An old fridge
- A temperature regulator, available online or from your local brew shop. The regulator goes into the wall, the refrigerator plugs into the regulator, and a probe goes into the fridge itself. You set the temperature with a dial gauge.
- A small humidifier that sits inside the fridge. It works the same as a temperature regulator. Or, for a little more money, you can get a combination regulator that covers both temperature and humidity. Auber Instruments makes one for about $130.
- A spray bottle with water. Even with the humidifier, I tend to spritz my salami every day or two at the start. This won't be necessary in humid places.

The whole shebang costs less than $300, and it lets you can control both temperature and humidity with precision.

# CORNED VENISON

**MAKES ▸** One 2- to 4-pound roast

**PREP TIME ▸** 5 days or so

**COOK TIME ▸** 3 hours

Corning venison at home is so good that every deer hunter out there ought to learn this technique—you'll get far more enjoyment out of the leg roasts from your venison. I typically use whole-muscle roasts from the hind leg to do this—big sirloin roasts, rump roasts, the "football roast," and such. But any big hunk of venison will work. The advantage of the whole-muscle roasts is that they have less sinew and connective tissue, which take hours to break down. I suppose you could use the backstrap, but then you'd have venison Canadian bacon.

The technique is simple. Brine your meat, then simmer it into tenderness. It takes several days, but it isn't labor-intensive at all. Corned venison is great hot or cold, with root vegetables, cabbage, cold in sandwiches (how I eat most of my corned venison), or chopped into hash.

Once made, you can keep corned venison in the fridge for a couple weeks or freeze it for a year.

One final tip. When you're done with the corned venison, leave it in the cooking broth. Store that in the fridge. Why? The broth keeps the venison moist. If you leave it out of the brine, the meat can get very dry, even crumbly.

Add everything but the roast to a pot and bring it to a boil. Turn off the heat and cover, then let it cool to room temperature while covered. This will take a few hours. Meanwhile, trim off any silverskin you find on the roast. Leave the fat. Once the brine is cool, find a container just about large enough to hold the roast, place the meat inside, and cover with the brine. You might have extra, which you can discard.

Make sure the roast is completely submerged in the brine; I use a clean stone to weigh the meat down. You can also flip the meat every day. Cover and put into the fridge for five to seven days, depending on the roast's size. A 2-pound roast might only need four days. The longer you soak, the saltier it will get, but you want the salt and nitrite to work its way to the center of the roast and that takes time, typically two days per pound of meat. Err on the side of extra days, not fewer.

After the allotted time has passed, you have corned venison. To cook and eat, rinse off the meat, then put the roast in a pot just large enough to hold it and cover with fresh water. You don't want too large a pot or the fresh water will leach out too much flavor from the meat; it's an osmosis thing. Partially cover the pot and simmer very gently—don't boil—for at least three hours and up to five hours. The meat itself will be cooked in an hour or less, but you want the sinews and connective tissue in the roast to soften, and that takes time.

Eat hot or cold. It's absolutely fantastic with good mustard and some sauerkraut on a sandwich.

**½ gallon water**
**½ cup kosher salt**
**⅓ cup sugar**
**½ ounce Insta Cure No. 1 (sodium nitrite)**
**1 tablespoon cracked black pepper**
**1 tablespoon toasted coriander seeds**
**6 bay leaves, crushed**
**1 tablespoon mustard seeds**
**1 tablespoon dried thyme**
**1 teaspoon caraway seeds**
**1 cinnamon stick**
**5 cloves garlic, chopped**
**One 2- to 5-pound venison roast**

## Dialing in the Cure

**The corned venison recipe here is the original, and it still works. But these days, I often switch to an equalization cure. With this, you weigh each roast in grams and then measure 1.5 percent of that weight in salt, plus another 0.25% (one quarter of one percent) in curing salt, mix the salts, then massage it into the meat. You then vacuum-seal the roast, with any stray salt that didn't stick to it, and put it in the fridge for several days. Flip the sealed meat each day. This method is foolproof in that it will never get too salty no matter how long you leave it.**

**The only downside is that you can lose salt in the simmering process, so when I make the spiced brine to cook the venison, I taste it before the meat goes in. If it tastes pleasantly salty, you're good to go.**

# CORNED VENISON CASSEROLE

This is a great use for leftover corned beef or venison, or you can make the meat just for this casserole. I like the homemade cream of chicken soup here, but you can use canned.

**SERVES** ▶ 8

**PREP TIME** ▶ 30 minutes

**COOK TIME** ▶ 45 minutes

12 ounces wide egg noodles

Salt

1 small head cabbage, chopped (or ½ large head)

1 white or yellow onion, chopped

3 tablespoons butter

2 pounds corned beef or venison, chopped or shredded

1 teaspoon dried savory or thyme

1 cup frozen peas

**FOR THE CREAM OF CHICKEN SOUP**

2 tablespoons butter

2 tablespoons flour, heaping

⅓ cup white wine

2 cups stock (chicken, grouse, pheasant, or quail)

2 tablespoons Dijon or other smooth mustard

¼ cup heavy cream

Salt

**FOR THE FINISH**

½ pound shredded cheddar cheese, divided

½ cup breadcrumbs, rye if possible

¼ cup melted butter

Preheat the oven to 350°F. Grease a casserole dish (9 by 13), with butter or lard. Boil the egg noodles in salty water until they're about half done, flexible but still a little crunchy at the center. Drain and set aside.

While the noodles are cooking, sauté the cabbage and onion in the butter until translucent, soft and barely starting to brown. Turn off the heat and mix in the corned beef, savory or thyme, and the frozen peas. Mix all this in with the half-cooked noodles.

### TO MAKE THE CREAM OF CHICKEN SOUP

To make the soup that will serve as the sauce, cook the butter with the flour over medium heat, stirring very often, until it turns a "dirty blonde" color, about 5 minutes. Keep an eye out while you are stirring—you don't want it to burn.

Pour in the white wine and stir. The mixture will seize up. Pour in the stock a little at a time, stirring constantly so it incorporates. Bring this to a simmer and ladle off a little into a cup. Mix this with the mustard into a slurry.

After the sauce has cooked about 5 minutes, add the slurry back into the pot and stir. The mustard will want to separate, so whisk or stir until it incorporates. Cook this another minute or two, the turn off the heat and stir in the cream. Add salt to taste.

### TO FINISH

Mix the soup and half the cheese with the meat-noodle-cabbage mixture, then pack it into the casserole dish.

Mix the breadcrumbs and melted butter and stir until incorporated. Sprinkle the rest of the cheese on top of the casserole, then the buttered breadcrumbs. Bake uncovered for 45 minutes. Let it set out of the oven for 5 to 10 minutes before serving.

**NOTE:** You can, of course, use canned cream of chicken soup. You will need a pint.

# VENISON PASTRAMI

**MAKES ▸** 2 pounds

**PREP TIME ▸** 3 days, to cure and dry

**COOK TIME ▸** 4 hours smoking time

I highly recommend that you use a single-muscle roast, ideally from the hind leg or even backstrap, for this recipe, as this is a lean smoked meat that you'll end up slicing thin and serving in a sandwich. If you have silver-skin or connective tissue in your roast, it won't soften and it'll get stuck in your teeth when you eat it. You've been warned.

A word on the salt and the Insta Cure. This cure is called an equalization cure, and it will never make your meat too salty. But you need to massage and press the salt into the roast, then, ideally, vacuum-seal it. If you don't have a vac sealer, put it in a freezer bag and remove all the air. Either way, you'll want to flip the roast every day as it cures. Err on a day or two too long rather than too little. You'll be fine. This method works on roasts up to about 5 pounds. Beyond that, the curing time runs into ten days or more.

Keep an eye on your venison's internal temperature when you're smoking it. A piece of backstrap can be ready in 90 minutes in a hot smoker, which to my mind isn't enough time on the smoke. Try to keep your smoker at 200°F or cooler; I like to keep it at 160°F, which lets me smoke the meat for a solid three to four hours.

What wood? Your choice. I prefer oak, maple, or hickory for this, followed by walnut, pecan, or cherry. Once you make your pastrami, it will keep a week or two, or you'll need to vacuum-seal and freeze it.

- A venison roast
- Kosher salt (see headnote)
- Insta Cure No. 1
- 1 teaspoon sugar
- ½ teaspoon dried thyme
- ¼ teaspoon celery seed
- ¼ teaspoon caraway seed
- ¼ teaspoon crushed juniper (optional)
- 3 tablespoons plus 1 teaspoon black pepper, divided
- ¼ cup brandy, red wine, vinegar or water
- 3 tablespoons coarsely ground coriander

Weigh your venison in grams. Then weigh out 1.5 to 2 percent pure salt—no iodide—ideally finely ground. Then weigh out 0.25% (one-quarter of one percent) of the weight of the roast in Insta Cure. This is a perfect amount and will give your pastrami the proper color and flavor.

Mix the salt, curing salt, and sugar, as well as the thyme, celery seed, caraway, juniper, and 1 teaspoon of black pepper, and grind them all together in a spice grinder. Pack the venison with this mixture, massaging it into the meat. Put the meat into a Ziploc bag or vacuum-seal it and set it in the fridge for three to seven days. A general rule is two days per pound of meat, but this will never get too salty.

Rinse the cure off the venison and pat it dry. It's fine if you have a little bit of the cure stuck to the meat, but you don't want too much. Put the venison on a rack in the fridge and let it dry uncovered for a day.

Dip the meat into the brandy—or really any other liquid you want—and then coat thoroughly in the remaining black pepper and coriander. I like to grind this myself so the texture is a little coarse, a little fine.

Smoke the venison at about 160°F to 200°F until the interior hits 145°F, which takes me about three hours. Let the pastrami cool and eat as lunch meat or on crackers.

## JERKY

Jerky, the ultimate road food. Meat snack. Beef leather. Chewy, savory, spicy, sweet, it's been my favorite thing to gnaw on ever since I ate biltong, the Mother of All Jerkies, in Zimbabwe thirty years ago. Making your own jerky at home is a snap—slice, brine, dry, eat. But making good jerky, I mean really good jerky, is harder than that.

I've made jerky a lot in recent years, and I've come to learn that nuances matter. How thick do you slice the meat? Across the grain or with it? What do you marinate it in? Or do you do a dry cure instead? How long is enough? How long is too long? Dry in an oven, smoker, or dehydrator? Again, how long? There is also the realm of ground meat jerky, which we'll get to later.

Slice thickness determines whether you'll have chewy jerky or the brittle stuff you need to moisten with your saliva before you can even begin to eat it. This latter stuff will last forever at room temperature.

Across the grain makes it easier to tear with your teeth, but the shorter strands are a little less satisfying as you gnaw them. Slicing with the grain can make for a challenging chew, but the fun lasts longer this way.

Brining, marinating, or dry-curing is virtually freestyle. So long as you have ample salt (or something salty, like soy sauce or Worcestershire sauce), you're in business. I'm not normally a fan of marinating meats, because marinades penetrate only about ⅛ inch into the meat (see page 67). But considering that I prefer to slice my meat for jerky about ¼ inch anyway, marinating works in this case. How long? Longer than you think you might need. Seasonings in jerky tend to fade a lot with the drying process, so you want it to get in there.

As for the drying process, a dehydrator beats an oven hands down. Even a low oven cooks the meat a bit too much, leaving it crispy. Of course, if you like crispy, go for it.

Through a fair bit of trial and error, I've come up with several satisfying recipes for venison jerky. They're not complicated, which is a bonus, and they pack a lot of flavor into the meat.

### Jerky Variations

Follow the same directions for the Chipotle Jerky (page 294), but use these alternate marinades.

#### Teriyaki Jerky

1¼ cups soy sauce
⅔ cup sugar
1 cup sake or other rice wine
½ cup mirin (optional)
¼ cup rice vinegar
2 cloves garlic, peeled and coarsely chopped
1 teaspoon Insta Cure No. 1

#### Sriracha Honey Lime Jerky

½ cup soy sauce
1 cup sriracha hot sauce
⅔ cup honey
½ cup freshly squeezed lime juice
1 teaspoon Insta Cure No. 1
1 tablespoon kosher salt

#### Mexican Carne Seca

3 tablespoons kosher salt
¼ cup freshly squeezed lime juice
1 tablespoon Mexican oregano
2 tablespoons guajillo chile powder, or 2 teaspoons cayenne

**NOTE:** For this recipe, you will want to slice the meat with the grain, not against it. And marinate it for only twenty-four hours.

# CHIPOTLE JERKY

**MAKES ▸** A lot

**PREP TIME ▸** 48 to 72 hours, for a good long marinating time

**COOK TIME ▸** 5 hours in the dehydrator

1 cup soy sauce

⅔ cup sugar

1 cup chopped onion

1 head garlic, peeled and coarsely chopped

One 7-ounce can of chipotles in adobo

Juice of 2 limes

1 teaspoon Insta Cure No. 1

2 tablespoons salt

5 to 6 pounds venison roast

The key to this recipe is the chipotle in adobo. Don't worry—it sounds more esoteric than it really is. It's basically smoked jalapeños canned in a rich, spicy adobo sauce. There are several makers of this magical stuff, and the little cans are widely available in Latin markets and most supermarkets that have a Hispanic food section. If all else fails, you can buy chipotles in adobo online.

You do need some curing salt to make sure this jerky completely safe. I use Insta Cure No. 1, which protects the meat as it slowly cooks in the dehydrator. You don't need this if you use an oven, but since I dehydrate at a relatively cool 145°F to 155°F, I use the nitrite.

The end result is a chewy, slightly thick jerky loaded with an almost "spicy BBQ" flavor. It's an addicting flavor—I ate three pieces one after the other, unconsciously, as I was trying to evaluate the flavor. That instinctive taking-another-bite is always a good sign.

Put the soy sauce, sugar, onion, garlic, chipotles, lime juice, curing salt, and enough water to fill the can of chipotles into a blender and blend until smooth. Taste and add salt if you need it—the marinade should taste pretty salty.

Cut the venison roast against the grain into roughly ¼-inch slices. Mix the marinade into the meat. The slices are going to want to stick to each other, so use your hands (wear gloves if you're sensitive to chiles) to make sure each side of every slice gets coated. These amounts are enough for up to 6 pounds of meat. Pack the mixture into a nonreactive (plastic, ceramic, or stainless steel) container, cover, and refrigerate for twenty-four to seventy-two hours. How long depends on your personal salt tolerance and on whether you plan on storing the finished jerky for months or not; I go three days.

When you're ready, lay the meat on dehydrator trays in one layer. Don't let the slices of meat touch. Set the dehydrator to 160°F for two hours, then drop it down to 145°F until the jerky is ready. When it's ready, the jerky will still be pliable but will fracture and crack a little when you bend it. All told, the jerky should be ready in about six hours. If you're planning to store this at room temperature for a long time, dry the meat until it is brittle.

If you're using an oven, set the oven as low as it will go and use something to prop open the door to let air circulate inside the oven. If you have a convection oven, use it.

Store it in the fridge for up to a month. Or freeze it until the Second Coming. I vacuum-seal jerky and take it on road trips.

# SMOKED VENISON JERKY

To make this jerky, I like to use slices, against the grain, from whole-muscle hind leg roasts. Backstrap is another good option. Don't use overly sinewy cuts. And do pay attention to your meat when slicing. No sinew or silverskin! For those of you who get a lot of deer in a year, backstrap is great for this. I mostly use roasts from the hind leg.

Adhere to the salt-to-meat ratio in this recipe, but feel free to play with the other spices. Some variations could be to add allspice or coriander, cinnamon, or use Tajin from a Mexican market.

Be sure to try a batch with just the salt and black pepper, at least once. It really shows off the quality of your venison.

**MAKES ▸** About 12 servings

**PREP TIME ▸** 24 to 48 hours

**COOK TIME ▸** 4 hours

½ cup freshly squeezed lime or lemon juice (see recipe)

½ cup salt

¼ cup paprika

2 tablespoons cayenne or other chile powder

2 tablespoons garlic powder, or 8 cloves garlic, minced and mashed

1 tablespoon black pepper

1 tablespoon dried oregano (optional)

1 tablespoon citric acid (optional)

5 pounds venison, sliced against the grain ¼ inch thick

Mix all the spices together in a bowl. If you're not using the citric acid powder (Fruit Fresh), wet the slices of the venison with the lime juice. Coat the venison with the spice mix, pressing and massaging it into the meat. Transfer to a covered container and put the container into the fridge for a day, and up to two days. More than that and things might get too salty.

Get your smoker going at about 165°F and no hotter than 200°F. Wood choice is up to you, but I like mesquite. Remove the meat from the container and shake off any excess spices; you do want some on there, though. Lay out the meat in the smoker so the slices aren't touching. Smoke until leathery, so not juicy and not brittle. Start checking on the meat at two hours, then every 20 minutes after that.

Once the jerky is to your liking, let it cool to room temperature before you put it in the fridge.

**NOTE:** Your jerky will keep for a few weeks at room temperature, and forever in the freezer.

**MAKES ▸** About ¾ pound, and can be scaled up

**PREP TIME ▸** 24 to 48 hours

**COOK TIME ▸** 4 to 8 hours, depending on your dehydrator

- 1¾ pounds venison
- ¼ pound bacon
- 1 cup dried cranberries or other berries
- 18 grams salt (about 2 tablespoons)
- 3 grams Insta Cure No. 1 (about ½ teaspoon)
- 2 teaspoons black pepper
- ½ teaspoon ground mace or nutmeg
- 1 tablespoon onion powder
- 1 tablespoon paprika, smoked if possible
- 2 to 3 tablespoons sugar
- ¼ cup water

# PEMMICAN-STYLE GROUND MEAT JERKY

Not all jerky needs to be made from intact pieces of meat. You can also make an excellent jerky-like product using ground venison. The very best of these is the Tanka Bar, a pemmican-like meat bar made by the Oglala Sioux Indians in South Dakota that's available online. The recipe here is a hat tip to the Tanka Bar.

You do need a special piece of equipment to do this right, however: a jerky gun, basically a caulking gun modified for food use. The one I use is made by Weston.

I like to grind the meat and fat for this right before making the jerky, but any ground venison will do. You'll want at least a little fat in the grind, however, because otherwise, the jerky will be crumbly and dry.

If you don't use bacon, you'll want to increase the salt to 25 grams. And if you have smoked salt, you'll want to use it.

Grind the venison, bacon, and dried cranberries through the fine die of your grinder. If you're using pre-ground venison, chop the dried cranberries and add them to the ground meat. Put the meat and cranberries in a large bowl and add all the remaining ingredients. Mix with your (very clean) hands until everything comes together and starts to stick to itself.

If you have a vacuum sealer, seal the mixture and set in the fridge for twenty-four to forty-eight hours. If you don't, pack the meat mixture into a lidded container, press some plastic wrap directly onto the surface, and let it sit that way.

The next day, separate the mixture into two or three chunks, depending on how big your jerky gun is. Pack it in and squeeze out lengths of jerky onto your dehydrator trays. Make sure they're separated from each other. Dehydrate at 150°F until the meat is mostly dry but still chewy.

This sort of jerky doesn't keep as long as traditional jerky because of the fat content. But it will keep for several weeks in the fridge, and it freezes well.

# VENISON SAUSAGE WITH SAGE AND JUNIPER

This is a sausage I was inspired to make after I returned from a deer-hunting trip to Catalina Island, off the coast of Los Angeles. I'm a firm believer in the cooking adage "what lives together in life can live together on the plate," and we found lots of native sages and juniper bushes on the island.

The two main players here are sage and juniper, boosted by the juniper herbiness of gin. It makes this sausage taste the way the hillsides of California smell on a warm summer's day. I add a touch of celery seed too, which seems to punch up the taste of the venison.

How to cook these sausages? Grill slowly or brown in a pan, then pan roast at 325°F for 20 minutes. You can also use these links in a stew or in a sausage, peppers, and onions sandwich.

**MAKES ▸** 5 pounds, about 20 to 22 links

**PREP TIME ▸** 90 minutes, if you have made sausages before; longer if you're a newbie

- 4 pounds venison
- 1 pound pork fat
- 10 to 15 feet hog casings
- 33 grams kosher salt (about 2 tablespoons)
- 3 grams Insta Cure No. 1 (optional)
- 15 grams ground juniper berries (about a tablespoon)
- 25 grams fresh chopped sage (about 2 tablespoons)
- 1 tablespoon black pepper
- 3 grams celery seed (about ½ teaspoon)
- ¼ cup gin
- ¼ cup cold water

Chop the venison and pork fat into 1-inch chunks, or however big you need to fit into your grinder. (Expert step: Mix the salt and curing salt with the meat—not the fat or any other ingredients—and refrigerate overnight. This helps develop myosin, which helps bind the sausage better later.)

Get out about 10 to 15 feet of hog casings and soak them in warm water. If you don't trust your source, run water through them to check for punctures or weak spots.

If you haven't already done so, combine the salt, curing salt, herbs, and spices with the meat and mix. Chill the meat and fat until it's almost frozen by putting it in the freezer for an hour or two.

Grind through your meat grinder using the coarse die; I use an 8 mm or a 10 mm die for this. If your room is warmer than 69°F, set the bowl for the ground meat into another bowl of ice to keep it cold. If the mixture is still below 38°F, you can grind a second time through the fine die; I use a 4.5 mm for this. If the meat mixture has warmed too much, put it into the freezer to chill and put the removable grinder parts (blade, die, hopper, etc.) into the fridge to stay cool. Clean the rest of the grinder and put into the freezer. Grind when the meat is very cold, about 32°F.

Add the gin and cold water and mix thoroughly using either a stand mixer on low for 60 to 90 seconds or with your (very clean) hands; I use my hands, which ache with cold as I do this (yours should, too).

Stuff the sausage into the casings. Twist off links by pinching a link and twisting it, first in one direction, and then, with the next link, in the other direction. Or you could tie them off with kitchen string.

Now look at the links, which will probably have air pockets in them. Use a sterile needle or sausage pricker (set it aglow in your stovetop flame) to puncture the casing over all the air pockets. Gently compress the links together to squeeze out the air pockets and rotate the links a bit more to tighten. This takes practice.

Hang the sausages in a cool place. At normal room temperatures, hang for two hours. But if you have a place where the temperatures are between 33°F and 40°F, hang for up to a day. Once the links have dried a bit, put them in the fridge until needed. They'll keep for a week. You can also smoke these sausages to an internal temperature of 150°F and they'll keep for about ten days. They also freeze well.

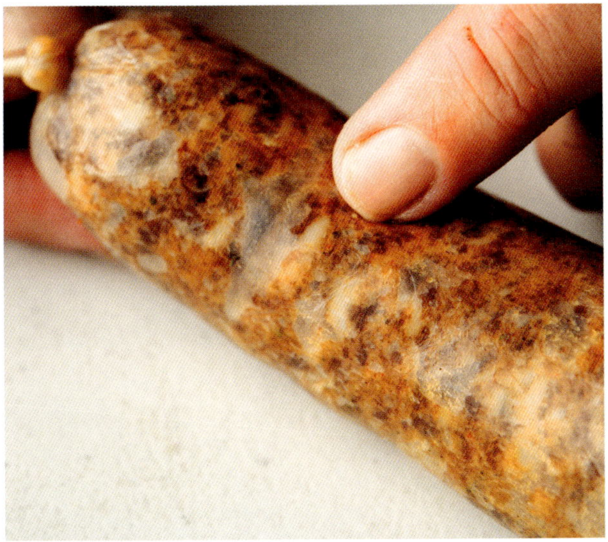

# BRITISH BANGERS

**MAKES ▸** About 5 pounds

**PREP TIME ▸** 90 minutes, if you have made sausages before; longer if you're a newbie

I had my first bangers and mash in the early 1990s at Lily Flanagan's, an Irish pub in Islip on Long Island. I remember it as generic sausage, with nice mashed potatoes and peas. Later, in 1995, on a thirty-six-hour layover in London, I had the real deal, a softish link with warm spices and an interesting bind that made it comforting to eat.

I later learned that the unusual mouthfeel of the banger is caused by the inclusion of some sort of grain in the link: breadcrumbs, oats, barley, or some such. I've heard various theories on why British charcuterie does this—virtually no other sausage-making nation does, with the exception of the famous Swedish potato sausage—ranging from scarcity during the World Wars to simple taste preference. I once thought it was some sort of scandalous cheapening of a good sausage. But I've come around. The addition of a grain in the mix can and does add something positive. Texture, sure, but also flavor. I'm partial to barley or oats coarsely ground in a coffee grinder.

There is no One True Banger, just as there is no single recipe for Italian sausage or Polish kielbasa. My version is adapted from a recipe for a Gloucester-style sausage I found in a charming little book called *British Charcuterie* by the prolific food writer Jennie Reekie.

Once you make these, the obvious thing to do with them is to make bangers and mash with peas. Just pull a page from your Thanksgiving playbook and make mashed potatoes, gravy, and peas in butter. That's it. You can also put these in a bun and serve with mustard and kraut or with pickled onions.

- 4 pounds venison, cut into chunks
- 10 to 15 feet hog casings
- 1 pound pork fat, or ½ pound pork fat and ½ pound venison fat, cut into chunks
- 36 grams kosher salt (about 2 tablespoons plus 1 teaspoon)
- 2 teaspoons fresh or dried thyme
- 2 teaspoons white pepper
- 1 teaspoon minced fresh sage
- 1 teaspoon porcini powder (optional)
- 1 teaspoon onion powder
- ½ teaspoon mace
- ½ teaspoon nutmeg
- 8 ounces coarsely ground oats, barley, or breadcrumbs
- ¾ cup malty beer

---

Get out about 10 to 15 feet of hog casings and soak them in warm water. If you don't trust your source, run water through them to check for punctures or weak spots.

Make sure all your equipment is cold by freezing the grinding plate, blades, and the bowl you will put the meat into for 30 minutes to an hour. Do the same for the meat and fat. When everything's nice and cold, mix the meat and fat with all the spices (leave out the oats and beer for the moment).

Grind through your meat grinder using the coarse die; I use an 8 mm or a 10 mm die for this. If your room is warmer than 69°F, set the bowl for the ground meat into another bowl of ice to keep it cold. If the mixture is still below 38°F, you can grind a second time through the fine die; I use a 4.5 mm for this. If the meat mixture has warmed too much, put it into the freezer to chill and put the removable grinder parts (blade, die, hopper, etc.) into the fridge to stay cool. Clean the rest of the grinder and put into the freezer. Grind when the meat is very cold, about 32°F.

Once the sausage has been ground twice, test the temperature again to make sure it's 35°F or colder. I prefer to chill the mix down to 28°F to 32°F for this next stage. Chill the mix, and when it's cold enough, take it out and add the oats and beer. Now, mix and knead this all up in a big bin or bowl with your (very clean) hands for a solid 2 minutes—your hands will ache with cold, which is good. You want everything to almost emulsify.

Stuff the sausage into the hog casings rather loosely. I like bangers to be about 6 to 8 inches long, but it's your choice. To twist them into links, tie off one end of the coil you made. Pinch off links with your hands and roll the link between them forward a couple times. Move down the coil and repeat, only this time roll backwards a few times. Repeat until you do the whole coil.

Now look at the links, which will probably have air pockets in them. Use a sterile needle or sausage pricker (set it aglow in your stovetop flame) to puncture the casing over all the air pockets. Gently compress the links together to squeeze out the air pockets and rotate the links a bit more to tighten; this takes practice.

Hang your links for at least an hour if your room is warm, and up to a day if you can hang them in a place that's 40°F or cooler. Let the sausages dry uncovered in the fridge overnight before you seal them up and freeze. Bangers will keep a week in the fridge and a year in the freezer.

# WISCONSIN RED BRATS

**MAKES ▶** About 5 pounds

**PREP TIME ▶** Overnight, plus about 2 hours

**COOK TIME ▶** 2 to 4 hours in the smoker

On *Wisconsin!* I'm a proud graduate of the University of Wisconsin, where I spent many an evening drinking beer, watching the Badgers, and eating red brats from State Street Brats in Madison. Red brats are smoky and addictive. Learn to make this link and you'll find yourself rooting for my Badgers, at least a little.

For the mustard seed, grind whole seeds a bit in a spice grinder to crack them up.

Get out about 10 to 15 feet of hog casings and soak them in warm water. If you don't trust your source, run water through them to check for punctures or weak spots.

Cut the venison and pork into chunks that will fit into your grinder. Mix with the salt, curing salt (Insta Cure No. 1), and sugar and refrigerate overnight. Doing this helps the sausage bind to itself later. You can skip the overnight rest, but your sausage won't be as firm in the casing.

When you're ready to make the sausage, freeze your grinder's grinding plate and blades and the bowl you'll put the meat into for 30 minutes to an hour. Do the same for the meat and fat. When everything's nice and cold—no warmer than 38°F—mix the meat and fat with the powdered milk and all the spices.

Grind it all through a coarse plate; I use a 10 mm plate. Test the temperature of the mixture, and if it's 35°F or colder, go ahead and grind half the mixture again through a fine die, like a 4.5 mm. Set it back with the rest of the ground meat mixture. If it's warmer than 35°F, put the mix back into the freezer to chill. This might take an hour or so if you've let the meat warm up too much. Use the time to clean up.

Once the sausage has been ground twice, test the temperature again to make sure it's 35°F or colder. I prefer to chill the mix down to 28°F to 32°F for this next stage. Chill the mix, and when it's cold enough, take it out and add the beer. Now, mix and knead this all up in a big bin or bowl with your (very clean) hands for a solid 2 minutes—your hands will ache with cold, which is good. You want everything to almost emulsify.

Stuff the sausage into hog casings rather loosely. Do this in a coil before you make the links. I like this sausage in links of about 6 to 8 inches long, but it's your choice. To twist them into individual sausages, tie off one end of the coil you made. Pinch off links with your hands and roll the link between them forward a few times. Move down the coil and repeat, only this time roll backward a few times. Repeat until you do the whole coil.

Now look at the links, which will probably have air pockets in them. Use a sterile needle or sausage pricker (set it aglow in your stovetop flame) to puncture the casing over all the air pockets. Gently compress the links together to squeeze out the air pockets and rotate the links a bit more to tighten. This takes practice.

Dry your links in a cool place for at least twenty-four hours and up to three days. I hang mine in a curing fridge set to 55°F, with about 75 percent humidity. The curing salt will protect them during this time. If you haven't used curing salt, dry the sausage uncovered in the fridge for a day.

To smoke the links, hang in a cool smoker and let the heat come up slowly until it hits about 200°F. Smoke the links until their internal temperature hits 155°F. This may take less than four hours, but internal temperature is more important. As soon as the sausages are cooked, submerge them in an ice water bath until cool. Pat dry and store in the fridge.

**3 pounds venison**

**10 to 15 feet hog casings**

**2 pounds very fatty pork shoulder or pork belly**

**35 grams kosher salt**

**5 grams Insta Cure No. 1**

**1 tablespoon sugar**

**25 grams powdered milk**

**3 tablespoons minced garlic**

**1 tablespoon freshly ground black pepper**

**2 teaspoons coarsely ground mustard seed**

**1½ teaspoons ground mace or nutmeg**

**1½ teaspoons dried sage**

**¾ cup cold lager beer**

"Of all the wonders of nature, a tree in summer is perhaps the most remarkable; with the possible exception of a moose singing 'Embraceable You' in spats."

—WOODY ALLEN

# TEXAS HOT LINKS

This is a Texas Hill Country classic, a reasonably spicy sausage usually made with pork, beef, venison, or a combination. You can amp up the cayenne if you want to make this legit spicy.

**MAKES** ▶ About 5 pounds

**PREP TIME** ▶ 2 hours

**COOK TIME** ▶ 4 hours in the smoker

- 3 pounds venison
- 2 pounds fatty pork shoulder or belly
- 34 grams salt (a little less than 2 tablespoons)
- 5 grams Insta Cure No. 1 (a little less than 1 teaspoon) (optional)
- 1 tablespoon sugar (optional)
- 2 tablespoons paprika
- 10 to 15 feet hog casings
- 1 tablespoon freshly ground black pepper
- 1 tablespoon cayenne
- 2 teaspoons thyme
- 6 bay leaves, ground fine
- 3 cloves garlic, minced
- ⅓ cup lager beer or ice water

Cut the venison and pork into chunks that will fit into your grinder. Mix with the salt, curing salt, and sugar. Let this sit in the fridge for as long as you can stand, up to overnight if you have time; it helps the sausage bind to itself better.

Get out about 10 to 15 feet of hog casings and soak them in warm water.

Mix the spices and garlic with the meat and fat and grind though a coarse die, about 10 mm. If you don't have that, grind with as coarse a die as you have. If your room is warmer than about 70°F, grind into a container that is set in ice to keep things very cold.

If the meat is still below 40°F, go ahead and grind again through a 6 mm die or similar. Tip: If you have some bread around, rip off a piece and make that the last thing in the grinder. It pushes out all of the rest of the meat so you don't waste any. If the meat is above 40°F, put it in the freezer for 30 minutes while you clean up everything.

Add the beer (or water) to the sausage mixer and mix with your (clean) hands, or a mixer with a paddle attachment set on low, for about 2 minutes. The sausage will adhere to itself and you will see whitish streaks in the bowl. Put the sausage in a sausage stuffer.

Thread a casing onto the stuffer, leaving a few inches as a "tail" so you can tie it off later. Stuff the whole casing at once, again leaving a tail at the other end. Repeat until you've stuffed all the sausage.

Make links by pinching them off and spinning them, first one way, then the other. This prevents them from unraveling when you hang the links to dry. You can also tie them off with twine. Tie off the ends of the casings.

Carefully compress the links to reveal air pockets and prick the links with a needle to remove them, gently compressing the meat.

Hang your sausages to dry for an hour at room temperature, or up to a day if you can do so in 40°F or below.

Smoke your hot links at 200°F or thereabouts until they reach about 150°F internal temperature. Then, either eat them or plunge them into a bath of ice water to stop the cooking. Dry them off and store in the fridge for a week, or freeze.

### NOTE

I really like adding a bit of binder to these links to get a better snap and bind. I use Butcher & Packer's "special meat binder," which you can buy online. You add it with the liquid, right before you mix.

# KABANOSY

**MAKES ▶** About 10 long links

**PREP TIME ▶** 4 hours

**COOK TIME ▶** 4 hours, plus hanging time afterward

Kabanosy is what a Slim Jim dreams about becoming when it grows up. It's lightly spiced with garlic, nutmeg, black pepper, and a hint of caraway, smoked over cherry, apple, or beech wood, then hung for a few days to dry. It is, quite simply, the world's greatest meat stick.

It's an unusual sausage because even though it's air-dried, you don't use starter cultures or Insta Cure No. 2, which is the sodium nitrate you normally use for dry-cured sausages. The drying process is too short for that. Traditionally, this is a pork sausage, but venison works with it. Once made, they'll keep in the fridge for a couple of weeks or so. After you vacuum-seal them or wrap them tightly, they'll freeze for up to a year without loss of quality.

To make a proper kabanosy, you'll need sheep casings. Many butcher shops have them, but they're harder to find than the regular hog casings. You can also buy sheep casings online. In addition, you'll need to smoke these links, preferably over cherry, apple, or beech wood. If you don't have any of these, oak, maple, or hickory would be fine.

2½ pounds pork, venison, wild boar, bear, or other meat

10 ounces pork fat

25 grams kosher salt (about 3 tablespoons)

3 grams Insta Cure No. 1 (about ½ teaspoon)

4 grams sugar (about 1 heaping teaspoon)

4 cloves garlic, minced

4 grams crushed black pepper (about 2 teaspoons)

2 grams nutmeg (about 1 heaping teaspoon)

2 grams caraway seed (2 teaspoons)

1 gram celery seed (about ¼ teaspoon)

⅓ cup ice water

20 feet sheep casings

Cut the meat and fat into pieces that will fit in your grinder. Mix all the salts and spices with the meat and fat. Put everything in the freezer for an hour to chill. Meanwhile, take out about 20 feet of sheep casings and soak them in tepid water.

Grind the mixture in the fine die of your grinder, making sure everything stays cold. If the meat warms beyond 40°F, stop and freeze everything for 30 minutes to cool it down. Put the ground meat into the fridge while you clean up.

Using a stand mixer or your (very clean) hands, add the ice water and mix the meat and fat—use the lowest setting on a stand mixer—until it binds, about 1 to 2 minutes. Again, put the meat into the fridge while you clean up.

Flush the sheep casings with warm water and set aside.

Put the meat mixture into your sausage stuffer and stuff into the sheep casings. Remember that sheep casings are weaker than hog casings, so you do not want to overstuff them. As you're stuffing, fill up a link between 12 inches and 24 inches, leaving plenty of extra casing on either end. Cut the casing and continue to make these large links until you've used all the meat.

Use a sterilized needle to pierce the casings wherever there are air pockets. Gently squeeze the meat in the casings to tighten. You may break some until you get the hang of it. If you do, put the meat back into the stuffer and make another link. Once all the links are firm in their casings, tie the ends together in a double or triple knot. Trim any excess casing.

Hang the links to dry in a cool place for several hours, depending on how warm it is. If the temperature is 70°F or above, hang for only an hour.

Move the links to a smoker and smoke until the interior of the meat hits 150°, keeping your smoker cool enough so that this takes about two to four hours. You want the links to get lots of smoke time.

Let the links cool, then move to a place to hang them. Ideally, this place is between 35°F and 60°F and dark. Hang the links for three to five days to let them dry out a bit. They're reasonably shelf-stable, but I keep them in the fridge. If for some reason you plan on keeping them more than a month or so, wrap tightly (or vacuum-seal) and freeze.

# SWEDISH STÅNGKORV

Stångkorv is a fascinating Swedish sausage that contains barley and is fermented until it gets tangy. It's great for breakfast and not terribly hard to make. I learned about this sausage in the book *The Nordic Cookbook* by Magnus Nilsson, which I highly recommend.

The addition of barley (cooked in salted water, drained, and cooled) in the grind kick-starts the fermentation process. After you make the sausages, you hang them in a warm, humid place for a couple of days to let the fermentation roll. Then you hang the links in a cool, drier place for another few days before eating or storing.

You shouldn't need to buy and use a separate bacterial starter to make stångkorv, but if you want to be double-dog sure you're getting the right lacto-fermentation going, I recommend using the starter LHP, which gives you strong tanginess.

What's the flavor? Addicting. I can't get enough of that tang, and the warming spices of clove and allspice really make stångkorv perfect for chilly morning breakfasts.

You should know that because of the barley, this sausage doesn't bind well. It's a lot like Swedish potato sausage, where the mixture is cased, but it will be crumbly, unlike, say, German Weisswurst.

I tend to either cook stångkorv cased and then tear into it like hash or uncase it before cooking and cook it like hash; you do still need to initially case stångkorv because of the fermenting and hanging time. It seems best as a breakfast sausage, with fried eggs and some form of potatoes, usually hash browns. It would also be excellent as part of a holiday stuffing or dressing or added to a stew.

Stångkorv will keep in the fridge for several weeks and freezes very well.

**MAKES ▶** About 5 pounds

**PREP TIME ▶** 90 minutes, plus 1 week to dry

- 2¼ pounds lean meat (pork, venison, beef, lamb, etc.)
- 17 ounces pork fat or pork belly
- 36 grams sea salt (or kosher salt), 1¼ ounces
- 6 ounces yellow onion, chopped
- Butter or oil, for frying
- 10 ounces cooked barley
- 10 feet hog casings
- 1 tablespoon freshly ground black pepper
- 2 teaspoons ground allspice
- 1 teaspoon ground cloves
- ½ cup ice water (distilled if possible)
- 4 grams LHP starter culture (optional)

Cut the meat and fat into chunks that will fit in your grinder. Mix with the salt, then put into a covered container in the fridge overnight, or up to a day.

Cook the onion in a little butter or oil until barely browned. Sprinkle with a little salt and set aside to cool. This can be done a day ahead.

Get about 10 feet of hog casings ready by soaking them in warm water. If you want, run fresh water through them to check for leaks and to flush any excess salt out of them.

Mix the meat, fat, cooked onion, and barley with the spices. Grind this through a very coarse die. I use 10 mm. If you have only coarse and fine options, use the coarse.

*continued*

If the meat mixture has warmed beyond 40°F, put it in the freezer while you clean up and get ready to grind again. When the meat mixture is cold enough—and this can be immediately after the first grind in some cases—grind it a second time through a 6 mm die or the coarse die one more time.

If you're using the starter culture, dissolve it in the distilled cold water (if you're not using the culture, the water need not be distilled). Let it sit about 15 minutes.

Mix the cold water with the meat mixture and work and knead it with your clean hands or a stand mixer on low for about 2 minutes. This sausage doesn't bind like a normal one because of the barley, but you want it to bind as best you can. Mixing does this.

Thread the casing onto the sausage stuffer tube and stuff it with the mixture. Stuff a whole coil before making links. When you're done, twist off links by spinning one away from you, then, working down the line, the next link toward you, then away from you, and so on.

Hang the links in your oven (turned off, of course), with a baking sheet underneath. Let them ferment like this for two to three days. Spritz them with water at least once a day. You want a warmish, stable, humid environment. They should start to smell nice—meaty, and tart-smelling, if there is such a thing.

Finally, hang the fermented links in a cool place, ideally dark and below 60°F, for at least a day, and ideally a week or even two. Then they're ready to eat or store. They keep in the fridge for a couple of weeks, and they freeze well.

**NOTE:** The weight of the barley is after cooking. This tends to be about 1 cup dried.

# MEXICAN-STYLE CHORIZO

Mexican chorizo is very different from its Spanish cousin, softer, spicier, and more floral. Making an authentic one is tricky if you don't have some of the ingredients. But if you can't find all of the ingredients, know that only a few are important. One such is achiote paste, which is available at any Mexican market, or you can buy it online. You do need cayenne and some other chile powder, but these are easily available in Latin markets—or you can grind dried chiles yourself, which is what I do.

**MAKES ▸** About 5 pounds

**PREP TIME ▸** 2 hours

- 4 pounds venison
- 1 pound pork fat
- 34 grams kosher salt (about 3 tablespoons)
- 15 grams sugar, about 1 tablespoon
- 6 cloves garlic, minced
- 6 grams oregano, about 2 tablespoons
- 5 grams ground cumin, about 2 teaspoons
- 3 grams chipotle powder, about 1 heaping teaspoon
- 5 grams cayenne, 1 tablespoon
- 28 grams pasilla, ancho, or mulato chile powder, about 3 tablespoons (optional)
- 2 tablespoons achiote paste
- ¼ cup red wine vinegar or freshly squeezed lime juice
- 10 to 15 feet hog casings

Cut the meat and fat into chunks that will fit into your meat grinder. Combine the salt, sugar, and all the dry spices (not the achiote paste) with the meat and fat, mix with your hands, and chill it until it's almost frozen by putting it in the freezer for an hour or so.

Get out about 10 to 15 feet of hog casings and soak them in warm water. If you don't trust your source, run water through them to check for punctures or weak spots. Mix the vinegar with the achiote paste and chill it in the fridge.

Grind the meat mixture through your meat grinder using a medium die—about 6.5 mm. If your room is warm, set the bowl for the ground meat into another bowl of ice to keep it cold. Make sure the meat mixture is very cold before moving on to the next step—you want it between 28°F and 35°F.

Add the achiote mixture and mix, using either a stand mixer on low or your hands, for 90 seconds. This is important to get the sausage to bind properly. Once it's mixed, put it back in the fridge and clean up.

Stuff the sausage into the casings all at once. To twist them into individual sausages, tie off one end of the coil you made. Pinch off links with your hands and roll the link between them forward a few times. Move down the coil and repeat, only this time, roll backward a few times. Repeat until you do the whole coil. Or you could tie them off with butcher's string.

Check the links for air pockets. Use a sterile needle or sausage pricker to puncture the casing over the air pockets. Gently compress the links together to squeeze out the air and rotate the links a bit more to tighten.

Hang the sausages in a cool place for up to four hours (the colder it is, the longer you can hang them). If it's warm out, hang for one hour. Once they've dried a bit, refrigerate. They will keep a week in the fridge. If you're freezing the sausages, wait a day before doing so. This will tighten up the links and help them keep their shape.

# BASIC VENISON SALAMI

With the possible exception of a whole dry-aged ham, to my mind, salami is the highest form of the butcher's art. The careful crafting of raw meat, salt, spices, and time creates something very different from a fresh sausage. It's not crazy to call it alchemy. But making salami is no joke. It takes time, attention to detail (and sanitation), plus a careful eye to troubleshoot problems. Doing this at home is not for beginners. Make fresh sausages until you're comfortable with the process before moving to this recipe.

When you do pluck up enough courage to make your own salami at home, this is the recipe you should start with. It's the classic, the "little black dress" of salami, flavored only with salt, black pepper, and a bit of garlic. The meat is the star here, not the spices. Every salami-making culture makes a version of this sausage, and recipes are similar whether you look to Spain or France or Italy or Hungary or Germany—although these last two nations tend to smoke their salami, too.

If you've never made fresh sausages before, come back when you've made a dozen or so batches. You need to be comfortable with the basic sausage-making process before you take the step of curing them. You also need some special equipment. Don't try to shortcut salami-making. You'll pay for it eventually.

First, you need a good grinder; I use a Weston. You need a sausage stuffer, too. Lots of companies make good ones. Can you hand-cut the meat and fat? Yes, but it requires a sharp knife and an awful lot of patience.

To hang your sausages for the few days it takes to ferment them, I use a simple wooden clothes-drying rack. I also buy "S" hooks from the local hardware store to hang the links. You'll need a humidifier both for the fermentation process and while your links are drying. Finally, you must have a curing chamber; I use an old fridge (see page 287).

The salami-making process is this: You make sausage, only with added sodium nitrate (Insta Cure No. 2) and a starter culture, then ferment the sausages at room temperature for a few days to let the good bacteria in the starter beat back any bad bugs within the meat. Do you need these two ingredients? Absolutely. Yeah, I hear you: "But can't salami be made without them?" Yes. But *we* can't. The people who can pull it off work in places where they've made salami for decades or even centuries, and the ambient air already has the good bacteria. It's like a sourdough. For you and me, adding nitrate and starter culture is our insurance policy against botulism and listeria.

The last stage is to hang the links to dry out slowly in the chamber or in a basement. The key to successful drying is to let the sausages dry slowly, little by little. Why? This does two things. First, it prevents the dreaded "case hardening," where the outside of the salami dries too fast and prevents the interior from drying properly. And second, the longer you cure your salami, the better it will taste.

Truly great salami has a distinct funk to it, like cheese. I've made a lot of decent salami, some mediocre and a few crappy ones. Only once in a while does everything work perfectly. It's part of the learning process, which never ends.

Follow this recipe, get decent equipment, and you should be fine. But remember: Sausage-making is a sprint; salami-making is a marathon. You must be careful and sanitary at the start—we're dealing with raw meat here—and you cannot forget about your salami while it cures or you may be very, very sad. Still, this ain't rocket science. You can make salami at home, and when you do, it's one of the most satisfying things you can make with your own two hands.

**MAKES ▶** About 5 pounds

**PREP TIME ▶** 3 hours to make the sausages, then at least 1 month to cure and dry

- 4 pounds venison
- 1 pound pork fatback
- 51 grams salt
- 6 grams Insta Cure No. 2
- 2 tablespoons minced fresh garlic
- 1 tablespoon minced fresh rosemary
- 1 tablespoon coarsely ground black pepper, divided
- 15 feet hog casings, preferably 38–42 mm wide
- ⅓ cup red wine
- ¼ cup distilled water
- 20 grams FRM-52 starter culture, or T-SPX culture

Start by setting out ½ to ⅔ pound of the venison and dicing it fine. Do the same for ¼ pound of the fat. I like doing this because it varies the grind within the sausage from very fine to chunky. To me, this is more interesting. You can run it all through the grinder if you prefer, or if you think someone will get all crazy if they see big pieces of fat in their salami. Cut the remaining fat and meat into chunks that will fit into your grinder. Trim as much sinew and silverskin as you can.

Put both the diced and chunked fat into separate containers in the fridge. Mix the salt and curing salt with the meat and put it into the fridge overnight, keeping the diced and chunked pieces separate. This overnight rest helps develop myosin, which will give you a tighter bind when you stuff the links later.

The next day, put the fat and your grinding equipment—blade, coarse and fine die, etc.—in the freezer. Mix the garlic, rosemary, and half the black pepper into the meat you plan on grinding. Put that in the freezer too. Let everything chill down until the meat hits about 30°F or so. It won't freeze solid because of the salt. Normally, this takes about 90 minutes. While you're waiting, soak about 15 feet of hog casings in a bowl of warm water and put the red wine in the fridge.

When the meat and fat are cold, take them out and mix together, but keep the diced meat and fat separate for now. Grind half to two-thirds of the mixture through the coarse die of the grinder, about 8 to 10 mm. Grind the rest through the fine die, about 4.5 mm. I do this to vary my grind, which makes for a better texture. Sometimes I do three-quarters fine and one-quarter coarse, depending on my mood. The key is variability.

Put the meat and fatback into the freezer while you clean up. Dissolve the starter culture with the distilled water.

*continued*

When the meat mixture is back below 35°F, you can mix it. I put the mixture into a big plastic bin with the diced fat and meat, the remaining black pepper, and the red wine and the starter culture mixture and mix it by hand for about 2 minutes. If you do this, you'll know the mixture's cold enough if your hands ache from the chill. Or you can put everything into a big stand mixer and mix on low for 90 seconds to 2 minutes. I prefer to mix by hand.

Put the sausage into the fridge while you clean up. Run some clean water through your casings to flush them and to see if you have any leaks. Cut lengths of casing of about 2 feet long and set all but one back in the water. Thread one onto your sausage stuffer.

Pack the sausage into your stuffer and get ready to make the salami. Leave 4 to 6 inches of casing hanging from the edge of the stuffer as a "tail"; you'll use this to tie off the salami in a bit. Start working the meat into the casing, using your fingers to flush any air out of the casing and to regulate the flow. I prefer straight links about a foot long or so. Remove the link from the stuffer and repeat with the remaining casings and sausage.

Now gently compress the meat within each casing, watching for air bubbles. Heat a needle or a sausage pricker in the flames of your stove to sterilize it and prick the links to let any trapped air out. Tie off both ends of the link in a double or triple knot (you don't need a specialized butterfly knot with hog casings) and then tie a loop of kitchen twine to one end, making sure the twine knot is underneath the casing knot you made. This will prevent the twine from slipping off. Hang your sausages from "S" hooks on a wooden rack.

To ferment your links, you'll need to keep them warm and moist. I do this by putting a humidifier under the hanging sausages and then tenting the whole shebang with big garbage bags that I've sliced open on one end. I also use a water sprayer to spritz my sausages a couple of times a day. Doing this prevents the casings from hardening. Keep your sausages hanging at room temperature (65°F to 80°F) in about 85 percent humidity for two to three days.

Now you need to dry your sausages and turn them into salami. Hang them in a place that is about 50°F to 60°F with about 80 to 90 percent humidity. In most cases, you will need to put a humidifier under your links. I also spritz them with water once a day for the first two weeks. After the first week of hanging, drop the humidity to 70 to 80 percent. On the third week, drop it again to 65 to 70 percent and hold it there until four to ten weeks have elapsed since the salami went into the chamber.

You now have salami. To store long-term, vacuum-seal them individually and keep in the fridge. They will last indefinitely this way, and the vacuum-sealing will keep them from becoming rock hard. You can also freeze them.

## The Many Colors of Mold

**When you cure meats, mold happens. Mold comes in many colors, each representing a different variety. In general, it's no big deal, especially since many people peel off the casing of their salami when they intend to eat it, even though the casing is perfectly edible. A general rule of thumb says that tight white mold is fine, fuzzy white mold is OK, green mold not great but not a disaster, and black mold is bad. If you should start getting green or black mold, wipe down your links with vinegar; you may need to scrub a bit to get all the mold off. Incidentally, smoked salami tend not to develop mold. One more note: If you have mold on your salami and you do the vac vacay I mention on page 286, the exterior of the links will get slimy when you take them out. In that case, you want to peel off the casing.**

# DUTCH SUMMER SAUSAGE

**B**oerenmetworst—literally, "farmer's dry sausage"—is a Dutch sausage that is dried and smoked, a proper "summer sausage" from the Old Country. You make the links, let them ferment for a few days, smoke them very gently—you don't want them to cook—then hang them to dry for a few weeks before eating.

The distinctive flavor of Dutch (and Afrikaner) sausages comes from the liberal use of coriander, ginger, cloves, and black pepper. Allspice is another common addition, and if you want to add some, you can mix in ½ teaspoon.

Note that if you want an Upper Midwest–style summer sausage, let the links hang for only two or three weeks, so they're still a little soft.

**MAKES ▸** About 5 pounds

**PREP TIME ▸** 3 hours to make the sausages, then at least 1 month to cure and dry

**COOK TIME ▸** 2 to 4 hours cold smoking

- 3½ pounds venison
- 1 pound fatty pork shoulder
- ½ pound pork fatback
- 10 grams dextrose (granulated sugar, if you can't get it)
- 51 grams salt
- 6 grams Insta Cure No. 2
- 1 teaspoon powdered ginger
- ½ teaspoon ground cloves
- 1 tablespoon cracked black pepper, divided
- 1 tablespoon coarsely ground coriander seed, divided
- 2 teaspoons coarsely ground mustard seed, divided
- 15 feet hog casings, preferably 38–42 mm wide
- ¼ cup malt vinegar
- ⅓ cup distilled water
- 10 grams F-LC or FRM-52 starter culture

Cut the meat and fat into chunks that will fit into your grinder. Trim as much sinew and silverskin as you can. Put the fat into a container in the fridge. Mix the dextrose, salt, and curing salt with the meats and put it into the fridge overnight. This helps develop myosin, which will give you a tighter bind when you stuff the links later.

The next day, put your grinding equipment—blade, coarse and fine die, etc.—into the freezer. Mix the ginger, cloves, and half of the remaining spices with the meat and fat. Put the mixture into the freezer and let everything chill down until it hits about 30°F or so. Because of the salt, it won't freeze solid. Normally, this takes about 90 minutes. While you're waiting, soak about 15 feet of hog casings in a bowl of warm water and put the malt vinegar in the fridge.

When the meat and fat are cold, take them out and grind through the coarse die of the grinder; I use a 10 mm plate. Test the temperature of the mixture, and if it's 35°F or colder, go ahead and grind it all again through a fine die, like a 4.5 mm. If it's warmer than 35°F, put the mix back into the freezer to chill. This might take an hour or so if you've let the meat warm up too much. Use the time to clean up and to dissolve your starter culture in the distilled water.

Once the sausage has been ground twice, test the temperature again to make sure it's 35°F or colder. I prefer to chill the mix down to 28°F to 32°F for this next stage. Chill the mix, and when it's cold enough, take it out and add the remaining spices, the vinegar, and the water-starter culture

*continued*

mixture. Now, mix and knead this all up in a big bin or bowl with your (very clean) hands for a solid 2 minutes—your hands will ache with cold, which is good. You want everything to almost emulsify.

Stuff the sausage into the hog casings rather loosely. For this sausage, you want long rings—you'll tie the ends together eventually. First make long links of about 2 feet long, with plenty of extra casing on either side. Do this with all the sausage before moving on.

When you're ready, gently compress the long links to fill the casing. Keep an eye out for air pockets. Use a sterile needle or sausage pricker (set it aglow in your stovetop flame) to puncture the casing over all the air pockets. Gently compress the links together to squeeze out the air pockets; this takes practice. Tie the ends of the casing together in a double or triple knot.

Hang the links from a clothes rack or some such. I use "S" rings you can buy from the hardware store to hang them from the clothes rack rods. You need to ferment your links, keeping them warm and moist. I do this by putting a humidifier under the hanging sausages and then tenting the whole shebang with big garbage bags that I've sliced open on one end. I also use a water sprayer to spritz my sausages a couple of times a day. Doing this prevents the casings from hardening. Keep your sausages hanging at room temperature (65°F to 80°F) at about 85 percent humidity for three days.

Move the sausages to your smoker and smoke them over very low heat for up to four hours of continuous smoke. It's vitally important that you do not cook your links here, so put ice in the water tray of the smoker, and smoke on a cold day or in the early morning. Do not let the smoker rise above 100°F. If it gets too hot, open the door of the smoker or take the links out.

Now you need to dry your sausages and turn them into salami. Hang them in a place that's about 50°F to 60°F with about 80 to 90 percent humidity. In most cases, you'll need to put a humidifier under your links. I also spritz them with water once a day for the first two weeks. After the first week of hanging, drop the humidity to 70 to 80 percent. On the third week, drop it again to 65 to 70 percent and hold it there until a total of four to eight weeks has elapsed since the salami went into the chamber.

To store long-term, vacuum-seal them individually and keep in the fridge. They will last indefinitely this way, and the vacuum-sealing will keep them from becoming rock hard. You can also freeze them.

# SPANISH CHORIZO

**MAKES ▸** About 5 pounds

**PREP TIME ▸** 3 hours to make the sausages, then at least 1 month to cure and dry

Chorizo is normally made with pork—except when it's made with "retired" bulls from the ring. But chorizo works great with venison, especially old bull moose or elk or rutty bucks.

Try to get Spanish smoked paprika for this recipe. Yes, you can use regular paprika, but it won't be nearly the same. If you want, you can add up to 1 tablespoon of hot paprika in place of one of the tablespoons of smoked paprika.

A word on the casings. This recipe calls for the widest hog casings available, easily obtainable online from Weston, The Sausage Maker, or Butcher & Packer (see "Special Equipment Needed," page 281). If you can only get standard hog casings, dry the salami for only three weeks.

Cut the meat and fat into chunks that will fit into your grinder. Trim as much sinew and silverskin as you can. Put the fat into a container in the fridge. Mix the dextrose, salt, and curing salt with the meats and put it into the fridge overnight. This helps develop myosin, which will give you a tighter bind when you stuff the links later.

The next day, put your grinding equipment—blade, coarse and fine die, etc.—into the freezer. Mix the spices with the meat and fat. Put the mixture into the freezer and let everything chill down until it hits about 30°F or so. It won't freeze solid because of the salt. Normally, this takes about 90 minutes. While you're waiting, soak about 15 feet of hog casings in a bowl of warm water and put the sherry in the fridge.

When the meat and fat are cold, take them out and grind through the coarse die of the grinder; I use a 10 mm plate. Test the temperature of the mixture, and if it's 35°F or colder, go ahead and grind half the mixture again through a fine die, like a 4.5 mm or something similar. If it's warmer than 35°F, put the mix back in the freezer to chill. This might take an hour or so if you've let the meat warm up too much. Use the time to clean up and to dissolve your starter culture in the distilled water.

Once the sausage has been ground, test the temperature again to make sure it's 35°F or colder. I prefer to chill the mix down to 28°F to 32°F for this next stage. Chill the mix, and when it's cold enough, take it out and add the sherry and the water-starter culture mixture. Now, mix and knead this all up in a big bin or bowl with your (very clean) hands for a solid 2 minutes—your hands will ache with cold, which is good. You want everything to almost emulsify.

Stuff the sausage into hog casings rather loosely. For this sausage, you want long rings—you'll tie the ends together eventually. First make long links of about 2 feet long, with plenty of extra casing on either side. Do this with all the sausage before moving on.

When you're ready, gently compress the long links to fill the casing. Keep an eye out for air pockets. Use a sterile needle or sausage pricker (set it aglow in your stovetop flame) to puncture the casing over all the air pockets. Gently compress the links together to squeeze out the air pockets; this takes practice. Tie the ends of the casing together in a double or triple knot.

Hang the links from a clothes rack or something similar. I use "S" rings you can buy from the hardware store to hang them from the clothes rack rods. Now you need to ferment your links, keeping them warm and moist. I do this by putting a humidifier under the hanging sausages and then tenting the whole shebang with big garbage bags that I've sliced open on one end. I also use a water sprayer to spritz my sausages a couple of times a day. Doing this prevents the casings from hardening. Keep your sausages hanging at room temperature (65°F to 80°F) for two days.

Now you need to dry your sausages and turn them into salami. Hang them in a place that is about 50°F to 60°F with about 80 to 90 percent humidity. In most cases, you'll need to put a humidifier under your links. I also spritz them with water once a day for the first two weeks. After the first week of hanging, drop the humidity to 70 to 80 percent On the third week drop it again to 65 to 70 percent and hold it there until a total of four to eight weeks has elapsed since the salami went into the chamber.

To store long-term, vacuum-seal them individually and keep in the fridge. They will last indefinitely this way, and the vacuum-sealing will keep them from becoming rock hard. You can also freeze them.

**4 pounds venison**

**1 pound pork fatback**

**12 grams dextrose (sugar, if you can't get it)**

**51 grams salt**

**6 grams Insta Cure No. 2**

**1 tablespoon cracked black pepper**

**3 tablespoons smoked paprika**

**15 feet hog casings, preferably 38–42 mm wide**

**1 teaspoon dried oregano**

**⅓ cup sherry or white wine**

**¼ cup distilled water**

**10 grams T-SPX or FRM-52 starter culture**

# SPICY SPANISH-STYLE RILLETTES

**SERVES ▸** 4 to 6

**PREP TIME ▸** 24 to 48 hours

**COOK TIME ▸** 6 to 8 hours

### FOR THE MEAT

2 pounds venison shoulder, neck, or shank

1 pig's foot (optional)

1 onion, chopped

2 bay leaves

A sprig of rosemary

A sprig of thyme

Stems from 1 bunch parsley

A handful of black peppercorns, cracked

Salt to taste

### TO FINISH

2 tablespoons sweet paprika

2 tablespoons Tabasco or other hot sauce

2 teaspoons smoked paprika

4 cloves garlic, minced

2 to 3 tablespoons sherry

Salt

Black pepper

Butter, duck fat, or lard (for longer storage)

These are fun, easy-to-make rillettes, like a loose pâté, that pack a ton of flavor. They keep a long time and are a perfect answer to party apps, potlucks, game day, or date night. Serve this slathered on good toasted bread or crackers.

Put the meat into a pot and cover with water. Bring to a boil and skim any froth that collects on the surface. When you've taken care of that, drop the heat to a bare simmer and add all the remaining ingredients for the meat. Let this simmer gently until the meat is falling off the bones, or, if it's boneless, when the meat begins to fall apart.

Remove the meat and let it cool enough to handle. Shred it and chop it coarsely. You don't want the fibers of the meat to be too long, or the rillettes will be stringy. Strain the cooking liquid and use it as stock for something else (it'll keep in the fridge a week, and it can be frozen).

Put the shredded meat into a large bowl and add the sweet paprika, hot sauce, smoked paprika, garlic, and sherry. Mix and add salt and black pepper to taste. You'll want to beat in as much duck fat, lard, or butter as you want. The fat needs to be solid but not cold. How much fat? Rillettes are a very rough spread, remember, so you want this mixture to be spreadable on toast. I usually use at least ½ cup of duck fat, but if I'm feeling luxurious, I'll use a full cup.

Once you've added all the fat in you want, you'll likely need to tinker with the salt, the sherry—which should be detectable in the final rillette—and the heat. Remember, you want this to be a little too salty, because when you eventually serve it cold, that saltiness will be tamed; humans don't perceive saltiness as much in cold foods.

Pack the rillettes into ramekins or small containers and let them set up in the fridge. For long-term storage, melt some lard or butter and pour a ¼-inch layer on top of the rillettes. Kept this way, they will keep in the fridge for several weeks. Once the protective layer of fat has hardened, you can also vacuum-seal the whole ramekin and freeze it for months.

# BRITISH GAME PIE

This is the classic British game pie, made with a hot-water crust and whatever wild game you have handy.

But to make them, you need to form the distinctive shape for a hand-raised pie. There are two choices: use a mold or dolly, or MacGyver it.

Using a pork pie tin or mold makes the process so much easier, to the point where I rarely made them before I bit the bullet and bought four. You can also wrap your dough around a pie dolly, which is another good option and can be cheaper because you wrap dough around the dolly, fill it, then make another pie with the same dolly.

The MacGyver method runs something like this: Grease a jar the size of your proposed game pie. Pint Mason jars are a good size, although the etching on them is an issue. Smooth glass jars work better. Wrap the dough around the greased jar, leaving about ½ inch of the jar exposed. Cut parchment paper to fit around the dough and tie with a string to hold the dough in place, then remove the jar. Chill this for 30 to 60 minutes before filling.

A traditional game pie uses a hot-water dough. This is a sturdy dough that you can tote around for a day or so at room temperature, or at least at English room temperature. It's fatty, and that fat is usually lard. Butter works too.

Anything goes with the filling. Whatever game floats your boat, your choice of herbs, mushrooms if you want, onions, and so on.

There's one critical ingredient to a good game pie: jelly. Not the sweet stuff but a gelatinous stock that sets up at room temperature. Its job is to close any air gaps in the pie—those air gaps can be breeding grounds for bad bacteria. The jellified stock helps a game pie keep longer.

Once you've baked your pies, remove from the oven, let them cool a little, then very carefully pour the hot, gelatin-rich stock in a hole you've made in the center, bit by bit, until it pools up. Let the pies cool completely, then chill overnight before eating. A game pie is normally eaten cold or at room temperature.

*continued*

**SERVES ▶** 8

**PREP TIME ▶** 1 hour

**COOK TIME ▶** 2 hours

**FOR THE FILLING**

- 8 slices bacon (optional)
- 1 large yellow onion, chopped
- ½ pound fresh mushrooms, chopped
- 1 pound meat, venison, grouse, pheasant, duck, whatever
- 1 pound pork shoulder
- 1 tablespoon ground juniper berries (optional)
- 1 tablespoon chopped lovage or parsley
- 2 teaspoons dried thyme
- 1 tablespoon black pepper
- A pinch of salt

**FOR THE DOUGH**

- 2 pounds all-purpose flour
- 2 teaspoons salt
- 12 ounces lard or butter
- 1½ cups water or milk

**TO FINISH**

- 2 eggs
- 2 tablespoons water or milk
- 2 cups gelatin-rich stock (see headnotes)

### TO MAKE THE FILLING

Fry the bacon in a large pan to render the fat. Remove the bacon when it's crispy. Eat a piece and chop up the rest. Use the fat to cook the onions and mushrooms. Cook over medium-high heat until nicely browned, about 10 minutes. Let this cool.

Chop or grind the game meat and pork shoulder. I prefer to grind the pork and dice the game meat, especially if I'm using the breasts of upland birds or waterfowl. Mix this with the cooled onions, bacon, and mushrooms, along with the herbs, spices, and a healthy pinch of salt, about a teaspoon or so.

### TO MAKE THE DOUGH

Mix the flour and salt in a large bowl. Heat the lard and milk or water in a pot to the steaming point, maybe 130°F tops, so not overly hot. Make a well in the center of the flour and pour the hot liquids in. Mix into a shaggy dough, then knead until it comes together. You want a soft dough, so you might need to add a little more water. If so, do so one tablespoon at a time.

Cut the dough into four equal pieces. Cut each piece into a one-third portion and a two-thirds portion. This is your pie and lid. Keep these pieces covered so they don't dry out when you are making each pie.

### TO MAKE THE PIES

Preheat your oven to 350°F. Roll out the large piece for a pie until it is about ¼ inch thick. Set it in the pie tin and press it all around to conform to the edges. You want a little to drape over the edges of the tin.

Fill the pie with filling, making a little mound at the top. Roll out the small piece of dough for the top and set that on the filling. Crimp the edges to seal and remove any excess dough.

Cut a hole in the top of the pie. Use the excess dough to make a little ring to line that hole. Repeat this whole process with the remaining dough and filling.

When all your pies are made, beat the eggs with water or milk to make an egg wash. Paint the tops of the pies with this. Set the tins on a baking sheet and bake for one hour.

Check on the pies. If the tops are getting too brown, cover them loosely with foil. Bake one more hour, or until the center of the pie reads 165°F on a thermometer. Remove the baking sheet from the oven and let the pies start to cool.

While that's happening, heat up your gelatin-rich stock. Use a funnel if you have one to fill the pies with this stock, little by little. It will fill any air pockets or gaps in the pie, and this makes the pies keep longer. When you're done, let the pies cool to room temperature before chilling overnight in the fridge. Eat cold or at room temperature.

**NOTE:** To make the gelatin-rich stock, you will want to dissolve 1 tablespoon of standard supermarket gelatin to every 2 cups of stock. This will help it set up. Do not use less than this amount, and you can go as high as 1 tablespoon per cup.

### MAKING PIES WITHOUT A TIN

If you're using a pie dolly, you'll want to cut the dough into six initial pieces instead of four because it's narrower, so you'll have more pies that are smaller. Grease the dolly with butter or lard, then wrap the dough around the dolly a little taller than you want the pie.

Cut a piece of parchment paper to fit around the sides of the pie, tie it in place with string, and carefully remove the dolly. Set this in the freezer for about 15 minutes to firm up, then remove the parchment paper, fill the pie and proceed as above.

These pies will keep for about ten days in the fridge.

# ICELANDIC VENISON "GRAVLAX"

**SERVES** ▶ 4 to 8, as an appetizer

**PREP TIME** ▶ 3 days

- One ½- to ¾-pound piece of venison backstrap or eye round
- 1 cup kosher salt, about 6 ounces
- ½ cup sugar, about 3 ounces
- 2 tablespoons dried thyme, or 4 tablespoons fresh
- 1 tablespoon minced fresh chives
- 1 tablespoon minced fresh rosemary
- 1 tablespoon black pepper

Made with lamb instead of venison, this is a traditional starter or snack in Iceland. It tastes somewhere between the totally raw and the cured, like the Deer Ham, Alpine Style recipe on page 326. Herbs are a major player here, and the meat is surprisingly substantial for being pounded so thin. It's truly a unique preparation, and it's worth the few days it takes to cure.

Serve with pickles, mustard, or a drizzle of vinegar—something acidic. Preserved mushrooms are excellent with it, as are the very un-Icelandic preserved artichoke hearts. A little coarse sea salt is a good touch, too. Once made, venison gravlax will keep for a week or more in the fridge and a year in the freezer if you vacuum-seal it.

Start by removing every little bit of silverskin and fat from the meat. Once the venison is trimmed, mix the salt and sugar in a nonreactive, lidded container (I use a plastic one), and bury the venison in the mixture. Refrigerate overnight.

The next day, rinse off the cure and pat the venison dry. Mix the herbs and pepper together and roll the meat in it. Do this several times, really pressing the herbs in. If you have a vacuum sealer, seal the venison and refrigerate it for at least twenty-four hours, and up to a week. If you don't have a vac sealer, wrap the meat tightly in two layers of plastic wrap and refrigerate.

To serve, cut off pieces about ¼ inch thick—the texture of the meat is such that you won't be able to slice it super thin—and place each piece between two pieces of plastic wrap. Pound them thin with a meat mallet, rubber mallet, or an empty wine bottle. Lay each slice on a plate and serve with the accompaniments mentioned in the headnote.

# DEER HAM, ALPINE STYLE

**V**enison hams present a problem. They're always skinned, and they rarely have much fat on them. Fortunately, there's a tradition in the Italian Alps of curing such a piece of meat. They cure legs of wild ibex and call the result *mocetta*.

Here in North America, think about doing this with antelope legs or legs from small whitetail or blacktail deer, like does or young bucks. Coues deer or Sitka blacktail would be ideal. Axis deer are a good choice, too.

Skinless hams cure easily but are tougher to age because they can dry out fast. You'll need to watch your humidity wherever you hang this thing. Start with about 90 percent humidity. As the meat ages, the humidity needs to drop week by week until you hit 60 percent humidity. Then you can let it rest for months. You're looking at a total of about five months for this project, tops. You can get away with hanging it less, but I wouldn't. There's something special about long-aged meats.

**MAKES ▶** 2 hams

**PREP TIME ▶** About 120 days

- ⅓ ounce juniper berries
- ⅓ ounce black pepper
- 1 tablespoon dried thyme
- 15 bay leaves
- 2 tablespoons fresh rosemary
- 1 ounce garlic powder
- 1 cup white sugar
- 10 grams Insta Cure No. 2
- 2 cups kosher salt
- 2 young deer hide legs

Grind together the juniper berries, black pepper, thyme, and bay leaves until fine. Mince the rosemary. Combine all the spices with the salts and mix. Divide this mixture in half. Put one part of the cure away in a sealed container.

Carefully rub half the mixture into the venison legs, making sure to get lots into the ball joint that connected the leg to the pelvis; this is where leg cuts often spoil. Massage the spices and salts into the meat.

Put the legs into a large container and refrigerate for two to three weeks. Drain off any liquid that seeps out of the meat. You'll know it's about done when the meat has firmed up quite a bit. Rinse off the cure and pat the legs dry.

Rub the legs with the second half of the cure. Return the legs to the container and refrigerate for another ten days or so. The longer you allow them to cure, the saltier the meat will be—and the longer it will last without spoiling.

When you're ready, rinse off the cure again and soak the legs in fresh water for an hour. This removes a little of the saltiness and results in a moister cure—you needed to cure with so much salt for so long to make sure it penetrated all the way through to the bone. The water soak removes some of that salt so it won't be overpowering when you ultimately serve the mocetta.

Hang for three to five months. You want a temperature between 50°F and 60°F (colder at the beginning and warmer near the end) and a humidity starting at about 90 percent and slowly decreasing—say, 5 percent a week—until you're at about 60 percent humidity.

Once it's ready, you can cut the meat from the bone and slice thin, or slice bone-in. Serve at room temperature with cheese and a husky red wine. Wrap closely and store in the fridge, or seal it and freeze it. The bones, when you're done, make fantastic stock.

# ACKNOWLEDGMENTS

Perhaps the hardest thing I faced when I first wrote this manuscript more than a decade ago, testing recipes and learning about our human relationship with the antlered (and horned) creatures of six continents, was knowing when to stop. The subject is so vast, the recipes so compelling, and our relationship with deer and their cousins so ingrained, that I just kept wanting to add more, and more, and more.

And here I am, ten years on, having added nearly thirty new recipes, still amazed at the vast array of venison dishes and their variations—and still wanting to add more, and more, and more. And though a cookbook, for practical reasons, can be only so long, the conversation we've begun with the first edition of *Buck Buck Moose* is, happily, unending—rich and varied and vital. The devoted readers of Hunter Angler Gardener Cook (huntgathercook.com) and To the Bone (tothebone.substack.com) continue to help me make these books better. It is to them that I wish first to extend my sincere gratitude.

Thanks also go, as before, to the 1,356 backers of the 2015 Kickstarter campaign who allowed me to make the first edition of this book. You truly kickstarted my career in self-publishing books on fish, game, and the regions of this country dear to me.

As I am a competent but not expert deer hunter, I want to thank Larry Robinson, Chris Niskanen, John Stallone, Corey LeHew, Phillip Loughlin, Joe Navari, Matt Greene, Tim Huber, Randy King, Tad Stout, and Ian Shaul for taking me out and showing me new things about chasing antlered critters. I hope to share the field with you all again someday soon.

I need to thank everyone who worked on this project. First, to all those who tested recipes for this book; there are lots of you, and I know who you are. Without you, these recipes would not be as good as they turned out to be. A hat tip to Gregory Berger, who designed our shirts and hoodies. To Richard Feit, who did the heavy lifting on the editing for this beast. And a huge huzzah to my sister Laura for not only designing this gorgeous book that you're holding but also for holding my hand through an often byzantine printing and production process.

Finally, I want to thank Holly Heyser, my former partner who is still a friend, for the gorgeous photography. Not only did she take most of the photos in this book and serve as guinea pig for most of the experimental recipes, she was also willing to re-edit the images for this second edition.

# SELECTED READING

Consider this collection to be an explorer's guide to the topic rather than a comprehensive bibliography. These are some of my favorite books about the arcana of charcuterie, butchery, and game cookery and for delving into the relationship between hunting and our humanity.

## Charcuterie, Butchery, and Game Cookery


Cameron, Angus, and Judith Jones. *The L.L. Bean Game & Fish Cookbook*. Random House, 1983.

Clarke, Eileen. *The Venison Cookbook*. Voyageur, 1996.

De Gouy, L. P. *The Derrydale Game Cookbook*. Derrydale, 2000.

Fearnley-Whittingstall, Hugh. *The River Cottage Meat Book*. Hodder and Stoughton, 2004.

Fromm, Eric, and Al Cambronne. *Gut it, Cut it, Cook It: The Deer Hunter's Guide to Processing & Preparing Venison*. Krause, 2009.

Griffiths, Jesse. *Afield: A Chef's Guide to Preparing and Cooking Wild Game and Fish*. Welcome Books, 2012.

Gutenbrunner, Kurt. *Neue Cuisine: The Elegant Tastes of Vienna: Recipes from Café Sabarsky, Wallse, and Blaue Gans*. Rizzoli, 2011.

Hasheider, Philip. *The Complete Book of Butchering, Smoking, Curing, and Sausage Making: How to Harvest your Livestock and Wild Game*. Voyageur, 2010.

Hunter, Michael. *The Hunter Chef Cookbook*. Penguin Canada, 2020.

Kutas, Rytek. *Great Sausage Making and Meat Curing*. The Sausage Maker, 2008.

Landers, Jackson. *The Beginner's Guide to Hunting Deer for Food*. Storey, 2011.

Leite, David. *The New Portuguese Table: Exciting Flavors from Europe's Western Coast*. Clarkson Potter, 2009.

Leysath, Scott. *The Sporting Chef's Better Venison Cookbook*. Krause, 2012.

Livingston, A. D. *Venison Cookbook*. Stackpole Books, 1993.

Marianski, Stanley, and Adam Marianski. *The Art of Making Fermented Sausages*. Outskirts Press, 2008

Marianski, Stanley, and Adam Marianski. *Home Production of Quality Meats and Sausages*. Bookmagic, 2010.

McGee, Harold. *On Food and Cooking: The Science and Lore of the Kitchen*. Scribner, 2004.

McGrail, Joie, and Bill McGrail. *The Catch and the Feast*. Weybright and Talley, 1969.

McLagan, Jennifer. *Odd Bits: How to Cook the Rest of the Animal*. Ten Speed Press, 2011.

Mettler, John J., Jr. *Basic Butchering of Livestock & Game*. Storey, 2003.

Nilsson, Magnus. *The Nordic Cookbook*. Phaidon, 2015.

Nolen, Jeremy, and Jessica Nolen. *New German Cooking: Recipes for Classics Revisited*. Chronicle Books, 2014.

Ruhlman, Michael, and Brian Polcyn. *Charcuterie: The Craft of Salting, Smoking, and Curing*. W. W. Norton, 2005.

Schwabe, Calvin W. *Unmentionable Cuisine*. University of Virginia Press, 1999.

Shaw, Hank. *Hunt, Gather, Cook*. Rodale, 2011.

Sheraton, Mimi. *The German Cookbook: A Complete Guide to Mastering Authentic German Cooking*. Random House, 1993.

Strybel, Robert, and Maria Strybel. *Polish Heritage Cookery*. Rev. and exp. Hippocrene Books, 2005.

Webster, Harold W., Jr. *The Complete Venison Cookbook*. Quail Ridge, 1996.

Wright, Clarissa Dickson, and Johnny Scott. *The Game Cookbook*. Kyle Books, 2005.


## Hunting and Humanity


Bulliet, Richard. *Hunters, Herders, and Hamburgers: The Past and Future of Human-Animal Relationships*. Columbia University Press, 2005.

Cambronne, Al. *Deerland: America's Hunt for Ecological Balance and the Essence of Wildness.* Lyons, 2013.

Fletcher, John. *Deer.* Reaktion Books, 2014.

Nelson, Richard. *Heart and Blood: Living with Deer in America.* Vintage, 1997.

Pickering, Travis Rayne. *Rough and Tumble: Aggression, Hunting, and Human Evolution.* University of California Press, 2013.

Stanford, Craig B. *The Hunting Apes: Meat Eating and the Origins of Human Behavior.* Princeton University Press, 1999.

Tattersall, Ian. *Masters of the Planet: The Search for Our Human Origins.* Palgrave Macmillan, 2012.

# RESOURCES

Many organizations work hard to expand, maintain, and restore habitat for deer, elk, and other big game animals here in North America. Consider joining them and becoming an active conservationist-hunter, and in the process, get a leg up on how to hunt and how to get access to hunting grounds for these animals. Here's a small sample of what's out there:

**Arizona Deer Association** (azdeer.org)
P.O. Box 21868, Mesa, AZ 85277, info@azdeer.org

**California Deer Association** (caldeer.org)
info@caldeer.org

**Minnesota Deer Hunters Association**
(mndeerhunters.com)
460 Peterson Road, Grand Rapids, MN 55744, (800) 450-3337

**Mule Deer Foundation** (muledeer.org)
1939 South 4130 West, Ste. H, Salt Lake City, UT 84104, askmdf@muledeer.org

**New Mexico Wildlife Federation** (nmwildlife.org)
3620 Wyoming Blvd NE, Suite 222, Albuquerque, NM 87111

**Rocky Mountain Elk Foundation** (rmef.org)
PO Box 8249, Missoula, MT 59807, (406) 523-4500

**Texas Wildlife Association** (texas-wildlife.org)
6644 FM 1102, New Braunfels, TX 78132

# INDEX

Note: Page references in **bold** indicate recipe photographs.

## D



## E



## F



## G



## H